The Future of Literacy in a Changing World

Revised Edition

SERIES ON
LITERACY: RESEARCH, POLICY AND PRACTICE

Volumes in the series include:

Literacy Among African-American Youth
    (Vivian L. Gadsden and Daniel A. Wagner, eds.)

What Makes Workers Learn *(Donald Hirsch and Daniel A. Wagner, eds.)*

International Perspectives on the School-to-Work Transition
    David Stern and Daniel A. Wagner (eds.)

Adult Basic Skills: Innovations in Measurement and Policy Analysis
    (Albert Tuijnman, Irwin Kirsch, and Daniel A. Wagner, eds.)

The Future of Literacy in a Changing World: Revised Edition
    (Daniel A. Wagner, ed.)

Forthcoming

Numeracy Development: A Guide for Adult Educators
    Iddo Gal (ed.)

Adult Literacy Research and Development Vol. 1: Learning and Instruction
    (Daniel A. Wagner, ed.)

Adult Literacy Research and Development Vol. 2: Programs and Policies
    (Daniel A. Wagner, ed.)

The Future of Literacy in a Changing World

Revised Edition

Edited by

Daniel A. Wagner
International Literacy Institute
National Center on Adult Literacy
University of Pennsylvania

HAMPTON PRESS, INC.
CRESSKILL, NEW JERSEY

Printed in the United States of America

Library of Congress Cataloging-in-Publication Data

The future of literacy in a changing world / edited by Daniel A. Wagner. -- Rev. ed.
    p. cm. -- (Series on literacy)
    Includes bibliographic references and indexes.
    ISBN 1-57273-082-X (cloth). -- ISBN 1-57273-083-8 (pbk.)
    1. Literacy. 2. Functional literacy. 3. Fundamental education.
4. Comparative education. I. Wagner, Daniel A., 1946-
II. Series
LC149.F87   1998
302.2'244--dc21   98-38340
                                          CIP

Hampton Press, Inc.
23 Broadway
Cresskill, NJ 07626

Contents

Series Preface

Daniel A. Wagner

International Literacy Institute
National Center on Adult Literacy
University of Pennsylvania

Although most peoples and cultures today utilize literacy as a way to conserve cultural knowledge, imbue contemporary information through education, and enrich their societal heritage, literacy—as a set of learned skills for producing and comprehending written language—is poorly controlled by large segments of many societies across the world.

Once thought to be a fully literate country—with a 1990 UN "literacy rate" at nearly 98%—the United States, according to recent studies, now is believed to have a literacy rate at which between one-fourth and one-third of adults are "functionally illiterate." Similar findings are coming in from around the world. Some specialists say that these discrepancies have more to do with changing definitions of literacy, whereas others say that previous claims were simply conjecture or based on poor methodologies for assessment. Both views are probably correct in part. What we do know is that changes in the globalization of economic exchange, industrial production, and worker retraining have put the acquisition of basic skills—of which literacy is clearly the most critical—at the center of national and international concern about education and development.

ON THIS VOLUME

This volume came out of a seminal international conference entitled "The Future of Literacy in a Changing World," held at the University of Pennsylvania in May 1985. It was the inaugural conference of the research center at Penn which is now called jointly the International Literacy Institute and the National Center on Adult Literacy.

That conference brought together a diverse array of academics and policymakers to take a new interdisciplinary look at the past, present, and future of literacy at what may now be seen as a turning point for the field. Up until the mid-1980s, the field could probably be characterized as primarily "insulated" within the (up until then) relatively closed confines of the field of adult education. But the field was beginning already to show the inputs from researchers in the allied fields of psychology, linguistics, anthropology, and the like. And leaders in the reading field (such as John Downing, to whose memory the first edition was dedicated) were also beginning to realize that the challenges of literacy were much more complex than simply producing more and better textbooks.

Now, more than 10 years later, with the tremendous growth in interest and publications in literacy, we can see that the cross-fertilization process has had important consequences, not only for research, but also for practice and policy. On the practice side, we now find teacher education programs embracing the complexities of culture and reading, language and bilingualism, and more. On the policy side, national and international agencies have begun to realize that the challenges of "fully literate" societies are ever-present; one consequence may be seen in the growth of national and international surveys of literacy in the 1990s and beyond.

Of course, this is not to say that this relatively small conference and its participants could see many of these growing trends as inevitable. But I think there was a sense that a significant transition was about to occur in the literacy field. Some would say, perhaps correctly, that we are still in the midst of this transition process. Only time will tell for certain.

A note on this publication. *The Future of Literacy in a Changing World* was first published in 1987 by Pergamon Press. That first edition sold out rather quickly, but the book continued to be used by scholars and in courses on literacy worldwide. We are pleased that Hampton Press has published this revised and updated edition. Most chapters have been updated and revised where possible in light of a decade of more recent research, except in the cases of several authors who are now deceased. Two new chapters (by R. Iredale and A. Gillette) of relevance to the general thrust of this book have been added to this edition.

ON THIS SERIES

Through what I believe to be an historical quirk of academic scholarship and arbitrary disciplinary divisions, research on literacy has tended to fall into a variety of unconnected research and specialty camps. Thus, under the rubric of "literacy," we find books on adult learning and adult education, cognitive dimensions of reading acquisition in children, oral versus literate societies, orthographies and psycholinguistic processes, the role of literacy in cultural preservation, the impact of literacy on income and social mobility, international education and development, and so on. These scholarly specialties are all valid, but they are remarkably insulated one from the other. Indeed, even the references utilized for these different approaches often take little note of what scholars and practitioners have produced in other areas.

The present series, *Literacy: Research, Policy and Practice*, is one attempt to break down the walls that partition literacy into such separate intellectual territories. In this series, we try to find interconnections not only among the three major segments of literacy specialists as denoted in the series subtitle, but also across the life span (children and adults) and across ethnic, linguistic, and cultural groups. This series, we hope, will provide an opportunity to make connections across various knowledge bases and expand the possibilities not only to achieve a better understanding of literacy in the past, present, and future, but also to lead to a future which is a more literate place to live.

Foreword

Dell A. Hymes
University of Virginia

The interest of this book can be suggested by interchanging two words of its title: "The changing of literacy in a future world." Let us assume that the human world does continue into the next century. It seems unlikely that the literacy of the next century will be what most of us who write about it now would most hope to see. Those who read this book, like those who write it, have lives in which the reading and writing of books matter. For most, one can hope, that gives some pleasure. For all who wish an academic identity, it is a necessity. Like the Cree who learn and maintain a syllabary to remain in contact with relatives at a distance (Bennett and Berry, this volume), we learn and maintain the production of written objects of a certain type so as to remain in contact with professionally significant others—prestations for appointment, promotion and tenure so as to enter or stay within such a community, tokens to send to people we admire and may never meet, rationales for conferences at which one can come to know interesting, unusual people, efforts to persuade that community, expressions of ourselves that only members of our far-flung community will understand, notifications to it that one is still here. For many of us, our lives are partly written down inside the covers of books we have sent or received or happened on. Some subset no doubt belongs to one or more of the interpretive communities (Purves) that do the puzzles in the Sunday *New York Times*, the *Nation, New Statesman, Times Literary Supplement, The Times* of London.

Campaigns for literacy in the de-developed cities of the United States, of course, have other concerns. Banks and corporations are concerned about employees who cannot move beyond entry-level positions. Mayors and civic groups are concerned about adults who cannot obtain entry-level positions at all, cannot manage the print of personal affairs. The heights of literacy are not in question, but rather a toe-hold, a literacy sufficient for self-support, a labor force sufficient for economic growth. Countries throughout the world seek to adapt their limited resources to economic pressures from without and within, to pressures of linguistic diversity without and within that have economic, political and religious implications.

Earlier in this century one typically thought of literacy as present or absent, or a difference between the literate and the illiterate. Missionaries, governments and agencies sought to eliminate the distinction. Much of the best-known discussion of literacy in the academy and general culture still speculates on the nature of literacy in terms of that categorical distinction, as a cultural or cognitive divide. It now seems entirely possible that the next century may see a world entirely literate, yet as divided as now between the well-to-do and the poor, as between countries and regions of the world, and within them. Thus, Fuller, Edwards, and Gorman find that investment in literacy did influence economic growth in Mexico, but only in urban centers. The effect in rural agrarian Mexico was slight at best. One can imagine that pattern repeated throughout the world: rising literacy and stable inequality.

This is the more likely, given, as Chall points out, that expectations as to the level of literacy needed have steadily risen. The concern in the United States must be addressed to adults who have literacy, but not enough. Sticht raises the prospect that technology itself will make higher literacy for such adults superfluous. With advances in technology, relatively low levels of literacy will suffice to use it, and technologies themselves will perform more and more of what is now performed by humans. As a result, those who are now external to technically advanced work are unlikely to be trained for it. The correlation between high and low literacy, male and female, majority and minority ethnic groups, developed and underdeveloped centers, will remain, perhaps increase.

There are three approaches to such disparity between people's abilities and literacy demands. Disparity may be accepted, and people simply matched to what they can read; one can seek to train people to read what they cannot; one can also redesign what is to be read. Anzalone explores technological aids to training, and Fan, Tong, and Song report on the redesign of Chinese characters. This throws into relief the pervasive problem of teaching itself. Many would agree with the principle assumed by Sticht (1987); namely that training should be meaningful (functional) for the student. Mangubhai, writing on the

South Pacific, and Nunes, writing on Brazil, document teaching that persistently fails to make literacy meaningful. Many would take meaningfulness to include taking into account where the student to be taught is at. Yet, for Hebrew in Israel, Feitelson describes an unsuitable pedagogy (whole-word method) that worked as long as Hebrew-literate parents could supplement it outside school, but that fails for children of immigrants, who cannot so supplement; and Nunes shows how failure for lower-class children in Brazil is almost guaranteed by a schedule of teaching and testing that ignores the stage they have reached. Downing urges that conventional pedagogies not be imposed, but their existence, at home and abroad, is partly a function of meaning in another sense, the meanings people associate with education, if it is to be considered education: that it take place in a school, that it evince certain forms. Investment in literacy is likely to reproduce the divisions of the social order if it is investment in a pedagogy which already does so.

As Wagner points out, the close interdependence of literacy and economic growth cannot be assumed. Historical studies have shown other motives than economic for high levels of literacy (e.g., a religious imperative in Lutheran Scandinavia), and contemporary discussions question whether increased literacy leads to economic growth, whether it can be readily achieved or afforded, what priority it is to have. The costs assessed must include the possibility that the introduction of literacy may introduce division and inequity among language communities (Schieffelin). In any case, at the level of international organizations, of national governments and agencies, of local governments and schools, whatever is done, what can even be learned about literacy, will be a function of the practices and interests of the institutions and persons involved. Those involved may assist or resist what comes from above or without.

Policies, of course, may change, as Ezzaki, Spratt and Wagner point out, making prediction rash.[1] Clearly, though, literacy in the next century will be what diverse communities make of it (Street)—a multiplicity of local configurations of functional consequence or practice, socially meaningful choice, and technological skill (Reder), of hierarchies of need-motivated activity, action, and operation (Scribner), emerging in interaction between those who seek to provide literacy and those who seek to acquire or extend or bracket or control it. A universal flowering of high literacy is unlikely, a continued polarization between haves and have-nots likely indeed.

Practical and theoretical insight into present and prospective literacy inequity will depend on an accumulation of relevant, well-described cases, and controlled comparison (Eggan, 1954; Hymes, 1980),

---

[1]Socialist regimes are likely to succeed in social mobilization that makes some level of literacy general (Cuba, Nicaragua), apart from technology.

identifying what is common and contrastive. Contributions to this book provide a number of relevant comparisons: medieval England: Malagasy as local adaptations of colonial literacy (Street); the Vai of Liberia: Brazilian peasants, similar in economic level, different in valuation of literacy (Nunes); Brazilian peasants: Brazilian middle-class expectations for literacy (Nunes); contrasting mother mediations of storybook reading (Teale and Sulzby); indigenous and immigrant families in relation to a common method of teaching reading in Israel (Feitelson); the effect of differing models of functional literacy in Kent, in New Zealand, and in Papua New Guinea (Downing). As in the ethnography of communication generally, such comparison interacts with both description and theory. It leads to the recognition of dimensions on which cases vary significantly, thus pointing up what is most relevant to describe, most promising of explanatory force, and can lead to a more precise identification of types of case, of what the presence of certain features is likely to entail as to the presence of others.[2] Central to all this will be accounts of repertoire: the *repertoire* of codes (languages, varieties, styles) available in a community or setting; the repertoire of channels; and, from the standpoint of communicative utility, the repertoire of persons, or recognized roles. The account of repertoire will map the connections between codes, channels and roles, and of course show the social meaning of each available choice (Reder) in relevant contexts. Among the Hmong of Philadelphia, for example, one would need to recognize three languages (Hmong, Laotian, English); at least four kinds of channel (oral face-to-face, oral recorded (exchanges of cassettes between communities in this country and between countries), print, handwriting; and, as resources as well, at least four communicative roles (transcriber, reader, interpreter, spokesperson) (these remarks draw on Weinstein, 1986). Such accounts will use concepts and models analogous to, or part of, models that have developed for multiplicity of language varieties, models to which writing has been sometimes essential, but not systematically, (e.g., diglossia, triglossia, polyglossia (with reference to societal codes), bilingualism, trilingualism, multilingualism (with reference to personal competencies) (cf. Platt, 1977).

These larger contexts are of course necessary to an understanding of the meaning of choice within repertoire. But choice within repertoire, while sometimes stable for a situation or set of participants, can also be dynamic, and must be observed. A teacher's self-report may acknowledge only what counts as writing—the approved tasks of the classroom, for example—and miss the pervasive presence of unofficial

---

[2]A possible initial framework is sketched in Hymes (1972); see also the last section of Hymes (1970).

writing, notes passed, games played, tasks mocked (Fiering, 1981). The interaction between literacy and oracy, the niches of each, may be complex and subtle, even in the highly literate environment of a university. Whether to phone or write or meet or use electronic mail;[3] if to phone, whether to do so oneself or have another place the call; if to write, the paper and letterhead, if any, to write by hand or type oneself or have another type: much of this may happen quickly, and be forgotten. And the modeling of literacy to others in the society by those most successful may not at all convey the necessity of literacy. Nunes notes the rich but often illiterate Brazilian landowners of the nineteenth century who hired others to tutor, read and write. The twentieth-century United States is familiar with autobiography "as told to," the leader with speech writers, the executive or star with equipment to record his or her voice for others to type. Those at the lower pole of the stratification of literacy may not have opportunity to observe the complex models; they may understandably take some of the visible models as showing that talent can make it to the top on its own, that literacy is something the successful can hire.

The prospect, then, is for complex diversification and stratification as the use of graphic representation of language radiates and adapts throughout the world. Polarization, inequality in literacy, may prove as acceptable as inequality in speaking. A liberal linguistics may abstract from the evident differences in what languages can do, and what users of language can do, and so not notice. A relativistic critique may not acknowledge that differences of opportunity and experience have as consequence persons who are in ability not the same, and so not reach the only truly radical position, namely that institutions should be changed, not only because they are unfair, but also because they do perduring harm. Certainly one must be alert to the popular tendency to blame the victim; one must also accept that there are victims, and that both institutions and persons must change. The obstacles will be great. Adherents of "correctness" will not give up their stake in deploring the decline of the language. If every adult is literate, even at a rather high level, distinctions will be noted, invented, if need be, as they have been for two centuries. In no known complex society, after all, do the present arrangements allow equality. Hierarchy is intrinsic. What could be more functional than a pattern of literacy in which everyone is allowed to go to school, and so considered to have an equal chance, then sorted out in terms of language, of something in which differences in resultant ability can be ascribed to the person, not the society?[4]

---

[3]On choices in regard to electronic mail, see the interesting work of Murray (1988).

[4]Cf. McDermott (1986) on failure as something schools may be organized to accomplish.

If inequity in literacy is not accepted, it will be of the greatest theoretical interest to determine why. Inequity in oracy is overlooked, and not regarded as a problem to be addressed by the world (cf. Hymes, 1973). For some cultures there was a myth that some people could not speak, and for some Europeans there have been places where other people could not adequately speak. Gradually, however, especially through the efforts of linguistic anthropologists such as Boas and Sapir, it came to be recognized that all languages are complex and capable of adaptation, are in principle potentially equivalent. This truth of potential has often been taken as a truth of realization. That sociocultural evolution has led to some languages differing from others in sheer order of magnitude of vocabulary, in elaboration of registers, styles and genres for the accomplishment of certain functions, is a fact of life in language planning and policy, but a fact about which mainstream linguistics has little to say. The core grammar of a language may still be discoverable even when there is no longer anyone alive who can use it to create an imagined narrative world. Scholars in the relatively new field of second language acquisition do address differential states of competence, and may ultimately bring about a change, if it is recognized, that differences in first language can be legitimately addressed. But for the present, "functional oracy" is not apparently a problem, while "functional literacy" is. Is the reason for the difference that it is not a problem for society to have people stay in their place with regard to oracy, but that it is with regard to literacy? Because literacy engages economic life in a different way?

If the meanings of literacy and oracy are interdependent, relative to each other, then it is worth remarking that the world's wealth of oracy has evidently declined. Those without literacy, or with little literacy, are seldom now participants in autonomous cultures, in which oracy skills could flourish as central. More commonly they live in circumstances of cultural marginality or subordination. We are coming to realize that the narrative traditions of many Native American communities have not been repetitious prose, but a kind of verse, embodying an often rich and subtle architecture (cf. Hymes, 1982, 1985, 1987a, 1987b, 1991b, 1992, 1995). Such potentialities have been found as well in stories told by African American children (D. Hymes, 1991b, 1995), suburban Philadelphians (Hymes, 1993), and many other users of English, including those of Ireland and Scotland (Glassie, 1982; V. Hymes, 1995), and narrators from a variety of other languages. These potentialities for organizing narrative in lines, marked by intonational contours and pauses, and grouped according to a few implicit, patterning sequences, may well be universal (Hymes, 1991b). They may be a kind of artistry that comes together with language everywhere. Yet biases associated with literacy may cause them to go unheard. One incident stands out in my mind. My wife and I were going by train to an international oracy conference in Norwich. We assumed that the others, like ourselves, were coming to call attention to the richness of oral art. And in the car in which we rode one man at the back held several others engrossed all the way from London with one story after another, as if in demonstration. Despite this happy omen, we were dismayed to discover that quite a few of those in attendance saw "oracy" as the name for something children had to be taught to have correctly. As if for them all the implicit intricate capacity for language itself with which normal children are born, that grows like a hidden forest from a few seeds, could not exist, only whatever visibly orderly garden might be planted from without.

And indeed, when an unfamiliar narrative capacity is present in a school setting, it is likely to be missed or rejected (e.g., Hymes, 1991a; Michaels, 1981, 1983). It is likely that many in the twentieth century will have a diminished oracy yet a merely threshold literacy.

There are efforts to cultivate both oracy and literacy together, and in more than one language, both spoken and written, as in the work of Sam Burnside and the Verbal Arts Centre in Londonderry in Northern Ireland. And where oracy in a language of valued heritage has declined, the literacy of others can be put to use to reclaim it. At the very least, what once was understood through hearing can be grasped by the eye. That is happening with some of the Native American traditions (cf. D. Hymes, 1992, 1995; Tedlock, 1972, 1990). Analysis can recover, space and arrangement on a page can show something of what voices have done.

To use a term familiar now with regard to Native American traditions, such work can be a kind of repatriation. It is especially appropriate for inheritors of the scholarly work which transcribed so much of the oracy of others to bring to these records the recognition now possible of the patterned, poetic nature of that oracy. For it is their predecessors who presented it to the world as prose. And exercises in the written transcription and presentation of oral narrative might be effective ways of preserving and promoting both in classrooms and communities.

Such a suggestion, of course, depends upon the mix already present and attitudes toward it, attitudes both channels and genres that make use of them. Many communities have their own combinations and interactions of oral tradition and instrumental writing—writing that is in part a continuation of open tradition (Finnegan 1977, 160-167; George, 1990; O'Keeffe, 1987, 1990), or specific in its expressive or other role (Besnier, 1988, 1989; Digges & Rappaport, 1992; Ferguson,1987). Such relations cannot be assumed, but have to be observed and investigated.

In the societies of the major industrialized nations the mix among modes of oracy and literacy hardly stands still. Some of us experience growing hostility from those who expect everyone to whom they want to communicate to be using e-mail by now, not "snail mail." At the other end of an aesthetic continuum the craft of calligraphy has not disappeared, but even appears at local fairs. Poetry has increasingly become again something written for the voice and performance. In some pockets of the United States, at least, someone coming from a world in Philadelphia, where others insist in having something in writing, may unwittingly insult someone in the world of Charlottesville by mildly asking the same thing. One has questioned another person's word. The upper reach of advanced science may be out of reach for someone who does not command the oral performance to which priority is given (Traweek, 1982). One can hope that awareness of continuing diversity and change will encourage further close studies of just what mix constitutes communicative competence in the niches to which it is hoped newcomers can aspire.

Whatever the changing of literacy in a future world, it is of the greatest importance to the general study of language, if such study wishes to understand the means of language available to humankind and what meanings such means can have in human lives. The mere existence of writing challenges the dogma that the goal of linguistics is to account for the acquisition of language, while meaning by language a spoken form alone, and modeling human abilities as varying within restricted parameters and emerging with a modicum of exposure to speech. To be sure, perhaps writing and reading can be more readily acquired if the circumstances of their acquisition more closely resemble those of speech, circumstances in which the use of these modes is likewise bound up with the satisfaction of intrinsic needs and interaction with significant others. It remains that the forms of writing in the world, though they may share certain organizational properties (Stevenson), differ sharply in what of linguistic form they select and group together for representation (segmental, syllabic, logographic, prosodic), and in the relation of what is represented and read to what is spoken and heard.

Writing has not sprung full-armed and unitary from the human brow, but has emerged late in human history, and in certain times and places and not others (cf. Marcus, 1992; Senner, 1989; Staal,1977). A modicum of exposure to graphic representations will not regularly elicit it. Forms of writing are historically dependent and culturally specific Yet one or another form of writing and printing and reading are becoming almost universally components of competence in language.

Literacy clearly cannot be acquired or understood, or its potential for human life realized, if it is treated, as some treat language, as separate from human life. Nor can the connection be regarded as merely the introduction, or execution, of language in a social context. The question of literacy makes indispensable a theory of language that addresses what is linguistic and what is social as mutually enabling, that encompasses not only what was once the only channel, but also what has become a channel of second nature for many, and a force for good or ill to the lives of all.

Among the Thompson Indians of British Columbia there has been a story that imagines writing as given by the one in charge of the world, Old One. He gave it to the trickster-transformer, Coyote, saying, "I will give you a paper. Carry it with you. When you need advice, consult it." After a while Coyote laid the paper down and forgot it; when he wanted it again, could not find it. "If Coyote had not lost it, the Indians would now know writing, and the whites would not have had the opportunity to obtain written language. It was because of the foolishness of Coyote.' (Teit, 1937).

The story imagines that writing as absent by accident, not inability. Those who contribute to work such as this book share such a view, of course, believing that the opportunity can be open to all, whatever the advice (wisdom) each wishes to provide, while recognizing as well that vital advice, worth preserving, often comes in speech, and that much that will be worth preserving is yet to be written and spoken.

ACKNOWLEDGEMENTS

I am grateful to my former colleague, Dan Wagner, for his invitation to add a few words to the book he brought together, and introduced himself so comprehensively.

REFERENCES

Besnier, N. (1988). The linguistic relationship of spoken and written Nukulaelae registers. *Language, 64*, 707-736.

Besnier, N. (1989). Literacy and feelings. *Text, 9*, 69-91.

Digges, D., & Rappaport, J. (1992). Literacy, orality, and ritual practice in Highland Colombia. In J. Boyarin (Ed.), *The ethnography of reading* (pp. 139-155). Berkeley and Los Angeles: University of California Press.

Eggan, F. (1954). Social anthropology and the method of controlled comparison. *American Anthropologist, 5*(6), 746-748, 758-759.

Ferguson, C. A. (1987). Literacy in a hunting-gathering society: The case of the Diyari. *Journal of Anthropological Research, 4*(3), 223-237.

Fiering, S. (1981). Unofficial writing. In D. Hymes (Ed.), *Ethnographic monitoring of children's acquisition of reading/language arts skills in and out of the classroom*. Final report to the National Institute of Education.

Finnegan, R. (1977). *Oral poetry. Its nature, significance and social context* (2nd ed.). Cambridge: Cambridge University Press.

George, K. M. (1990). Felling a song with a new ax: Writing and the reshaping of ritual song performance in Upland Sulawesi. *Journal of American Folklore, 103*(407), 3-23.

Glassie H. (1982). *Irish folk history. Texts from the north.* Philadelphia: University of Pennsylvania Press.

Hymes, D. (1970). Linguistic aspects of comparative political research. In R. Holt & J. Turner (Eds.), *The methodology of comparative research* (pp. 295-341). New York: Holt, Rinehart and Winston. (Reprinted, Basil Blackwell, 1986).

Hymes, D. (1972). Models of the interaction of language and social setting. In J. J. Gumperz & D. Hymes (Eds.), *Directions in sociolinguistics* (pp. 35-71). New York: Holt, Rinehart and Winston. (Reprinted, Oxford: Basil Blackwell, 1986).

Hymes, D. (1973, Summer). Speech and language: On the origins and foundations of inequality among speakers. *Daedalus,* pp. 59-86. (Proceedings of the American Academy of Arts and Sciences 102(3).

Hymes, D. (1980). Educational ethnology. *Anthropology and Education Quarterly, 1*(1), 3-8

Hymes, D. (1982). Narrative form as 'grammar' of experience: Native Americans and a glimpse of English. *Journal of Education, 164*(2), 121-142.

Hymes, D. (1985). Language, memory, and selective performance: Cultee's 'Salmon's myth' as twice told to Boas. *Journal of American Folklore, 98*(390), 391-434.

Hymes, D. (1987a). Anthologies and narrators. In B. Swann & A. Krupat (Eds.), *Recovering the word. Essays on Native American literature* (pp. 41-84). Berkeley and Los Angeles: University of California Press.

Hymes, D. (1987b). A theory of irony and a pattern of Chinookan verbal humor. In J. Verscheuren & M. Bertucelli-Papi (Eds.), *The pragmatic perspective. Selected papers from the 1985 International Pragmatics Conference* (pp.293-338). Amsterdam and Philadelphia: John Benjamins.

Hymes, D. (1991a). Ethnopoetics and sociolinguistics: Three stories by African-American children. In I. G. Malcolm (Ed.), *Linguistics in the service of society* (pp. 155-170). Perth, Australia: Institute of Applied Language Studies, Edith Cowan University.

Hymes, D. (1991b). Is poetics original and functional? *Language & Communication, 11*(112), 49-51.

Hymes, D. (1992). Using all there is to use. In B. Swann (Ed.), *On the translation of Native American literatures.* Washington, DC: Smithsonian Institution.

Hymes, D. (1993). Inequality in language: Taking for granted. In J. E. Alatis (Ed.), *Language communication and social meaning* (pp. 23-40). Washington, DC: Georgetown University Press.

Hymes, D. (1995). "The Sun's myth," "Coyote, master of life, true to life," "Seal and her younger daughter lived there." In B. Swann (Ed.), *Coming to light. Contemporary translations of Native American literatures of North America.* New York: Random House.

Hymes, V. (1995). Experimental folklore revisited. In R. D. Abrahams (Ed.), *Fields of folklore: Essays in honor of Kenneth Goldstein.* Bloomington, IN: The Trickster Press.

Marcus, J. (1992). *Mesoamerican writing systems: Propaganda, myth and history in four ancient civilizations.* Princeton, NJ: Princeton University Press.

McDermott, R. (1986). Achieving school failure: An anthropological approach to illiteracy and social stratification. In G. D. Spindler (Ed.), *Education and cultural process: Anthropological approaches* (rev. ed). Prospect Heights, IL: Waveland Press.

Michaels, S. (1981). "Sharing time": Children's narrative styles and differential access to literacy. *Language in Society, 10,* 104-111.

Michaels, S. (1983). Influences on children's narratives. *The Quarterly Newsletter of Comparative Human Cognition, 5*(2),30-34.

Murray, D. E. (1988). The context of oral and written language: A framework for mode and medium switching. *Language in Society, 17,* 351-373.

O'Keeffe, K. O'B. (1987). Orality and the developing text of Caedmon's Hymn. *Speculum, 62*(1), 1-20.

O'Keeffe, K. O'B. (1990). *Visible song. Transitional literacy in Old English verse.* Cambridge: Cambridge University Press.

Platt, J. T. (1977). A model for polyglossia and multilingualism (with special reference to Singapore and Malaysia). *Language in Society, 6,* 361-378.

Senner, W. (Ed.). (1989). *The origins of writing.* Lincoln: University of Nebraska Press.

Staal, F. (1989). The independence of rationality from literacy. *European Journal of Sociology, 30,* 301-310.

Sticht, T. G. (1987). Literacy, cognitive robotics and general technology training for marginally literate adults. In D. A. Wagner (Ed.), *The future of literacy in a changing world* (pp. 289-301). London: Pergamon.

Tedlock, D. (1972). *Finding the center. Narrative poetry of the Zuni Indians.* New York: Dial Press. Reprinted, Lincoln: University of Nebraska Press, 1978.

Tedlock, D. (1990). From voice and ear to hand and eye. *Journal of American Folklore, 103*(408), 133-156.

Teit, J. A. (1937). More Thompson Indian tales. *Journal of American Folklore, 50*, 173-190.

Traweek, S. (1982). Gossip in science. Paper presented in the section Culture, text, and social action: Papers in memory of Michelle Zimbalist Rosaldo, American Anthropological Association annual meeting, Washington, DC.

Weinstein, G. (1986) *From mountain tops to city streets: An ethnographic investigation of literacy and social process among the Hmong of Philadelphia*. Doctoral dissertation, University of Pennsylvania, Graduate School of Education.

Contributors

Manzoor Ahmed, from Bangladesh, was the Senior Education Adviser of UNICEF at its New York headquarters and now heads the UNICEF office in Japan. He has earlier served as UNICEF's representative in China and Ethiopia. He taught at the Institute of Education and Research of Dhaka University and was Educational Adviser in the Ministry of Education in Pakistan. He also worked as a senior researcher with the International Council for Educational Development.

Stephen Anzalone is Director of Research and Evaluation at the Education Development Center in Washington, DC. Dr. Anzalone worked for numerous years on the applications of technology to educational problems in the developing world, with a special focus on Africa.

Jo Anne H. Bennett trained as a social anthropologist. She is currently an Adjunct Assistant Professor in the Department of Psychology at Queen's University, Kingston, Ontario. Her earlier (pre-doctoral) research focused on the cognitive effects of Quranic, Western, and traditional education in a predominantly Muslim town in northern Ghana. Along with J. W. Berry she was engaged in a study of the uses, traditions, and values surrounding the Cree syllabic script in northern Ontario, Canada.

John W. Berry is a Professor of Psychology at Queen's University. He received his Ph.D. from the University of Edinburgh in 1966. Has been a lecturer at the University of Sydney, a Fellow of Netherlands Institute for Advanced Study, and a visiting Professor at the Universities of Nice, Geneva, Bergen and Oxford. He is a fellow of the Canadian Psychological

Association, and Fellow and past president of the International Association for Cross-Cultural Psychology. He specializes in the areas of cross-cultural, multicultural, social and cognitive psychology.

Meta E. Bogle is a lecturer in Language Education with principal responsibility for the programme in Literacy Studies in the Faculty of Arts and Education. She coordinates Literacy Studies through Distance Education and makes an input in the Institutions Staff Development programme. Her research interests include literacy acquisition from a communication perspective, and the reconceptualization of teaching-learning for teacher training and development.

Jeanne Chall is Professor Emerita of Education and former Director, Reading Laboratory, Harvard University. She is author of numerous books and articles, including the now classic *Learning to Read: The Great Debate, Stages of Reading Development,* and is co-author, with Edgar Dale, of the *Dale-Chall Readability Formula* and, with John Carroll, of *Toward a Literate Society.*

John Downing (deceased) was Professor Emeritus of Educational Psychology at the University of Victoria, Canada. His research and writing were in two main fields: cognitive factors in literacy acquisition and cross-cultural comparisons of literacy behavior. In 1984 he was awarded the International Citation of Merit by the International Reading Association. In 1987 he was elected to the Reading Hall of Fame of the International Reading Association.

John H. Y. Edwards is professor of economics at Tulane University in New Orleans. He works principally on public finance and education issues in Latin America.

Abdelkader Ezzaki received his Ph.D. in the psychology of reading at Temple University, and is Professor and Chair of the English Department at the Faculté des Sciences de l'Education of the Université Mohamed V in Rabat, Morocco. His interests include the study of literacy, and language teaching methodologies.

Liu Fan (deceased) was head of the Section of Developmental Psychology of the Chinese Psychological Association and former head of the Section on Developmental Psychology of the Institute of Psychology of the Chinese Academy of Sciences in Beijing.

Dina Feitelson (deceased) was Professor of Education at the University of Haifa, Israel, and Director of the Infant School Program of the Israeli Ministry of Education. Her study, "The causes of school failure among first graders," was awarded the Israel Prize and led eventually to sweeping changes in approaches to reaching beginning reading. Her work concerned school-community relations, the developmental role of play, reading comprehension, and recreational reading. She published extensively in both Hebrew and English.

Bruce Fuller is Associate Professor of public policy and education at University of California at Berkeley and codirector of the PACE research center. His current work focuses on family poverty and early education policy. Mr. Fuller is currently codirecting a Berkeley-Yale initiative to assess how young children's lives are being affected by welfare reform. Mr. Fuller also writes in the area of decentralization and education policy, including school choice and charter schools. He taught at Harvard University until 1996. Mr. Fuller has worked on education and family policy issues within the World Bank and the California legislature.

Arthur Gillette received his Ed.D. from the School of Education at the University of Massachusetts in international comparative education. He has worked at UNESCO as Programme Officer in Youth and Sports Division 1953-1967; on youth questions in Ethiopia 1967-1968 and Chile 1997; Programme Officer in the Youth and Sports Division 1972-1981; Executive Assistant to Assistant Director General for Social Sciences 1981-1982; Senior Programme Officer in Literacy Division 1982-1988; and Director of Youth and Sports Division since 1992.

Kathleen Gorman is Associate Professor of psychology at the University of New Hampshire. Her work focuses on early education and child development in Third World or impoverished settings.

Dell H. Hymes is an anthropologist and linguist who has been active in the development of sociolinguistics. He was for numerous years Professor of Linguistics and subsequently Dean of the Graduate School of Education at the University of Pennsylvania; and is currently Professor at the University of Virginia. Among his published works are *Foundations of Sociolinguistics* (1974) and *Language in Education: Ethnolinguistic Essays* (1980).

Roger Iredale, Emeritus Professor of International Education, the University of Manchester (UK), was for fifteen years an education adviser at the UK Overseas Development Administration, the government department responsible for the British aid program. For ten of these years he was the Chief Education Adviser to Ministers for Overseas Development. He is currently working as an independent consultant.

Jacqueline Landau is an educational consultant in the Philadelphia area. She works with schools and school districts on issues related to second language learning, assessment, and program evaluation.

Susan Lytle is Associate Professor of Education and Director of the masters and doctoral Program in Reading/Writing/Literacy and of the Philadelphia Writing Project at the University of Pennsylvania. Her research centers on practitioner inquiry and the professional development of urban teachers, literacy learning in adolescence and adulthood, and the literacies of women. She is co-author of *Inside/Outside: Teacher Research and Knowledge* (Teachers College Press, 1993), and author of several monographs and numerous other publications related to literacy teaching and learning.

Francis Mangubhai is the Head of Centre for Language Learning and Teaching at the University of Southern Queensland, Australia, For many years he worked in the South Pacific, and was the Director of the Institute of Education at the University of South Pacific. He has authored and co-authored a number of ESL textbooks for the South Pacific, many of which are still being used. His research interests are in the area of second language reading, second language learning, cultural aspects of second language learning, and the social aspects of literacy.

Terezinha Nunes is Professor of Education in the Institute of Education, University of London, and Head of the Child Development and Learning Department. Recent research on literacy has focused on morphological aspects of spelling and the development of spelling among children with reading difficulties. Other research interests are the development of children's understanding of mathematical concepts including hearing and deaf children.

Alan C. Purves (deceased) was Professor in the Department of Program Development and Evaluation, School of Education, State University of New York at Albany. Prior to that he was a Professor at the University of Illinois and at Indiana University. He was a member of, and later chairman of, the Specialist Committee in Literature for the IEA Six-Subject Survey, and later Chairman of the International Project Council for the IEA Study of Written Composition. He has written and edited numerous volumes dealing with international comparative studies in education.

Stephen Reder received his BA from Stanford and Ph.D. from the Rockefeller University in Psychology. He is interested in the comparative study of the development of language, literacy and communication skills as well as in learning processes occurring in the workplace. Dr. Reder is Professor at Portland State University in Portland, Oregon.

Bambi B. Schieffelin is Professor of Anthropology at New York University. She has carried out field work on language use and literacy in Papua New Guinea among the Kaluli and in Philadelphia among Sino-Vietnamese and in New York City with Haitian families. In addition to her book *The Give and Take of Everyday Life: Language Socialization of Kaluli Children* (1990, Cambridge University Press), she has co-edited (with Elinor Ochs) *Language Socialization Across Cultures* (1986, Cambridge University Press) and (with K. Woolard and P. Kroskrity) *Language Ideologies* (1998, Oxford University Press).

Sylvia Scribner (deceased) was Professor of Developmental Psychology at the Graduate Center of the City University of New York. She was a principal contributor to research in the broad domain of the cultural context of literacy and cognition. She published (with M. Cole) *The Psychology of Literacy* (1981), and numerous other papers in cognition and practice.

Jun Song is a researcher in the Section of Developmental Psychology of the Institute of Psychology of the Chinese Academy of Sciences. He is especially interested in the development of reading skills among elementary school children.

Jennifer E. Spratt received her Ph.D. from the Graduate School of Education, University of Pennsylvania (1988). She has worked for the last decade in international educational development at the Research Triangle Institute in North Carolina. Currently Program Area Director of Policy Support Systems at RTI's Center for International Development, Dr. Spratt has focused her technical work on assistance to basic education planning, policy research and analysis, and policy formulation, most recently in Haiti Egypt, Guinea, and Barbados.

Harold W. Stevenson is Professor of Psychology at the University of Michigan. His research in recent years has been on the correlates of achievement in reading and mathematics of Chinese, Japanese and American elementary schoolchildren; he is currently conducting a longitudinal study of reading skills among these groups.

Brian V. Street read a first degree in English Literature and then took a conversion course in Social Anthropology at Oxford, completing a D.Phil. there in 1970 linking the two disciplines. He then undertook anthropological field work in Iran during the 1970s, focusing on literacy and education in village life. He taught social anthropology in the University of Sussex for many years. He recently joined Kings College, University of London, as Professor of Education.

Elizabeth Sulzby is Professor in the School of Education at the University of Michigan. For the past 20 years she has studied emergent literacy and the transition to conventional literacy. She has studied early literacy development across diverse groups, including children from low income homes of midwestern, Appalachian, Spanish-English bilingual, and African-American backgrounds. Recently, she has continued her in-home studies of the internalization of storybook reading in Rotterdam, The Netherlands (with A. G. Bus and M. H. van IJzendoorn) and with children whose language is typically developing or SLI (specific language impaired, with J. Kaderavek).

William H. Teale is Professor of Education at the University of Illinois at Chicago, where he teaches courses on reading, writing, and early childhood and also serves as Director of the UIC Literacy Clinic. His research, which has focused on topics such as storybook reading and the literacy environments of poor children from a variety of sociocultural backgrounds, has been conducted in diverse settings that range from classrooms and child care to homes and public libraries. For seven years, Dr. Teale served as editor of *Language Arts*, a journal of the National Council of Teachers of English.

Lequan Tong is currently head of one of the sections of the Institute for Applied Linguistics of the Chinese Academy of Social Sciences in Beijing. His main research interest is in the study of learning to read Chinese. Earlier in his career he was a model teacher of reading in the Beijing schools.

Daniel A. Wagner is Professor of Education and Director of the International Literacy Institute (ILI), co-sponsored by UNESCO and the University of Pennsylvania, where is also Director of the National Center on Adult Literacy. Among his books are: *World Literacy in the Year 2000: Research and Policy Dimensions* (1992), *Literacy: Developing the Future* (1992), *Literacy, Culture and Development* (1993), and *Literacy: An International Handbook* (1999).

I

INTRODUCTION

1

Literacy Futures, Revisited: Five Common Problems from Industrialized and Developing Countries

Daniel A. Wagner
University of Pennsylvania

Conscious of the need to arouse awareness, nationally and internationally, that the struggle against illiteracy can be won, to demonstrate solidarity with those working on behalf of the thousand million adult illiterates in the world, and to vigorously mobilize the resources and will to eradicate illiteracy before the end of this century . . . [we] hereby adopt this Declaration. (The Udaipur Literacy Declaration of 1982, cited in Bhola, 1984, p. 201)

Reduction of the adult literacy rate . . . to, say, one-half its 1990 level by the year 2000, with sufficient emphasis on female literacy to significantly reduce the current disparity between male and female illiterate. (Target 6; Report on World Conference on Education for All, Jomtien, 1990)

I. INTRODUCTION

The "eradication" of illiteracy by the year 2000, as mentioned in the above citation, was adopted as a goal of UNESCO and a significant number of its member states more than 20 years ago (and even earlier). At the 1990 Jomtien conference it could be seen that the UN agencies and others scaled back promises of a fully literate world, by choosing a target of cutting illiteracy rates in half by the year 2000—a much more modest goal. The chapters in the first edition of this volume were written in 1985 (published in 1987), five years before Jomtien, and more than a decade before the appearance of this revised and expanded volume. In the first edition I claimed that the "main concern of this paper is not whether the year 2000 is too optimistic, bur rather how we can better understand the set of constraints on the promotion of literacy across the vast number of contexts extant in the contemporary industrialized and developing world."

These words, I believe, have stood up fairly well against the test of time. We should not and cannot view illiteracy in terms we might ascribe to a *medical* model, in which the germs of illiteracy must be wiped out. An alternative view, and the one ascribed to in the present discussion (and throughout much of the volume), is that literacy is a sociocultural phenomenon, which, like culture itself, cannot be radically changed by individual or political willpower; and that any intervention should be accompanied by serious consideration of the cultural contexts in which illiteracy and literacy are embedded. While numerous efforts have been undertaken in both research and practice in the past decade, the fundamental problems (and statistics) of how literacy have actually changed rather little. whether in industrialized or developing countries. Indeed, it would be fair to say that the concern about low literacy and illiteracy is probably greater today than ever before, due in large part to increasingly competitive economies (Wagner, 1992, 1995).

A central paradox in efforts to reduce illiteracy in today's world is that so much effort has been invested and so little knowledge gained about how best to achieve success. The well-known Experimental World Literacy Program (UNESCO, 1976), ended with very little information being used by subsequent literacy programs (Gillette, this volume). And, after several decades of international attention and investment, the adult illiteracy rates of most developing countries remain relatively stable (roughly 35-55% in Africa and Asia; cf. Wagner, 1992), and population growth has meant that the actual number of illiterates has grown dramatically (from 760 million in 1970 to 1000 million in 1995). At the same time, interest in the nature and functions of literacy has greatly increased within the scientific community, although research findings are still inadequately known or disseminated within the policy-making community.

The present discussion, including the chapters in this volume, is an attempt to bring together some of the disparate elements of knowledge which have been the foci of research in varied societies across the world. It is my view that, while there is tremendous cultural variation, a number of the basic "problems" of literacy cut across every society and, therefore, provide an opportunity for synthesis. This seeming contradiction between cultural specificity and world-wide universals is one of the elements that makes the domain of literacy research both exciting and, at times, frustrating. Neither researchers nor policymakers are sure when they can apply what is learned from one context to another. This sense of uncertainty provides the rationale for an attempt, in this Introduction, to focus on what may be thought to be common problems in discussions concerning literacy in almost any context. Five such problems are considered: definitions; acquisition; retention; individual consequences; and social consequences. Finally, I provide a brief epilogue which attempts to gauge the validity of the claims made in this chapter, with the advantage that only hindsight can bequeath.

II. THE PROBLEM OF DEFINITIONS

A person is functionally literate when he has acquired the knowledge and skills in reading and writing which enable him to engage effectively in all those activities in which literacy is normally assumed in his culture or group. (Gray, 1956, p. 19)

[L]iteracy is a characteristic acquired by individuals in varying degrees from just above none to an indeterminate upper level. Some individuals are more literate or less literate than others, but it is really not possible to speak of literate and illiterate persons as two distinct categories. (UNESCO, 1957, p. 18)

It appears that a functional competence (in literacy) has been defined so that it is merely sufficient to bring its possessor within the reach of bureaucratic modes of communication and authority. (Levine, 1982, p. 261)

Literacy is not simply . . . a set of isolated skills associated with reading and writing, but more importantly . . . the application of those skills for specific purposes in specific contexts. . . . There is no single measure or specific point on a single scale that separate the "literate" from the "illiterate." Literacy can no longer be defined simply as the ability to sign one's name, completion of a particular year of schooling, or attainment of a specified reading grade level. (Kirsch & Jungeblut, 1986)

With the multitude of experts and published books on the topic, one would suppose that there would be a fair amount of agreement as to how to define the term "literacy." On the one hand, most specialists would agree that the term connotes aspects of reading and writing; on the other hand, major debates continue to revolve around such issues as what specific abilities or knowledge count as literacy, and what "levels" can and should be defined for measurement. Thus, UNESCO, an organization which has devoted much energy and resources to promoting literacy, has opted for the rather general notion of "functional literacy," as defined by Gray (1956).

While functional literacy has a great deal of appeal because of its implied adaptability to a given cultural context, the term is inadequately defined for measurement purposes. For example, it is unclear in an industrialized nation like Great Britain what level of literacy should be required of all citizens; does a coal miner have different needs than a barrister? Similarly, in a Third World country, does an illiterate woman need to learn to read and write in order to take her prescribed medicine correctly, or is it more functional (and cost-effective) to have her school-going son read the instructions to her? The use of the term *functionality*, based on norms of a given society, fails precisely because adequate norms are so difficult to establish.

What might be an adequate definition of literacy? Is it, as implied by Levine (1982), a competency which just permits the individual to be controlled (and propagandized) by government media and bureaucracies? My personal predilection is to accept the concept embedded in the 1957 UNESCO statement (above), and the work of Kirsch and his colleagues (1986, 1993), which both describe literacy as a fuzzy continuum of abilities (and potentially concepts dealing with literacy) which goes from zero to some undefined upper limit. Since there exist dozens of orthographies for hundreds of languages in which innumerable context-specific styles are in use every day, it would seem ill advised to select a universal operational definition, either at minimum or maximum needed. As done today in some countries, the use of newspaper reading skills as a functional baseline may seriously *underestimate* literacy if the emphasis is on comprehension of text (especially if the text is in a national language not well understood by the individual). Such tests may *overestimate* literacy if the individual, as is often the case, is asked simply to read aloud the passage, with little or no attempt at the measurement of comprehension.

Only in the decade since this volume was first published have there been systematic attempts to design a battery of tests from low literacy ability to high literacy ability which would be applicable across the complete range of possible languages and literacies in any society, such that such a continuum of measurement possibilities might be achieved. Specialists (primarily in industrialized countries) have begun to develop uniform methods to assess literacy within and across different societies (Elley, 1992; Kirsch, Jungeblut, Jenkins, & Kolstad, 1993; OECD & Statistics Canada, 1995). Yet, UNESCO (1994) still relies almost entirely on data provided by its member countries in order to provide worldwide statistical comparisons; these countries typically rely on national census information, which may judge literacy ability by self-assessment questionnaires, years of primary schooling, or even by more simplistic estimates. Most specialists now agree that such measures are basically unreliable or unuseful indicators of real literacy ability. Nonetheless, little change in literacy measurement has been forthcoming for a variety of reasons, including sensitive political questions concerning literacy progress in many countries. This remains the case even though a number of propositions have been put forth to provide relatively low cost assessments of literacy through sampling in household surveys (Wagner, 1992) or through proxy measures of literacy (Murray, 1997).

At least part of the controversy over the definition of literacy lies in how people have attempted to study literacy in the first place. The methodologies chosen, which span the social sciences, usually reflect the disciplinary training of the investigator. Thus, we find that anthropologists such as Street and Schieffelin (both this volume), provide in-depth ethnographic accounts of single communities, while trying to understand how literacy is woven into the fabric of community cultural life. In this work, little attempt is made at quantifying levels of particular literacy abilities, though rough qualitative self-assessments by community members are used in conjunction with other social indicators. While cognizant of cultural context, psychologists such as Carraher and Ezzaki et al. (both this volume), have chosen to look at the relationship between various measurable literacy abilities and certain social background variables. While anthropologists typically use qualitative description to construct a persuasive argument, psychologists tend to use inferential statistics to substantiate claims beyond a numerical level of uncertainty. Both these approaches (as well as history, linguistics, sociology, and computer science) have value in helping us to understand literacy. It often seems that the typical divisions that separate the disciplines from one another make it difficult, in the single domain of literacy, for common agreement to be achieved. There is no easy resolution to this problem, but it is clear that a broad-based conception (if not an exact definition) of literacy is required not only for a valid understanding of the term, but also for appropriate policy actions.

III. THE PROBLEM OF ACQUISITION

Six stages (of reading) are hypothesized . . . , from a kind of pseudo-reading to reading that is highly creative. . . . Individuals vary in their progression, yet most who are educated in typical schools tend to progress largely through the stages within (certain) age limits. . . . Among adult illiterates, the typical time periods for each of the stages is uncertain. Hypothetically they, too, tend to follow largely the same course of development, although like others with special needs, they have more success with some stages (of reading) than with others. (Chall, 1983, p. 9)

Children growing up in literate societies, surrounded by the printed word, begin to read and write long before they start school. They become aware of many of the uses of written language, they develop a sense of the written forms, and they begin to make sense of print and to experiment with communication through writing. Until recently, this growth into literacy has not been expected or appreciated, even by professional educationists. (Goodman, 1985, p. 57)

[T]he mistrust which blacks (in the United States) have toward the school and the conflict between them and these schools reduce the degree to which black parents and their children are able to accept the goals, standards, and instructional approaches of the schools as legitimate, and hence, their internalization or convictions of the need to cooperate with the school and follow their rules of behavior for achievement (of literacy) as conceived by and required by the schools. (Ogbu, 1980, p. 26)

The study of literacy acquisition appears, based on the research literature, to be heavily biased in favor of research undertaken in the industrialized world. Much of this research might be better termed the acquisition of reading and writing skills, with a heavy emphasis on the relationship between cognitive skills, such as perception and memory, and reading skills, such as decoding and comprehension (cf. Chall and Downing, both this volume). Most of this work has been carried out with school-aged children, rather than with adolescents or adults. Surprisingly little research on literacy acquisition has been undertaken in the Third World; and that which is undertaken has typically focused more on adult acquisition than on children's learning to read. This latter phenomenon is a result, quite probably, of the emphasis by Western and international organizations on promoting adult literacy in the developing world, while until quite recently ignoring adult illiteracy problems in Western societies. In the decade since the first edition of this volume, there has been an upsurge in research on adult literacy in industrialized countries (e.g., Hirsch & Wagner, 1994; Stern & Wagner, 1999; Tuijnman, Kirsch, & Wagner, 1997; Wagner & Venezky, 1995).

Despite these gaps in the research literature, some synthetic statements may be proposed as to how literacy is acquired across different societies. More than a decade ago, Downing (1974) published *Comparative Reading,* which surveyed the acquisition of reading skills across different languages and different orthographies. We know that mastery of the spoken language is a typical prerequisite for fluent reading comprehension in that language, though there exist many exceptions. For example, many Islamic scholars can read and interpret the Quran, even though they cannot speak classical Arabic, the language in which the Quran is written (Wagner, 1983); and, of course, many individuals can read and write languages which they may not speak fluently. Chall claims (this volume) that there are universal stages through which the individual must progress in order to be a fluent and comprehending reader, ranging from word decoding to understanding the intent of the person who wrote the passage. While some would take issue with Chall's precise stages, or would make counterclaims as to the interactive nature of literacy abilities and stages, most specialists would agree that there are a variety of different abilities that need to be acquired for a given written language, and that a good proportion of these must be mastered before fluent reading can be accomplished.

A consensus on the issue of reading *abilities* is rather important, since there are also those who would suggest that literacy is more like language in the sense that specific abilities do not need to be learned, but the individual must be able to interact with a "literate environment" (a term which is itself often ill-defined) in order to acquire literacy (cf. Goodman, 1985). This latter approach stems in part from the popular perception of a high correlation between literate parents and their children in many societies, but, as such, does not imply direct causation. It is likely that literate parents provide a variety of additional opportunities for their children to learn reading abilities including reading practice, but also better schools, more textbooks, and the attitudes and values which help children learn in school (e.g., Gadsden & Wagner, 1994). However, in the Third World, we know that many parents are illiterate, and yet their children do learn how to read and write (see Ezzaki et al., this volume; and Wagner, 1993). The question for specialists is how to best understand the range of abilities required by the social context for a given written language and how these abilities might be acquired.

One lacuna in the available research literature is the fact that very little research has been undertaken on the relationship between childhood and adult literacy acquisition. In both the industrialized and developing countries there is a great need for this type of research, which would provide many insights concerning the relation between cognitive and knowledge-based skills, social factors and reading achievement. Since adults have a much more complete repertoire of cognitive and linguistic skills and general knowledge than most beginning readers of primary-school age, it ought to be possible to tease out the range of cognitive and social prerequisites of learning to read. As yet, little research has been undertaken along these lines.

Finally, Ogbu (1980) and others have stressed the importance of class structure and ethnicity/race as explications of differential motivation among young literacy learners. Ogbu claims convincingly that many minority children in America are simply unmotivated to learn to read and write in the cultural structure of the school. This approach is increasingly popular in that it avoids blaming the child for specific cognitive deficits, while focusing attention on change in the structure of the school. This view has been making some progress among Third World social scientists, particularly in the area of language planning; but little psychometric research has been carried out on reading acquisition in the Third World which would substantiate claims of the structural approach.

IV. THE PROBLEM OF RETENTION

[V]ery few empirical studies of retention of (literacy and) of basic skills have been under taken, compatibility among studies is minimal, and there are enormous problems in making valid comparisons between countries of different levels of development and between adults and children. (IDRC, 1979, p. 71)

The term educational "wastage" is very common in the literature on international and comparative education, particularly with respect to the Third World. This term typically refers to the loss, usually by dropping out, of children who do not finish what is thought to be the minimum educational curriculum of a given country (often 5-8 years of primary school). Most specialists who work within this area gather data on the number of children who enter school each year, the number who progress on to the next grade, those who repeat a given year (quite common in many Third World countries), and those who quit school altogether. The concept of wastage, then, refers to those children for whom an economic *investment* in educational resources has already been made, but who, literally, waste that investment by not completing the appropriate level of studies.

The issue of literacy retention becomes crucial here, for it is *not*, presumably, the number of school leavers or graduates that really counts for a society, but what they *learn* and *retain* from their school years, such as literacy and numeracy skills. When students drop out of an educational program a society is wasting its resources because those individuals (children or adults, if in an adult education program) will not reach some presumed threshold of minimum learning such that what has been acquired will not be lost. Thus, retention of learning (or literacy, in particular) is a key goal of educational planners around the world; the special attention given to this issue in the Third World, as contrasted with the industrialized world, appears to be due to the simple fact that educational resources are much more scarce in the former. An obvious question might be: what, indeed, is the threshold of learning required for literacy to be retained in one or another society?

Up until the mid-1980s, there were only three scientific studies published on this question (Hartley, 1984; National Educational Testing Center, 1982; Roy & Kapoor, 1975). Though it is beyond the scope of this brief review to consider these publications in detail, methodological problems contained in each of them render clear answers on the issue of retention, as posed above, impossible. We know very little about what might be termed the "trajectory" of literacy ability, once it has been acquired. This is as complex a topic as acquisition because the same sorts of localized societal and cognitive factors intervene in the retention process. What are the effects of practice on literacy ability? What type of materials, what type of motivation, and how many years are required to *retain* fluent or partially fluent reading and writing. In what types of schools and programs? Such questions provide a rich and important area of inquiry. Nonetheless, little research has been undertaken in this area.

Ten years later, several new studies on literacy retention have been published, the most thorough to date stemming from the Morocco Literacy Project, described in part in the contribution by Ezzaki et al. (this volume). This Project "tracked" children who had dropped out of primary school before receiving their school certificate, and followed (and tested) these children for another two or three years. The results of this study demonstrate that there was relatively little skill loss among the sample population, irrespective of the type of skill level achieved and type of post-literacy practice (cf. Wagner et al., 1989; Wagner, 1993). A more recent study, undertaken in the United States among low literate adults, showed similar results (Wagner, in press).

V. THE PROBLEM OF INDIVIDUAL CONSEQUENCES

What does illiteracy mean to the illiterate? . . . [T]he map of illiteracy closely coincides with the maps of poverty, malnutrition, ill-health, infant mortality, etc. Hence, in the typical case, the illiterate is not only unable to read and write, but he—or more usually she—is poor, hungry, (and) vulnerable to illness. . . . In these circumstances, does his or her literacy really matter? Would he or she even list illiteracy among life's major problems? . . . Hence, the best argument for doing something about illiteracy is not that it is part of the immense problem of inequality in our world, but that literacy can be part of the answer to remedying it. (Gillette & Ryan, 1985, p. 21)

An individual needs a minimum level of mastery in order to "pass" as literate in public and keep intact his or her self-respect; as schools and literacy programs become more effective in equipping their students with these skills, the effective threshold of acceptability will be raised accordingly. There is, quite simply, no finite level of attainment, even within a specific society, which is capable of eliminating the disadvantages of illiteracy or semi-literacy by permitting the less literate to compete on equal terms for employment and enjoy parity of status with the more literate. (Levine, 1982, p. 260)

The above quotations are perspectives typical of two opposing sides of the arguments concerning the necessity of literacy at the individual level, but each perspective leaves out an essential ingredient. Gillette and Ryan admit that other problems might have a higher salience and importance to the world's poor, but nonetheless claim that literacy can somehow be part of the remedy (yet another medical metaphor), without specifying what is the real linkage between literacy and other types of benefits, such as health. In contrast, Levine treats literacy like IQ scores in that, since the latter is a normed average, it is impossible to raise the national IQ because it will always stay at 100, even if many individuals obtain more correct answers in a given year. In the same way, by improving national literacy rates, one is simply putting the norm at a higher level, which, on the whole, will maintain most individuals at their same *relative* level compared to others. Levine's argument, of course, denies the real possibility that literacy ability might have some concrete utility beyond one's social status relative to his or her neighbor or classmate.

Does either contention truly represent the real problems of individuals living in situations where a change from low to higher literacy will make a concrete difference in life? The only way to determine an answer is to do more ethnographic and case studies which delve into the actual lives of individuals (e.g., Reder, this volume). Looking at the "average literacy rate" and comparing this with other health indicators, or estimating "employability" from such a rate, only obscures the diversity of human plights. Our own work in rural low-literate Morocco has demonstrated that those with higher literacy tend to be better off economically, but also that an in creasing number of parents believe that more education and more literacy will not necessarily lead to greater wealth, since more and more school graduates have not found work. A common perception is that both *some* literacy and *some* level of education are needed by *some* individuals in *every* family (or extended family) to meet the tasks required by government bureaucracy, but not everyone need be literate in order to accomplish such tasks (cf. Wagner, 1993a; Wagner, Messick, & Spratt, 1986). Similar mixed views and beliefs about the advantages of literacy and disadvantages of illiteracy have been found in studies within the United States (e.g., Wagner, 1993b).

VI. THE PROBLEM OF SOCIAL CONSEQUENCES

[T]here is no real sense in which a level of education in the active population of a country can be said to be technically 'required' to permit the achieved level of economic growth of that country. That sort of argument grossly exaggerates the contribution of manipulative and cognitive skills in the performance of economic functions, and ignores the fact that such skills are largely acquired by on-the-job training. . . . (Blaug, 1985, p. 25)

[A]dopting different criteria (for literacy) for different regions and communities would ensure the perpetuation of educational inequalities and the differential access to life opportunities with which these standards are associated. (Scribner, 1985, p. 10)

Since World War II perhaps the most compelling argument for human resources development is that literacy and schooling will lead to economic growth in countries which are able to make a sufficient investment. This is the approach sometimes referred to as investment in human capital (e.g., Psacharopoulos & Woodhall, 1985; Shultz, 1981). Anderson and Bowman (1965), for example, went so far as to say that an 80% national adult literacy rate would be necessary for rapid economic development, while a 40% literacy rate would be required for a minimal amount of economic development. Naturally, this type of claim makes use of aggregated data across many countries of the world, based on a significant correlation between GNP and literacy rates. Naturally, claiming causality using such correlations is a very hazardous approach. On the contrary, one would probably be just as correct in claiming that literacy rates, like infant mortality rates, are prime indicators of the degree of economic development in most countries. If social and economic progress are being attained, then one usually finds that literacy rates climb and infant mortality rates drop. Blaug (1985), who was at one time a supporter of human capital theory, has changed his earlier position, coming to the conclusion (cited above) that neither years of schooling nor specific literacy rates have any direct effect on economic growth.

It would seem that the intellectual tide is turning against those who argued that universal literacy would have important economic outcomes. Increasing numbers of policymakers in the area of educational planning are wondering if nations can bear the burden of ever-expanding educational costs with fixed or lowered economic resources. Mixed with economic arguments, we hear increasing reference to moral imperatives in both the developing and industrialized worlds (e.g. Bhola, 1984; Kozol, 1985); yet there are many moral imperatives in today's world (e.g., life, liberty, health, and literacy), and choosing among them is not, strictly speaking, a scientific enterprise. Nonetheless, the association of literacy with health, nutrition, and other social goods is such that it is unlikely that governments will cease efforts at universalizing literacy and primary education. Moreover, high rates of literacy have taken generations to achieve, in spite of the rhetoric of the literature on literacy campaigns and educational revolutions (cf. Wagner, 1986a). As we have seen in the realm of economic development, literacy development has not taken place over night. Literacy certainly brings economic and social benefits; but the question that Blaug and others raise is whether, on the whole, the costs of obtaining high levels of literacy outweigh the benefits. This debate within even the supporters of literacy work shows, as we approach the year 2000, little sign of abating.

The issue, as I see it, is not whether to promote literacy, but rather in what manner. Even if we had conclusive evidence of the economic benefits of literacy, the question for literacy and development specialists ought to be: How can we most efficiently achieve appropriate literacy levels with the available economic and social resources? Here, the emphasis is on efficiency and appropriateness, domains in which specialists can play a crucial role. A campaign may be efficient in a country undergoing revolutionary change, such as Nicaragua, where schools had been closed for years and urban high school students were available for rural teaching. But such a campaign may be relatively less efficient in a country like Zimbabwe, where public schooling has a long and organized history, and it is difficult and expensive to provide teachers for the less literate countryside. What is appropriate, of course, brings forth a whole series of qualifiers, such as: for whom, in which language, for what purpose, using what methods, and so on.

VII. CONCLUSION: TOWARD A KNOWABLE FUTURE OF LITERACY

Meaningful adaptation is actively evolved good design for local circumstances, not merely muddling through with inherited features poorly suited to current needs. (Gould, 1985, p. 12)

[I]deal literacy is simultaneously adaptive, socially empowering and self-enhancing. (Scribner, 1985, p. 7)

[The] great mass of reading research should be relegated to the shelves by those focusing on Third World adult literacy problems. (International Development Research Centre, 1979, p. 55)

Will the world, as proposed by UNESCO, be literate in the year 2000 or even 2025? If the above analysis has some validity, the chances are small to nonexistent. More importantly, the question itself is, as implied earlier, the wrong one. More realistic is the following: What are the prospects for a *knowable* and *doable* future of literacy by the year 2000 or 2025? Here, we can be more optimistic. The emphasis on what may be known is central, since, until recently, so little has been known about how literacy is acquired, valued, and retained, particularly in low-literate environments around the world. In order to have a realistic policy goal of increasing literacy, we need to have a clearer understanding of it as a sociocultural phenomenon. As Gould (1985) suggests, in a quite different arena, simply "muddling through" without paying attention to local circumstances is a strategy destined to fail. Those who would promote short-term media-oriented campaigns with only modest adaptations to the local contexts for literacy have two major problems to contend with: first, campaigns are typically top-down government-sponsored approaches where citizens may have at least an ambivalent relationship with central authorities; second, the notion of short-term programming, while convenient for ideologues, runs counter to the notion that adaptation and flexibility in programming will be critical for success, and fails to recognize that literacy is a cultural phenomenon that cannot be imposed or maintained through short-term interventions.

As noted by IDRC (above), much of the research on literacy has been, until fairly recently, irrelevant to those who are interested in its promotion around the world. One prime reason for this paradox (as in other areas of Third World inquiry) is that researchers have been motivated more by theoretically derived questions than by questions based on policy needs (cf. Wagner, 1986b). The picture has begun to change, especially in the 1990s, as publications on literacy have proliferated. The idea of a knowable future of literacy is not just a researcher's desire to do more research, but a necessity for anyone interested in helping to increase literacy in a practical and long-lasting manner.

Another central theme evoked in this discussion is that of the relationship between literacy problems and literacy solutions seen in a systemic and global fashion, and which takes into account what we have learned about the varied nature of literacies in contemporary societies. There has been a historical tendency to treat literacy in the industrialized and developing worlds as completely different and unrelated, with different causes and different effects. We now know that this is not so. What varies are the specific contexts for literacy, with many parallels existing within and across different countries. Thus, we find that the low-literate individual must cope with a similar set of problems concerning the accomplishment of literacy tasks in many different countries (such as dealing with government bureaucracy), but he or she may be able to resolve his or her literacy needs through a culturally-specific set of heuristics (such as a literate uncle or a walk-in clinic). We may agree, for example, that beginning readers of alphabetic scripts—whether adults or children—must understand how to make blends of letters, so as to map written codes onto the spoken language. On the other hand, we now know that newly literate adults may be able to accomplish this task much more quickly than children, due to a more advanced array of cognitive and linguistic skills. We may agree that most people now acquire literacy in formal school settings, and that subsequent failure to achieve literacy is usually due to failure and/or dropping out of school. Yet, the solution to keeping children in school settings may vary from solutions such as Quranic preschooling in a Muslim country (cf. Wagner et al., 1986) to work-placements linked with schooling in a European country (cf. Hirsch & Wagner, 1994).

In sum, the future of literacy will depend on the efforts of and common interests among, many sectors of the world's societies, and as much on the non-literate populations as on the literate ones. Policy makers should not simply decide that all must be literate by such and such a date. A sensitive balance and effective communication must be sought. Within this framework the role of literacy research, as evidenced in the present Volume, is to provide the kind of knowledge about literacy which will be crucial for the efforts of the future.

VIII. POSTSCRIPT

The field of literacy is more informed now than it was a decade or more ago. Scholarship has advanced, and so have the number of people who UNESCO identifies as "literate" across the world. Unfortunately, with population growth taken into account, little real progress can be claimed in reducing "illiteracy" and "low literacy" in most countries, especially in the developing world. This chapter tries to suggest that such findings should come as no surprise. Literacy work in the field is even more problematic than the research perspectives pointed to in this chapter. Resources for adult literacy (and even children's literacy in school contexts) are slim and often declining in real terms around the world. Politicians often express their frustration that more has not been achieved with the investments provided. Such is the fate of social and educational programs that often promise more that they can reasonably deliver.

Nonetheless, the future of literacy and for literacy is not dim. We know more now than we did before. If we could perhaps reduce our promises and our expectations, and invest wisely in the areas of literacy promotion that are likely to produce the greatest individual and societal gains, public confidence would rise concomitantly. The challenge of a fully literate world remains, and will certainly be with us for decades to come.

REFERENCES

Anderson, C.A., & Bowman, M.J. (1965). *Education and economic development*. London: Frank Cass.

Bhola, H.S. (1984). *Campaigning for literacy: Eight national experiences of the twentieth century, with a memorandum to decision makers*. Paris: UNESCO.

Blaug, M. (1985). Where are we now in the economics of education? *Economics of Education Review, 4*, 17-28.

Chall, J. S. (1983). *Stages of reading development*. New York: McGraw-Hill.

Downing, J. (1973). *Comparative reading*. New York: Macmillan.

Elley, W. (1992). *How in the world do students read: IEA study of reading literacy*. Hamburg: IEA.

Gadsden, V., & Wagner, D.A. (Eds.). (1994). *Literacy among African-American youth*. Cresskill, NJ: Hampton Press.

Gillette, A., & Ryan, J. (1985). Eleven issues in literacy for the 1990's. *Assignment Children, 63/64*, 1-44.

Goodman, K.S. (1985). Growing into literacy. *Prospects, 15*, 57-65.

Gould, S.J. (1985) Mysteries of the panda. *New York Review of Books, 32*(13), 12-14.

Gray, W.S. (1956). *The teaching of reading and writing*. Paris. UNESCO.

Hartley, M.J. (1984) *Achievement and wastage: An analysis of the retention of basic skills in primary education. Final report of the international study of the retention of literacy and numeracy: An Egyptian case study (preliminary version)*. Washington, D.C: The World Bank.

Heath, S.B. (1983). *Ways with words*. New York: Cambridge University Press.

Hirsch, D., & Wagner, D.A. (Eds.). (1994). *What makes workers learn? The role of incentives in workplace education and training*. Cresskill, NJ: Hampton Press.

International Development Research Centre. (1979). *The world of literacy: Policy research and action*. Ottawa: IDRC.

Kirsch, I., & Jungeblut, A. (1986). *Literacy: Profiles of America's young adults*. Final report of the National Assessment of Educational Progress. Princeton, NJ: Educational Testing Service.

Kirsch, I., Jungeblut, A., Jenkins, L., & Kolstad, A. (1993). *Adult literacy in America: A first look at the results of the National Adult Literacy Survey*. Washington, DC: National Center for Educational Statistics, U.S. Department of Education.

Kozol, J. (1985). *Illiterate America*. New York: Doubleday.

Levine, K. (1982). Functional literacy: Fond illusions and false economies. *Harvard Educational Review, 52*, 249-266.

Murray, T.S. (1997). Proxy measurement of adult basic skills: Lessons from Canada. In A. Tuijnman, I. Kirsch, & D.A. Wagner (Eds.), *Adult basic skills: Innovations in measurement and policy analysis* (pp. 163-185). Cresskill, NJ: Hampton Press.

National Educational Testing Center. (1982). *Literacy retention among dropouts from the Philippine elementary schools*. Manila: Philippine Ministry of Education, Culture and Sports.

OECD and Statistics Canada. (1995). *Literacy, economy and society*. Paris: OECD.

Ogbu, J.U. (1980). *Literacy in subordinate cultures: The case of Black Americans*. Paper presented at the Literacy Conference of the Library of Congress, Washington, DC.

Psacharopoulos, G., & Woodhall, M. (1985). *Education for development: An analysis of investment choices*. New York: Oxford University Press.

Roy, P., & Kapoor, J.M. (1975). *The retention of literacy*. New Delhi: Macmillan of India.

Scribner, S. (1985). Literacy in three metaphors. *American Journal of Education, 93*(1), 6-21.

Shultz, T.W. (1981). *Investing in people: The economics of population quality*. Berkeley: University of California Press.

Stern, D., & Wagner, D.A. (Eds.). (1999). *International perspectives on the school-to-work transition*. Cresskill, NJ: Hampton Press.

Tuijnman, A., Kirsch, I., & Wagner, D.A. (Eds.). (1997). *Adult basic skills: Innovations in measurement and policy analysis*. Cresskill, NJ: Hampton Press.

UNESCO. (1957). *World illiteracy at mid-century.* Paris: UNESCO.
UNESCO. (1976). *The experimental world literacy program: A critical assessment.* Paris: UNESCO/UNDP.
UNESCO. (1978). *Revised recommendation concerning the international standardization of educational statistics.* Paris: UNESCO.
UNESCO. (1985). *The current literacy situation in the world.* Paris: UNESCO.
UNESCO. (1994). *World education report.* Paris: UNESCO.
Wagner, D.A. (1983). Indigenous education and literacy in the Third World. In D.A. Wagner (Ed.), *Child development and international development: Research-policy interfaces.* San Francisco: Jossey-Bass.
Wagner, D.A. (1986a). Review of H.S. Bhola, *Campaigning for literacy.* (1985) and V. Miller, *Between struggle and hope: The Nicaraguan literacy campaign* (1985). *Comparative Education Review,* April, 450-454.
Wagner, D.A. (1986b). Child development research and the Third World: A future of mutual interest? *American Psychologist, 41,* 298-301.
Wagner, D.A. (1992). Literacy: Developing the future. *UNESCO Yearbook of Education,* Vol. 43. Paris: UNESCO.
Wagner, D.A. (1993a). *Literacy, culture and development: Becoming literate in Morocco.* New York: Cambridge University Press.
Wagner, D.A. (1993b, September). Myths and misconceptions in adult literacy: A research and development perspective. *Adult Learning,* 9-11.
Wagner, D.A. (1994). *Use it or lose it?: The problem of adult literacy skill retention* (NCAL Technical Rep. TR94-07). Philadelphia: University of Pennsylvania.
Wagner, D.A. (1995). Literacy and development: Rationales, myths, innovations, and future directions. *International Journal of Educational Development, 15,* 341-362
Wagner, D.A. (in press). Literacy retention: Comparisons across age, time and culture. In S.G. Paris & H. Wellman (Eds.), *Global prospects for education, culture and schooling.* Washington, DC: American Psychological Association.
Wagner, D.A., Messick, B.M., & Spratt, J.E. (1986). Studying literacy in Morocco. In B.B. Schieffelin & P. Gilmore (Eds.), *The acquisition of literacy: Ethnographic perspectives.* Norwood, NJ: Ablex.
Wagner, D.A., Spratt, J.E., Klein, G., & Ezzaki, A. (1989). The myth of literacy relapse: Literacy retention among fifth-grade Moroccan school leavers. *International Journal of Educational Development, 9,* 307-315.
Wagner, D.A., & Venezky, R.L. (1995). *Adult literacy: The next generation* (NCAL Whitepaper report). Philadelphia, PA: National Center on Adult Literacy.
WCEFA (1990). *World conference on education for all.* New York: United Nations.

II

THEORETICAL PERSPECTIVES ON COMPARATIVE LITERACY

2

Introduction

Sylvia Scribner[†]
City University of New York

As we know from experience in many fields, a comparative approach offers an opportunity to tackle basic questions concerning constancy and variety in human affairs that cannot be addressed by concentration on a single setting. In the case of literacy development it is evident that countries can best benefit from each other's experience if comparative research sorts out those aspects of literacy that are constant across cultures ("universals") and those that vary ("culture-specific" features). Universals and differences, of course, are only determinable within a particular theoretical framework and disciplinary perspective. The chapters that follow clearly illustrate this contingency relationship. Brian Street draws on cultural anthropology and evidence from historical and ethnographic case studies to argue that the model of a universal literacy, defined in technical terms, is inconsistent with actual social practices; the functions and meanings of literacy, and its impact on social relationships, vary with the power structure and belief systems in a given society. John Downing distills an extensive body of research, conducted primarily by psychologists, to support the thesis that basic processes of literacy acquisition are universal, although effective educational practices need to take into account the specific features of literacy use and learning in particular communities. Jeanne Chall, on the basis of psychological studies of reading, maintains that an invariant sequence characterizes reading development, not only among children of all societies, but among adults as well.

[†]Deceased

An interesting feature of these contributions is that analyses conducted primarily from the psychologist's perspective emphasize the universal aspects of literacy, while those contributed by social and historical scientists stress variety and relativity. As several contributors to this volume (e.g., Reder, Wagner) observe, there is an unresolved and underlying tension between models of literacy based on studies of psychological processes and models based on social processes at the macrolevel. They do not seem to fit well together into a larger picture, and sometimes generate conflicting implications for literacy programs and policies.

This problem of integrating findings generated from psychological and social sciences is not unique to scholars of literacy. It reflects basic theoretical problems of long standing for which over the years various resolutions have been proposed (see Leacock, 1985, for a historical review of efforts in anthropology to provide an integrative frame; Wertsch & Lee, 1984, cite similar efforts in psychology). In these brief notes I want to draw attention to several current theoretical projects which I think offer useful constructs for an integrative framework for social and psychological approaches to literacy research. The two projects concern the clarification of the problem of integrative levels: a problem in the philosophy of science; and the development of an activity approach to theory and research in psychology. I will give a very sketchy presentation of these approaches here, and then consider what kinds of questions they pose for literacy research.

THE LEVELS CONCEPT

Initially introduced as a way of ordering phenomena in biology (Woodger, 1929; Needham, 1937) the concept of levels of organization has been elaborated as a general methodological approach in many sciences (see Aronson, 1984, for a historical review and analysis). This approach views all material entities and processes as being organized hierarchically in progressively more complex systems or levels of integration. Principal levels are frequently and roughly characterized as the physical level, the biological, the psychological and the social levels, although other and more differentiated schemes have also been proposed. Each level has its own unique properties which cannot be predicted from knowledge of lower level processes; thus processes on a societal level cannot be explained by reducing them to psychological or physiological processes. At the same time, knowledge of lower-level processes is essential for understanding higher-level processes, since these continue to be operative in the higher level system. Full understanding of a given phenomenon often hinges on a grasp of the relationship of levels to each other: how do higher levels modify processes at a lower level? How do levels become integrated into more complex systems? Here formidable problems arise. Concretization of the levels approach for a particular inquiry makes enormous demands on still-scant theoretical resources. Some progress, however, has been made in formulating general principles of attack. Tobach (in press) has contributed the critical insight that if these concepts are to be fruitful, levels and their relationships need to be analyzed, not "in general" but with respect to a particular scientific category or question.

Now what does this mean for the present discussion? I think it suggests first, that phenomena in literacy learning and practice cannot be considered as *either* psychological *or* social but as particular integrations of processes operating on both these levels. Second, it suggests that, to examine the integration of these processes, we need to pursue the analysis, not with respect to literacy "in general", but with respect to some particular unit or aspect of literacy. A prior requirement, then, is to conceptualize literacy within some theory which offers applicable units of analysis, around which we can seek to integrate the knowledge gained through social practice and through research in many disciplines. The theory of activity developed by psychologists and philosophers working in the tradition of L. S. Vygotsky is such a foundational theory (see Leont'ev, 1978, 1981; Wertsch & Lee, 1984, for expositions).

ACTIVITY THEORY

Activity theory holds that the integral units of human life—humans interacting with each other and the world—can be conceptualized as *activities* which serve to fulfill distinctive motives. In the course of activities, people engage in goal-directed *actions*, carried out for particular purposes under particular conditions and with particular technical means. The *operations* which compose actions may be, and typically are, both mental and behavioral, and vary with both subjective and objective conditions and means. I emphasize the terms *activities, actions,* and *operations* since the theory holds these to be the structural units of human behavior, and, accordingly, units of analysis for the behavioral sciences. These units are non-additive: an activity may be realized by different actions (one can satisfy hunger by catching fish or opening a can of soup), and, conversely, one and the same action may realize different activities (a fisherman may try to land a big fish to feed a family or to win a sportsman's prize). Actions and operations are similarly non-contingent, since various operations are often available to meet the same goal, and the same operations may contribute to attainment of different goals.

Consider literacy in this light (see Scribner & Cole, 1981, for a fuller but somewhat different elaboration of an activity approach to literacy). We may conceptualize literacy as a set of activities satisfying distinctive motives related to the written language: creating distinctive genres of communication, for example, or transmitting information over time and space. Literacy can also be conceptualized as actions, in this case acts of reading or writing carried out for particular purposes. According to our guiding framework, literacy actions may realize literacy activities, but they may also, and more frequently do, realize other activities with a broad array of motivations—educative (getting through school), religious-ideological (becoming a holy person) or political (organizing a social movement). Literacy may also be considered as operations—namely, the set of processes and procedures by which reading and writing actions are executed in a given time and place.

It is immediately evident from this analysis that literacy—considered on all of these scales—is always profoundly and pervasively social in nature. Literacy activities come into being (acquire "motivational" power) through larger political, economic and cultural forces in a given society; neither their structure nor function can be understood outside of their societal context. Literacy actions are similarly profoundly and pervasively social, since the purposes for which people read and write, and the settings in which these actions take place are socially organized and maintained, and the activities whose motives they realize are socially generated. As for operations, these, too, take shape around the particular symbolic systems (language and orthography) in a culture or social setting and the technical means for producing written language available within the community (whether stylus and stone, or terminal key and computer screen).

Where do psychological processes come in? I would maintain that psychological processes are integrated with sociocultural processes throughout all of these structural units. Consider activities. Motivations for literacy activities are acquired by individuals in the course of their own personal life histories as members of a social group. As for actions, it is similarly the case that the purposes and goals of literacy actions (particular acts of reading and writing) must make sense to individuals who undertake, or refrain from undertaking, them (that is, they must be seen to realize some motive). And, patently, individuals must acquire the knowledge and perceptual and intellectual skills (operations) involved in acquiring and using a given culture's means of literacy and modal literacy actions. Note that this framework is a departure from the more common approach of equating the "psychological" with "microprocesses" and the "cultural" with "macro-processes." That equation leads to a separatist view—as though psychological processes could be separated from sociocultural processes and "lead a life on their own."

It is perfectly clear that the complexity of literacy is not about to yield to a schematic application of a theoretical approach, which is itself in an early stage, more valuable for offering constructs than providing testable theories. Still, the perspective raises interesting suggestions about future directions in an integrated approach to literacy research.

In attempting to integrate knowledge derived from practice and research in various disciplines, it is useful to sort out the structural units of literacy which are objects of concern and analysis. One source of underlying tension between psychological analyses of literacy, and historical, social and cultural analyses, may be the mismatch between the units of literacy each has traditionally emphasized. Social sciences customarily probe the factors generating and sustaining literacy activities, and examine the social forces regulating their distribution. Ethnographic research, in addition, contributes highly detailed case studies on the organization of literacy actions in various social contexts—the sorts of reading or writing projects members of a cultural system engage in and the purposes these satisfy. In psychological research, investigators have overwhelmingly devoted their energies to analyzing perceptual, linguistic, and cognitive processes implicated in reading and writing, which we have referred to here as operations.

The problem of integrating the great bulk of psychological research into social analyses of literacy—and into direct programs—thus revolves around an assessment of how knowledge about reading and writing operations relate to larger questions about literacy. Clearly it does. For example, if research indicates that the beginning reading process is lengthened by the heavy memorization demands a script such as Chinese imposes on learners, then educators and policy-makers attempting to extend popular literacy may well want to consider some measures of script modification. But useful information on the kind of modification to make, and when and how it might be implemented, will not flow directly from research on reading operations. These questions require attention to social and psychological analyses on literacy activity and action levels as well. How might instructional activities be affected? Will current literacy teachers be motivated to teach a script they may not value? Will script changes restrict the kinds of reading available to new literates? And, if so, how will this affect the purposes for which they chose to learn how to read in the first place? As this line of analysis indicates, an activity frame of reference not only provides some guidelines for piecing together research pieces, but enlarges the realm of research questions which might contribute to literacy programs.

From the vantage point of a psychologist, two arenas of exploration are especially challenging. One has to do with the level of actions. Wagner (Wagner et al., 1986) and others in this volume (e.g., Street,

Bennett and Berry, and Reder) have deepened our understanding of the diversity and modal types of reading actions that are undertaken in various cultural settings. The array of purposes for which people engage in reading in their "indigenous settings" may be more or less compatible with the purposes for which reading actions are undertaken in school. How do the purposes of school-based reading actions come to make sense to students whose every day activities do not encompass such purposes? What are the processes of goal formation?

Finally, though I have not seen studies of this kind in collections of papers on literacy, social psychological research on such issues as group dynamics, the autonomization of motives, and the formation of ideologies may have much to contribute to our understanding of the origin and history of literacy activities.

REFERENCES

Aronson, L.R. (1984). Levels of integration and organization: A revaluation of the evolutionary scale. In G. Greenberg & E. Tobach (Eds.), *Behavioral evolution and integrative levels*. Hillsdale, NJ: Lawrence Erlbaum.

Leacock, E. (1985). The individual and society in anthropological theory. *Dialectical Anthropology, 9.*

Leont'ev, A.N (1978). *Activity, consciousness, and personating.* Englewood Cliffs, NJ: Prentice-Hall.

Leont'ev, A.N. (1981). Sign and activity. In J. V. Wertsch (Ed.), *The concept of activity in Soviet psychology.* White Plains, NY: M.E. Sharpe.

Needham, J. (1937). *Integrative levels: A revaluation of the idea of progress.* Oxford: Clarendon Press.

Scribner, S., & Cole, M. (1981). *The psychology of literacy.* Cambridge, MA: Harvard University Press.

Tobach, E. (in press). Integrative levels in the comparative psychology of cognition, language and consciousness. In G. Greenberg & E. Tobach (Eds.), *Cognition, language and consciousness: Integrative levels.* Hillsdale, NJ: Lawrence Erlbaum.

Wagner, D.A. Messick, B.M., & Spratt, J. (1986). Studying literacy in Morocco. In B.B. Schieffelin (Ed.), *The acquisition of literacy: Ethnographic perspectives.* Norwood, NJ: Ablex.

Wertsch, J.V. (Ed.). (1979). *The concept of activity in Soviet psychology.* White Plains, NY: M.E. Sharpe.

Wertsch, J.V., & Lee, B. (1984). The multiple levels of analysis in a theory of action. *Human Development, 27,* 3-14, 193-196.

Woodger, J.H. (1929). *Biological principles.* London: Routledge & Kegan Paul.

3

Comparative Perspectives on World Literacy

John Downing†
University of Victoria, B.C., Canada

I. INTRODUCTION

The comparative method of study has led to progress in many disciplines. Comparing different phenomena leads to the discovery of universal characteristics that lie beneath the surface of apparent diversity. When these universals are recognized, each of the different varieties of the category are better understood and can be more effectively brought under deliberate control.

When one makes such a comparative approach to the study of literacy behavior, one recognizes more clearly that reading is reading no matter what the surface differences in orthography—logographies, syllabaries, alphabets. Likewise, writing is writing in any orthography. Literacy is learned only once in an individual's lifetime, just as oracy is learned once only. When the skills of oracy or literacy have been learned, they are readily transferable to other languages despite surface differences.

The proposition put forward in this chapter is that the universal psychological processes of literacy acquisition can be determined irre-

---

†Deceased

spective of the specific languages and writing systems in which literacy develops. These universals exist beneath the surface of a diversity of literate cultures and they exist as potentials in preliterate people. In this chapter these cross-language and cross-cultural universals will be described firstly in terms of sociolinguistic features and secondly in respect of the common human psychology of the learning of skills. In both these areas affective as well as cognitive factors will be seen to be significant. The chapter concludes with some practical suggestions for improving literacy programs in the future.

Universal Characteristics of Literacy Acquisition

It is sometimes argued that, because "literacy is not a universal of human life", it is not learned in a universal manner in the way that cognitive operations such as conservation or temporal representation are. Feldman's (1980) view that universals in cognitive development occur because of universal human biological characteristics and universal features of the physical environment and that these cognitive universals do not require any special environment for them to develop is cited. On this premise, it is claimed that since some societies have no written language and some individuals in literate societies remain illiterate, literacy acquisition cannot be based on cognitive universals.

The theoretical position taken in this chapter is that literacy acquisition is indeed a universal process. The fact that some societies do not develop literacy because they have no written language does not constitute negative evidence to this position. As Piaget (1959) pointed out originally in the 1920s in his *Language and Thought of the Child*, the universal stages of cognitive development and the ages at which they occur depend on individuals' experiences of the appropriate environment. Thus, if literacy exists in the environment, one would expect to find universal characteristics in people's responses to it. If literacy is not present in the environment, people's potential universal responses to it still exist though, as yet, they remain undeveloped. The same is true, of course, of spoken language. Children who are deprived of experiences of speech do not learn this universal human skill despite their potential capability.

In searching for these universal features of the literacy acquisition process, one must be very careful not to assume that observations of how children learn to read and write in one's own culture and language can be generalized to other cultures and languages. For example, it would be dangerous to assume that a conception of stages of reading development based on observations of children's reading only in American schools, for instance, could designate universal steps in the acquisition of reading skill. Although such a stage theory might be an accurate description of children's behavior in response to the curriculum of reading instruction found in the majority of schools in the United States, it would be scientifically un acceptable as having universal application, without evidence from cross cultural research on literacy learning.

A cross-cultural or comparative approach is essential to sift out the true universals from the linguistic or cultural specifics. Only by making comparisons between the literacy behaviors of people in differing cultures and in varying languages can one understand the fundamental and universal processes of reading and writing, and how these develop. This was the aim of the original *Comparative reading* project (Downing, 1973) and it is the aim of this present chapter which is a new effort in that direction.

Literacy as One Mode of Language Behavior

In his contribution to this volume, Street emphasizes the overlap and interaction of the oral and literate modes of language and he rejects the notion of any "great divide" between them. Street's position is amply supported by the contemporary research literature of the social sciences. Although there are important differences between spoken language and written language, they are obviously related and influence one another (Akinnaso, 1981). Thus, oracy and literacy are varieties of language behavior. Hence one should expect that the universal laws of learning in general, and the universal principles of language learning in particular, must apply to literacy as well as to oracy. There may be some specific characteristics of literacy due to its primarily visible features in contrast to the primarily acoustic features of speech but, since both oracy and literacy are related modes of language behavior, they must share many patterns which will be reflected in the acquisition process.

The author of this chapter inserted the word "primarily" before the words "visible" and "acoustic" in the last sentence in the preceding paragraph because of a rather dramatic experience he had of the overlap between the oral and literate modes of language. He was conducting a group discussion about speech with some men in a preliterate village in Papua New Guinea when the conversation turned spontaneously to visible language. These Agoyei speakers, who had no previous experience of written language, provided a long list of non-verbal gestures with conventional meanings in their culture. These preliterate people had other visible symbols, too, which could be "read" by their peers, e.g. a pig's tusk inserted through the nose symbolized the social status of initiation. Clearly, a dividing line between oral and literate modes of languages is highly artificial. It is more appropriate to apply principles of language development in general to the particular linguistic facet of literacy acquisition.

II. SOCIOLINGUISTIC UNIVERSALS

In current social psychology it is commonly agreed that general language development depends on three variables:

A.   the *socialization process* of the child in his/her early years;
B.   the development of language *functions* in the child;
C.   the availability of an *adequate model* of these language functions in the child's environment (Hamers & Blanc, 1982).

A. The Socialization Process

That the socialization process is a vital factor in literacy acquisition as well as in general language development is stressed by Street in his contribution to this volume. His "ideological model" emphasizes the significance of the socialization process in the construction of the meaning of literacy for participants.

Three social psychological mechanisms in the socialization process are especially significant for language development: identification, internalization, and self-image formation.

In *identification* children model their language on the persons in their environment with whom they identify. That this mechanism works equally in literacy development is highlighted in Carraher's contribution to this volume, where she discusses how a child's identification with a parent who is a college instructor creates quite different expectations of literacy requirements from those produced by identifying with a parent who is a housemaid. The second of these two children arrives in the classroom cognitively unprepared for many of the tasks of learning how to read and write. They will seem to him/her to be arbitrary and pointless.

In *internalization* the child internalizes the social values associated with the common behavior in the community, and some of these values will be specifically linked to language. Purves' contribution to this volume provides compelling evidence that, when a person becomes literate, he/she enrolls in a literate community and follows its customs. Of course these communities and their customs vary, but the internalization process is a universal one.

The way in which cultural values may influence the child's expectations of literacy was brought out in the *Comparative reading* project which compared children's literacy experiences in fourteen different countries (Downing, 1973). It was found that pressures on the child to learn literacy skills are much greater in some countries than in others, and that these differences are based on cultural values. In the scale of values literacy is given a higher priority in some cultures, e.g. U.S.A.,

Japan, than it is in others, e.g. Argentina, Sweden. These differences arise because other goals are relatively more or less important in the culture. In Argentina, family poverty forces children out of school to find more immediate ways to survive economically. In primary education in Sweden, personality development has higher priority than learning academic skills. Of course, the effect of such differences in children's internalization of social values regarding literacy education cannot be measured directly by statistical literacy rates. This variable interacts with many others in the literacy learner's environment.

The third social psychological mechanism in the socialization process in language development is *self-image formation*. The child will come to recognize that certain aspects of language are used as social markers and his/her self-image will conform with them. This phenomenon is readily observable in social differences in literacy behavior. In nineteenth-century England, for example, the upper and lower social classes were in agreement that the latter should not engage in any literate behavior. Goody (1968) cites many examples of such social restrictions on access to literacy. One of these is a chronic problem in many Third World countries today—the social assumption of the inappropriateness of literacy in women. In the *Comparative reading* project it was found that the pattern of sex differences in reading achievement differed from one country to another. In the United States girls were generally superior to boys. In Britain sex differences were not important. In Germany, India and Nigeria boys achieved better than girls. These results led to the hypothesis that the social roles of boys and girls in regard to the appropriateness of literacy behavior varied from country to country (Downing, 1973). Later, a specially designed empirical study supported this hypothesis. For example, whereas males in Canada and the U.S.A. Learn early to allocate reading to the feminine social role, males in Denmark and Japan persistently regard reading as masculine at all ages (Downing et al., 1979).

B. Development of Language Functions

Halliday (1975) showed that the very beginnings of language come from the child's problem-solving behavior to serve evolving needs and developmental tasks. The child learns the language of the people in the environment as a by-product of striving for these other goals. Grammar is learned, in Halliday's view, because it functions to enlarge the child's scope for controlling the environment. Bruner (1975b) describes how language develops as a specialized and conventionalized extension of communication through earlier cooperative action. Thus the initial development of an aspect of language comes as a solution to the problem of improving some function already present in the child's social behavior.

Furthermore, functional language thus developed does not remain a mere tool, but becomes active in the improvement of that function. It is important also for literacy specialists to bear in mind that a specific language structure develops only if it serves a function for the individual. If he or she does not experience a need for a particular communicative function, then the corresponding linguistic structure will not develop (Bruner, 1975a, 1975b; Hamers & Blanc, 1982; Karmiloff-Smith, 1979).

That literacy similarly develops naturally as a solution to the problem of improving some function has been demonstrated by the findings of studies of preschool children's invented spellings and spontaneous attempts at written expression and communication (Read, 1978). If such social psychological findings are taken seriously, it must be accepted that literacy will not take root in individuals unless it serves some already existing function for them. Literacy will not grow in individuals unless they experience literate activities which increase their competency in existing functions. Neglect of these principles is one of the prime causes of failure in the teaching of reading and writing in industrialized and developed nations alike. In Third World countries there have been too many cases of literacy campaigns which failed because they were not functional for the people. In industrialized countries too many children develop mediocre or poor reading and writing skills because classroom instruction consists of ritual drills instead of communication activities truly relevant for the students. It should be a cardinal principle of all literacy instruction that its activities must have genuine communicative functions for the students (Downing, 1970). For example, both children and adults can be involved in practical projects which incorporate reading to find out the answer to practical problems in the project and writing to obtain information from outsiders as genuine parts of a real-life functional literacy task. Simulated functional literacy situations may serve where the reality is not available. But experience and/or observation of the functions of literacy are essential.

C. Availability of Adequate Models

No aspect of language can develop without the presence of an adequate model of that linguistic trait in the child's environment. If a language function is manifest in the child's surroundings, he/she will readily develop that language function. If it is absent or infrequent, development will not occur in the child, or it will be feeble. Note that this phenomenon is not merely a matter of the child imitating the adult's language. Instead, what happens is that the child observes how the model achieves a purpose with language. Then the child attempts to perform the same linguistic skill.

That these findings from the social psychology of language development apply equally well to literacy acquisition is well supported by research in industrialized countries. (For a review, see Downing and Leong, 1982, pp. 280-283.) For example, Morris (1966), in her survey of Kent, England, found public library membership in 61% of the mothers and 49% of the fathers of good readers, while for the poor readers the corresponding figures were only 15% and 13% respectively. Also the parents of over 40% of the good readers had plenty of adult books in the home compared with less than 4% of the homes of the poor readers. Another example of this effect of available models which may be closer to the Third World situation is Clay's (1976) research in New Zealand. She found that West Samoan immigrants made better progress in learning to read than native Maoris, and she attributed this to the differences in the modeling of the parents in these two cultures. The West Samoan parents regularly engaged in Bible-reading sessions at home, and they also shared the activities of reading and writing letters in communicating with relatives in the home country. The Maori children did not have these experiences.

The author of this chapter recently obtained some empirical data on the influence of observable models of functioning literacy. Two preliterate cultures in Papua New Guinea were compared. One, an Agoyei-speaking village, was isolated geographically and had no access to a literate environment. The other, a Gadsup-speaking village, was connected by road with a small market town in which written language (not Gadsup) and people reading and writing it were observable. On a test of children's concepts of literacy the Agoyei children scored around zero, as would be expected, but the Gadsup children had positive scores and among them the older children, who had had more opportunities to observe functioning literacy at the market, had significantly higher scores than the younger children with less experience of this kind.

In the industrialized countries the lack of adequate models of functioning literacy is a handicap only for a minority (though a sizeable one) of the population. In Third World countries this problem may be more serious, varying in degree, as in the Agoyei and Gadsup examples from Papua New Guinea cited above.

III. HOW CAN THESE SOCIOLINGUISTIC PROBLEMS BE SOLVED?

The preceding paragraph may seem pessimistic. The question that may be posed by literacy specialists in Third World countries is *how can people of preliterate cultures be exposed to adequate models of functioning literacy?* Fortunately, two social psychological findings exist that can be applied in these daunting circumstances: (1) valorization and (2) motivation through feedback.

Valorization

The key to the solution to this problem lies in the social psychological findings on *valorization*. This term refers to society's attribution of positive value to an activity or institution. Here the concern is with the social valorization of language because it functions to fulfill the goals of a human group. Where adequate models of functioning literacy are available, valorization is transmitted to children through the modeling process described in the preceding section. But in many cultures in Third World countries literacy has not been socially valorized because it is not a traditional language activity.

Fortunately new non-traditional behavior can be valorized by a social group. For example, in industrialized countries a whole field of applied social-psychological research has been devoted to the study of learned or acquired valorization through persuasion—advertising and propaganda. In market research this has often been described as "motivation research"—studying the motives of potential consumers of a product in order to create a sales pitch which will trigger one or more of such motives. In the same way, literacy may be "sold" to potential consumers by attaching it to existing motivations.

Examples of acquired valorization of literacy can be cited also for Third World countries in cultures where literacy is not valorized through tradition. For instance, literacy was valorized for women tea-pickers in Kenya when they wanted to form a union and they had to know how to read and write in order to be taken seriously by the male union leaders (Bruchhaus, 1984). In Indonesia learning groups in a literacy campaign were valorized through the support of cultural leaders. Learning groups grew fast in villages where the village chiefs were aware of the need for literacy, and very slowly otherwise. This finding led the literacy campaign organizers to make deliberate efforts to educate the leaders and the literate persons in the village on the value of literacy as a means to motivating the illiterates themselves (Napitupulu, 1982). The successes of the literacy campaigns in Cuba, Nicaragua and the U.S.S.R. clearly were due to a very important degree to the valorization of literacy as part of a social revolution.

Motivation Through Feedback

The feedback mechanism is very important in the social psychology of language development. When people are successful in using language to fulfill a function they will attach value to that linguistic activity and they will become more motivated to use it for that particular function. In contrast, if a language activity fails to facilitate a particular function it will lose value for that particular function.

It is very important to note that the psychological mechanism of feedback operates through self-evaluation of one's own attempts to perform a skill. An apprentice cannot get feedback to improve his/her skill unless he/she *uses* or *does* something in an attempt to perform that skill. Note also that, in natural learning situations, learners progress most of the time by making attempts to perform the skill as a whole. They adjust their actions in accordance with the feedback that they receive from perceiving their results. Educators never question that the skill of oracy develops always as a result of children's functional use of natural speaking and listening activities and the feedback that they receive from the results of their own actions. Yet, in the formal teaching of literacy, all too frequently these fundamental principles of language learning are ignored when written language is presented to beginners in terms of letters and separate words which have no function for the students. The negative effect of such atomistic methods of instruction has been brought out particularly well by Goodman (1976). He criticizes "instructional reading programs that begin with bits and pieces abstracted from language, like words or letters, on the theory that they're making learning simpler," but "in fact make learning to read harder," because it "isn't language any more" (p. 59). Goodman was writing from the perspective of an industrialized country, but such atomistic teaching methods have been imitated all too well by educators in the developing countries. For example, Oommen's (1973) description of reading instruction in India showed how such atomistic approaches presented children with reading as an almost meaningless ritual divorced from their past experience of real life and language and only mystically related to any educational aspirations they might have had.

IV. PSYCHOLINGUISTIC UNIVERSALS

Now the focus of this chapter shifts from social psychology to the general psychology of learning. The preceding section viewed literacy through sociolinguistic spectacles; now it is the turn for psycholinguistic lenses.

Reading as a Skill

For psychologists, literacy behavior belongs in the category of "skill". Literacy comprises two basic skills—reading and writing. These are intricately related to one another and also to the two basic skills of oracy—listening and speaking which also are interrelated (Downing & Leong, 1982). Skill acquisition is one of the best-researched areas of human behavior in psychology. It is also one of the most useful for practical applications. For example, driving a car, plumbing, swimming, playing football or chess are all skills. To the layman these may seem quite different types of behavior but, as Whiting (1975) points out, though "verbal, mental, perceptual, social and motor are common adjectives in relation to skills," it would "be wrong . . . to assume that the processes involved in learning any of these skill categories are essentially different from the learning of another" (p. 6). Whiting and den Brinker (1982) emphasize that all skills, including those that appear to be predominantly motor, "have a cognitive involvement, i.e., they are intelligently carried out" (p. 218).

Thus, in addition to the sociolinguistic universals of literacy discussed in the preceding section of this chapter one can expect to find psychological universals of literacy acquisition which are shared with other types of skill. In everyday life any skill is acquired through the individual's application of innate learning processes to the perceived task of mastering its performance. Also skills cannibalize other behaviors. Skills are certainly not genetically programmed, but some of the behaviors which they cannibalize may be more or less determined by genetic factors. For example, Orton (1925, 1937), in his classic neuropsychological studies of disorders of reading and writing, recognized that the skill of reading and the skill of writing are not unique or independent. Individuals who display symptoms of dyslexia or dysgraphia, in addition, exhibit other related disordered behaviors arising from a common underlying handicapped behavioral module cannibalized by the reading or writing skill. The handicap may be determined genetically or through environmental experience. This cannibalization process was also implicit in Holmes's (1970) classic theory of literacy acquisition when he wrote that "reading is an audiovisual verbal-processing skill of symbolic reasoning, sustained by the intrafacilitations of an intricate hierarchy of substrata factors *that have been mobilized* as a psychological working system and *pressed into service* in accordance with the purpose of the reader" (pp. 187-188; italics added).

A review of the research literature on skill acquisition in general leads to the conclusion that the most important finding of relevance to literacy learning in particular is that there is a universal pattern of skill development (Downing & Leong, 1982). Each step in the growth of any skill, by the addition and development of its subskills, passes progressively through three overlapping phases which may be termed: (1) cognitive; (2) mastering; and (3) automaticity.

The initial cognitive phase is when the learner tries to figure out what he or she should attempt to do in performing the skill. Cronbach (1977) called it, "getting in mind just what is to be done" (p. 396). Luria (1976) described it as "getting a preliminary fix" (p. 117). In the mastering phase, as the learner improves comprehension of the task, he/she works to perfect the performance of the skill. Learners practice until they achieve a high level of accuracy with almost no errors. But mastery is not sufficient for the practical use of a skill. Practice must continue beyond mastery to the condition of overlearning which produces automaticity. When automaticity has been achieved the skill does not deteriorate, even if it is not used for many years. It will quickly recover when it is needed again.

A very common error in literacy education has been to consider only the mastering phase, and to overlook the cognitive and automaticity phases. If the cognitive phase is ignored in the teaching program, literacy learners are unable to apply themselves to practice for mastery because they are floundering in the flood of new concepts introduced in the literacy instruction (Downing, 1982, 1984b, 1986). They remain trapped by cognitive confusion and may begin to doubt their own mental capacity to comprehend the tasks of literacy. Neglect of the automaticity phase is a deficiency which has been observed in some literacy campaigns. It produces the phenomenon of "exliterates"—people who have lost their literacy skills, although they had received literacy certificates, for instance, only the year previously. For example, Balpuri (1958) found that a representative sample of adults in India who had received literacy certificates could not comprehend a few paragraphs containing 73 common words 1 year later. This finding indicates that they had not reached automaticity when the campaign period ended and no follow-up materials had been provided afterwards (Downing, 1979).

Language Awareness

During the past 20 years there has been a remarkably rapid growth in research on a hitherto somewhat neglected aspect of language—people's awareness of their own and others' linguistic behavior. Such phenomena are often labeled "metalinguistic" if they are related to awareness of linguistic units such as the phoneme or the word. But the term "metacognitive" is more encompassing since it may be used to describe people's awareness of such aspects of literacy as its functions. Empirical evidence of the existence of this language awareness in the development of oracy and literacy has been found in many different countries and languages. (For reviews, see Downing & Valtin, 1984; Yaden & Templeton, 1986.) Language awareness is very important for the cognitive phase of acquiring the many sub-skills of literacy because, in learning how to perform the tasks of reading and writing, learners need to reflect about features of language that are symbolized in its visible form and they need to reflect about the functions of language that are served by reading and writing.

Mattingly (1984) has suggested that one important cause of individual differences in success and failure in literacy acquisition may be variable development of this linguistic awareness. In learning oracy, all children everywhere must become linguistically aware to a certain prerequisite level, but some children driven by an instinctive linguistic curiosity continue expanding their awareness indefinitely, while others abandon this acquisition once they are adequately equipped for the purposes of ordinary communication. Thus children enter the tasks of learning how to read and write with varying degrees of linguistic awareness. Mattingly proposes that, in consequence, they will vary in their capacity to reflect about literacy tasks in the cognitive phase of acquiring the many new subskills they are faced with in the introductory stage. Beginners whose linguistic awareness is minimal will be unprepared for the tasks of literacy acquisition. For them, "the orthography will seem a mysterious and arbitrary way to represent sentences" (p. 24).

In becoming aware of language activities and objects when faced with literacy, two kinds of conceptual representation develop which are essential for reasoning about reading and writing tasks: (1) functional concepts—the purposes of these skills; (2) featural concepts—the characteristics of speech that are symbolized in writing. Literacy learners have to become curious about the intentions of writers. Why do they make those visible symbols? The answer will have two parts: (1) they intend to communicate some meaning; (2) they intend to code certain features of speech. As Ferreiro and Teberosky (1979) concluded from their study of the stages of literacy development in children in Argentina, "Reading is not deciphering; writing is not copying." The real task of acquiring literacy is the "intelligent construction" of these two skills (pp. 344-345).

Numerous studies have shown that literacy learners approach the tasks of reading and writing with only partially developed concepts of their functions and features. Vygotsky (1962) reported that school beginners in post-revolutionary Russia had only a vague idea of the functions of writing. Reid (1966) found that Scottish beginners had a general lack of any idea of the purpose of written language and that they did not possess such concepts as "word" or "sound" (phoneme) essential for understanding their teacher's instruction. Luria (1946) explained the Russian findings of this phenomenon by analogy. He wrote that the beginner "is still not able to make the word and verbal relations an object of his consciousness. In this period a word may be used but not noticed by the child, and it frequently seems like a glass window through which the child looks at the surrounding world without making the word itself an object of his consciousness and without suspecting that it has its own existence, its own structural features" (p. 61). These early studies have been confirmed by many more recent investigations. (For reviews see Dopstadt, Laubscher, & Ruperez, 1980; Downing, 1984b, 1986; Templeton & Spivey, 1980.)

Although there is now rather general agreement among researchers that there is a strong relationship between language awareness and reading achievement, there has been some debate about their causal connection (Ehri, 1984; Valtin, 1984). However, the research evidence has increasingly pointed to an interactive connection (Ferreiro, 1982; Hamilton & Barton, 1983; Morais et al., 1979; Raban, 1984; A. Sinclair & H. Sinclair, in press; and Sultmann et al., 1983). This is what one would expect from established findings from psychological research on the general course of concept development. For example, Piaget (1977) showed how concepts develop as a result of challenges from experiences that contradict a person's existing conceptual systems.

The interactive causal relationship between linguistic awareness and the acquisition of literacy is confirmed by the data obtained in the Papua New Guinea studies completed recently by the author of this chapter. The preliterate Agoyei children readily solved the problem of analyzing their speech into phoneme sound units despite their total lack of exposure to written language. Thus linguistic awareness has primacy in the causal connection with literacy development. Furthermore, in the Telei and Hakö villages which have schools and where some literacy is observable in the environment, scores on tests of linguistic awareness administered to children just entering school in 1982 were highly correlated with achievements on reading tests administered 3 years later in 1985. Children who were superior in linguistic awareness on entering school in 1982 were the best readers in 1985. Children who scored lowest on linguistic awareness in 1982 were the poorest readers in 1985. The fact that no preschool reading occurs in these environments and that there was a 3-year interval between the administration of the linguistic awareness test and the testing of reading indicates that linguistic awareness is a causal factor in reading achievement. On the other hand, different experiences of literacy lead to different levels of linguistic awareness. Children in the literate villages had higher linguistic awareness scores than children in the non literate village. Also children taught to read in their mother tongue had higher linguistic awareness scores than children taught in an unfamiliar language (English).

Thus there is not a simple cause-and-effect relationship between linguistic awareness and the acquisition of literacy. They mutually assist one another. Beginners start with some degree of linguistic awareness derived from their previous experiences of oracy. This linguistic awareness has the causal priority. Understanding the tasks of reading and writing does de pend on the development of linguistic awareness. But the new tasks of literacy acquisition pose problems and puzzles which stimulate the concept formation process in the development of language awareness. The relationship is a spiral one, each enhancing the other as they grow.

Factors Influencing Language Awareness

If language awareness is necessary for the cognitive phase of learning literacy subskills, the practical educator will want answers to two questions: (1) How can I foster language awareness? (2) What negative influences on the growth of language awareness should be avoided? Re search in this area is only in its early stages. Nevertheless, it is already,clear that educators can take positive steps to foster language awareness, and they can take preventive action against negative influences on it.

Kokora (1985) provided an excellent example of how readiness for school tasks can be fostered in deliberately planned preschool experiences. His innovative experiment in rural areas of the Ivory Coast was concerned with developing children's thought and language to cope with the tasks that they would meet later when they entered school. It provides a model for what could be done more specifically in developing concepts and metalanguage as a preparation for the cognitive phase of literacy learning.

In the Soviet Union, Elkonin (1973) and his colleagues developed a range of methods for developing children's metalinguistic concepts at the kindergarten and primary school level. Some of Elkonin's methods have been tried out with success in Canada (Bell, 1982; Ollila, Johnson, & Downing, 1974). The essence of these methods is to make the abstract metalinguistic concepts of speech more concrete, or, using Luria's analogy, to make the "glass window" of speech opaque. For example, in one kindergarten game each child is asked to "be" a word in a given sentence. The teacher asks these children to form a line in front of the class to form the sentence. At first, there is some confusion. The children may arrange themselves in the wrong order. But the teacher helps them to sort out the puzzle. After only a few games of this kind these children will have increased their linguistic awareness of speech considerably. They will know that a spoken sentence is a set of words in a certain temporal arrangement and they will have begun to think about the spatial representation of that temporal arrangement. Elkonin's essential point is that these metalinguistic concepts should be learned *before* the teacher wants to use them in literacy instruction. With this enhanced language awareness the beginner has an armory of linguistic concepts for solving the puzzles of the cognitive phase of subskill learning.

Unfortunately, many traditional teaching methods and parenting customs continue to prevent or delay children's development of language awareness. For example, Elkonin expresses strong disapproval of the adults in the U.S.S.R. who drill children to learn the names of the alphabet by rote. He argues that this delays children's growth of understanding of metalinguistic concepts of speech and writing. Three independent experiments in the United States have confirmed that teaching letter names provides no benefit in children's reading achievements (Johnson, 1970; Ohnmacht, 1969; Samuels, 1971). The confusing effect of teaching pre schoolers letter names before the letters are functional has even been elevated to the "letter-name strategy" in studies of young American children's invented spelling in their early attempts at writing (Read, 1978), e.g. *FET* for "feet" because of the letter *E*'s name. Letter-name confusion has been shown to be the main cause of the letter reversal symptom in dyslexia (Vellutino, 1977; Bigsby, 1985).

Kokora (1985) made a very important observation in his report on the Ivory Coast mother-tongue preschool experiment. He stated that the language ability needed to think logically, and to express verbally the child's thought processes, becomes a very critical issue if the meta-language is different from his/her daily language use. In the rural areas of the Ivory Coast, French, the language of school instruction, is spoken and read by only 4% of the rural population, which represents over 70% of the total population of the country. This mismatch between the mother-tongue of the literacy learner and the language of school instruction is indeed a very serious cause of confusion in the cognitive phase of literacy learning (see also Ezzaki, Spratt and Wagner in this volume).

The damaging effect of this language mismatch has been found also in Papua New Guinea. In that developing country about 40% of children cannot attend school because there is none in their area. Most of the rest have their school instruction in English, but in recent years several experimental mother-tongue schools have been established. Children in these different conditions were compared on a test of children's ability to learn the metalinguistic concept of the phoneme in speech (developed by Liberman et al., 1974). The best achievements on this aspect of language awareness were those of the children receiving literacy instruction in their mother-tongue. But what was even more interesting was that the un schooled children developed awareness of this linguistic unit more rapidly than children who were at school and being given phonics instruction in English. From these empirical findings it may be concluded that mother tongue instruction taps the child's existing linguistic awareness, whereas second-language instruction not only fails to exploit the available linguistic awareness but also causes cognitive confusion by introducing exemplars that do not fit the child's developing concepts of speech elements (Downing, 1984b). The longer-term effects of language mismatch and its consequent cognitive confusion are shown by the results of reading tests administered 3 years after the linguistic awareness testing described above. In comparison with children who started reading in an unfamiliar language (English), children who had their first 2 years of instruction in their mother-tongue became superior readers not only in that language but also in a second language, Tok Pisin. Although they had 1 or 2 years less instruction in English, the mother-tongue beginners had equal scores, and were faster and more confident in reading English than those who had been taught reading only in English from the start.

These results provide a theoretical explanation for the general finding that initial literacy instruction in a second-language retards the develop ment of reading skill (Garcia de Lorenzo, 1975; Larson & Davis, 1981; Macnamara, 1966; Modiano, 1973; Österberg, 1961). The cause of this delay is both cognitive and affective. Not only does teaching initial literacy in a second language confuse the child metalinguistically, but also it flies in the face of the social psychological and sociolinguistic principles discussed in the first section of this paper.

Affective Variables

In the preceding paragraph it was noted that negative affect or emotion as well as cognitive confusion may lead to poor literacy achievements when instruction is delivered in an unfamiliar language instead of the mother-tongue. Teaching written language in an alien language may be perceived by students and their community as a rejection of their mother-tongue. As was described in an earlier section of this chapter, the individual identifies with the mother-tongue and it becomes a part of his/her cultural identity. Hence what is perceived as a rejection of this identity amounts to an attack on the personality, and this arouses negative emotion and resistance. Unfortunately, quite often teachers not only do not use students' mother-tongue for instruction but also they overtly attack.it through ridicule or even punishment for its use in classrooms, leading to even greater negative effects on literacy acquisition (Goodman, 1969; Spolsky, 1970; Tax, 1965).

In Stewart's (1975) experiment negative emotions forestalled the anticipated cognitive benefit of introducing literacy in the mother-tongue. Stewart tried to replicate the successful mother tongue experiment reported by Österberg (1961). In Österberg's empirical study in

Sweden an experimental group was introduced to literacy in the local dialect. The students achieved significantly higher levels of reading and writing than a control group instructed in Standard Swedish. Österberg noted the positive affect observed in the experimental classes in contrast to the usual negative affect in the control classes. When Stewart attempted to replicate this experiment with Black American dialect-speaking children in Washington, D.C., it was a failure, because, unlike the proud speakers of the dialect in Sweden, the Black American community at that time rejected their own mother-tongue dialect as being worthy of formal schooling. According to Stewart, these Black dialect speakers were ready to condemn their own children to school failure because of their unwillingness to accord recognition to their own culture in the school curriculum. Searle (1972) described a similar devalorization of the mother-tongue in Tobago. The contrasting emotional attitudes in the Österberg and Stewart experiments bring out the great importance of the affective variable in literacy programs.

Note that the distinction between the cognitive domain and the affective domain is arbitrary and abstract. In everyday life behavior they are usually inextricably interwoven. For example, one must *know* the value of literacy before one can be *motivated* to achieve it. The present chapter is in effect a restatement of the cognitive clarity theory of literacy acquisition which was described originally in *Reading and Reasoning* (Downing, 1979), and has been revised in the light of more recent research findings (Downing, 1984a; Downing & Downing, 1983; Downing & Fijalkow, 1984). The central postulate of the theory remains unchanged, i.e. the literacy learning process consists in the discovery of (a) the functions and (b) the coding rules of the writing system. Knowledge of the functions of literacy is given the priority position because awareness of functions has both motivational and cognitive consequences for the learner. Until learners of literacy are aware of its functions they cannot be intrinsically motivated to learn the skills of reading and writing. With regard to cognitive consequences, until learners develop awareness of the various purposes of reading, and how they can adapt their reading style to different purposes, they remain inflexible plodding decoders.

V. THE FUTURE OF WORLD LITERACY

Rather than an end in itself. literacy should be regarded as a way of preparing man for a social. civic and-economic role that goes far beyond the limits of rudimentary literacy training, consisting merely in the teaching of reading and writing. The very process of learning to read and write should be made an opportunity for acquiring information that can immediately be used to improve living standards; reading and writing should not lead only to elementary general knowledge but to training for work. increased productivity, a greater participation in civil life and a better understanding of the surrounding world, and should ultimately open the way to basic human knowledge. (Proposal for the goals of literacy, World Conference of Ministers of Education on the Eradication of Illiteracy, Teheran, 1965)

Although this declaration of literacy goals is more than 30 years old it remains freshly relevant to current ideals. It will endure for many years to come because those ideals will continue to be extremely difficult to attain on a world basis. Nevertheless, the slow but steady progress that has been made in the growth of literacy in many countries is encouragement to literacy specialists to persist in their efforts. They certainly should not allow their efforts to be undermined by the cynicism that has become fashionable in some quarters regarding the effects of literacy. Claims that literacy has not delivered the benefits expected have been made in some publications (e.g. Calhoun, 1973; Sanderson, 1972) but the variables determining economic and social development are far more complex than envisioned in these weak historical and statistical methods.

Literacy may best be regarded as *one* of the *potential forces* favoring development. As Akinnaso (1981) puts it: "As a psycho-social phenomenon, literacy is seen as a highly potent catalyst of cultural change" (p. 169). But the outcome depends on other variables also in the situation. Take, for instance, the debate on whether or not literacy causes cognitive development. It may be that this effect of literacy sometimes does occur and sometimes does not occur because of the presence or absence of other variables in the situation. As Gough (1968) stated:

Literacy is for the most part an enabling rather than a causal factor, making possible the development of complex political structures, syllogistic reasoning, scientific enquiry, linear conception of reality, scholarly specialisation, artistic elaboration. . . . Whether, and to what extent, these will in fact develop depends apparently on concomitant factors of ecology; inter-societal relations, and internal ideological and social structural responses to these. (p. 153)

Professionals in the literacy field have to work toward the practical goal of helping people to acquire this *enabling* factor, as Gough calls it. This does not mean that professionals should leave the overall policy decisions to the politicians and administrators and serve only in developing methods to implement them. For example, whether literacy should be introduced in the mother-tongue or in a second language is not only a matter of political expediency or administrative convenience. Professionals should have input into such a decision. They have expert knowledge on the relative effectiveness of delivery of literacy instruction in the mother-tongue or second language. Of course, the policy-maker has to consider other variables in the politics of education, but professionals have a duty to bring their expert knowledge to bear on policy-makers.

Both in the industrialized countries and in the developing countries the most common cause of poor educational results is the failure of politicians and administrators to act on the results of scientific research on human behavior. Such failure would not be tolerated in fields where the outcomes were more immediately obvious. Akinnaso (1981) puts his finger on this chronic and widespread limitation on literacy education:

> The contemporary problem with literacy programs stems from the lack of fit between these new orientations [from scientific research] and educational policies. In talking about literacy problems, educational leaders often show little or no awareness of current research findings and of the change in literacy standards and expectations. (p. 182)

It is instructive to observe that some of the most promising progress toward the goals of literacy outlined in the quotation given at the beginning of this section is happening outside formal educational systems. Volunteer literacy workers in non-formal situations seem quicker to utilize research knowledge from the social and behavioral sciences, perhaps because their attention is not distracted by administrative and political considerations.

Note how in tune with our discussion of the social psychology of literacy is this simple statement in a description of Summer Institute of Linguistics (SIL), literacy programs in Ghana: "Fundamental to any programme that seeks to promote literacy in societies where reading and writing is not already an established habit and value is the question 'What is the relevance of literacy to daily life?'" (Bendor-Samuel & Bendor-Samuel, 1983, p. 8).

Note how another SIL volunteer applies scientific research findings on mother-tongue versus second language literacy learning to the practical problems of developing countries. Wendell (1982) writes that authors of literacy materials must pay close attention to two basic factors: "(1) it must be in the language of the people for whom it is intended, and (2) the content must clearly reflect the culture of the people for whom it is intended" (p. 169). She continues by indicating how this can be put into practice: "The fastest and surest way of obtaining desirable reading material is to train native speakers of the target language to write their thoughts, experiences, and stories in their own language and in their own indigenous style. These may be written by their own hand or dictated to someone else who can write" (pp. 169-170). Wendell's book on *Bootstrap Literature* is a practical guide on how to do this, and it is being implemented. For example, in Papua New Guinea SIL has instituted a National Literacy Course to train people who want to create literature in the mother-tongue (Patrick, 1984).

These quotations may seem rather homely and artless in the context of this volume on the complex topic of the application of science to literacy in a technologically rapidly changing world. But in fact these simple words demonstrate how the findings of research can be boiled down to straight forward and uncomplex answers to practical problems in developing countries. Indeed, it is refreshing and encouraging to observe the directness with which such voluntary literacy organizations can implement new research findings from the social and behavioral sciences. Hopefully, they provide models which may be utilized eventually by governments on a wider scale. In many developing countries volunteer educators have traditionally been the pioneers who blazed the trail and laid the foundations for national education in later years.

In this volume several contributors demonstrate how governments of various developing countries are making strong efforts to spread literacy and raise literacy standards. A tremendous amount of human energy and money is being invested in such efforts. This must be applauded even though professionals sense that much of it may be wasted.

In the observation of this author, wastage occurs because, instead of distilling out the simple practical principles from scientific research, as is done by the Bendor-Samuels, and Wendell in the quotations cited above, government educational institutions often tend to oversimplify the problem by passing over the research and theory and going directly to what they consider to be "practical." Rather than important theoretical and research findings, they import "practical" methods of instruction from the industrialized countries. Perhaps they assume that the foreign practices are based on research findings from the same foreign source (a vain hope, unfortunately).

Such uncritical importation of educational practices from one country to another can be very wasteful even when both countries belong in the same category of industrialized nations. For example, the "open school" program with its accompanying characteristics of individualized instruction and flexibility of scheduling developed with great success in England. But when it was suddenly adopted as a fad in American public schools in the 1960s it failed dismally because it was so out of tune with the cultural traditions of American formal education. Quite apart from the waste of teachers' and students' efforts, millions of dollars were thrown away on school buildings without classroom walls which the American importers believed (mistakenly) to be a prerequisite of open schools. Uncritical importation of educational practices is a recipe for waste. The same cause of wastage can be seen frequently in developing countries in the uncritical importation of so-called "successful practical" methods of teaching, teacher training and so forth.

Sometimes this uncritical importation of educational practices occurs in the transition from a colonial administration to independence for a developing country. For example, the Australian administration of Papua New Guinea decreed that teachers must not teach in a village where the teacher had the same mother-tongue as the students. It was assumed that this policy would force both teacher and children to communicate in English. But actually it more often produced a different result. A long standing joke among educators in Papua New Guinea is that "we do this to make children learn English but they learn Pidgin".

Educators in developing countries should be much less modest than they are about their own expertise. No foreign expert knows more about their people and children than the local educators in their own culture and nation. They should be especially skeptical about "practical" methods which are proffered by foreign experts. They may be quite *impracticable* for the needs of people in the developing country.

Educators need to be skeptical about the findings of research from other countries too. In particular they must ask: "Are these findings ethnocentric or linguacentric? Do they sift out universal human traits or are they limited to the linguistic and cultural circumstances of the country where the research was conducted?"

There would be much surer grounds for optimism for the future of world literacy if policy-makers would reduce the importation of ready-made "practical" educational methods and, instead, combine the findings of scientific research on human behavior and language with local knowledge of their people's culture and language. Social and behavioral scientists around the world already possess a valuable store of research findings, surprisingly little of which has as yet been applied in literacy instruction. In this chapter an attempt has been made to distill just a few important sociolinguistic and psycholinguistic universals discernible in that store. These admittedly may be colored by my own research and theoretical position, but I believe that policy-makers both in the industrialized countries and in the developing countries could get a much higher return for their investment of human energy and money if they would pay more attention to such universals. More specifically, they should make two major changes in their planning of literacy programs: (1) involve more high level scientific consultants—professionals from relevant disciplines who are steeped in knowledge of such universals; and (2) be much more skeptical about conventional school methods and materials for teaching reading and writing. Literacy education everywhere is bogged down by the prescientific folklore of the pedagogy of industrialized countries.

ACKNOWLEDGEMENTS

The research in Papua New Guinea was funded by the Social Sciences and Humanities Research Council of Canada.

REFERENCES

Akinnaso, F.N. (1981). The consequences of literacy in pragmatic and theoretical perspectives. *Anthropology and Education Quarterly, 12,* 163-200.

Balpuri, S. (1958). Wither adult education in India? *Fundamental and Adult Education, 10,* 171-3.

Bell, A.A.L. (1982). *Phoneme segmentation in the acquisition of reading.* Masters thesis. Department of Psychological Foundations, University of Victoria, Canada.

Bendor-Samuel, D., & Bendor-Samuel, M. (1983). *Community literacy programmes in Northern Ghana.* Dallas, TX: Summer Institute of Linguistics.

Bigsby, P. (1985). The nature of reversible letter confusions in dyslexic and normal readers: Misperception or mislabelling? *British Journal of Educational Psychology, 55,* 264-72.

Bruchhaus, E. (1984). One billion reasons to continue our efforts. *Convergence, 17*(3), 46-50.

Bruner, J.S. (1975a). Language as an instrument of thought. In A. Davies (Ed.), *Problems of language and learning* London: Heinemann.

Bruner, J.S. (1975b). The ontogenesis of speech acts. *Journal of Child Language, 2,* 1-19.

Calhoun, D. (1973). *The intelligence of a people.* Princeton, NJ: Princeton University Press.

Clay, M.M. (1976). Early childhood and cultural diversity in New Zealand. *Reading Teacher, 29,* 333-342.

Cronbach, L.J. (1977). *Educational psychology* (3rd ed). New York: Harcourt Brace Jovanovich.

Dopstadt, N., Laubscher, F., & Ruperez, R. (1980). *La representation de la phrase ecrite chez l'enfant de 6 a 8 ans.* Masters thesis, Psychology Department, L'Université Toulouse-le-Mirail, France.

Downing, J. (1970). Relevance versus ritual in reading. *Reading, 4* (June), 4-12.

Downing, J. (1973). *Comparative reading* New York: Macmillan.
Downing, J. (1979). *Reading and reasoning.* New York: Springer-Verlag.
Downing, J. (1982). Cognitive clarity and reading disabilities. In J.P. Das, R. Mulcahy, & A.E. Wall (Eds.), *Theory and research in learning disability.* New York: Plenum.
Downing, J. (1984a). A source of cognitive confusion for beginning readers. *Reading Teacher, 37,* 366-70.
Downing, J. (1984b). Task awareness in the development of reading skill. In J. Downing & R. Valtin (Eds.), *Language awareness and learning to read.* New York: Springer-Verlag.
Downing, J. (1986). Cognitive clarity: A unifying and cross-cultural theory for language awareness phenomena in reading. In D.B. Yaden, Jr. & W. S. Templeton (Eds.), *Metalinguistic awareness and beginning literacy: Conceptualizing what it means to read and write.* Exeter, NH: Heinemann.
Downing, J., & Downing, M. (1983). Metacognitive readiness for literacy learning. *Papua New Guinea Journal of Education 19,* 17-40.
Downing, J., & Fijalkow, J. (1984). *Lire et Raisonner.* Toulouse, France: Editions Privat.
Downing, J., & Leong, C.K. (1982). *Psychology of reading.* New York: Macmillan.
Downing, J., & Valtin, R. (Eds.). (1984). *Language awareness and learning to read.* New York: Springer-Verlag.
Downing, J., Dwyer, C.A., Feitelson, D., Jansen, M., Kemppainen, R., Matihaldi, H., Reggi, D.R., Sakamoto T., Taylor, H., Thackray, D. V., & Thomson, D. (1979). A cross-national survey of cultural expectations and sex-role standards in reading. *Journal of Research in Reading, 2,* 8-23.
Ehri, L.C. (1984). How orthography alters spoken language competencies in children learning to read and spell. In J. Downing & R. Valtin (Eds.), *Language awareness and learning to read.* New York: Springer-Verlag.
Elkonin, D.B. (1973). U.S.S.R. In J. Downing (Ed.), *Comparative reading.* New York: Macmillan.
Feldman, D.H. (1980). *Beyond universals in cognitive development.* Norwood, NJ: Ablex.
Ferreiro, E. (1986). The interplay between information and assimilation in beginning literacy. In W. Teale & E. Sulzby (Eds.), *Emergent literacy.* Norwood, NJ: Ablex.
Ferreiro, E., & Teberosky, A. (1979). *Los sistemas de escritura en el desarrollo del niño.* Mexico DF: Siglo Veintiuno Editores, sa. (English translation, *Literacy before schooling.* Exeter, NH: Heinemann, 1982).
Garcia de Lorenzo, M.E. (1975). Frontier dialect: A challenge to education. *Reading Teacher, 28,* 653-8.
Goodman, K.S. (1969). Dialect barriers to reading comprehension. In J.C. Baratz & R.W. Shuy (Eds.), *Teaching Black children to read.* Washington, DC: Center for Applied Linguistics.

Goodman, K.S. (1976). What we know about reading. In P.D. Allen & D.J. Watson (Eds.), *Findings of research in miscue analysis: Classroom applications.* Urbana, IL: National Council of Teachers of English.

Goody, J. (1968). *Literacy in traditional societies.* Cambridge, England: Cambridge University Press.

Gough, K. (1968). Literacy in Kerala. In J. Goody (Ed.), *Literacy in traditional societies.* Cambridge, England: Cambridge University Press.

Halliday, M.A.K. (1975). *Learning how to mean.* London: Edward Arnold.

Hamers, J.F., & Blanc, M. (1982). Towards a social-psychological model of bilingual development. *Journal of Language and Social Psychology, 1,* 29-49.

Hamilton, M. E., & Barton, D. (1983). Adults' definitions of "word": The effects of literacy and development. *Journal of Pragmatics, 7,* 581-594.

Holmes, J.A. (1970). The substrata-factor theory of reading: Some experimental evidence. In H. Singer & R.B. Ruddell (Eds.), *Theoretical models and processes of reading.* Newark, DE: International Reading Association.

Johnson, R.J. (1970). *The effect of training in letter names on success in beginning reading for children of differing abilities.* Paper presented at the annual convention of the American Educational Research Association.

Karmiloff-Smith, A. (1979). *A functional approach to child language.* Cambridge, England: Cambridge University Press.

Kokora, P. (1985). Paper presented at the conference on The Future of Literacy in a Changing World. University of Pennsylvania, Philadelphia, Pennsylvania, May 9-12, 1985.

Larson, M.L., & Davis, P.M. (1981). *Bilingual education: An experience in Peruvian Amazonia.* Washington, DC: Center for Applied Linguistics, and Dallas, TX: Summer Institute of Linguistics.

Liberman, I.Y., Shankweiler, D., Fischer, F.W., & Carter, B. (1974). Explicit syllable and phoneme segmentation in the young child. *Journal of Experimental Child Psychology, 18,* 201-212.

Luria, A.R. (1946). On the pathology of grammatical operations (in Russian). *Izvestija APN RSFSR,* No. 17. (English translation in J. Downing (Ed.). (in press), *Cognitive psychology and reading in the USSR.* Amsterdam, The Netherlands: North-Holland.

Luria, A.R. (1976). *Cognitive development: Its cultural and social foundations.* Cambridge, MA: Harvard University Press.

Macnamara, J. (1966). *Bilingualism and primary education.* Edinburgh, Scotland: Edinburgh University Press.

Mattingly, I.G. (1984). Reading, linguistic awareness and language acquisition. In J. Downing & R. Valtin (Eds.), *Language awareness and learning to read.* New York: Springer-Verlag.

Modiano, N. (1973). *Indian education in the Chiapas Highlands.* New York: Holt, Rinehart and Winston.

Morais, J., Cary, L., Alegria, J., & Bertelson, P. (1979). Does awareness of speech as a sequence of phones arise spontaneously? *Cognition, 7,* 323-331.

Morris, J.M. (1966). *Standards and progress in reading*. Slough, England: National Foundation for Educational Research.

Napitupulu, W.P. (1982). Each one teach ten: Literacy in Indonesia. *Prospects, 12*, 213-20.

Ohnmacht, D.D. (1969). *The effects of letter knowledge on achievement in reading in the first grade*. Paper presented at the annual convention of the American Educational Research Association.

Ollila, L., Johnson, T., & Downing, J. (1974). Adapting Russian methods of auditory discrimination training for English. *Elementary English, 51*, 1138-1141, 1145.

Orton, S.T. (1925). "Word blindness" in school children. *Archives of Neurology and Psychiatry, 14*, 581-615.

Orton, S.T. (1937). *Reading, writing, and speech problems in children*. New York: Norton.

Österberg, T. (1961). *Bilingualism and the first school language*. Umeå, Sweden: Västerbottens Tryckeri, AB.

Patrick, H. (1984). A national literacy course. *Read, 19*, 37-39.

Piaget, J. (1959). *The language and thought of the child*. London: Routledge & Kegan Paul.

Piaget, J. (1977). *The development of thought: Equilibration of cognitive structures*. New York: Viking.

Raban, B. (1984). *Children's understanding of written language at seven years of age*. Unpublished manuscript. Reading, England: School of Education, University of Reading.

Read, C. (1978). Children's awareness of language, with emphasis on sound systems. In A. Sinclair, R.J. Jarvella, & W.J.M. Levelt (Eds.), *The child's conception of language*. New York: Springer-Verlag.

Reid, J.F. (1966). Learning to think about reading. *Educational Research, 9*, 56-62.

Samuels, S.J. (1971). Letter-name versus letter-sound knowledge in learning to read. *Reading Teacher, 24*, 604-608.

Sanderson, M. (1972). Literacy and social mobility in the industrial revolution in England. *Past and Present, 56*, 75-103.

Searle C. (1972). *The forsaken lover*. London: Routledge & Kegan Paul.

Sinclair, A., & Sinclair, H. (in press). Preschool children's interpretation of written numbers. *Human Learning*.

Spolsky, B. (1970). *Literacy in the vernacular: The Navajo reading study*. Paper presented at the annual meeting of the American Anthropological Association.

Stewart, W.A. (1975). Teaching Blacks to read against their will. In P.A. Luelsdorff (Ed.), *Linguistic perspectives on Black English*. Regensburg, Germany: Verlag Hans Carl.

Sultmann, W.F., Elkins, J., Miller, S., & Byrne, M. (1983). Linguistic awareness and early reading. *Reading Psychology, 4*, 327-335.

Tax, S. (1965). Group identity and educating the disadvantaged. In *Language programs for the disadvantaged*. Champaign, IL: National Council of Teachers of English.

Templeton, S., & Spivey, E.M. (1980). The concept of word in young children as a function of level of cognitive development. *Research in the Teaching of English, 14*, 265-278.

Valtin, R. (1984). The development of metalinguistic abilities in children learning to read and write. In J. Downing & R. Valtin (Eds.), *Language awareness and learning to read*. New York: Springer-Verlag.

Vellutino, F.R. (1977). Alternative conceptualizations of dyslexia: Evidence in support of a verbal deficit hypothesis. *Harvard Educational Review, 47*, 334-354.

Vygotsky, L.S. (1962). *Thought and language*. Cambridge, MA: MIT Press.

Wendell, M.M. (1982). *Bootstrap literature: Preliterate societies do it themselves*. Newark, DE: International Reading Association.

Whiting, H.T.A. (1975). *Concepts in skill learning*. London: Lepus.

Whiting, H.T.A., & den Brinker, B.D. (1982). Images of the act. In J.P. Das, R. Mulcahy, & A.E. Wall (Eds.), *Theory and research in learning disability*. New York: Plenum.

Yaden, D.B., Jr., & Templeton, W.S. (Eds.). (1986). *Metalinguistic awareness and beginning literacy: Conceptualizing what it means to read and write*. Exeter, NH: Heinemann.

4

Literacy and Social Change: The Significance of Social Context in the Development of Literacy Programmes

Brian V. Street
King's College, University of London, U.K.

I. INTRODUCTION

Those concerned with the "future of literacy" must ask themselves what are the consequences for social groups and for whole societies of acquiring literacy. We need first, however, to consider the framework within which such questions are asked. The questions that have mostly been asked by agencies attempting to introduce literacy to societies where it has not been widespread, have generally stemmed from emphasis on the technical problems of acquisition and how these can be overcome. In earlier work (Street, 1984), the term "autonomous" model of literacy was proposed to describe theories which treat literacy as an "independent" or "autonomous" variable, somehow divorced from the social and ideological contexts that give it meaning. From the perspective of the "autonomous" model, the question for agencies and those conducting literacy campaigns becomes: how can people be taught to decode written signs, and, for example, avoid spelling problems. This approach assumes that the social consequences of literacy are given—greater opportunity for jobs, social mobility, fuller lives, etc.—and that what the agencies need to address is the question of how literacy is to be imparted. This, however, takes too much for granted regarding the social implications of the process of literacy acquisition: there are other questions that need to be addressed prior to the apparently technical ones, questions derived from an alternative, "ideological" model of literacy. It is useful to explore some of the implications of these models, and of the questions which arise from them, for the "future of literacy" and for the conduct of literacy campaigns.

The "autonomous" model, dominant in UNESCO and other agencies concerned with literacy, tends to be based on the "essay-text" form of literacy and to generalize broadly from what is in fact a narrow, culture specific practice. The model assumes a single direction in which literacy development can be traced, and associates it with "progress," "civilization," individual liberty, and social mobility. It isolates literacy as an independent variable and then claims to be able to study its consequences. These consequences are classically represented in terms of economic "take-off" or in terms of cognitive skills. An "ideological" model, on the other hand, forces one to be more wary of grand generalizations and cherished assumptions about literacy "in itself." Those who subscribe to this second model concentrate on the specific social practices of reading and writing. They recognize the ideological and therefore culturally embedded nature of such practices. The model stresses the significance of the socialization process in the construction of the meaning of literacy for participants, and is therefore concerned with the general social institutions through which this process takes place and not just the specific "educational" ones. It distinguishes claims for the consequences of literacy from its real significance for social groups. It treats skeptically claims by Western liberal educators for the "openness," "rationality" and critical awareness of what they teach, and investigates the role of such teaching in social control and the hegemony of a ruling class. It concentrates on the overlap and interaction of oral and literate modes rather than stressing a "great divide." The investigation of literacy practices from this perspective necessarily entails an ethnographic approach, which provides closely detailed accounts of the whole cultural context in which those practices have meaning. Until there are far more such accounts available one should be wary of making any generalizations about literacy as such.

The term "ideological" is appropriate to describe this approach, rather than the less contentious or loaded terms such as "cultural," "sociological," etc., because it signals quite explicitly that literacy practices are located not only within cultural wholes but also within power structures. The very emphasis on the "neutrality" and "autonomy" of literacy by many writers is "ideological" in the sense of disguising this power dimension: any ethnographic account of literacy will, in fact, bring out its significance for power, authority and social differentiation, in terms of the author's own interpretation of these concepts. Since all approaches to literacy in practice will involve some such bias, it is better scholarship to admit to and expose the particular "ideological" framework being employed from the very beginning—it can then be opened to scrutiny, challenged and refined in ways which are more difficult when the ideology remains hidden. This is to use the term "ideological" not in its old-fashioned Marxist (and current anti-Marxist) sense of "false consciousness" and simple-minded dogma, but rather in the sense employed within contemporary studies of discourse, in anthropology, sociolinguistics and cultural studies, which focus on the tension between authority and power on the one hand and individual resistance and creativity on the other (Asad, 1980; Bourdieu & Passeron, 1977; Centre for Contemporary Cultural Studies, 1980; Fairclough, 1992; Grillo, 1990; Mace, 1979). This tension operates through the medium of a variety of cultural practices, including particularly language and, of course, literacy. It is in this sense that it is important to approach the study of literacy in terms of an explicit "ideological" model. This approach does not attempt to deny technical skill or the cognitive aspects of reading and writing, but rather understands that they are encapsulated within cultural wholes and within structures of power. Those who adopt an "autonomous" model are responsible for setting up a false polarity between these aspects of literacy practice by suggesting that the "technical" aspects can be isolated and the "cultural bits" added on later. In that sense the "ideological" model subsumes rather than excludes the work undertaken within the "autonomous" model.

II. THE TRANSMISSION OF LITERACY

These models may be tested more directly against the immediate practical questions that are raised by consideration of the "future of literacy," particularly with reference to comparative material from industrialized and developing nations and to the questions raised by literacy campaigns, conducted both within and across nation-states. There are a number of ways in which the acquisition of literacy affects a society. For social groups with virtually no prior exposure to literacy it is likely that the dominant feature of acquisition will be not so much the consequence of literacy *per se* but the impact of the culture on the bearers of that literacy. By definition, literacy is being transferred from a different culture, so that those receiving it will be more conscious of the nature and power of that culture than of the mere technical aspects of reading and writing. Very often this process has involved some transfer of "Western" values to a Third World society. This aspect of literacy acquisition can be called, for convenience, "colonial" literacy, and this chapter considers some contemporary examples of this, as well as citing some historical ones for comparison.

It is not always the case, however, that literacy is transferred from an alien society to indigenous "illiterates." In many situations it is a dominant group within a society that is responsible for spreading literacy to other members of that society and to subcultures within it. This has been the paradigm in many European cases of literacy transmission, as in France and Britain where bourgeois groups justified the expense of providing widespread literacy in terms of the spread of certain dominant class values (cf. Donald, 1981: Furet & Ozouf, 1984; Houston, 1990). The "technical" advantages in terms of manpower skills, and so forth, were encapsulated within these values. In order to distinguish it from "colonial literacy," this second kind of literacy transfer can be termed "dominant" literacy and this chapter considers some examples in contemporary literacy campaigns, with particular reference to the author's own anthropological field work in Iran during the 1970s.

A. "Colonial" Literacy

1. Medieval England

In order to bring out the ways in which the acquisition of literacy has to do with deeper aspects of ideology, culture and epistemology rather than just being an empirical matter of extending "skills" and "knowledge," it may be helpful to begin with an instance well removed in time from the present and thus, perhaps, less charged than many contemporary examples. Clanchy (1979), in his description of how the Normans introduced literacy in medieval England, argues that what was required was a shift to a "literate mentality." By this he means to indicate that the shift involves a way of thinking, a whole cultural outlook, an ideology, rather than simply a change in technical processes. Members of the culture, at least at certain levels of the hierarchy, came to share new assumptions about the status of the written word and its significance for claims about truth. In the eleventh century, rights to land and claims to truth were validated through, for instance, the display of swords and other such symbols of authority, through use of seals and through the oral testimony of a jury. By the fourteenth century certain classes of people, such as knights and local gentry, were referring, as a matter of course, to such literate material as "pipe rolls," documents validated by a notary or letters that were dated precisely. A shift of this kind did not happen simply: it involved profound changes in people's sense of identity and in what they took to be the basis of knowledge. For instance, the spread of commercial documentation required the development of a system of dating. When a businessman wrote a letter he had to learn to put the date on it, for a number of reasons—in order to establish a basis for a sequence of further correspondence, in order to enable the letter to be retrieved easily later, and also so that the truth of the claims made in it could be tested against other evidence from the time. The dating of a letter, then, was not just a "technical" matter but had legal and practical significance.

Moreover, during this era, development of the new convention of dating impinged upon deeply held religious beliefs. In medieval England the conceptual basis for the division of time was provided by Christian theology. Dating a document placed its maker in temporal and geographical perspective: it involved expressing an opinion about the writer's place in the world. The birth of Christ was the central reference point for current dating but this was a sacramental matter and not one to be lightly applied to temporal or commercial matters. The writer of a commercial document could not, then, simply date it with reference to the Christian calendar without giving possible offense both to the clergy and to the writer's own deeply held beliefs. Clanchy describes how a compromise developed, whereby secular dating was organized with reference to such events as the crowning of a king, while the religious calendar remained independent of commercial practice. The boundaries between the sacred and the profane were kept distinct within the new literate practices which were thereby accommodated to the belief system of the society into which they were being introduced. Clanchy, indeed, argues that the new "mentality" became accepted precisely because it happened in such gradual ways, and did not therefore represent a great shock to traditional beliefs, even though over time the cumulative effect was quite radical. There is a lesson here for contemporary literacy agencies, in judging how far to take account of local perceptions and how far to simply impose their own "outside" view of literacy.

Clanchy also describes how the very form of written texts is associated with deeply held beliefs, and how the transition from one system to another was achieved in Norman times by the "mixing" of elements of the new and the old. What had given written texts legitimacy in the pre-Norman period had been their association with Christian truth. A Bible was a sacred object not only because of the content of the words on the page, but also in its material form and context. Certain Bibles, highly illuminated and preserved in monasteries, were held in esteem as reflections of the glory of God, the elaborate artwork cherished not simply on aesthetic grounds but as proof of the Beauty and Goodness of the Creator. When commercial documents began to circulate in greater numbers, there was some ambivalence, during the period of transition, as to how far they required embellishment and illumination as marks of the truth value of their content. Later, commercial and legal users of documents hence took to embellishing their writing, in order to try to acquire some of that status, and as a means to easing the transition from previous custom to new practices. Some of this has carried over into contemporary England in the way in which some legal and constitutional manuscripts are illuminated, the embellishments signifying their status and often having as much formal importance as the words on the page. Recognizing the problems associated with claiming validity for their assertions, politicians and others play upon the variety of ways in which different media of communication are taken to signify the truth.

In other parts of the contemporary world, too, the introduction or spread of literacy practices is associated with theological and epistemological problems of the kind cited by Clanchy (Goody, 1986; Probst, 1993). Researchers and agencies need to ask questions that would elicit similar information about the compromises or breakdown that these problems may lead to, and to find ways of describing and analyzing this level of the literacy process across different cultures. Clanchy's work, in a sense, provides a useful model for this endeavor, even though the conditions of medieval England are obviously very different from those of the modern world. Both the way in which he approaches the material, in terms of the concept of a "literate mentality," and some of the examples themselves, have general applicability. An analysis of one or two more recent examples will bring this point out more fully. These examples owe much to the "ethnographic" approach to literacy, whereby literacy practices are described as part of social wholes, in a way traditionally developed by social and cultural anthropologists. These methods and the material they generate suggest important questions and levels of understanding that can usefully be applied to both the research and practice involved in contemporary literacy campaigns.

2. Malagasy

Maurice Bloch (1989) uses a combination of contemporary anthropological fieldwork and analysis of historical documents in order to explain the sudden growth of historical manuscripts in Madagascar in the nineteenth century. In doing so he brings out some general aspects of the development of literacy in colonial contexts, that has relevance to the contemporary situation and the current discussion. As in many non-European societies in this period, missionaries were the first to contribute to mass literacy in Madagascar.[1] Roman script and printing were introduced to Madagascar by the London Missionary Society from the 1820s, supplanting Arabic which had been used for astrological and administrative purposes. The missionaries translated the Bible and wrote it down in Malagasy. At first the new literacy continued to be used mainly for administration, as well as for religious purposes. But from 1835 onwards the political situation changed dramatically. The London Missionary Society was expelled, Christianity was banned, the spread of literacy was seriously restricted and the schools closed. Yet both Christianity and literacy flourished in this period, which was one of the most productive for Malagasy literature. While administrative uses of literacy continued, the main development was in the production of historical and ethnographic manuscripts, many of which have survived until today.

Bloch explains these developments partly with reference to the knowledge he himself acquired during field work on the island in the 1960s, amongst a group called the Merina. In Merina culture, knowledge was validated through being passed on from one generation to another. Elders passed on knowledge to their juniors and at the same time affirmed their political authority over those to whom it was being transmitted. The status of the elders was multi-faceted, and their authority depended upon a variety of social conventions: display of knowledge alone would be irrelevant or ridiculous, but in the context of the power structure it represented a claim to power. The missionaries, with their "Bible," were seen as making claims regarding their own authority, similar to those which Malagasy elders were accustomed to make through indigenous genealogies and stories. The Bible was seen as similarly consisting of accounts of the history and customs of the missionaries' ancestors, together with their genealogies, as indeed it does, and the accounts appeared, therefore, to be challenging those of the Merina themselves.

By asserting this knowledge the missionaries were seen to be overtly claiming a high place in the power structure and subordinating local authorities. As in Clanchy's example from medieval England, the significance of new forms of documentation lay in their location in a power structure rather than in the intrinsic qualities of the medium itself. Indeed, Bloch stresses that the significance of the written medium of communication lay not "in the fact that it represented a different kind

---

[1]Compare Clammer (1978) on nineteenth-century Fiji, where missionaries took printing presses with them to the island and allowed locals access only to what they chose to print, namely catechisms and Bibles.

of knowledge to the oral knowledge of elders, but because it represented a more powerful, impressive, efficient form of the same kind of knowledge. A new technology had been harnessed for an old purpose to make a competing claim" (p. 11). The Merina, then, responded to the missionaries' Bible by writing their own "Bibles," with their own histories and genealogies and accounts of important legitimating events. This was what the Christian Bible consisted of, and it had likewise been part of the oral tradition in Malagasy. The adoption of written forms represented a continuation of traditional oral practice in the medium of literacy, a way of fighting back against the newcomers with their own weapons.

As in many responses to outside domination, the Merina pragmatically adopted aspects of the alien culture to their own conventions, while rejecting the Europeans' implied position of superiority in the power structure. As Bloch states: "They used writing in this way, principally for administrative purposes, but also for ideological purposes. They therefore used writing in their reassertion of their history and customs against the political threat of outside predators, in the old way for these purposes" (p. 12). The written word, like oral knowledge, was carefully transmitted from authoritative person to authoritative person:

> What the Malagasy did in 19th century Madagascar with literacy was to use it as a tool for a kind of ideological practice which they had done before, orally. . . . Literary knowledge did not act on its own, rather people used literacy for their own purposes. The people who were using literacy were part of a system of social relations and therefore it was in terms of that system of social relations that literacy was significant and its relation to knowledge was in terms of these uses. Literacy did not desocialise knowledge, as implied by Goody. (Bloch, 1985, p. 12)

Goody (1968) has argued that the advent of literacy creates a new distinction, between myth and history where "history" refers to "true" accounts of the past, unsullied by the particular social interests of those recording it. What the Malagasy example shows is that myth and history are both embedded within particular social conventions, and they do not necessarily correlate directly either with a distinction between truth and falsity or with that between orality and literacy. Both Christian uses of the text of the Bible and Malagasy uses of their own manuscripts served to maintain social conventions related to the assertion of power and the validation of knowledge. The ways in which myths are employed to validate present political positions does not necessarily change when they are written down. They do not automatically become altered or subjected to historical scholarship, for instance. The Malagasy could easily accommodate literate forms of communication, without the meaning or functions of the texts being radically changed. The development of literacy in itself did not alter the traditional bases of knowledge. Whereas Goody—and many development agencies—have assumed that the acquisition of literacy leads to a new kind of knowledge, more "objective" and related to historical truth rather than myth, the evidence from ethnographic research suggests a more complex picture. As Bloch says: "There is no such thing as non-social knowledge, whether literate or not" (p. 13).

The situations in Malagasy and in medieval England can both be taken as examples of "colonial" literacy. Members of an outside culture introduced their particular form of literacy to a colonized people as part of a much wider process of domination. In both cases the introduction of certain literacy practices is to be understood in terms of that wider domination: in Malagasy, as part of the missionaries' attempt to spread their own religion and of the colonial administration to set up bureaucratic structures through which they could rule. In Medieval England, the Normans introduced certain legal and bureaucratic forms of literacy in order to centralize their authority and to shift the basis for validating rights in land away from local sources. In both cases, however, we find something more than a simple imposition of dominant views on a passive indigenous population. Rather, local peoples find pragmatic ways of adopting elements of the new ideology, or of the new forms in which literacy is introduced, to indigenous belief and practice. In both cases, too, there was some degree of indigenous literacy prior to the colonial incursion, so that what was new was the particular forms which their uses of literacy took, rather than simply the presence of literacy itself.

B. "Dominant" Literacy

In most examples of colonialism one finds, similarly, that the subjugated peoples have had some acquaintance with literacy, notably in cases of Muslim groups and others with religions of the "Book." One would expect to find similar complex processes of adaptation, resistance and encapsulation when foreign forms of literacy are introduced in these contexts. This is also the case in countries not under direct colonial rule, but where some degree of indigenous differentiation of power and control means that the recipients of literacy campaigns are in practice experiencing "foreign" cultural forms. In many cases the main agency of transmission today tends to be national governments and indigenous experts, frequently drawn from a narrow class or cultural base. On the one hand these situations frequently reproduce features of the "colonial" situation, such as for instance in the employment of educators from Western countries in local literacy campaigns. As participants at the

Persepolis UNESCO Conference on Literacy (and the followers of Paulo Freire) have made clear, governments in the developing world and their internal agencies are often wedded to major features of Western culture and style (Freire, 1978, 1985; UNESCO, 1975). Furthermore, at a structural level, these countries are often economically dependent on the Western economic order, through multinationals, export dependency, loans and aid (Lloyd, 1971; Worsley, 1984). Very often, then, literacy is being introduced along with a whole range of features of Western society—forms of industrialization, bureaucracy, formal schooling, medicine, and so forth.

On the other hand, beyond these obvious features of the "colonial" model of literacy transmission, it is also important to take account of a degree of "internal domination" in the ways in which literacy campaigns are being conducted. The primary dimensions of this new power structure involve hegemony of urban areas over rural, of men over women and of central elites over local populations. In order to understand the processes of literacy transmission in these contexts it is not enough simply to analyze the role of colonialism or of neo-colonialism, but also to develop ways of knowing about these local power structures and cultures.

Just as in the overtly colonial situations described above for Malagasy and medieval England, there was local resistance and pragmatic adaptation to or modification of colonial literacy, so the contemporary situation of "internal domination" is characterized by complex forms of adaptation to the new literacy practices being introduced. Again the model of literacy needs to be elaborated in order to make sense of this complexity and to understand what literacy means to the people acquiring it.

III. THE CASE OF IRAN

An interesting, and perhaps extreme, example of "internal domination" is to be found in many of the literacy campaigns conducted under the Shah in Iran during the 1960s and 1970s. Many campaigns were addressed to women as the main socializing agents and, in the eyes of many, the major "barriers to change." In order to "get at" the children, it was believed, it was necessary to "alter" their mothers. One Iranian educationalist who played an important role in the campaigns in Khorosan province suggested that "The psychological attitudes of the Iranian villagers create a great obstacle to rural reconstruction" (Gharib, 1966, p. 88). This psychological attitude, he believed, stemmed largely from the influence of mothers. While the father was considered to be an authoritarian head of the family, he was usually out at work all day and it was the mother who passed on values to the child. She, according to Gharib, was "permissive," had poor standards of health and hygiene and had a passive belief in fate. As a result, Gharib states, "Family life remains the most stubborn core of resistance to change; [the home] contradicts the principles taught at school [and it is necessary to educate] mothers as well as daughters" (p. 88). Hashemi (1966) agrees that "It is in the home that attitudes are fixed, ways of life established and traditions continued. The profound change in patterns of behaviour and expectations depends on a great part upon the attitude of the home-maker" (p. 98). The education of women, then, is central to education and development: "their education might be the way for removing remaining social, cultural and psychological barriers to the advancement of a nation" (Hashemi, 1966, p. 107).

It was the role of the teacher in the village to make these changes come about, in particular by challenging the conservatism of rural women: "The task of the teacher in rural areas is not so much that of giving instruction in the classroom but of providing an integrated education in social habits, agriculture techniques and the creation of a new attitude of mind" (Gharib, 1966, p. 45). Teams of trained women teachers could be drafted into villages to transform values. Unfortunately for the proponents of this scheme, women were reluctant to move far from home to train as teachers. In 1964, when Hashemi and Gharib were writing, only 9% of rural teachers were women and only 18% of their pupils were girls. Moreover, most teachers were reared and educated in cities and this, Gharib comments, made them "usually unable to perform their task adequately," since their task was defined as becoming rural community leaders and transforming values. Gharib's solution was to set up Rural Teacher Training Colleges in local communities, so that rural people could be brought in, given some teaching experience and knowledge and then, before they became wedded to urban ideas and used their education to migrate, they would be sent back to the villages to teach fellow peasants.

From an educator's point of view Gharib's proposals had much merit, and were certainly an improvement on earlier authoritarian, urban-based practice that failed to recognize the importance of women in education. But, in a context where the national drive was towards rapid Westernization, and where most urban Iranians shared the views outlined above regarding "backward" villagers, there was a crucial ambivalence in Gharib's proposals similar to that found in many such campaigns. The ambivalence lies on the one hand in the fact that, if the process was to be one of major indoctrination, changing fundamental beliefs and practices and the very bases of knowledge amongst the majority of the population, then a few rural teachers trained in rural areas and insulated to some extent from urban influences were not likely to have much impact. On the other hand, the introduction of urban teachers to rural areas was already creating resistance and resentment.

There was also a deep ambivalence amongst villagers towards the state education system and the forms of literacy it transmitted. They saw urban teachers as looking down on them, as interested in their own urban advancement rather than in educating villagers, and as failing to understand rural values and material needs, all of which was indeed true. Nevertheless, it tended to be assumed that one or two boys in each family would take advantage of the State education system, go on to higher levels of schooling and university in the city to obtain urban jobs. The main image of the new employment to which such education could lead was that it involved working at desks in clean, modern offices, with high salaries and security, in overt contrast with rural dependence on the vagaries of the climate and the general discomfort of working in the fields. So the urban teachers in the village found some village boys motivated to attend and learn. But the majority, it was assumed, would remain in the villages, work in the fields or orchards and support their aging parents.

For girls the likelihood of continuing their education was even more remote. It was assumed that they would marry young, and that their major function was to rear children and look after the household. Each year a few girls would pass through to the top grades of the local village school and a decision would have to be made as to whether they could continue their education in urban schools. There were a number of factors to be taken into account. The family would need to have relatives whom they could trust in the town, or a house of their own, so that the girl had somewhere to live and someone to chaperone her while studying there. The parents would have to be committed to breaking tradition by allowing her to continue: the most likely job she could get would be as a teacher and, for many villagers, this was self-evidently a low-status occupation, given the low pay and poor standards of the teachers they encountered. There would also, of course, be problems in finding an appropriate husband.

All of this is familiar from many other parts of the world, but it indicates the importance of understanding local beliefs and values and local perceptions of literacy, rather than simply imposing them from outside. The effect of all of these factors, as regards both boys and girls, was a mixed and somewhat confused situation. Many boys who did "succeed" in the education system found themselves without jobs of the kind their parents envisaged, as the Iranian economy began to break down in the later part of the 1970s. In the village where I worked, in which ownership of orchards and sale of fruit provided a relatively lucrative source of income, educated boys might be better off returning to organize their plots in the village than hanging around disaffected and underemployed in the city. But their new literacy, and the aspirations developed through their urban education, did not prepare them for this kind of work. On the other hand, many who stayed in the village found that their education at the local *maktab*, or Quranic school, prepared them better for the new, "commercial" literacy required of village entrepreneurs than would the new State education. Moreover, these youths might finish up both wealthier and with more security than those trained in the "modern" literacy of the State education system (cf. Street, 1984).

For girls too the picture was uneven. Some girls from the village did continue with their education in the city each year, and there were large numbers of women studying at the local university. Many village women with whom I spoke saw the advantages of schooling and literacy, and said that they would have liked it for themselves, and some older women did take advantage of the adult literacy classes that were being provided by central agencies. Women themselves had views on these matters, and were not simply the passive instruments of conservatism caricatured by outside, male educators.

Moreover, there was already a long tradition of forms of education and literacy in rural Iran, so that urban educators were not simply working on unsophisticated or "uneducated" minds (cf. Arasteh, 1960). The villagers were already accustomed to the educational traditions imparted through the "*maktabs*," and in many cases these were supplemented by local "reading groups," in which people gathered at each others' homes to read *suras* of the Quran and passages from the commentaries, as a basis for discussion and interpretation. These processes provided the basis for village literacy well before Western-style and state interventions. In the *maktab* the mullah would provide basic knowledge of the Quran, mostly through rote learning for younger pupils, although even here the process was not as one-dimensional and mindless as many Western caricatures of it have suggested. At one level the students were learning many of the hidden conventions of literacy: the ordering of words on a page: the indicating of meaning by precise placing of words, whether in margins, as headings or across the main text at an angle; the indication of the beginning and ending of words by different forms of a letter.

In this sense, then, *maktab* students cannot be deemed "illiterate," although they may well appear so in government and formal school tests designed to examine other, less "hidden" skills. What students of the *maktab* acquired as part of their *maktab* literacy was not an obvious, or even a universal, aspect of literacy skills: it was a specific skill derived from the specific nature of the literacy materials they used, and of the context of learning in which they encountered them (cf. also Wagner, Messick, & Spratt, 1986). Many of these aspects of literacy learning are not taught in modern, State schools, so one cannot simply equate village learning and literacy with "backward" conservatism and modern schooling with "progress" and critical thought, as many are wont to do. For instance, despite the stereotypes that associate Quranic learning with mindless repetition, that imparted in the villages of Iran frequently involved some discussion and analysis, and did give scope for interpretation and criticism, particularly at higher stages.

The skills and processes developed within *maktab* literacy were, in terms of Western pedagogy, "hidden" rather than explicit, but they provided and important basis for some villagers to build on them a form of "commercial" literacy that enabled them to cash in on the oil boom of the 1970s. With the help of this "commercial" literacy they created an infrastructure for the production and distribution of village fruit to urban areas as demand increased. The *tajers* or middlemen adapted their *maktab* literacy to these new requirements: this involved signing cheques, writing out bills, labeling boxes, listing customers and their deals in exercise books, recording fruit held in store, etc. In all of these transactions, use was being made of the "hidden" literacy skills acquired within *maktab* literacy. These skills were being elaborated in new ways, and new conventions were being adopted specific to the expanded commercial enterprises. This involved, for instance, the attention to layout as a factor in construction meaning that had been learned through reading of the Quran and the commentaries.

Local perceptions and uses of literacy, then, many differ from those of the dominant culture, and must be taken into account in order to understand the literacy experience of different peoples. All of this represents a different picture from that presented by those urban educators who see only "ignorance" or "backwardness" in the village. The overemphasis, in Iran, on this urban perspective on literacy, meant that educators failed to identify those features of local literacy and culture most likely to facilitate adaptation to the new economic order of the country in the 1970s. Rather than seeking to impose a particular literacy and ideology on rural life, as the quotes above from Iranian educators suggest was the dominant viewpoint, observers might have looked at how the villagers themselves perceived the different literacies to which they were exposed and how they made pragmatic adaptations to serve their particular interests, in a similar way to the Malagasy situation. These examples also suggest that, in most cases in the contemporary world, literacy is not being introduced entirely fresh to "illiterate" populations. Rather, most people have some experience of forms of literacy, whether as in these cases, through traditional religious texts, or as in many other circumstances, through exposure, however minimal, to the commercial literacy of local elites or neighboring cultures. In all of these cases the reality is of a mix of oral and literate conventions, and the introduction of specific forms of literacy through education and agency campaigns represents a shift in those conventions rather than the introduction of an entirely new process.

IV. CONCLUSION

If one would like to anticipate some aspects of the "future of literacy," ethnographic methods and theories about culture and change would need to be applied to the different literacies currently practiced and experienced by people from different class and cultural backgrounds (see Street, 1994). This involves, in the first instance, developing respect for this variety rather than attempting to impose a single, uniform "autonomous" model on local practice. The conflict between these two views of literacy has important implications for the conduct of literacy campaigns, and I shall conclude with a brief examination of some of the arguments currently being conducted by a number of literacy specialists.

Some specialists, such as Heribert Hinzen of the German Adult Education Association, have argued that literacy planners should look more closely at "research being done by anthropologists on the variety of literacy practices in different cultures and the relationship between literacy and education development" (Hinzen, 1984). He urges that education and literacy campaigns be rooted in and developed from these cultures themselves, rather than simply being imposed in terms of the cultural values of the campaigners themselves.

This view is challenged by H. S. Bhola, who characterizes Hinzen's approach as "cultural relativism" and he identifies within it a "new paternalism." It involves those already educated and literate in "telling the Third World that their illiterates are not ignorant but wise; that being illiterate can be dignified in its own peculiar way" (Bhola, 1984b, p. 3). Bhola sees this as an attempt to "freeze" indigenous values and techniques at the expense of teaching "new communication skills brought to us by literacy" (p. 3). Bhola's perspective is, however, itself patronizing to many "Third World" societies, since it ignores the communication skills and forms of literacy that already exist there, as was evident from the examples of Malagasy and Iran cited above. What the ethnographic evidence suggests is that the major change brought by literacy campaigns is not simply in the introduction of new communication skills but in the particular, often Western-oriented forms of literacy and of ideology being imparted, and in the altering of the previous "mix" of orality and literacy in the receiving culture.

It is not, as Bhola's approach might lead us to believe, a simple choice between "freezing" traditional values on the one hand or of crude "modernism" on the other. Rather the issue is that of sensitivity to indigenous cultures and recognition of the dynamic process of their interaction with dominant cultures and literacies. The reality, in such situations, is of pragmatic adaptation, particularly on the part of the less powerful party, to the new skills, conventions and ideologies being introduced. The particular "literacy" being imparted through campaigns, whether conducted by national governments or by colonial powers, involves conventions and assumptions alien to those socialized into indigenous forms of literacy. The outcome is most often a mix of new and old convention: in reality, there is continuous interaction and change, and people frequently maintain a number of different literacies side by side, using them for different purposes, as Wagner and colleagues have discovered in Morocco (Wagner, 1993; Wagner et al., 1986, and in this volume) and Scribner and Cole in Liberia (1981). Indeed linguists, psychologists and anthropologists are just beginning to describe these processes in more sophisticated and less culturally biased ways (Wagner, 1983; Olson et al., 1985; Heath, 1983; Bledsoe & Robey 1986; Street, 1987, 1994). Those involved in practical, literacy campaigns on the ground would do well to take advantage of this contemporary research, and to abandon outdated and ethnocentric models of literacy that can only distort practical efforts.

Some specialists still maintain that this kind of research is "neither possible nor necessary in the policy-making world" (Bhola, 1984b, p. 3). Rather, they put their faith in the cultural ideals and literacy conventions of the dominant, usually Western-oriented, classes in Third World countries and see the "future of literacy" as being bound up with the strategic and practical problems of how their view of literacy can be spread to the masses. Bhola, for instance, argues-that the only strategy commensurate with the size of the problem of illiteracy today is the national, mass-scale literacy campaign (Bhola, 1984a). Ethnographic research, however, suggests that local literacies are too substantial to be simply "accommodated" to a single dominant "autonomous" model. The complexity of the situation is disguised when literacy planners devise mass campaigns that treat local variation as something to be at best tolerated and, as in some of the cases cited above, denigrated.

Indeed in some recent literacy campaigns, such as that in Nicaragua, planners and politicians have discovered for themselves that local experience cannot be simply "accommodated" while it is assumed to be inferior, backward and a "barrier to progress," and they have very ideology of the campaign itself (Freeland, 1985, 1995; Miller, 1985). They have provided a response to the advocates of the "autonomous" model of literacy on the political level similar to that being developed here on a theoretical level: namely a recognition that literacy is part of ideological practice and will no more conform to the grand designs of central planners than will the members of the different cultures that happen to be defined within a given nation-state. Others would do well to follow their example. For the way in which "local variations" are "accommodated" to the hegemonic character of central campaigns will provide the fundamental question for those concerned with the "future of literacy" in the next decades. Such questions can only be answered if we conduct more research into the varieties of literacy and forms of communication to be found in the contemporary world, in terms of the "ideological" rather than the "autonomous" model of literacy. In the field of literacy neither theory nor practice can be divorced from their ideological roots.

REFERENCES

Arasteh, R. (1960). *Education and tradition in Iran*. Leiden: Brill.

Asad, T. (1980). Anthropology and the analysis of ideology, *Man*, n.s., 14(4).

Bhola, H.S. (1984a). *Campaigning for literacy*. Paris: UNESCO.

Bhola, H.S. (1984b). Letter to *Unesco Adult Information Notes*, No. 3.

Bledsoe, C., & Robey, K. (1986). Arabic literacy and secrecy among the Mende of Sierra Leone, *Man*, 21, 202-26.

Bloch, M. (1989). Literacy and enlightenment. In K. Scousboe & M. Larsen (Eds.), *Literacy and society*, Akademsig Forlag, Centre for Research in the Humanities, Copenhagen University.

Bourdieu, P., & Passeron, J.-C. (1977) *Reproduction in education, society and culture*. London: Sage.

Centre for Contemporary Cultural Studies (1980). *Language, culture, media*. London: Hutchinson.

Clammer, J. (1978). *Literacy and social change: A case study of Fiji*. Leiden: Brill

Clanchy, M. (1979). *From memory to written record 1066 1307*. London: Edward Arnold.

Donald, J. (1981). Language, literacy and schooling. Open University course No. U203. *Popular Culture*.

Fairclough, N. (1992). *Discourse and social change*. London: Polity Press.

Freeland, J. (1985). The literacy campaign on the Atlantic Coast of Nicaragua. *World University Service News*, Nos. 1 and 2.

Freeland, J. (1995). The literacy campaign on the Atlantic Coast of Nicaragua. *World University Service News*, Nos. 1 and 2.

Freire, P. (1978). *The pedagogy of the oppressed*. New York: Seabury Press.

Freire, P. (1985). *The politics of education: Culture, power and liberation*. London: Macmillan.

Furet, F., & Ozouf, J. (1984). *Reading and writing: Literacy in France from Calvin to Jules Ferry.* Cambridge, MA: Cambridge University Press.

Gharib, G.S. (1966). *Training teachers for rural elementary schools in Iran.* Masters thesis, University of Beirut.

Goody, J. (1968). *Literacy in traditional societies.* Cambridge, MA: Cambridge University Press.

Goody, J. (1977). *The domestication of the savage mind.* Cambridge, MA: Cambridge University Press.

Goody, J. (1986). *The logic of writing and the organization of society,* Cambridge, MA: Cambridge University Press.

Goody, J. (1987). *The interface between the written and the oral.* Cambridge, MA: Cambridge University Press.

Grillo, R. (1990) *Dominant languages.* Cambridge, MA: Cambridge University Press.

Hashemi, M. (1966). Adult education in rural Iran: Problems and prospects. Masters thesis, University of Beirut.

Heath, S.B. (1983). *Ways with words.* Cambridge, MA: Cambridge University Press.

Hinzen, H. (1984). *Letter to Network Literacy,* Vol. 1.

Houston, R. (1990). *Literacy in early modern Europe,* London: Longman.

Lloyd, P. (1971). *Classes, crises and coups.* London: Granada.

Mace, J. (1979). *Working with words* London: Chameleon.

Miller, V. (1985). *Between struggle and hope: The Nicaraguan literacy crusade.* Boulder, CO: Westview Press.

Olson, D., Torrence, N., & Hildyard, A. (Eds.). (1985). *Literacy, language and learning.* Cambridge, MA: Cambridge University Press.

Probst, P. (1993). The letter and spirit: Literacy in the aladura movement in Nigeria. In B. Street (Ed.), *Cross-cultural approaches to literacy.* Cambridge, MA: Cambridge University Press.

Scribner, S., & Cole, M. (1981). *The psychology of literacy.* Cambridge, MA: Harvard University Press.

Street, B. (1984) *Literacy in theory and practice.* Cambridge, MA: Cambridge University Press.

Street, B.V. (1987). Literacy practices and literacy myths. In R. Saljo (Ed.), *The written code and conceptions of reality.* Springen Press.

Street, B.V. (Ed.). (1994) *Cross-cultural approvals to literacy.* Cambridge: Cambridge University Press.

UNESCO. (1975). *Final report for International Symposium for Literacy, Persepolis.* Iran.

Wagner, D.A. (Ed.). (1983). Literacy and ethnicity. *International Journal for the Sociology of Language,* 42.

Wagner, D. (1993). *Culture, literacy and development.* Cambridge, MA: Cambridge University Press.

Wagner, D. A., Messick, B., & Spratt, J. (1986) Studying literacy in Morocco. In B.B. Schieffelin & P. Gilmore (Eds.), *The acquisition of literacy: Ethnographic perspectives.* Norwood, NJ: Ablex.

Worsley, P. (1984) *The three worlds.* London: Weidenfeld & Nicolson.

5

Developing
Literacy . . . in
Children and Adults

Jeanne S. Chall
Harvard University

I. INTRODUCTION

Adult literacy in the United States seems to present an ever-growing challenge—greater perhaps than the acknowledged challenge of literacy among those still in school. The problems in adult literacy have grown as the field has come to include the full range of reading ability—from beginning reading to highly competent and skilled reading. This broad range of competency has not always been the province of adult literacy. Not too long ago, before World War II, those who developed adult literacy programs were concerned mainly with adults who were completely illiterate, usually newcomers to the United States. Most adult students who attended these literacy classes had attended school for fewer than 4 or 5 years, and if they spoke another language before English, they were usually not literate in it.

For these adult illiterates the goal was to advance from reading nothing to reading something. What exactly that something was to be was not always clear. But one might guess that it was relatively little—enough to pass a literacy test for voting, to read simple signs, to write one's name and address, and perhaps to read the headlines and captions in a tabloid.

World War II marked an important change. The greater complexity of the military technology, the use of more difficult instructional manuals, and the more complex organizations and procedures required more than "a little bit of literacy." The tasks required a level of literacy closer to that of typical elementary school graduates.

In the 40 years since World War II literacy needs have advanced even more—from that of an elementary school student to that of a typical high school graduate. The education attainments, according to United States census data, have advanced in a similar direction, from an average attainment of 8th grade in 1940 to an average of nearly 12th grade in 1980.

Thus the nature of adult students in the United States seeking help with literacy has changed vastly. Some still seek help with basic literacy; but this group is shrinking in comparison with those whose literacy needs go beyond the beginnings.

The changing nature of the adult student is perhaps one of the main reasons for the confusion over the extent of adult illiteracy in the United States. The layman, and even the student of literacy, is often confused by the numbers cited. Some say there are 13 million illiterates in the United States. Others say 26 million. And yet a truer estimate would be even higher, perhaps half of the adult population, if we included the "new illiterates"—those whose literacy does not reach that needed for a high tech world.

There are several other reasons why adult literacy presents an ever greater problem and uncertainty than that of literacy among those in school.

One is the tendency to underplay development and progression in the curriculum of adult literacy programs. The grading of instructional materials was never too popular with adult programs, and it has become even less popular in programs that stress the individual and motivation. There has also been a tendency to underplay assessment and evaluation. There are few tests specifically meant for adults. Indeed, at the advanced levels (high school and college), standardized reading tests for regular high school and college students are generally used. It is only at the middle and upper elementary levels where several special achievement tests for adults have been constructed within the recent past. But even with the availability of these tests there seems to be a hesitation in using them for evaluating group or individual gains or for judging the effectiveness of programs. No doubt this stems from a great respect for adult students and a fear that a low score on a reading test, for example, might be interpreted as a judgment not only of the adult student's inadequate reading, but of his/her knowledge or intelligence.

Another difficulty stems, I believe, from a lack of clarity as to what should be taught and when it should be taught. Does reading progress in the same manner and at the same pace for adult students as for elementary and high school students? Some have argued that it could not be the same, what with the adults' greater language, cognitive abilities, and experience. For example, an average child at age 6 first learning to read has been estimated to have a meaning vocabulary of about 5000 words, while the average adult's meaning vocabulary, even when that adult is not literate, has been estimated to be in the tens of thousands (Lorge & Chall, 1963). Thus, since the adult illiterate who first learns to read has a larger vocabulary than the 6-year-old, and since vocabulary knowledge has long been known to be highly correlated with reading achievement (R. L. Thorndike, 1973-74), it is often suggested that adults might learn to read by a different process than children (Weber, 1975).

Still another challenge is the rapidly changing structure of our economy, which has brought unemployment to many in traditionally skilled work in heavy industry. Economists speak of ultimately absorbing many into the new electronic industries, after they have been retrained. Although it is not yet clear what such retraining will involve, it would seem likely that the level of literacy required in these new jobs will be greater than that needed for skilled, heavy-industry jobs; closer, in fact, to levels typical for secondary school, or junior college, graduates. Similar to the young people of today whose educational standards and expectations are being raised, the standards for adults are also rising. The need for retraining adults in the higher literacy will probably be an increasing responsibility of adult education.

Thus it seems as if, in a 40-year period, the field of adult literacy has expanded its original responsibilities—from basic adult literacy (ranging from approximately a 4th- to an 8th-grade reading level) to a high technical level (approximately 12th-grade reading level).

In the remainder of this chapter I will consider what it means to read at these various literacy levels, what they imply for adults whose job and responsibilities require higher levels of literacy, and what this means for instruction, testing and evaluation, and diagnosis.

Let us assume, for the time being, that adult literacy encompasses about the same range of proficiency as that of children and young people. It may be useful, therefore, to understand the broad sweep of reading development—from its beginnings to its most mature and highly skilled forms. For in essence, the main goal of adult literacy programs is to bring adults up from lower literacy levels to higher ones. As an introduction to developing levels, let us examine Table 5.1, samples of text representing increasing levels of literacy, from *Stages of Reading Development* (Chall, 1983a, p. 39).

If we look at the passages which range in reading difficulty from a low-to an advanced-literacy level (Stages 1-5; or reading grade equivalents of 1st grade through college graduate level) we note changes in vocabulary and concepts, in sentence structure and length, and in cognitive demands.

The easier passages, those requiring lower levels of literacy to be read and understood, use words that are generally familiar, common, concrete, and short. The passages at higher levels have more words that are unfamiliar, difficult, technical, abstract, and long. The sentence structure also changes—from short, simple sentences in the easier passages to longer, more complex sentences in the more difficult selections. The passages change in still other ways—the ideas tend to become more removed from common, everyday happenings. While the ideas are usually concrete or elemental at the earlier levels, they become more abstract at the later stages, requiring more analytic and critical thought. These excerpts suggest that reading at successive levels of proficiency depends on ever more difficult and varied language, more complex and abstract ideas, and more advanced reading skills.

TABLE 5.1. Samples of Writing From Beginning to Advanced Levels of Literacy.*

Stage 1	"May I go?" said Fay. "May I please go with you?"
Stage 2	Spring was coming to Tait Primary School. On the new high way big trucks went by the school all day.
Stage 3A	She smoothed her hair behind her ear as she lowered her hand. I could see she was eyeing beauty and trying to figure out a way to write about being beautiful without sounding even more conceited than she already was.
Stage 3B	Early in the history of the world, men found that they could not communicate well by using only sign language. In some way that cannot be traced with any certainty, they devised spoken language. No matter what phenomena he is interested in, the scientist employs two main tools—theory and empirical research. Theory employs reason, language, and logic to suggest possible, or predict probable, relationships among various data gathered from the -concrete world of experience.
Stage 5	One of the objections to the hypothesis that a satisfying after-effect of a mental connection works back upon it to strength en it is that nobody has shown how this action does or could occur. It is the purpose of this article to show how a mechanism which is as possible psychologically as any of the mechanisms proposed to recount for facilitation, inhibition, fatigue, strengthening by repetition, or other forms of modification could enable such an after-effect to cause such a strengthening.

*From Chall (1983a), p. 39.

To move from one of these levels or stages to the next higher ones takes considerable development and change. Table 5.2 presents brief descriptions of the six reading stages, from the developmental scheme by Chall (1983a).

The reading stages cover the range from pre-reading to highly mature, expert reading. Individuals may vary in the rate of their progression. Some move quickly; others more slowly; but most tend to follow the same sequence of progression.

TABLE 5.2. What is Learned at Six Reading Stages.*

Stage level and designation	Reading grade levels	Essential learnings
Stage 0 pre-reading	Below 1st grade reading level	Introduction to nature and function of print. Reads common signs and labels, learns letters and some sounds. Can write one's name.
Stage 1 decoding	Reading grade levels 1 and beginning 2	Letter-sound correspondences, knowledge of the alphabetic principle and skill in its use. Identifies about 1000 of the commonest words in the language. Can read very simple texts.
Stage 2 fluency	Reading grade levels 2 to 3	Integrates knowledge and skills acquired in Stages 0 and 1. Relies on context and meaning as well as on decoding (phonics) for identifying new words. Reads with greater fluency. By the end of Stage 2 can recognize about 3000 familiar words and derivatives.
Stage 3 learning the new	Reading grade levels 4 to 8	Can use reading as a tool for "learning the new"—information, ideas, attitudes and values. Growth in background knowledge, meaning vocabulary, and cognitive abilities.
Stage 4 multiple viewpoints	High school-reading grade levels 9 to 12	Ability to read widely a broad range of complex materials—expository and narrative—from a variety of viewpoints and at a variety of levels of comprehension—inferential, critical as well as literal.
Stage 5 construction and reconstruction	College and beyond	Reading for one's own needs and purposes (professional, and personal, civic) to integrate one's knowledge with that of others, and to create new knowledge.

*From Chall (1983a), p. 39.

How well and how fast a person progresses through the stages—whether a child or an adult—depends upon the interaction of individual and environmental factors. That is, the individuals' abilities and freedom from handicaps, their schooling, home experiences, and the communities in which they live.

Overall, these six stages can be divided into two major levels: the pre reading/decoding/fluency level (Stages 0, 1 and 2) and the level of learning the new/multiple viewpoints/reconstruction (Stages 3, 4 and 5). In terms of reading grade equivalents, the break seems to come at about a 4th-grade reading level (the beginning of Stage 3). A pre-grade 4 reading level can be said to represent the "oral tradition," in the sense that text rarely goes beyond the language and knowledge that the reader already has through listening, direct experience, TV, and so forth. We can view reading beyond grade 4 reading level as comprising the literary tradition—when the reading matter goes beyond what is already known. Thus, grade 4 reading level can be seen as the beginning of a long progression in the reading of texts that are ever more complicated, literary, abstract, and technical; and that require more world knowledge and ever more sophisticated language and cognitive abilities to engage in the interpretations and critical reactions expected for such materials.

II. ADULT COMPARED TO CHILD LITERACY

The above descriptions of the reading stages are greatly shortened versions of the more extensive descriptions. Because of space limitations it is also not possible to include relevant research evidence (Chall, 1983a).

For present purposes it is hoped that the stages can be considered as a metaphor, a scheme for helping us get a picture of what reading is and how it changes in the life of individuals—from its beginnings to its advanced forms.

The course of the development of reading is, I think, essentially the same for adults and children. Their instructional needs are also broadly similar as they progress, except for the content of the instructional materials, particularly at the early stages. Let us consider a few similarities and differences in what adult and child beginners need to learn. According to the stages scheme, the major task to be learned by both the 6-year-old beginner and the 40-year-old beginner is to recognize in print the words they already know when heard or spoken. If they have any difficulty in understanding the sentences or stories they can read, it usually stems from the fact that they cannot recognize the words, or they cannot read fluently enough. It is their limited or inadequate knowledge of the alphabetic principle and its automatic use in recognizing words that keeps the adult an illiterate or the child preliterate in a world in which he is surrounded by print.

Some adult educators, as well as early childhood educators, have a different view, tending to see the beginner as lacking primarily in concepts, ideas and knowledge, or motivation to read.[1] The view that the first and major need of adult illiterates is knowledge and maturation stems from many sources. One of these may come from the enthusiastic acceptance of the theories of Paulo Freire (1970, 1974, 1985), which focus first on the political consciousness of adult illiterates, as the first step in literacy training. But it is often overlooked that Freire's adult learners had little or no previous schooling, while the typical adult seeking basic literacy in the United States today has been to school for a number of years and is considerably more sophisticated. There is also a tendency to overlook the fact that Paulo Freire's programs for teaching reading to beginners were developed with great care to teach decoding. This was done through teaching the most vital words first, words which also facilitated the teaching and learning of the alphabetic principle. Thus, word recognition and decoding are a vital aspect of the Freire program, along with political consciousness and motivation. This is in contrast to many of our reading programs for adult beginners which assume that interesting and vital content will lead naturally to word recognition and knowledge and skill in the use of the alphabetic principle.

Syntheses of the research evidence over the past 70 years (as well as the characteristics of successful beginning reading programs for adults and children) have concluded that early systematic teaching and learning of word recognition and decoding produces better results than emphasis on meaning (Anderson et al., 1985; Chall, 1983b). The oral reading errors of adult beginning readers in our Reading Laboratory are quite similar to those of younger beginners. Some teachers contend that recognition and decoding are not essential problems of most adult beginners because adults have more experience and more mature language than child beginners. If so, one may ask why these adults have not picked up reading informally in a world of print—in signs, labels, newspapers, TV commercials, and the like—which they would easily understand, *if* they could read them.

Of course, adult beginners do have greater language skills and knowledge than do most child beginners. But then again, children are

---

[1]The illiterate students (child or adult) may also not speak English. This presents still another problem of teaching the English language, as well as the reading of it. But here, too, it is not concepts and knowledge that are usually lacking, but the expression of them in the new language. These students also need to learn to recognize and decode English words in print, as well as to speak and understand them, if they are to learn to read.

also considerably more advanced in their understanding and speaking knowledge of language than they are in the language they can read. The typical child entering first grade knows about 5000 words when he hears them (Lorge & Chall, 1963). But it will take about 3 years of reading instruction before he can read them.

Still other similarities may be found when adult and child beginning readers are compared. At first view it would appear that among illiterate adults a sense of failure may be more common. But not all children are or feel successful. Indeed, a long history of studies has found that from 10-15% of elementary, high school, and college students are significantly below grade or intellectual potential in reading. Overall, perhaps about one-third of all students in school are significantly behind in reading and experience a psychological sense of failure. It is from this group that the various adult literacy programs ultimately get their clients (Carroll & Chall, 1975).

Adults who are learning at Stages 1 and 2 do suffer a disadvantage as compared to children at these levels. Such low-literate adults often do not have enough to read in terms of interesting, enticing books, informative magazines, and newspapers at their level of reading skill. More materials exist for children at their appropriate level of knowledge and reading level, although these books are not always accessible to them. A wide variety of appropriate literacy materials, easily available, is needed for those moving from decoding to fluency whether one makes this transition as a child or as an adult.

Adults first learning to read can, of course, gain some practice by reading children's books to their own children. For progress in Stage 1 and particularly in Stage 2, when automatic recognition of words and fluency are developed, readers—whether children or adults—need to read a lot.

At Stage 3 even fewer differences are found. If the adults have considerable language ability and general knowledge they should have little difficulty with Stage 3—assuming word recognition and decoding are in good form, and some fluency has been acquired. But some children also fall within this category. They have very extensive vocabularies and background knowledge, and once their decoding, recognition and fluency are developed, they can more easily move through Stage 3, where they can read to gain new information—new ideas, attitudes, and values.

At Stages 4 and 5, again, there seem to be few differences between the younger and older students. For both groups the challenge is to master abstraction, thought, complex language, broad knowledge, an extensive vocabulary, more efficient reading skills and a greater ability to analyze, to read critically and creatively. Theoretically, it takes the typical student 12 to 16 years or more to progress from Stage 1 through 5. Can all typical students reach Stage 5, even when they start reading in grade 1? Would it take as long for adults who start at Stage 1 as adults? Can Stages 4 and 5 be reached by those who start to learn at Stage 1 or 2 as adults? There is little evidence, and a great need for answers to these and related questions.

One might hypothesize that most adults would need less time to progress through these stages. The lower the stage, perhaps the less time it should take for adults as compared to children. Thus Stages 1 and 2 may be mastered relatively quickly, in a few weeks or months, depending upon the student's motivation and the excellence of the methods, materials, and the teaching. There will probably be a slowing up at Stage 2, unless adequate reading materials are available for practice.

If Stage 3 instruction concentrates on work-type reading in an area in which the adult students are knowledgeable and experienced, the time of learning may be shorter than that needed by children (Sticht, 1975). But the reading may not transfer to other content areas, even if the material is at the same reading level. Thus there has been a trend to call for teaching reading in each of the broad content areas (Herber, 1978). Most children need 8 years to read at an 8th grade level. It may take some adults less time; but if they have not acquired general knowledge and a vocabulary in broad cultural areas, it may even take them longer (see in this context E. D. Hirsch's concept of cultural literacy, 1987).

Acquiring the skills and abilities of Stage 4 may take adults even longer, unless they already have the cultural experiences, the language, and thought processes usually needed for reading high school level texts (see Tables 1 and 2). If adult students have not attended high school it may take considerable time for them to acquire the background of knowledge and skills taught there. We may get further insight into the great task involved in acquiring Stage 4 reading achievement when we consider what it takes to read and understand *The New York Times*, a newspaper cited as a criterion for advanced literacy needed today (Carroll & Chall, 1975). It requires a broad general vocabulary, sophisticated syntax, specialized vocabulary and knowledge of history, geography, current events, and so forth.

The situation is similar for Stage 5. Generally, Stage 5 reading requires not only advanced reading skills and strategies, but even more—a considerable knowledge of the world and of one's culture acquired formally or informally, from which one is able to construct and reconstruct knowledge for one's own purposes.

Many of the skills and abilities needed at the early levels can be taught in workbook exercises, readers, and through computer software. Yet, it would seem that for the full development of reading, particularly at Stages 3, 4 and 5, a broad education, including wide reading of non-text materials as well as textbooks, is essential.

Thus, if reading is seen as a broad, developing process in adults as in children, it requires more than a few weeks or months of intensive instruction—mostly at Stages 1 and 2—for decoding and fluency. To reach a stage of literacy that is of use for work, citizenship and one's own personal needs—and for continued learning from print—considerably more time for learning and practice is needed. For most children, proceeding through elementary, high school and college brings about this development. For adults enrolled in literacy and adult education programs this progression is not as explicit, but needs to be made so.

III. STANDARDS OF LITERACY

How well should adults read? What are the minimal standards of literacy today? In the next decade? There has been much difference of opinion on these questions—some call for higher standards; others for lower. On the other hand, there appears to be some agreement that universal literacy goals are a relatively recent phenomenon even among industrialized nations. The majority of the populations of most of the industrialized nations were illiterate up until about 100 years ago; and among the Third World nations literacy is enjoyed only by a small percentage, even today (see other chapters in this volume).

The numbers and proportion of people who are literate, and the extent and quality of their literacy, increased as societies moved from an agricultural base to an industrial one, and more recently to a post-industrial, information age. The "simpler" the society, the more elementary the literacy skills needed. Those few who could read in simple, agricultural societies probably read on a level characterized by Stage 1 or 2—for example, the reading of simple, familiar texts such as would be sufficient for religious purposes—the reading of prayers and psalms that had previously been memorized (see Street, this volume).

As production and societies became more complex, a level permitting greater problem-solving and analysis was required. This would be close to Stage 4, a high school reading level. Such a level was needed by more people during the past decade, a time variously called the start of the post-industrial age, the computer age, the information age.

The studies of Sticht and his associates (1973) tend to confirm the recent increases in literacy needs. They found from a series of studies that job-related text materials in the army ranged from a 10th- to a 12th-grade level—higher than had been expected. They also found that the higher the reading levels of the personnel, the more frequent the use of job-related printed materials, and the higher their ratings on job proficiency tests.

In a more recent update of these studies, Sticht (1982) calls for a developmental rather than a remedial view toward adults needing assistance with literacy, since literate parents are more effective in influencing the reading ability of their children than those who are illiterate or barely literate.

Similar findings were reported by Mikulecky (1981) for industrial workers and students. He found that technical workers faced more difficult job-related literacy demands than did students in technical schools. Workers also reported reading more for job-related tasks than students for school-related tasks. Workers read an average of 143 minutes per day compared to 98 minutes for high school and 135 minutes for technical school students. The workers also read more difficult materials than the students, with even the blue-collar manuals and directions averaging a 10th-grade level of difficulty.

IV. TRENDS IN ADULT LITERACY

Are adult literacy standards improving? It is hard to assess since there are no systematic testing programs for adult literacy classes as there are for those in school. Trends for school-age groups can be estimated from the National Assessment scores, the Scholastic Aptitude Tests, Standardized Reading Achievement Tests, and from comparisons on special tests.[2]

Can one estimate trends in adult literacy? Can we say that more progress has been made by some adult groups than perhaps by others? Without the availability of national test data, one can do so only with caution. Yet, because of the importance of such knowledge, one can, however, attempt a *relative* estimate by comparing three adult groups seeking assistance with their literacy.[3]

The first group may be called "adult illiterates," those who need work at Stages 1 or 2 (reading grade levels 0 to 3)—basic decoding and reading of simple texts.

The second group is composed of those adults who have mastered the basic decoding skills, and still need practice in using reading as a tool for learning. These adults are usually referred to as functionally illiterate. That is, they can read something but *not* what they need in

---

[2]See, in this connection the report of National Assessment for Educational Progress (Kirsch & Jungeblut, 1986).

[3]Based on *Stages of Reading Development* (Chall, 1983a).

order to function or "to survive." In grade level standards they read at about a 4th- or 5th-grade level (a Stage 3 level).

The third group is composed of the "new illiterates," those who have "survival" or functional literacy but who do not yet read on a high school graduate level, one that permits problem-solving and is more functional for a technological society (Stage 4).

Historically, the need for adult basic literacy was recognized and provided for first in the United States; functional literacy was a later concern; and the latest is the concern for the newer and higher literacy.

The gains in adult literacy seem to vary by these levels. The greatest gains seem to be at the basic literacy level, where there has been a steady decline in the percentage of total illiterates (as seen from the decline in numbers who have completed less than 5 years of schooling) according to the 1980 as compared to the 1970 census (U.S. Bureau of the Census, 1970 and 1980).

The next larger gains, I believe, have been among those classified as functional literates, with larger numbers of adults completing 8th grade in 1980 than in 1970.

The greatest problems exist, in my view, among the "new illiterates," whose abilities and skills, although substantial and even above the average adult level of 50 years ago, are not sufficient in a world that continues to become more complex and requires from its workers a literacy that implies not only taking information off the page, but making inferences, reasoning critically, and the like. Thus it would seem that the literacy needs among adults as among students of school age have some parallels—the greater needs are now at the higher levels.

The National Academy of Education Reading Committee Report, *Toward a Literate Society* (Carroll & Chall, 1975) suggested similar needs. A 12th-grade reading level, they suggested, is essential for today. It implies an ability to read *The New York Times* or *Time Magazine* critically and analytically. No-one seems to know for sure what numbers of illiterates fall within the three groups noted above. The numbers suggested by The Network (Andover, Mass.) have some merit: 1 million estimated for basic literacy group, 22 to 26 million for the functionally literate group and 51 million for the "new illiterates."

That modern man and woman, whether at work or as a citizen, needs more than the coping and survival skills of functional literacy was made evident to me when I served as expert consultant in two class-action lawsuits. Both concerned a mismatch between the readability levels of materials needed to be read and the reading ability of adults who needed to read the materials. One was concerned with federal housing contracts, the other with notices about food stamps.

For both, the readability levels of the materials (contracts and notices) were on about a college level, while the persons for whom they were intended could read only on a high functional level—about a 7th- to 8th-grade reading level.

There has been a considerable effort during the past several decades to make documents more readable for the millions of adults with limited reading ability. But the problem is far from being solved; and it seems likely that the problem cannot be solved fully through simpler documents, for the nature of the information and ideas is what makes the text difficult. Anyone trying to make sense of the notices on divestiture from AT & T would know that a readability estimate of a 9th- to 10th-grade level did not quite do justice to its complexity.

Thus, it would appear that for work, for citizenship, and for personal survival, a literacy level on at least a 12th-grade reading level (Stage 4) seems to be needed. What is it about a 12th-grade reading level (or Stage 4) that makes it a challenge to both high school students and adults? This reading level requires an extensive general and specialized vocabulary, considerable background knowledge, ability to reason and to think critically. Also necessary are efficient rate of reading, and strategies for gaining ideas from what is read. A 12th-grade reading level means the ability to use reading to solve problems as well as to gain information about how others solve problems. Put in these terms it is easier to understand why moving from an elementary to a high school level (from Stages 3 to 4) is a considerable challenge, requiring much reading of difficult materials of a great range of subject matter. This requires long practice as well as direct instruction.

That many high school graduates do not meet this level is evident from the National Assessment scores, SAT verbal scores, and on scores on most standardized achievement tests.

V. READING DISABILITY, DYSLEXIA, AND LEARNING DISABILITIES

There is still another problem area that is of importance in a consideration of the status of adult literacy—that of severe difficulty in learning to read, called by various names—reading disability, dyslexia, or learning disability. Various government committees basing their estimates on a long history of research have reported that-about 10-15% of children and adults have severe difficulty in learning to read (Carroll & Chall, 1975).

Recent studies and clinical reports indicate that while many of these students tend to drop out of school earlier than those without such problems, increasing numbers now stay in school and many continue on to college.

I have often wondered why the literature on adult literacy tends to pay little attention, if at all, to adults with reading disability, learning disability, or dyslexia. The vast research on reading disability, much of it concerned during the past two decades with neurological causes, seems not to be considered as a factor in adult literacy problems (Hunter & Harman, 1979; Lerche, 1985). And yet it is well known that many adults with literacy problems had severe reading difficulty in elementary and high school, and they continue to have difficulty as adults. Thus it would seem that the research, as well as the diagnostic and remediation practices, used with those having reading disability are also relevant for adult literacy.

It should be recognized that those adults who still have severe reading disability can learn to read, although they have done poorly previously. Although popular opinion is that if one has not learned to read by high school, one will never learn, the research indicates otherwise. Significant gains from remedial instruction have been made at all ages. Comparisons with control groups indicate that there are immediate and long-term gains when remedial treatment is given (Smith, 1979). Remedial programs in community and 4-year colleges are also effective (Cross, 1981).

VI. RESEARCH AND THE USES OF RESEARCH

It would seem that learning to read is a similar process whether one is a child or an adult. Adults may be able to move faster at the basic literacy stage, but the pace tends to slow down when they reach the functional literacy and problem-solving stages—as it does among children (Chall & Snow, 1982).

Since the development of literacy among school-age students has a longer history, and a richer research base, it would seem to me that much can be used from this research and experience to the advantage of adult literacy.

I am aware that this suggestion may be met with some anxiety by many adult educators who have sought to separate themselves from childhood education. The desire to separate stems, I believe, from a realistic base. For too long elementary school methods and materials were those used for adult illiterates. Few special adult materials were available.

There seems also to be a sensitivity about using standard tests with adults. And yet one wonders how it is possible to measure progress or lack of progress, and how one can plan individual programs without tests. There is also a need for diagnostic testing in adult programs. Unless it is known what the needs are—the strengths and weaknesses on specific reading components—it would seem difficult to be as effective as one needs to be.

Some other of the recent findings for children would be helpful in understanding adult literacy. First, recent research indicates that wide and frequent reading contributes to higher reading scores and to higher language development (Chomsky, 1972; Chall & Snow, 1982). Research also indicates that students benefit from challenging levels of instructional material from which they receive teacher instruction (Chall, Conard, & Harris, 1977; Chall, Conard, & Harris-Sharples, 1983).

There is a great need for research on adult reading, and with an eye towards comparisons with the large research base on childhood reading. Thus we should inquire as to the relation between adult and child reading on different reading levels. Do they differ in the kinds of errors or miscues? At the different reading stages? Do they differ in their patterns of strengths and weaknesses at the different stages? Is the amount of direct instruction needed the same? Are the independent reading needs the same for adults and children at similar reading stages?

Research is especially needed on how more students and adults can be brought to a 12th-grade level. With what kind of help and programs can it be achieved? Can those of average cognitive functioning make it, if given the proper amounts and kind of instruction? It seems that too many do not, at the present.

Perhaps the most important need, however, is to know more about the influence of cognition on reading and the influence of reading on cognition among both children and adults. Descriptions of the higher stages of reading, particularly, are similar to descriptions of higher levels of reasoning. This relationship has been known a long time (E. L. Thorndike, 1917; R. L. Thorndike, 1973; 1973-74). Both Thorndikes characterized reading comprehension as reasoning, which is related as highly to tested intelligence as to other aspects of reading comprehension. If reading is reasoning, is it possible to enhance mental ability through training in reading? The findings here are somewhat contradictory (Luria, 1976; Scribner & Cole, 1981). But it would seem to be important to pursue the question for solving our present educational problems, for improving our economic productivity, and for coping with our social and human problems.

VII. EPILOGUE: 1987 TO 1997

I present here some of the major trends in adult as compared to child literacy from 1987 to 1997.

Perhaps the most important trend is the growth in adult literacy—in the number of variety of programs designed to improve adult literacy and in the increase in the surveys and research (see Cohen,

Golonka, Maynard, Ooms, & Owen, 1995; Kirsch & Jungeblut, 1992; Kirsch, Jungeblut, Jenkins, & Kolstad, 1993; Wagner & Venezky, 1995).

The Differences Between Child and Adult Literacy

In the 1987 chapter, while I noted differences between child and adult literacy, I focused on the similarities. In 1990 Mary E. Curtis focused on the differences—in word recognition, knowledge of word meanings and reading comprehension (Curtis, 1990).

With regard to word recognition, Curtis notes that the relationship between accuracy and fluency differs for children and adults. Adults who read accurately at a 4th grade level do so at a slower pace than 4th grade children. Overall adults tend to be less fluent than children. This is important because the lack of fluency slows down comprehension.

There also are differences in knowledge of word meanings (Curtis, 1990). At the 4th grade level, and often higher, adults are more likely than children to know hard words. But these words are often not "totally known" since less skilled adult readers often know the harder words only in the context of how then first met the words. Thus adults with limited skill often apply incomplete or incorrect knowledge about word meaning.

With regard to reading comprehension, adults as compared to children, tend to do better on silent reading comprehension than on word recognition. They can do this because of their better comprehension strategies.

Adults and children also tend to differ on the relationship between listening and reading comprehension. Up until the eighth grade, children's listening comprehension exceeds their reading comprehension. For adults who are learning to read, the differences between listening and reading comprehension are not as great (Curtis, 1990).

Adult Reading Problems

Another development during the past seven years is an increase in concern for the reading problems among adults—their diagnosis and treatment. In the 1987 chapter I reported a hesitancy among specialists in adult literacy toward viewing adult reading difficulties in terms of reading and learning disabilities, as is common among children. In the seven years since, there has been a growing recognition of serious difficulty in learning to read among adults, particularly among those below a functional literacy level, similar to that found among children.

In the 1995 report by Cohen *et al.*, learning disabilities among adults is given a page and a half. They note that they are "very prevalent within the welfare population and constitute a major—but largely unacknowledged—barrier to successful education and employment," and furthermore, "Adults with learning disabilities (LD) is the largest of the disabilities groups (Interagency Committee on Learning Disabilities, 1987) and there is evidence of a high incidence of learning disabilities and functional illiteracy among the economically disadvantaged population" (Cohen et. al., 1995, p. 8).

A test that helps distinguish adults whose main problem is either with reading-learning disability or with language was developed in 1992 (DARTTS) (Roswell & Chall, 1992). The assessment, which focuses on aspects of reading and related language skills, reveals two patterns of adult reading. One pattern is similar to profiles of younger students clinically diagnosed as having a reading or learning disability—higher word meaning and reading comprehension and lower word recognition, analysis and oral reading. Most adults with this pattern are native speakers of English who have a long history of reading difficulty. The other pattern is found among adults with higher scores in word recognition, analysis and spelling, and lower scores in word meaning and silent reading comprehension. For most of these adults, English is their second language (Chall, 1994).

Awareness of these two patterns helps teachers conceptualize the needs of the adults with whom they work. It also helps them clarify to their adult clients what their needs are. The anxieties of the adult clients lessen as they realize that their overall reading proficiency could be improved by thinking of their reading as stemming from certain strengths and weaknesses that can, with practice, be strengthened.

Research

The past decade has brought research on the various aspects of adult literacy. There has been a growing interest in the extent and nature of the literacy needed by adults and children in order to cope with modern and historical documents. A considerable gap has been found between the literacy levels required to read and understand these documents and the reading abilities of most young people and adults in America today. Most historical documents and much public information in print requires a higher reading level than that attained by most adults and young people (Chall, 1990; Chall & Henry, 1991; Stotsky, 1991).

A history of literacy from 1880 to 1990 provides a rich background for the scholar and the practitioner. As was common among many adult literacy researchers in the 1980s and 1990s, Kaestle, Damon-

Moore, Stedman, Tinsley, and Trollinger (1991) used a continuum of literacy—from low to high—instead of distinguishing only between literacy and illiteracy. The various levels of literacy are treated historically and related to schooling and the reading of newspapers, magazines, and books. They also consider the relation of literacy to social class and the number of books and other printed materials in the home.

Other analyses have shown considerable gaps between needs and literacy attainment for both those of school age and adults—and particularly among the poor, minorities, bilinguals, and the learning disabled (see Chall, 1994; Cohen et al., 1995; Venezky, Wagner, & Ciliberti, 1990; Wagner & Venezky, 1995).

A growing development in adult literacy hardly known a decade is family literacy—the combining of adult literacy with the teaching of young children. Also of growing importance have been job and work based literacy programs and other projects aimed at promoting literacy and employment. (For a comprehensive overview of such programs see Cohen et al., 1995.)

Overall Trends

Overall, this past decade has added to our knowledge of research and practice of adult literacy. We know more than we knew seven years ago. But we are still lacking some of the most fundamental knowledge about teaching adults to read and write that has been known for more than a century in teaching literacy to children. According to Venezky, "We know very little about the effectiveness of different literacy programs . . . the literacy field has not yet been able to specify or assess clear measures of successful performance" (Venezky, 1992, cited in Cohen et al., 1995, p. 18; see also Venezky, 1997).

It is hoped that the next decade will bring such knowledge along with simple diagnostic and treatment procedures to use with adults who seek help.

REFERENCES

Anderson, R.C., Hiebert, E.H., Scott, J.A., & Wilkinson, I.A.G. (1985). *Becoming a nation of readers: The report of the commission on reading.* Washington, DC: The National Institute of Education.

Carroll, J.B., & Chall, J.S. (1975). *Toward a literate society.* New York: McGraw-Hill.

Chall, J.S. (1983a). *Stages of reading development.* New York: McGraw-Hill.

Chall, J.S. (1983b). Literacy: Trends and explanations. *Educational Researcher,* 12(9), 3-8.

Chall, J.S. (1990). Policy implications of literacy definitions. In R.L. Venezky, D.A. Wagner, & B.S. Ciliberti (Eds.), *Toward defining literacy* (pp. 54-62). Newark, DE: International Reading Association.

Chall, J.S. (1994). Patterns of adult reading. *Learning Disabilities: A Multidisciplinary Journal, 5*(1), 29-33.

Chall, J.S., & Henry, D. (1991). Reading and civic literacy: Are we literate enough to meet our civic responsibilities? In S. Stotsky (Ed.), *Connecting civic education and language education: The contemporary challenge.* New York: Teachers College Press.

Chall, J.S., Conard, S., & Harris, S. (1977). *An analysis of textbooks in relation to declining S.A.T. scores.* New York: College Entrance Examination Board.

Chall, J.S., Conard S., & Harris-Sharples, S. (1983, September). *Textbooks and challenge: An inquiry into textbook difficulty, reading achievement, and knowledge acquisition* [Final report to the Spencer Foundation].

Chall, J.S., & Snow, C. (1982, December 22). *Families and literacy: The contribution of out-of-school experiences to children's acquisition of literacy* [Final report to the National Institute of Education].

Chomsky, C. (1972). Stages in language development and reading exposure. *Harvard Educational Review, 42*(1).

Cohen, E., Golonka, S., Maynard, R., Ooms, T., & Owen, T. (1995). *Welfare reform and literacy: Are we making the connection?* (Tech. rep.). Philadelphia: University of Pennsylvania, National Center on Adult Literacy.

Cross, P. (1981). *Adults as learners.* San Francisco: Jossey-Bass.

Curtis, M.E. (1990, May). *Developing literacy in children and adults: Are there differences?* Paper presented at the International Reading Association, Newark, DE.

Freire, P. (1970). *Pedagogy of the oppressed.* New York: Seabury Press.

Freire, P. (1974). *Education for critical consciousness.* London: Sheed & Ward.

Freire, P. (1985). *The politics of education: Culture, power and liberation.* South Hadley, MA: Bergin and Garvey.

Herber, H. (1978). *Teaching reading in the content areas* (2nd ed.). Englewood Cliffs, NJ: Prentice-Hall.

Hirsch, E.D. (1987). *Cultural literacy: What every American needs to know.* New York: Houghton Mifflin.

Hunter, C., & Harman, D. (1979). *Adult illiteracy in the United States.* New York: McGraw-Hill.

Kaestle, C.F., Damon-Moore, H., Stedman, L.C., Tinsley, K., & Trollinger, W.V., Jr. (1991). *Literacy in the United States: Readers and reading since 1880.* New Haven: Yale University Press.

Kirsch, I.S., & Jungeblut, A. (1986). *Literacy: Profiles of America's young adults* [Final report of the National Assessment of Educational Progress]. Princeton, NJ: ETS.

Kirsch, I., Jungeblut, A., Jenkins, L., & Kolstad, A. (1993, September). *Adult literacy in America.* U.S. Department of Labor, Washington, DC.

Lerche, R. (1985). *Effective adult literacy programs*. New York: Cambridge Adult Education

Lorge, I., & Chall, J.S. (1963). Estimating the size of vocabularies of children and adults: An analysis of methodological issues. *Journal of Experimental Education, 32,* 147-157.

Luria, A.R. (1976). *Cognitive development: Cultural and social foundations.* Cambridge, MA: Harvard University Press.

Mikulecky, L. (1981, December). The mismatch between school training and job literacy demands. *The Vocational Guidance Quarterly.*

Roswell, F., & Chall, J.S. (1992). *Diagnostic assessments of reading and trial teaching strategies (DARTTS).* Chicago: Riverside Publishing Company.

Scribner, S., & Cole, M. (1981). *Psychology of literacy.* Cambridge, MA: Harvard University Press.

Smith, L. (1979). *An evaluation of studies of long term effects of remedial reading programs.* Unpublished doctoral dissertation, Harvard Graduate School of Education.

Sticht, T.G. (1975). *Reading for working.* Alexandria, VA: Human Resources Research Organization.

Sticht, T.G. (1982). Literacy at work. *Reading/Language Research, 1,* 219-243.

Sticht, T.G., Caylor, J.S., Fox, L.C., Hauke, R.N., James, J.H., Snyder, S.S., & Kern, R.P. (1973, December). *HumRRO's literacy research for the U.S. Army: Developing functional literacy training.* Alexandria, VA: Human Resources Research Organization.

Stotsky, S. (Ed.). (1991). *Connecting civic education and language education: The contemporary challenge.* New York: Teachers College Press.

Thorndike, E.L. (1917). Reading as reasoning: A study of mistakes in paragraph reading. *Journal of Educational Psychology, 8,* 323-332.

Thorndike, R.L. (1973). Reading comprehension in education in fifteen countries. *International Studies in Evaluation III.* Stockholm: Almquist and Wiksell.

Thorndike, R.L. (1973-74). Reading as reasoning. *Reading Research Quarterly, 9,* 135-147.

United States. Bureau of the Census (1970). *1970 census.* Washington, DC: U.S. Department of Commerce.

United States. Bureau of the Census (1980). *1980 census.* Washington, DC: U.S. Department of Commerce.

Venezky, R.L. (1997). Literacy assessment in the service of literacy policy. In A.C. Tuijuman, I.S. Kirsch, & D.A. Wagner (Eds.), *Adult basic skills* (pp. 311-336). Cresskill, NJ: Hampton Press.

Venezky, R.L., Wagner, D.A., & Ciliberti, B.S. (Eds.). (1990). *Toward defining literacy.* Newark, DE: International Reading Association.

Wagner, D.A., & Venezky, R.L. (1995). *Adult literacy: The next generation.* Philadelphia: University of Pennsylvania, National Center on Adult Literacy.

Weber, R. (1975). Adult illiteracy in the United States. In J.B. Carroll & J. S. Chall (Eds.), *Toward a literate society.* New York: McGraw-Hill.

III

LITERACY ACQUISITION IN CULTURAL CONTEXT

6

Introduction

Meta E. Bogle
University of the West Indies

It has become commonplace for national development to be linked to education, with education frequently measured in terms of literacy. Thus, the educated have been those who have learned to read and write. In this scheme of things, the acquisition of literacy, both by individuals and whole societies, has been presented as universally desirable and even essential. Though what literacy is may now be accepted as variable, one gets the sense that the process of acquisition of literacy is perceived as following some universal path. As yet, it is not quite clear what that path is, as global variation in the achievement of literacy attests. This state of knowledge regarding literacy acquisition is at the root of the ever-rising concern with, and search for, methods and materials for making people literate.

The study of literacy acquisition has traditionally been in connection with the reading process in which the essential focus has been on the input from materials and pedagogies. This input was first conceived of primarily in linguistic terms, with a good deal of attention being given to features of the writing system. When the characteristics of the individual learner became central to research, the perspective was predominantly psychological, and failure was often viewed in terms of individual deficits. It is my view that literacy acquisition is a more complex process than may be suggested by a focus on deficits; and a more comprehensive view is needed.

The chapters in this section may be viewed in the context of the search for such a comprehensive view. When this introduction was being prepared for the first publication of the contributions, they were seen as part of an emerging literature (Heath, 1983; Taylor, 1983; Wells, 1981, 1986) which makes a case for looking at learner characteristics from a somewhat different perspective. Since that time, an intensified focus on emergent literacy has increased the body of literature contributing to a broader understanding of literacy acquisition by children. In some ways the chapters in this Section had looked ahead to some of these developments.

While drawing on experiences in different geographical locations and focusing on different components of literacy, these chapters offer an opportunity for an analysis of literacy acquisition in children, and identify issues relevant both to the acquisition and future of literacy. Several contributors, by implication at least, raise the issue of reading failure as an appropriate basis for the analysis of literacy acquisition, and that of relevant research models in the acquisition of literacy.

The contributions by Fan, Tong, and Song and Stevenson focus on the analysis of literacy acquisition by attending to the features of the writing system. There is a cognitive orientation to their analysis, with an emphasis on skills related to accessing the writing system. Of course, an issue here is whether the writing system is ever an independent entity. Indeed, Fan et al. question the existence of any such independence by suggesting a possible influence of semantic content in the processing of symbolic form to achieve comprehension.

More recently, the literature presenting the research has shown a sharpened focus on the ecology of learning as it applied to literacy acquisition as an instance of learning. Morrow (1991), for instance, suggests the possible influence of voluntary literacy activities on acquisition. Neuman and Roskos (1991, 1993) suggest that a combination of this and the child's active engagement with an adult exerts a positive influence on the child's literacy development. Parent or family involvement has been positively identified with the presence of emergent literacy abilities. Central is the idea that children's literacy acquisition is enhanced when they experience literacy as a meaningful event in which they are somewhat like apprentices observing the expert and afforded the opportunity to participate. This trend has followed the lead of researchers like Heath (1983) and Taylor (1983), among others, in looking beyond literacy acquisition through the culture of school to the more functional, derived from the routines and demands of real life—to the large cultural context. Here the emphasis is on ownership by the individual (Neuman & Roskos, 1992).

From the vantage point of these developments, cognitive issues with respect to literacy acquisition are nested in the context of a larger culture rather than in the culture of the school. The universals, then, are in the cultural base of literacy acquisition which makes issues of the writing system culturally determined as suggested by Fan, Tong, and Song. It is that larger cultural context which provides the frame of reference for learning to be literate and which gives rise and relevance to the concept of "literacies." As yet the research does not seem to have extensively examined in a wide range of circumstances the thesis that differences between urban and rural cultures in any given territory may create different literacies which in turn may offer a challenge to the identification of national standards of childhood literacy. An attendant fundamental, and as yet unaddressed issue, is that of the nature of the influence of perceptions of the status and role of the child on the patterns and processes of acquisition, and th extent to which these perceptions constitute a "culture of childhood."

Stevenson claims that a fundamental task, regardless of the writing system, is that of dividing symbol strings into manageable segments which are then integrated into meaningful entities, may then be not as much a universal as it is a description of an approach available to those whose cultural contexts make this step functional and meaningful. This is suggested by the contributions of Fan, Tong, and Song and Nunes. While it is clear from all the contributions that learners do things with the writing system as they acquire literacy, it is not clear that they all do the same thing; nor is it clear how they do it. Taken together, the contributions suggest the strong possibility of alternative analytical paths.

The ecology of literacy acquisition is central to the claims made by Nunes who writes from the Brazilian context, though she seems to make the claim in reverse. At the same time, both the Nunes and the Teale and Sulzby contributions offer an analysis of literacy acquisition from an individual perspective. An issue central to that perspective is motivation—a process of initiating, sustaining, and ordering activity. This is not a new issue in literacy research nor in education more generally. It is an issue which draws on the notion of context as complex. In delivering literacy to children, context has typically been conceived in terms of conditions external to the individual and functioning as a kind of vehicle for learning. Here the chapters draw attention to another dimension of context which includes the individual's (in this case the learner's) perceptions of those "external" conditions—perceptions which derive from social practices. Social practices distinguish cultures, whether at the level of home, school, social group, or society. An important feature of context conceived of in this way is that it is dynamic; the components are in interaction, yielding subprocesses as part of the larger process which we call culture. From this kind of relationship the individual comes to learning situations "pre-adapted" (as Wells, 1991, remarks with reference to language learning) to the task.

Thus the literacy practices of the parents in Nunes' study provide their children with the raison d'etre for the acquisition of literacy. The chapter by Teale and Sulzby suggests that motivation to acquire literacy also comes from opportunities the learner has to internalize ways of interacting with print. Thus cultural practices like storybook reading have the potential for creating the environment of interaction which will facilitate literacy acquisition. Stevenson, in his conclusion, acknowledges this potential when he notes that at the level of perceptions of problems and solutions in acquiring literacy, children's school and home experiences seem to be implicated in the view of both mothers and teachers.

The Teale and Sulzby chapter makes the further suggestion that the motivation may also be associated with the relative independence and creativity in exploration and reenactment which a particular cultural practice affords the young learner. The suggestion is that in such contexts of relative independence that the learner can experiment with his or her insights. If this is the route, then it is possible that such opportunity has the potential for creating the kind of needed continuity between the home and school situations. When school situations do not deliberately show "how to do it," the learner with access to the relevant cultural practices can independently engage his or her insights. Of course, this makes a statement about the need for sensitivity to existing relevant cultural practices and in some way echoes the call of Harste, Woodward, and Burke for a linking of curriculum with the exploration and expansion of the human potential and with what happens mentally to the learner as a language user in that exploration.

In drawing attention to the relevance of the contribution from the home culture, Teale and Sulzby as well as Nunes attach significance to the nature and quality of the interaction through which the young child becomes pre-adapted in the home to the acquisition of literacy in school. The issue may not be so much that the activity should be storybook reading, as that it should reflect the authentic function of literacy of the home and simultaneously offer the young insights into how it is done. The children in Nunes' study benefited from their parents' experience with receiving letters. What is accessible and what is mediated are cultural artifacts. What may be the relevance of access and mediation where literacy activities are confined to a specific constituency—the constituency of adults? What may be the relevance where there is no tradition of producing reading materials addressed to children, or where the quality of available books assumes the acquisition of literacy at a level usually credited to older children in literate societies?

Nunes suggests a link between parents who acquire just enough literacy to save embarrassment and the likely lack of achievement of their children. As a motivation for acquiring literacy, face-saving cannot be expected to be accessible to young children. It seems that a necessary condition for the successful delivery of strategies and conditions helpful to the acquisition of literacy is that communication should take place, and the content of that communication delivered at a level which is meaningful to the child. The "literacy giver" in such inter actions cannot be expected to give more than she or he knows. This reality distinguishes Charlene from Hannah in the Teale and Sulzby chapter, and raises the issue of who plays the role of "literacy giver." The demands of the situations of interaction are for more than access to literacy; the young child needs to be able to identify with the "giver" as well as to be allowed the opportunity for independent reenactment in ways relevant to the particular cultural practice.

These issues hinted at in this introduction and associated with the chapters in this Section identify dimensions on which to analyze the contexts in which literacy is acquired. From this will arise the important task of extracting principles underlying the acquisition of literacy, and identifying, in a range of cultures, the activity or activities through which these principles are worked out. Cultural context will exist as a framework in which to engage this analysis and introduce a way of cataloguing the literacy agendas of groups and of individuals who grow up in these cultures. Of course, literacy which depends heavily on a school-based delivery system may very well not reach the disinherited bulge in the population of many developing countries. It may be that the future of literacy is assured only to the extent that the cultural underpinning of literacy acquisition is recognized.

REFERENCES

Harste, J.C., Woodward, V.A., & Burke, C.L. (1984). *Language stories and literacy lessons*. Portsmouth, NH: Heinemann.

Heath, S.B. (1983). *Ways with words: Language, life and work in communities and classrooms*. Cambridge: Cambridge University Press.

Morrow, L.M. (1991). Relationships among physical design of play centers, teachers' emphasis on literacy in play, and children's literacy behaviors during play. In J. Zutell & S. McCormick (Eds.), *Learner factors/teacher factors: Issues in literacy research and instruction* (pp. 127-139). Chicago: National Reading Conference.

Neuman, S.B., & Roskos, K. (1991). Peers as literacy informants: A description of young children's literacy conversations in play. *Early Childhood Research Quarterly, 6,* 233-248.

Neuman, S.B., & Roskos, K. (1992). Literacy objects as cultural tools: Effects on children's literacy behaviors in play. *Reading Research Quarterly, 27*, 203-225.

Neuman, S.B., & Roskos, K. (1993). Access to print for children of poverty: Differential effects of adult mediation and literacy-enriched play settings on environmental and functional print tasks. *American Educational Research Journal, 30*, 95-122.

Taylor, D. (1983). *Family literacy: Young children learning to read and write.* London: Heinemann Educational Books.

Wells, G. (1981). Learning through interaction: The study of language development. Cambridge: Cambridge University Press.

Wells, G. (1981). *Learning through interaction: The study of language development.* Cambridge: Cambridge University Press.

Wells, G. (1986). Styles of interaction and opportunities of learning. In A. Cashdan (Ed.), *Literacy: Teaching and learning language skills.* Oxford: Basil Blackwell.

7

The Characteristics of the Chinese Language and Children's Learning to Read and Write

Liu Fan, Lequan Tong, and Jun Song
Academia Sinica, Beijing, People's Republic of China

INTRODUCTION

Most children in China begin to learn Chinese characters at the age of 6. Thereafter they gradually learn words and sentences so as to have a good command of written Chinese language. At the outset, learning Chinese is difficult, and pupils must spend much time and effort studying during the first 3 years of primary school. Special principles govern Chinese children's learning of the Chinese language. These principles are closely related to the characteristics of the Chinese language and to the cognitive abilities of children. Since the 1950s much work has been done by psychologists in this domain, yielding data that are useful for understanding the process of learning the written language. These data provide the psychological basis for the improvement of literacy instruction.

II. PREPARATORY STAGE FOR READING: LEARNING CHARACTERS

A. Characters and Memorizing

To read Chinese one must first learn the characters. The Chinese character is a kind of ideograph. Unlike alphabetic writing that can be read on
the basis of spelling, it is difficult to find the pronunciation cues at the
initial stage and therefore children have to memorize mechanically.
Moreover, Chinese characters are numerous; in the *Zhong Hua Dictionary*
we find more than 50,000 characters. According to a survey (Tong, Song,
Li, & Feng, 1974), young people with a high school level of education
can read about 3700 characters, and university students about 4500 characters. They can read books and newspapers but sometimes they write
characters incorrectly or mispronounce them. This is a rather serious
problem, and some call learning characters a stumbling block.

The many ideas proposed for solving this problem can be categorized into two types. The first is to change the object of study—the
writing system—by simplifying the characters. The second is to use an
alphabetic writing system instead of ideographs. This second idea
would be equivalent to replacing the characters with an alphabet, an
idea that is still under discussion. To simplify Chinese characters would
mean reducing the number of strokes in a character and eliminating
complicated variants. Since 1949 the government of the People's
Republic of China has published a list of about 500 simplified characters,
bringing convenience to children and adults (see Table 7.1).

When these characters were simplified, psychologists in China
performed research on the methods and principles of simplification,
suggesting homonymous displacement to be an effective way of simplifying characters (Research Group for the Writing System Reformation,
1977). Another line of research is also important. What cognitive abilities
do Chinese children utilize when they recognize characters, or how can
they learn faster through learning the rules of character structure?
Chinese psychologists are particularly interested in these questions.

TABLE 7.1. Simplified and Complex Characters.

Pronunciation	feng	bian	nong	chen	yu
Simplified character	丰	边	农	尘	吁
Complex character	豐	邊	農	塵	籲
Meaning	rich	side	farming	dust	appeal

There are six methods of constructing Chinese characters: pictographs, pictophonetics, self-explanatories, associate compounds, phonetic loans, and synonyms. Among these, 80% of the characters are pictophonetics. These consist of two parts. One part indicates the meaning of the character for example " 氵 " relates to water and " 扌 " relates to hand. The second part, usually a simple character, indicates the pronunciation (see Table 7.2). In this kind of character, there are some connections among pronunciation, meaning and the form of the character, which supply memorizing cues to children. Thus, redundancy in parts and simple characters is an important merit of Chinese characters. In our primary schools the concentrated method of learning Chinese characters has been recently introduced. This method stresses the structural rules of pictophonetics. It breaks down the barrier that new characters must exclusively come out in sentences, and puts together the characters that have the same pronunciation. In this way children can draw inferences about other cases from one instance, and can learn characters much faster.

TABLE 7.2. Pictophonetic Characters.

	方	芳	仿	坊	房	放
fang:	square	fragrant	imitate	lane	house	place
	胡	葫	湖	蝴	猢	糊
hu:	(a surname)	calabash	lake	butterfly	monkey	paste

B. The Skill of Analyzing Character Forms

For a child who does not know any characters there is no difference between a character and a nonsense figure formed of lines. He has to look for the threads of meaning on the basis of living experience. In one experiment (Tong, Song, Li, & Feng, 1979) we found that children learned " 壶 " (kettle) on the basis of the form of this character because it looks like a hot-water bottle. They learned jujube (" 枣 ") on the basis of the two dots which look like two jujubes. Memory of this kind is not very taxing, and children did not really master the skill of analyzing character forms by root forms for such words.

Once children know the strokes and the order of strokes of characters they progress faster. Once they can recognize characters by their structure the children have mastered the initial skill of analyzing character forms, but the result is influenced by whether the strokes are many or few. By the time they have learned 100-200 characters, children have gradually learned that many characters are made from two or three parts. These parts are formed with strokes, but they are general and can be used as a whole (for example, 月·皿·古·里). During this period children rely mainly on these parts, not on the strokes. At this stage the teacher ought to give each of the parts a name. The children would thereby be able to use linguistic code to analyze and memorize character, thus increasing their skill.

C. Characters and Writing

Our research has shown that children's memorization of characters is influenced by strokes and parts of characters (Tong et al., 1979). This influence, however, varies with the task. For instance, the reproduction of simple characters is easier than for complicated characters. In recognition, however, there is no marked difference between simple and complicated characters. We assume that recognition is on the basis of the characteristics and outline of a character, and reproduction must be on the basis of its every detail. Thus, it is a rather difficult task for children to learn to write characters.

Every Chinese character is like a square. When writing a character, the child has to draw a clear distinction between top and bottom, right and left, inside and outside. Writing characters is a process in which vision motion plays an important role. In a recent experiment (Tong, 1983), the feedback of vision motion was deprived, and the results indicated that writing was very difficult, especially when the child could not see where his pen point was put on the paper. This is because the end of one stroke and the beginning of the next are disconnected in a character. It seems that writing Chinese is more difficult than writing in an alphabet, because the order of strokes is more important. In China, primary school teachers have considerable experience in teaching children to write. They know that to strengthen the guidance of writing can make children's memorization more precise.

III. FROM CHARACTER LEARNING TO WORD UNDERSTANDING

A. Characters and Words in Chinese

A Chinese word is constructed of one or more characters. Although the Chinese vocabulary, like that of any other well-developed language (such as English), is huge, the number of characters from which its words are constructed is relatively small. About 3500 characters may be sufficient for reading non-expert newspapers and magazines, and among these only 2000 characters are quite frequently used. The number of words a child has to learn in alphabetic writing would presumably be far larger for reading the same text.

In the Chinese vocabulary a great proportion of words consist of two-syllable words that are composed of two characters serving as morphemes. Thus, a great number of Chinese words could be composed of a relatively small number of characters as Table 7.3 indicates. To comprehend the twelve words listed in the table, only seven characters had to be learned in advance. Furthermore, these characters can be used to compose still more words. When new words such as television (" 电视 "), astronavigation (" 航天 "), and rocket (" 火箭 ") appeared to denote new things and events, these words were typically composed of familiar characters from which one can roughly infer their meaning even though one had never seen these words before.

B. Children's Understanding and Mastering of Words

The above-mentioned characteristics may be helpful in learning Chinese words. Using a picture vocabulary test (Feng, Song, & Tong, 1981), we measured the vocabulary ability of preschool children and found that their development of word comprehension was quite fast. Children age 4-6 years could not only comprehend frequently used words, especially the nouns in spoken language, but also could infer the meaning of some words that were mainly used in written language from the familiar characters they contained [e.g., the character " 斗 " (fight) to infer to the meaning of " 斗殴 " (scuffle)] and identify the corresponding picture. These results indicate that Chinese youngsters might possess a larger vocabulary than that of English-speaking children of the same age.

TABLE 7.3. Compound Words.

	公 male	母 female	大 big	小 small
牛 ox	公牛 bull	母牛 cow	大牛 cattle	小牛 calf
羊 sheep	公羊 ram	母羊 ewe	大羊 sheep	小羊 lamb
猪 pig	公猪 boar	母猪 sow	大猪 pig	小猪 piglet

The classifier quantitative is a special part of speech in Chinese. There are different quantitatives for different verbs and nouns. All countable verb actions and nouns have corresponding classifier quantitatives. An example of these classifiers would be the word "head" in the English phrase "five head of cattle". Shao, Zhu et al. (1982) have found that children's ability to grasp quantitatives increased with age, and was closely correlated with cognitive development. The quantitatives used by 4-year-olds showed that there was no differentiation at that age. Thus, 4-year-olds used "ge" (个) and "zhi" (只), two general classifiers, indiscriminately in most situations. Five-year-olds began to be aware of the collocation of quantitatives and nouns, but the collocation tended to be inappropriate. Most of the 7-year-olds could correctly use quantitatives, but those whose cognitive ability was less developed misused them occasionally.

To what extent a child had comprehended the meaning of a word can be detected from his generalization of its meaning. In one study (Feng, Song, & Tong, 1980), children in the 2nd through 5th grades were told to read nine groups of sentences, each group composed of three sentences. They were required to summarize the ideas of the three sentences in each group with one sentence. In doing so they had to summarize the meaning of several words in these sentences, such as "magpie," "swallow" and "eagle" with one word "bird." We found that, although the ability to generalize improved with age, the rate of improvement was not the same at every age. From 8.5 to 9 and from 11 to 12 years of age, the improvement was more obvious than at other ages. Significantly, the 8.5 and 9 year groups were from two classes of the same grade in the same school. They used the same textbooks and had learned the same number of characters. The children differed only in 6 months of chronological age. Whether the difference in the generalization between them reflected a sudden change in their language development or cognitive development is a problem of much interest.

Does the way of constructing words in different languages really affect the size of children's vocabulary and their learning of words? If it does, then what is their relation to cognitive development? For us, this would be a problem of interest. But before any comparative study of this kind is undertaken, an appropriate measure of language ability will be necessary. Because of cultural factors the vocabulary tests commonly used in Western countries are not adequate for this purpose.

C. Comprehension of Written Sentences

The structure of written Chinese also has its own characteristics. As in English, Chinese depends on word order to represent the relationship among words and constituents. Because morphological change in the Chinese language is less developed than in English this dependency is more strict in Chinese. The grammatical meaning, such as gender, number, or case of nouns or the tense of verbs, is expressed with functional words in Chinese. Therefore the processing of Chinese sentences might well differ from other alphabetic languages. Furthermore, though complex sentences are used in Chinese as in other in languages, simple and short sentences are more commonly used. Complicated ideas are generally expressed with several simple sentences rather than with one complex sentence. Moreover, the Chinese version of a given text is shorter than that of other languages. It is estimated that the Chinese version is about two-thirds the length of the English version of the same text. This characteristic may surely produce some effect on reading.

Because of the difficulty imposed by the large number of characters, the learning of written Chinese had always focused on characters. Recently there have been clear improvements in teaching methods in this respect, and it has gradually come to be recognized that the memorizing of a certain number of characters, although perhaps a necessary preparation for reading, is not the same as possessing reading skills. Thus the study of sentence comprehension has come to receive more attention.

One study explored the effect of "expectancy" in reading (Song & Tong, 1982). Children were taught to read short sentences presented tachistoscopically. The subjects were 26 pupils from each of the 2nd and 4th grades. The 24 short sentences were of two types, 12 sentences each. Type A sentences expressed ideas more likely to correspond to the expectancy of children. Type B sentences were variations of those in type A, expressing ideas that were somewhat unexpected but still rational (see Table 7.4).

Each sentence was presented for one-fifteenth of a second. After each presentation the child had to read aloud, as well as possible, the sentence he observed. The number of presentations required for reading correctly was taken as the index of the degree of difficulty in reading a given sentence. A significant difference in the reading of these two types of sentences was found. It is clear that the expectancy of the child did affect reading behavior. Therefore the semantic content of the sentence may be an important factor affecting reading performance. The effect of sentence structure on reading is a topic requiring further study. From the same experiment it was also found that the strategy used, and the perceptual span of the child, were additional factors that clearly influenced reading performance. Generally speaking, the more advanced 4th-graders could see a sentence in an order from left to right and could see a large unit at each presentation, such as a word, half of a sentence, or even a short whole sentence. The direction of attention of the 2nd-

TABLE 7.4. Two Types of Sentences.

Type A	Type B
老牛吃青草。	老牛吃白菜。
The ox eats grass.	The ox eats cabbage.
鉛笔在桌上。	鉛笔在桌下。
The pencil is on the desk.	The pencil is under the desk.
阿姨讲故事。	阿姨听故事。
The nurse tells a story.	The nurse listens to a story.
老师教學生。	学生教老师。
The teacher teaches the pupils.	The pupil teaches the teacher.

graders tended not to be so definite. They might see only a single character at each presentation, although there were clear individual differences and some of the 4th-grade pupils were similar to the 2nd-graders. What causes these kinds of differences? What effect do different response patterns have on comprehension? These are questions to be answered in further investigations.

IV. CONCLUSIONS

We have briefly described the characteristics of the Chinese language and its writing system, and some aspects of how Chinese children learn to read and write Chinese. One can see that these characteristics make the learning of Chinese rather different from that of other languages (Song & Tong, 1981). In order to know about the uniqueness of Chinese language and literacy, and to better understand literacy in other languages, it would be helpful to undertake comparative studies.

REFERENCES

Feng, S., Song, J., & Tong, L. (1980). An experimental study on children's ability to generalize terms in sentences groups. *Acta Psychologica Sinica,* **2.**

Feng, S., Song, J., & Tong, L. (1981). An exploratory study of the word comprehension in preschool children. *Selected Papers of the Chinese Psychological Society.*

Research Group for the Writing System Reformation (Institute of Psychology and Printing House, Academia Sinica). (1977). An attempt at simplifying the Chinese characters. *Guang Ming Daily,* August 12, October 7.

Shao, W., Zhu, M. et al. (1982). *Characteristics of quantitatives in 4-7-year-old Chinese children.* Paper presented at the Annual Meeting of Developmental and Educational Psychology.

Song, J., & Tong, L. (1981). Comparative study of remembering the Chinese characters and Uighur words. *Selected Papers of the Chinese Psychological Society.*

Song, J., & Tong, L. (1982). *The effect of expectancy in reading.* Paper presented at the Annual Meeting of Developmental and Educational Psychology.

Tong, L. (1983). *The effect of feedback in writing Chinese characters.* Unpublished paper, Academia Sinica, Beijing, PRC.

Tong, L., Song, J., Li, W., & Feng, S. (1974). *A survey of the number of characters used by literates.* Unpublished paper, Academia Sinica, Beijing, PRC.

Tong, L., Song J., Li, W., & Feng, S. (1979). The influence of the number of strokes and the parts of speech on remembering Chinese characters. *Acta Psychologica Sinica*, 2.

8

Illiteracy in a Literate Society: Understanding Reading Failures in Brazil

Terezinha Nunes
University of London

I. INTRODUCTION

Literacy comprises a set of skills. But being literate is also a "way of being," a way of carrying out social transactions in a literate society. Not being able to read in a non-literate society is the regular state of affairs. However, in a literate society it is a mark of class; it defines job opportunities and level of pay. It defines one's prestige and status in many ways. When society institutionalizes literacy in some way—for example, by restricting voting rights to literate individuals—it implicitly creates a system of values since all individuals must be literate in order to fully participate in this society.

This chapter discusses literacy both as a skill and as a way of being. It attempts to examine how cognitive and social aspects of literacy interact in producing school failure in Brazil at rates so high that illiteracy has not been reduced proportionally to the expansion of the school system over time. A brief historical look at literacy in Brazil is provided initially, in order to show how the official sanctioning of illiteracy was introduced in Brazil and how the expansion of the school system did not affect rates of illiteracy in the expected way. This section is followed by a description of literacy as a skill which aims at providing a basis for the final section—an analysis of how social and cognitive factors interact in maintaining illiteracy in Brazil.

II. ILLITERACY IN BRAZIL: SOME HISTORICAL INFORMATION[1]

When the Portuguese arrived in Brazil in 1500 they found there several groups of non-literate Amerindians. The Jesuit missions established the first schools for Indian children, which were designed principally for the transmission of a religious faith. Schools were not a concern of the Portuguese in this colony for three centuries. It was only in 1808, when the Portuguese royal family fled to Brazil from Napoleon's army, that public education became an issue. Still, there was no concern with elementary education: instead, *colleges* and *secondary schools* were created to serve the local elite who hitherto had studied, if at all, in Europe.

After Brazil's independence from Portugal in 1822, the national constitution declared a minimum schooling of 4 years for all children to be the responsibility of the central government. However, beyond such legislation not much was done. The rural aristocracy was basically composed of *illiterate* landowners. For their children, and those of the urban bourgeoisie, education took the form of private tutorship, occasionally followed by further education in secondary schools and colleges. Following the Portuguese bureaucratic tradition, a system of registering births, marriage and other contracts was also set up at this time. Birth and marriage certificates could be issued officially by the church through their records of baptism and the religious marriage. These were the only documents needed (but not always possessed) by the propertyless. The rich but often illiterate landowners had at their disposal learned individuals, who acted as tutors for their children and read and wrote for them because they often needed other types of documents such as land and slave property certificates.

When the Republic replaced the Monarchy, in 1889, criteria for voting rights had to be set up. There was a period of intense debate about these rights since the Brazilian elite did not want to risk their

[1]The historical description presented here is primarily based on the excellent work by Paiva (1972).

power with the advent of democratic elections. Voting rights were given to immigrants from different European countries, but those unable to read and write were not allowed to register as voters. With this restriction, the elites were able to propose a "democratic" election while retaining extensive influence in government since 80% of the population was illiterate, illiteracy predominating among the lower classes. The ostensive criterion for determining literacy for the purpose of obtaining voting rights was decoding a simple message, but the *de facto* criterion seems to have been—as it is until this day—the ability to write one's name. Some historians (Paiva, 1972; Rodrigues, 1965) have suggested that the incorporation of this discrimination in the Constitution in 1891 represents the sanctioning of the prejudices against the illiterate, who have come to be viewed as lacking judgement. As one writer put it, "[before], not being able to read did not imply anything about the individual's good sense, dignity, knowledge, skills, and intelligence; it did not constitute a barrier to his economic productivity" (Rodrigues, 1965, in Paiva, 1972).

Census data make it clear that only after World War I did the government give serious consideration to the problem of illiteracy. In 1890, fully 82% of Brazilians above age 15 were illiterate. By 1920 this proportion was virtually unchanged: 78%. These data stand in strong contrast to the American case, for example, where educators noted with dismay that 30% of the military men tested at the time of the World War I could not read well enough to understand instructions in an intelligence test (Resnick & Resnick, 1977). A much stronger criterion for literacy was used in the latter case—understanding instructions rather than writing one's name—and rates of literacy were still much higher than in Brazil.

The post-war climate was one of enthusiasm towards the role of education in building a fairer society (Paiva, 1972; Cunha, 1980). A liberal revolution overthrew the conservatives in power, and for almost a decade the political rhetoric was very favorable toward elementary education. The percentage of children attending school at the elementary level almost quadrupled between 1920 and 1937, rising from 10% to 37% as a result of regional investments in education. However, with the establishment of a totalitarian regime in 1937 voting rights were sharply curtailed, and popular engagement in political life was no longer held as an ideal. Almost no investments were made in elementary education. A census in 1940 indicated that more than half of the population was still illiterate. For the first time a special fund from federal revenues for elementary education was created by law. It became operative in 1945, four decades ago, and four and a half centuries after the discovery of Brazil by Europeans.

Increased investments by both federal and international institutions (USAID, UNESCO) helped raise the proportion of school-aged children attending school from 57% in 1945 to 90% in 1964. The concern with elementary education was, however, mainly quantitative. A 4-year follow-up study of schoolchildren matriculated in first grade in 1958 revealed that, despite larger enrollment, 42% of the children were not promoted to second grade (Cunha, 1980). When results such as these became widely known, several theories were put forth to explain such massive school failure. These theories aimed at explaining reading failure since the criterion for passing at the end of 1st grade is loosely defined as "being able to read and write words with simple syllabic structures" (i.e. consonant-vowel patterns).

III. LITERACY AS A SKILL

Explaining this failure *en masse* in the acquisition of literacy skills was a task taken up in the early 1960s mainly by educators and psychologists. The explanation for failure, it was thought, must be found in the limited abilities of the children who fail. In 1968 a distinguished psychologist and pioneer in the field of reading research in Brazil closed her book— entitled *Alfabetizacao: Disfuncoes Psiconeurologicas* (Learning to Read: Psychoneurological Dysfunctions)—by expressing her hope that her work would contribute to the understanding of the causes of this massive reading failure (Poppovic, 1968). The causes investigated then were predominantly of a psychological nature. Large numbers of poor children, who were failing these "reading readiness" tests, were labeled "deficient" and were excluded from regular reading instruction, either through referral to special education classes insufficient in number to meet the demands of this sudden rise in rates of "deficiency", or through being kept in the regular classrooms but working under teachers who had very low expectations for them.

In the next decade, however, educators started facing the fact that failure was not independent of social class. Two types of approaches to the problem then emerged. On one hand, some authors (Silva, 1979; Novaes, 1977) were inclined to treat this school failure as a consequence of extremely poor development resulting from nutritional and stimulation deficits. They suggested that medical (nutritional and health care) and psychological intervention were the route to solving reading failure. At the same time there arose a cultural deprivation approach (Poppovic, Esposito, & Campos, 1975; Poppovic, 1981; Brandao, 1982). Schools were criticized as unprepared for their culturally deprived clientele. The solution to the problem was seen in the introduction into school curricula of programs for training perceptual and motor activities for the development of pre-reading skills. These explanations reflected the academic battles under way in other countries facing similar problems: American schools were concerned with the question of lower reading achievement after desegregation; English schools were facing the discrimination of their system with regard to working-class children; and French schools were also facing high rates of reading failure among poor children. There were essentially two sorts of theorists: those who believed that children failed as a result of their limited capacities, and those who believed in the children's capacities but could offer no explanation for their failure in school. Theoretical battles were often waged without a careful analysis of the purported reading skills themselves. What were poor children capable or incapable of? A good description of reading acquisition was still missing.

IV. READING AND WRITING IN PORTUGUESE

Portuguese, like Spanish but unlike English, is a language with clear syllable boundaries and a fair amount of consistency in the written-to spoken correspondence, especially at the syllabic level. Literacy in Portuguese, however, seems to call for the same basic skills as in other languages, as is the case of metalinguistic knowledge (see, for e.g., Downing & Oliver, 1973-74, and Bradley & Bryant, 1983, for English; and Carraher & Rego, 1981, 1983, with respect to Portuguese).

Literacy skills are based upon a generative ability (for a detailed discussion of this argument, see Carraher, 1985), which can be used in different ways by calling into play elements of a different nature, such as the meaning of the word, syllables, phones or morphemes.[2] Different phases in the development of literacy skills can perhaps be defined through an analysis of the way in which this generative capacity is being deployed (Ferreiro & Teberosky, 1979; Marsh et al., 1980, 1981; Frith, 1984; Carraher, 1985). As the child becomes engaged in the task of learning how to read, the very basis of this learning process, i.e. the child's metalinguistic knowledge, changes through the contact with written language, which offers information about language not easily accessible in oral language. The newly acquired metalinguistic knowledge will, in turn, provide the basis for new approaches to reading and writing.

The literature available on reading/writing acquisition in Portuguese is suggestive of the following phases in the development of reading/writing skills. At first, children seem to look through word form at word meaning and base their conceptions of writing upon word

---

[2]It is beyond the scope of this chapter to discuss in detail experimental evidence regarding the present description of literacy as a skill in Portuguese.

meaning. They judge word similarity and length on the basis of meaning and expect, accordingly, that words which are similar in meaning ought to be written in similar ways, and that words which refer to large or long objects will also be long (Carraher & Rego, 1981, 1983, 1984). Children who judge word similarity and word length on the basis of word meanings are much less likely to succeed in learning how to read at the end of one year of instruction than children who do not show semantic responding to metalinguistic tasks at the outset of reading instruction (Carraher & Rego, 1983, 1984).

When children first build word concepts which take word form into account, they systematically relate the spoken to the written word by using a syllabic breakdown of the word (Ferreiro & Teberosky, 1979; Carraher & Rego, 1983). They spell by matching one letter to each syllable of the word, and even read in the same way words for which they have memorized the spelling (e.g. their own names). Probably because vowels are often taught at the outset of reading instruction, and there are so few of them, all easily recognizable as units in spoken Portuguese, many children at this phase write non-memorized words by representing each vowel sound in the spoken word. This performance is a clear display of their generative ability and of their use of the syllable as the unit of analysis for writing purposes.

A third phase in the development of reading/writing skills can be called, after Ferreiro and Teberosky (1979), the alphabetic phase. Writing here calls into play an analysis of phones, and children use in their written words roughly as many letters as there are phonemes in their pronunciation of the word (see also Read, 1978; Chomsky, 1977). Phonological spelling errors are plentiful in this phase, attesting to the generative power of the child's writing skills and its alphabetic nature (Marsh, Friedman, & Welch, 1980). Carraher (1985) observed that about 40% of the spelling errors by first-graders were of this type. The differences between the spoken and the written forms of language are the major source of phonological errors in Portuguese. Regional and class-related variations in spoken language may be seen as determining a higher incidence of phonological errors in the northeast of Brazil as compared to some states in the south, and among poor children in any region as compared to children from wealthier homes. Among highly literate individuals, phonological errors are often viewed as a sign of "ignorance."

With the exposure to written language, children end up discovering the differences between spoken and written language. A new type of spelling error is then observed, which can be termed as "overcorrection" error. Overcorrection errors are indicative of the child's attempts to coordinate the phonological with the morphological aspects of words. An interesting example from Portuguese is the consistent overcorrection used by children when they spell the perfect tense of certain verbs. This tense marker should be spelled with the ending -iu. However, non-stressed final /u/s in Portuguese are often spelled with the letter "o". Many children end up by creating the morpheme -io, which they use as the ending for past tense, consistently misspelling these verb forms. Overcorrection errors increase in proportion with the child's growing ability; in a longitudinal study of one child's writing, Carraher (1985) found that these errors represented 6.7% of the total number of errors made by the child after 4 months of reading instruction and 53.8% after 22 months of reading instruction.

V. GROWING UP TO BE A LITERATE ADULT

A cognitive analysis of reading processes should not make one lose sight of other important aspects of literacy and its acquisition—namely, the importance of social factors which show up in the lower achievement of poor children in different cultures. Sociologists such as Bourdieu and Passeron (1977) and Willis (1977), when discussing the class-related selectivity of the school system, have insisted upon the importance of analyzing how socioeconomic factors are mediated by cultural practices which influence individual action. Sociological analyses have exposed the difficulties of mobility in our class system: working-class children grow up to get working-class jobs, avoid learning in school, and reject academic values which they consider appropriate only for the "weak" (Willis, 1977). Sociological analyses have also revealed the discriminatory nature of school systems, their function in maintaining the system of classes in Western societies and spreading an ideology of success of the fittest, which justifies the class system (Althusser, 1980).

What sort of literacy one achieves is intimately related to whom one identifies with. A Brazilian college instructor may complain that her students "can't read" when they fail to understand an assigned theoretical paper, yet asserts that her maid, who decodes recipes with difficulty, "can read." Expectations of a college student's reading and writing skills are markedly different from expectations of a domestic worker's skills. If the latter can take down telephone messages and cook from recipes she is literate for her purposes. Growing up and identifying with parents who are college instructors or maids most certainly creates different expectations with regard to what type of literacy one will live with as an adult. How literacy is viewed by parents may be an important factor in creating both the motivation for and occasion to practice literacy skills.

Carraher (1984) interviewed a sample of 42 mothers whose children were attending first grade in a lower-class neighborhood school with failure rates of about 40% in the previous years. The purposes of the interviews were to obtain a description of the sample according to some socioeconomic variables, to assess mothers' attitudes towards and uses of literacy skills, and obtain information about children's daily routines and their opportunities for using/needing literacy. The sample was formed primarily by migrants who had lived in the community for 7.1 years on average. The level of instruction of fathers showed a range of variation from illiterates (25%) to high school (7.5%), with a median level of instruction equivalent to 3.2 years. The level of instruction of mothers showed a range of variation from illiterate (27%, according to self-reports and the ability displayed in decoding a simple written message) to incomplete college education (2.5%), with the median level of instruction equal to 2.6 years. Family income varied from one to five minimum-wages. Type of employment of fathers was as follows: 40% unskilled manual laborers; 12.5% bricklayers; 25% skilled manual workers; 2.5% managers of own business; 20% absent fathers, no information was obtained. Among mothers, 45% contributed to the family's income but only 12.5% were formally employed; the remainder worked in the informal sector of the economy, doing jobs such as laundry, sewing, cooking, and house-cleaning for others without formal hiring. The number of children per family ranged from 1 to 14, with a mean equal to 5.9. The target-children's age ranged from 7 to 11, with a mean of 7.9 years. This brief description of the sample shows that there was enough variation among the interviewed families with regard to macrostructural variables to allow for the observation of significant relationships between these variables and school success.

With respect to attitudes and uses of literacy, only 27% of the mothers expressed the belief that literacy leads to better occupational levels while the value of literacy for daily life purposes was recognized by 85% of the mothers. When asked about literacy, these mothers clearly referred to it as reading and writing for very simple purposes—which is what they themselves, when literate, use their skills for. The most common use of reading and writing in their daily lives was for correspondence with relatives: 75% of the mothers asserted that they used reading and/or writing for this purpose. In contrast, only 39% reported reading newspapers, books, magazines or the bible; 32% reported using writing as a memory aid and 17% reported at least one other use of reading and writing. When we later looked at the relationship between schooling and occupational levels in this group it became clear that it was necessary for mothers to complete at least fourth grade in order to have access to employment levels not accessible to the illiterate (Carraher, 1984). Since the simple literacy skills the mothers had been referring to are acquired in first and second grades, the amount of schooling needed for them to climb up the ladder of occupational levels is higher than that required for the acquisition of the type of literacy they had in mind when answering our questions. Middle- and upper-class mothers, on the other hand, expressed a strong belief in the value of school for promoting their children's access to higher occupational levels in Brazil (Weber, 1976). However, the level of instruction these mothers referred to was college level, which in Brazil confers professional degrees. Literacy is thought of by these mothers as an elementary tool used throughout a school system for learning. In this social milieu, reading and writing are not aspired to—they are taken for granted just as are proper clothing, hygiene and politeness.

When the attitudes toward literacy were examined in this study it became clear that, from the lower-class mother's viewpoint, literacy serves mostly a face-saving function (Carraher, 1984). People do not like to be embarrassed by displaying their illiteracy in public situations. Illiteracy is treated as a stigma which strongly devaluates the person, an attitude which is revealed in such statements as "A person who can't read may as well be blind because he doesn't know half the world around him and has to ask others," or "I'd like to be able to read so I could go into a bar and read what type of food they have and wouldn't have to say I don't know how to read." We have often come across reports by literate lower-class individuals who stated that in certain situations they had failed to ask for directions for fear of being taken for illiterate. If it is true that children grow up to be literate by identifying with their parents' attitudes toward, and motivations for, being literate in particular ways, it is unlikely that children who grow up with this view of literacy will be highly motivated for reading and writing: in the poor children's lives there are few opportunities of displaying illiteracy in public since their daily activities (games and occupations with which they help their families, such as house chores) do not call for reading or writing. Moreover, the uses of literacy reported by mothers in their own daily lives do not seem to open new privileges or possibilities of entertainment to their children. Children's books were virtually non-existent in the homes, and children were rarely read to; only 19% of the mothers reported reading to their children.

The relationship between the variables used to define the socioeconomic characteristics of the families and the children's passing or failing in school at the end of first grade was analyzed, showing the following trends: (1) even though there was noticeable variation in the socioeconomic variables, there was not a significant correlation between family income and school success; (b) there was not a significant correlation between parental level of instruction and school success but, in this case, correlation approached significance; (c) there was no significant correlation between the number of children in the family, the number of people in the household, and the child's position in the family and school success. Thus, while macrostructural variables play an important role in predicting school failure when one studies society as a whole, these variables do not seem to play the same role within that portion of society which is particularly afflicted by school failure.

On the other hand, the association between uses of reading and writing at home and school success showed several interesting results. Children whose mothers reported reading stories or letters to them were significantly more likely to succeed than to fail in school (cf. Teale & Sulzby, this volume). There was also a positive and significant association between mothers' reports of receiving letters from relatives and children's success in school. This association is particularly interesting since it cuts across levels of parental education; in fact some of these mothers reported having to ask someone else (e.g. neighbor, older child) to read their letters for them since they were, themselves, illiterate.

Heath (1983) described the uses of literacy in three different communities in rural United States. She convincingly argued that uses of literacy among mainstreamers and their way of living prepared their children for the type of literacy they would have to cope with in school. Attitudes toward, and uses of, literacy among people from two poor neighboring communities, on the other hand, did not play the same positive role of pre-training their children for life and literacy in school.

The most impressive evidence regarding the importance of the personal meaning of literacy for its development, however, comes from Scribner and Cole's (1981) description of Vai literacy in Liberia, where children acquire English literacy in school and Arabic literacy for religious purposes. Despite competition with English and Arabic, 20-25% of adult males (Scribner & Cole, 1978) were literate in Vai, although Vai script was only taught outside of formal schooling. Since Vai literacy is acquired under informal conditions of instruction, it is most likely that what favors the acquisition of Vai literacy is the meaning it has for those who learn it. Writing is a part of life for certain Vai men; as a consequence women rarely learn it. Vai men learn Vai script in order to replace their fathers in their business, and to correspond with girlfriends and relatives living in other villages. Scribner and Cole (1981) report that there was usually a specific motive prompting the learner—one also found in our studies in Brazil—the interest in keeping one's secrets through being able to read one's own letters. It seems possible to conclude that what keeps Vai literacy going is its functional significance in the culture.

A finding of the work by Scribner and Cole which is relevant for the Brazilian case under discussion—poor children's massive failure in reading acquisition—is that the cognitive requirements of reading acquisition are likely to be present in "culturally deprived" people; the living conditions Scribner and Cole describe as predominant among the Vai are similar to those termed "cultural deprivation" in Brazil, involving deficient health conditions (infant mortality exceeds 50%), lack of print in the environment (Vai is almost never printed) and high rates of illiteracy in the community. In spite of these conditions and the non-institutionalization of Vai reading instruction, the Vai writing system has been maintained in use for the last 100-150 years.

VI. CONCLUSIONS

If we look now at the interrelationships between literacy as a skill and social interactions related to literacy, it is possible to attempt to find some answers to the question "Why are there so many illiterate people in literate societies?" In the case of Brazil the 1980 census still showed 26% of the population aged 15 or above to be illiterate according to self-reports. Don't we all share the abilities to accomplish basic reading and writing? Why do poor Brazilian children fail to acquire literacy even according to the least strict criteria? Some answers may be suggested on the basis of the previous discussion.

First, motivation may be lacking. We saw in the case of poor Brazilian children that very few of them may have gone into school with some personal meaning for literacy since very few mothers[3] read to their children. Brazilian schools do not take upon themselves the task of making literacy meaningful to children. Carraher (1984) observed nine first-grade teachers in two schools for a total period of 35 hours during reading instruction periods. On no occasion did any of the teachers bring their pupils to use reading or writing functionally in the classroom. This shows that reading and writing were never used to accomplish anything, but were always the purpose of the school task. Teachers did not read to children as a form of entertainment, for instance by reading stories. Nor did they use written material such as magazines or newspapers for finding or providing information. Reading and writing were exclusively used in activities which aimed at practicing reading and spelling, such as copying, building up words with particular syllables, or writing

---

[3]Some people will be concerned about the role of fathers. It is not possible to discuss here in detail the degree to which fathers are uninvolved with their children's school work in particular, and education in general, in Brazil; it may be sufficient to mention that the interview questioned whether anyone read to the child, and the response was largely that either the mother did or no-one did. In a few isolated cases an older sibling *and* the mother read to the child.

from dictation. This total absence of functional uses of literacy in the classroom is even more striking when one considers that teachers know that many children come from homes where literacy may not be used. These observations have been recently replicated by Buarque (1986) with 12 other first-grade teachers observed for a total of 60 hours during reading instruction periods; Buarque reports one instance of reading a story—and this with the purpose of asking children some specific questions at the end, the story not being particularly interesting nor having the purpose of entertaining the children.

Second, reading instruction may be out of pace with poor children's development of reading/writing skills. Carraher and Rego (1984) observed that most poor children in their sample came into reading instruction giving semantic responses to questions about word form. Reading instruction provides them with opportunities for reflections upon word form, and they tend to "catch up" with their teachers' expectations (teachers are not aware of the difficulty of focusing upon word form and simply assume that children will be doing so during reading instruction) by the end of the year. However, by the time they do so it may be too late: they move into the syllabic phase of writing and display a performance which is again out of pace with their teachers' expectations, since teachers evaluate children on the basis of their ability to write alphabetically. Carraher and Rego (1984) followed three groups of children during their first year of reading instruction, evaluating them on at least two occasions. Two groups were composed of middle- and upper-class children undergoing reading instruction according to either a syllabic or a phonemic teaching method. The third group was formed of lower-class children receiving instruction according to a syllabic method. Children's ability to judge word length and similarity (considering word form and disregarding word meaning) were classified into three levels, ranging from responses based primarily upon word meaning to responses totally independent of word meaning. The percentages of children in each group falling into the highest level of performance are presented in Figure 8.1.

Three trends may be pointed out:

1. Children of the same socioeconomic group (schools 1 and 2 were middle-class schools) varied in their rate of development of metalinguistic knowledge during the year according to the teaching method they were exposed to, with syllabic instruction (school 1) proving superior to phonemic instruction (school 2) in this case;
2. Despite their higher age level at the beginning of the year, poor children (school 3) started reading instruction signifi-

cantly behind middle- and upper-class children with respect to metalinguistic knowledge, a trend which may be explained by the fact that middle- and upper-class children typically attend at least 1 or 2 years of preschool, during which their reading instruction is started;

3. Poor children showed very little progress with regard to abandoning semantic responding during the first term of reading instruction but tended to catch up at the end of the year.

Thus, poor children's marked disadvantage in metalinguistic knowledge could be partially responsible for their lack of success at the end of the year. However, their results in this task also suggest that their prospects of succeeding in the following year are very good—an expectation which is not confirmed by official statistics: Children who have failed reading instruction once are more likely to fail again than those who are starting afresh (Cunha, 1980).

Third, the slower development of poor children in metalinguistic knowledge and their slower development of literacy skills provides Brazilian teachers with "evidence" to support their views regarding the imputed lack of capacity among poor children. Since teachers in Brazil typically know nothing about other writing systems, nor about the development of children's reading skills involving a syllabic phase

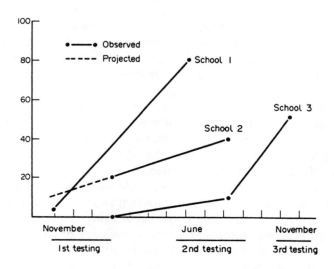

Figure 8.1. Percentage of children at the highest level of performance in a task of metalinguistic knowledge. Schools 1 (syllabic instruction) and 2 (phonemic instruction) were middle-class; school 3 was lower-class. (From Carraher & Rego, 1984)

before the alphabetic one is achieved, they are often at loss when a pupils' performance reflects a syllabic conception of writing. We showed some teachers in a seminar a writing sample produced by a child who consistently used one letter to represent each syllable, choosing invariably the correct vowel according to her pronunciation of the word (e.g. /patu/ was spelled as "au"; /furmiga/ was spelled as "uia"), and asked what they thought of that way of writing. They interpreted the child's production as attesting to a lack of capacity in perceiving consonants. However, research has shown syllabic conceptions of writing to be good predictors of success at the end of the year (Ferreiro & Teberosky, 1979). Even spelling according to regional pronunciation—which is typical of the alphabetic phase in the development of writing- is commonly viewed by teachers as reflecting deficiencies. When Brazilian teachers face such performance in the classroom they tend to ignore the children who display it, assigning them to corners of the room with other "weak" students (Rosemberg, 1982, and Buarque, 1985, have independently observed this phenomenon). These "weak students," excluded from regular reading instruction, will then be given "perceptual and motor development tasks," which their teachers believe will improve their pre-reading skills.

A fourth source of failure for poor children in the acquisition of literacy skills resides in the variations of language spoken by the poor. No-one speaks the ideal form of a language which is the model for writing. While many distinctions between the written and the varieties of spoken language follow regional patterns, many others are class-associated, there being greater discrepancies between written Portuguese and poor children's language than between written Portuguese and middle- and upper-class children's language. Poor children with a phonemic spelling strategy will thus make more spelling errors than middle- and upper-class children with the same spelling strategy, and they will only correct these errors when they further develop their competence in writing. Galifret-Granjon (1984) has pointed out the existence of a similar problem in France, and suggested that a strong emphasis on spelling in the early schools years represents the adoption of class-biased criteria for the evaluation of school performance.

In short, it appears that poor children grow up with a conception of literacy that fails to motivate them for learning how to read. Schools, however, seem to assume that reading is valuable to anyone, and do not promote in the learner the knowledge of its relevance while carrying on reading instruction. Moreover, educators are as yet unaware that a learner may not start out learning how to read with a full conception of what the writing system in his community is—a conception which must be learned as a part of reading acquisition. Children who start out under the teacher's expectations, even if they catch up later, will provide the teacher with "evidence" of their disabilities, and will be excluded from regular reading instruction—a procedure which will most likely interfere with children's learning about the writing system. Finally, when poor children develop alphabetic conceptions of writing—a conception which is sufficient for reading, although not spelling, in Portuguese—their spelling errors are plentiful and are treated as renewed "evidence" of ignorance. A large proportion of poor children will then be retained by the school system, yielding such high rates of failure that only 36.8% of all Brazilian children who enter first grade will be promoted into third grade 2 years later, having proven to their teacher's satisfaction that they have, in these 2 years, mastered basic reading and spelling skills.

A last question to be asked is: Can schools function with enough autonomy from the rest of society to break this chain of events promoting reading failure, or must one change the whole society first? In other words, is it possible to promote greater success in learning to read by changing competence and beliefs in schools, or is reading failure a by-product of a class-differentiated society in a developing nation? Experiments on a small and large scale are presently being carried out in Brazil, which attempt to decrease reading failure from within the school system itself. Government units are investing in teacher education and publication of new research on reading in ways that make this research accessible to teachers. Researchers are progressively more committed to carrying out action research by working with teachers and observing the effects of teacher and curriculum changes upon their children's reading acquisition process. There is a clearer commitment from the government to reduce illiteracy by appropriately teaching children at their entrance into the system.

At a macro-level, however, there have been some important changes also. Educators such as Paulo Freire and Darcy Ribeiro have accepted a more prominent role in the politics of education. Educational reforms are being studied for all levels. The most significant one for reading acquisition is under way in three states, where children are automatically promoted at the end of one year of reading instruction and will only be evaluated at the end of the second year. This policy, which assumes that time is the best remedy, may have very positive effects when it is combined with effective changes in the classroom.

The new liberal government has given the illiterate the right to vote—a decision which may have an impact upon literacy, albeit rather indirect. It is a time of change in many ways. It remains to be seen how reading failure will be affected.

POSTSCRIPT

The positive note on which this chapter ended eight years ago was to some extent borne out by later events. The positive changes witnessed by those involved with literacy research and teaching in Brazil can be documented in many ways.

First, the research production on literacy has increased significantly, illustrating the greater involvement of researchers and federal funds in the analysis of literacy learning in Brazil. Soares (1990), in an overview of articles on literacy published in Brazilian educational journals in the last decades, offers the following figures: 12 items for 1950-59; 12 items for 1960-69; 42 items for 1970-79; 164 items for 1980-89. Although these figures are modest if compared to the production in developed countries, they clearly indicate that there is a greater awareness of the need for studies investigating literacy learning in Brazil.

Second, the focus of the research also seems to be shifting with significant consequences for researchers' and teachers' views of children who show little progress at the beginning of the year. Soares (1990) indicates that between 1950 and 1979, fully one third of the literature consisted of investigations of methods for teaching literacy whereas there are only three papers dealing with the process of children's development in literacy learning. In contrast, 47% of the papers between 1980-89 were concerned with the psychogenesis of literacy, must of which are directly or indirectly inspired in the constructivist approach put forth by Ferreiro and Teberosky (1979). The significance of this shift for the interpretation of children's initial difficulties in literacy learning was pointed out by do Nascimento (1990) and Nunes (1990) on the basis of different analyses of the current scenario. Do Nascimento observed that children's spelling errors are interpreted differently by researchers, who often use the word *error* in quotes, thereby indicating that some of the children's production may be viewed as an error only because they do not conform to the conventional system. However, these researchers point out that, when these productions are considered in and of themselves, they are perfectly sensible and cannot be interpreted as symptoms of any deficiency. Phonetic transcription of the children's spoken dialect are the most common example of these "errors". Nunes suggested that, as a result of the constructivist approach to literacy, many teachers have learned to look for children's progress in a much more positive manner, even if the children's written productions reveal a syllabic rather than an alphabetic conception of written Portuguese. This positive attitude was illustrated in the work of Buarque and Rego (1994) in a series of papers about intervention projects in the Northeast and by Hickel (1992) in a paper about literacy learning in the extreme South. Marzola (1992) proposed a more radical interpretation of these changes and suggested that there is a paradigm shift in literacy teaching in Brazil, away from mechanistic models that focused on methods and attributed difficulties to individual differences moving to a constructivist approach that pays little attention to individual differences and centers its analyses on the process of emergent literacy. The beneficiary of these changes is expected to be the learner, whose difficulties would no longer be attributed to neuropsychological dysfunctions.

Third, there is also a much greater awareness of literacy as a form of social action, where motivation and pragmatic rules must be taken into account. Many school based intervention projects about literacy learning emphasize the need to use reading for a purpose in the classroom (see, for e.g., Pedrosa & Dubeux, 1994; Rego & Dubeux, 1994; Pereira, 1990.) The variety of literacy practices introduced in these projects tends to relate to the different types of clientele engaged in the programs. In the work of Rego and Dubeux, the pupils were young school children (pre-school and grades 1 and 2), and consequently stories played a major role in the choice of activities in which the pupils were engaged; the reading of newspapers was also included as part of social studies activities. In the work of Pereira, the pupils were older school children (grade 4), whose probable life trajectories would involve their participation in the work force quite soon. Texts chosen in this case included job announcements (self-presentation) as writing material, besides fiction. This introduction of purposeful material had clearly documented effects in the project by Rego and Dubeux (1992), where the children who participated in the program showed better reading and writing ability at the end of grades 1 and 2 and significantly lower drop out rates in comparison with a control group.

To conclude, I would like to add that, although there is reason for a positive view of the changes illustrated above, it is still too soon to evaluate what the impact of these changes on illiteracy rates will be in the long run. The participation of committed educationalists such as Paulo Freire, Esther Grossi, Silke Weber, and others in the political arena has enabled some major urban centers to engage whole school systems in innovative literacy projects and thereby significantly alter the failure and drop out rates within the first few years of school. This positive impact has illustrated the strong connections between politics and education in the Brazilian context. Will these accomplishments be maintained and expanded on by the newly elected neo-liberal government? Will the progress made in these local foci of activity be spread enough to significantly affect illiteracy rates?

ACKNOWLEDGEMENT

I am thankful to David Carraher, who read several versions of this paper and helped me with his insightful comments, and to Allan Luke and Peter Bryant, whose criticism of my previous views of the development of reading competence led to major changes in my understanding of this question. I am also thankful to Daniel Wagner, for his careful work as editor, which went beyond the normal obligations of editors.

REFERENCES

Althusser L. (1980). *Posicoes-2*. Rio de Janeiro: Edicoes Graal.

Bourdieu P., & Passeron, J. C. (1977). *Reproduction in education, society and culture*. London: Sage.

Bradley, L., & Bryant, P.E. (1983). Categorizing sounds and learning to read: A causal conexion. *Nature, 301*, 419-420.

Brandao, Z. (1982). A formacao dos professores e a questao da educacao das criancas das camadas populares. *Cadernos de Pesquisa, 40*, 54-57.

Buarque, L.L. (1986). Estilos de desempenho de professores de primeira serie e seus efeitos sobre a aprendizagem. Recife, Brazil: Universidade Federal de Pernambuco, Master's thesis.

Buarque, L.L., & Rego, L.L.B. (1994a). *Alfabetizacao e Construtivismo, Teoria e pratica*. Recife, Brazil: Editora da UFPE.

Buarque, L.L., & Rego, L.L.B. (1994b). Classes de repentes: Uma experiencia de alfabetizacao. In L.L. Buarque & L.L.B. Rego (Eds.), *Alfabetizacao e construtivismo. Teoria e pratica* (pp. 100-118). Recife, Brazil: Editora da UFPE.

Carraher, T.N. (1984). Face-saving and literacy in Brazil. *Sociological Abstracts, 32*, 40-41.

Carraher, T.N. (1985). Exploracoes psicologicas sobre o desenvolvimento da ortografia em portugues. *Psicologia: Teoria e Pesquisa, 4*, 269-285.

Carraher, T.N., & Rego, L.L.B. (1981). O realismo nominal como obstaculo na aprendizagem da leitura. *Cadernos de Pesquisa 39*, 3-10.

Carraher, T.N. & Rego, L.L.B. (1983). Understanding the alphabetic system. In D. Rogers & J. Sloboda (Eds.), *Acquisition of symbolic skills* (pp. 163-170). New York: Plenum Press.

Carraher, T.N., & Rego, L.L.B. (1984). Desenvolvimento cognitivo e alfabetizacao. *Revista Brasileira de Estudos Pedagogicos, 65*, 38-55.

Chomsky, C.C. (1977). Approaching reading through invented spelling. In L.B. Resnick & P.A. Weaver (Eds.), *Theory and practice of early reading*. Hillsdale, NJ: Erlbaum.

Cunha, L.A. (1980). *Educacao e desenvolvimento social no Brasil*. Rio de Janeiro: Francisco Alves.

do Nascimento, M.A. d. O.M. (1990). Da analise dos "erros" aos mecanismos envolvidos na aprendizagem da escrita. *Educacacao em Revista, 12*, 33-43.

Downing, J., & Oliver, P. (1973-74). The child's conception of "a word". *Reading Research Quarterly, 9,* 568-582.

Ferreiro, E., & Teberosky, A. (1979). *Los sistemas de escritura en el dsarollo del nino.* Mexico D. F.: Siglo Veintiuno.

Frith, U. (1984). Beneath the surface of developmental dyslexia. In K. Patterson, J. Marshall, & M. Coltheart (Eds.), *Surface Dyslexia.* London: Erlbaum.

Galifret-Granjon, N. (1984). A lingua escrita como objeto de aprendizagem. In J. de Ajuriaguerra et al. (Eds.), *A dislexia em questao. Dificuldades e fracassos e fracassos na aprendizagem da lingua escrita* (pp. 17-29). Porto Alegre, Brazil: Artes Medicas.

Heath, S.B. (1983). *Ways with words. Language, life, and work in communities and classrooms.* Cambridge: Cambridge University Press.

Hickel, N. (1992). A inteligencia e um processo e nao um dom: fica-se inteligente porque se aprende. In E. P. Grossi & J. Bordini (Eds.), *Paixao de aprender* (pp. 53-58). Petropolis, Brazil: Vozes.

Marsh, G., Friedman, M.P., & Welch, V. (1980). Development of strategies in learning to spell. In U. Frith (Ed.), *Cognitive processes in spelling.* London: Academic Press.

Marsh, G., Friedman, M. P., Welch, V., & Desberg, P. (1981). A cognitive developmental theory of reading acquisition. In T.G. Waller & G.E. Machinnon (Eds.), *Reading research: Advances in theory and practice.* New York: Academic Press.

Marzola, N. (1992) A formacao de professores num processo de mudanca da alfabetizacao. In E.P. Grossi & J. Bordini (Eds.), *Paixao de aprender* (pp. 79-82). Petropolis, Brazil: Vozes.

Novaes, M.H. (1977). *Psicologia do Ensino-Aprendizagem.* Sao Paulo: Atlas.

Nunes, T. (1990). Construtivismo e alfabetizacao: Um balanco critico. *Educacacao em Revista, 12,* 21-32.

Paiva, V.P. (1972). *Educacao popular e educacao de adultos. Contribuicao a historia da educacao Brasileira.* Rio de Janeiro: Loyola.

Pedrosa, I., & Dubeux, M.H. (1994). Acompanhando a conquista da leitura e da escrita: O que as criancas aprendem? In L. L. Buarque & L. L. B. Rego (Eds.), *Alfabetizacao e construtivismo. Teoria e pratica* (pp. 79-99). Recife, Brazil: Editora da UFPE.

Pereira, V.W. (1990). Ensino de lingua portuguesa e pratica social. *Educacao, 19,* 23-44.

Poppovic, A.M. (1968). *Alfabetizacao. Disfuncoes psiconeurologicas.* Sao Paulo: Vetor.

Poppovic, A.M. (1981). Enfrentando o fracasso escolar. *Revista da Associacao Nacional de Educacao, 1,* 17-21.

Poppovic, A.M., Esposito, Y.L., & Campos, M.M.M. (1975). Marginalizacao cultural: Subsidios para um curriculo pre-escolar. *Cadernos de Pesquisa, 7,* 11-60.

Read, C. (1978). Children's awareness of language, with emphasis on sound systems. In A. Sinclair, R.J. Jarvella, & W.J.M. Levelt (Eds.), *The child's conception of language.* New York: Springer-Verlag.

Rego, L.L.B., & Dubeux, M.H. (1994). Resultados de uma intervencao pedagogica no pre-escolar e no primeiro grau menor. In L.L. Buarque & L. L. B. Rego (Eds.), *Alfabetizacoa e construtivismo. Teoria e pratica* (pp. 66-78). Recife, Brazil: Editora da UFPE.

Resnick, D.P., & Resnick, L.B. (1977). The nature of literacy: An historical exploration. *Harvard Educational Review, 47,* 370-385.

Rodrigues, J.H. (1965). *Conciliacao e reforma no Brasil, um desafio historico politico.* Rio de Janeiro: Civilizacao Brasileira.

Rosemberg, L. (1982). Educacao e desigualdade social. In. J.M.C. de Carvalho (Ed.), *Concurso nacional de pesquisa em educacao. Os doze trabalhos premiados.* Curitiba, Brazil: Secretaria de Educacao/FUNDEPAR.

Soares, M.B. (1990). Alfabetizacoa: Em busca de um metodo? *Educacacao em Revista, 12,* 44-50.

Scribner, S., & Cole, M. (1978). Literacy without schooling: Testing for intellectual effects. *Harvard Educational Review, 48,* 448-461.

Scribner, S., & Cole, M. (1981). *The psychology of literacy.* Cambridge, MA: Harvard University Press.

Silva, A.C. da. (1979). Probreza, desenvolvimento mental e desempenho escolar, *Cadernos de Pesquisa, 29,* 7-9.

Weber, S. (1976). *Aspiracoes a educacao.* Petropolis, Brazil, Vozes.

Willis, P. (1977). *Learning to labor: How working class kids get working class jobs.* New York: Columbia University Press.

9

Literacy Acquisition in Early Childhood: The Roles of Access and Mediation in Storybook Reading

William H. Teale
The University of Illinois, Chicago

Elizabeth Sulzby
The University of Michigan

I. INTRODUCTION

During the past century research on beginning reading and writing tended to focus on the first year or two of formal literacy instruction in school, because it is usually during this period that most children become able to read and write in conventional ways. Much of the beginning literacy research in the United States, like that of many other literate societies, stemmed from, rather than led to, instructional practices (Teale & Sulzby, 1986). That is, reading research has to a large degree centered on identifying which methods of teaching beginning reading worked best.

In recent years attention has focused increasingly upon the *emergent literacy* of children, from infancy up to school entry. Three periods of research prior to the current focus on emergent literacy can be identified. At the turn of the century the literacy of young children (up to school entry at age 6) was disregarded or treated with "benign neglect." Then, in the 1930s the notion of *reading readiness* began to be examined through research studies and implemented through instructional practices in schools. Reading readiness was first interpreted in the context of *maturation*, the research question being "When can/should the child be taught to read?" The third era, close on the heels of reading readiness as maturation was reading readiness interpreted as *experience*. The question underlying the research of this era was "What can be done to increase children's readiness for reading instruction?"

During the present period, for the first time, research began to lead, rather than merely follow, instruction. The era of emergent literacy treats young children as being in the process of becoming literate long before school entry, and long before the children's reading and writing behaviors are conventional (Ferreiro & Teberosky, 1982; Goodman, 1980; Harste, Woodward, & Burke, 1984; Sulzby, 1985; Taylor, 1983; Teale, 1986). From current research it can be concluded, for example, that children acquire written as well as oral language during the period before they are able to read and write conventionally (Scollon & Scollon, 1981; Sulzby, 1986), and they develop reading and writing abilities concurrently and interrelatedly (Ferreiro & Teberosky, 1982; Sulzby & Teale, 1987).

Children learn written language through active engagement with their world, particularly through language interactions with adults (Heath, 1983; Snow & Ninio, 1986; Teale, 1982). Rather than being the product of "lessons in literacy," this literacy learning takes place in real-life settings for real-life activities (Heath, 1983; Taylor, 1983; Teale, 1986). Much as the studies of Brown (1973) and other researchers in the 1960s and 1970s changed the prevailing conception of oral language acquisition, the evidence gathered over the past decade has caused theoreticians and researchers to change their ways of conceptualizing literacy development in early childhood. Young children's literacy development, like oral language development, can be described as a process of "guided reinvention" (Lock, 1980).

Our own investigations of early childhood literacy acquisition have focused on English-Spanish-speaking children, from infancy through age 7, in homes and schools in the United States. This chapter addresses the roles that access and mediation play in the emergent literacy of young children. The discussion is based primarily upon our studies of children's storybook reading, but also includes findings from other investigators' research on young children's reading and writing.

II. PRESCHOOLERS' HOME LITERACY ENVIRONMENTS

The backdrop for our research on young children's storybook reading is provided by a series of observational studies of home literacy environments. Heath's ethnography of communication in two working-class communities (one white, one black) and one mainstream community in the Piedmont, Carolinas, showed reading and writing to be intimately connected with the histories and current day-to-day lives of the members of each community (Heath, 1983). Taylor (1983) studied the family literacy of six white, middle-class families in suburban towns around New York City, also observing that reading and writing were used "to solve practical problems and to maintain social relations." The research of Teale and his colleagues focused on the literacy occurring in the lives of 24 low-income Anglo, Black and Mexican American children in the San Diego, California area (Teale, 1986). Findings from naturalistic observations reflected the results of Heath and Taylor: reading and writing functioned not as isolated events but as components of the social activity of the adults and children. In sum these studies indicated that literacy is embedded in the culture of the family and community.

The conclusion that literacy functions primarily as an aspect of human activity (rather than a set of isolated skills) has influenced our research in several ways. First it indicates that development of the mental operations involved in reading and writing cannot be fully understood without also understanding the contexts in which literacy is experienced. Analyses of these contexts show that literacy serves a variety of functions, and that the different functions and uses of literacy tend to be associated with different types of texts and information (Heath, 1983; Teale, 1986). For example, Teale reported that literacy connected with activities labeled Daily Living Routines (the recurrent practices of everyday life, e.g., obtaining food and maintaining shelter) tended to involve materials like applications, directions, advertisements, and "nontextual" materials such as labels, signs, checks, and schedules. On the other hand, texts associated with the activities Religion, Participating in Information Networks (the practice of achieving or maintaining membership in certain groups), and, for certain types of employment, Work, are often more extended pieces of narrative or expository discourse. The child's developing conceptions of, and skills in, reading and writing would be influenced, then, by the types of literacy-mediated activities which s/he had experienced. These studies have shown that children have differential access to the variety of functions and uses of literacy.

Another aspect of the child's experience—mediation—is shown by the observational studies of home literacy environments to be crucial for development. Unlike the basic concepts of intelligence (e.g., Piaget's conservation), literacy is not a universal that is achieved spontaneously. Rather, literacy is, in Feldman's (1980) terms, a cultural achievement. As such it requires "some form of instruction," or mediation, by a literate person. Typically, literacy is mediated for a child by the parent, and the nature of the mediation can differ across cultural groups, with pronounced effects upon the young child's literacy learning (Heath, 1982, 1983, 1986).

Thus, recent ethnographic studies of young children's home literacy environments have highlighted the importance of the twin issues of access and mediation for literacy development in early childhood. The significance of these factors is predicted by Vygotsky's theory of development (Vygotsky, 1978, 1981). For Vygotsky the foundations of cognition are social in nature. He proposed that individuals' higher psychological processes (such as reading and writing) were reflections of social processes in which they participated at earlier points in their development. Cultural routines—what is done in the way of literacy activities and how adults serve to mediate the activities for children—will, then, directly determine the young child's developing conceptions of and strategies for reading and writing.

III. ACCESS, MEDIATION, AND STORYBOOK READING

Within the relatively literate society of the United States where our work has been conducted, storybook reading has become an activity that organizes literacy experience in a way beneficial to young children's literacy learning. Although storybook reading could mean a child reading to himself or herself, it is meant here as a shorthand term to stand for occasions during which an adult reads to a child who is not yet reading conventionally (i.e. by him or herself). Storybook reading is a cultural practice: (1) it has evolved culturally and (2) it is a recurrent, goal-directed activity constructed and maintained by particular groups of human beings. Furthermore, the practice in America is normally conducted with materials written specifically for young children.

A. Access

It was suggested earlier that a child may have access to literacy without having literacy mediated for him or her. In theory it is also possible to have access to storybook reading without any mediation, though anecdotal evidence suggests that such cases are relatively rare. There may, for example, be children's books available in the home but no regular storybook reading activity. We have observed (and had reported to us) instances of homes that contain considerable numbers of children's books, but in which the parents do not read to the children. Children in such situations would have access to the materials of storybook reading but not to the activity itself. Also, one child could have the opportunity to observe another child being read to, but not be read to himself or herself. In homes where storybook reading is a cultural practice there has yet to be reported a documented observation of a case in which, by the time the children reach school age, one child in the family has been read to but another has not. However, there is certainly evidence that siblings have different amounts of experience in being read to. In general, though, the issue of access to storybook reading implies, in reality, participation in storybook reading. But what does access to storybook reading provide?

Three decades of research results have clearly established that early childhood experience in being read to is positively correlated with reading readiness and reading achievement in school (Burroughs, 1972; Durkin, 1974-75; Fodor, 1966; Irwin, 1960; Moon & Wells, 1979). Wells' (1982, 1985) most recent work showed that for the children in the Bristol Language Development Project, of the most frequently occurring preschool literacy activities, only listening to storybook readings was significantly associated with reading achievement in school. Wells argued that connections between storybook reading and reading achievement are causal as well as correlational. Other researchers have also documented connections between being read to and becoming literate (Feitelson, this volume; Snow & Goldfield, 1983; Teale, 1984). Thus, although control led experimental studies on the effects of parent-child storybook reading have yet to be performed, there is considerable evidence that the activity is intimately associated with growth in literacy acquisition. Furthermore, children in different social and cultural groups in a wide variety of countries have differing degrees of access to storybook reading.

Children who are read to tend to develop concepts about books and reading more readily. For example, they understand directionality in reading, they have learned that the print not the picture contains the story that is being read, they are able to locate a word, and so forth. Children who are read to also exhibit independent preconventional reading behaviors. These behaviors, or independent reenactments, have been shown to play an integral part of the process of learning to read (Holdaway, 1979; Sulzby, 1985).

Sulzby (1983, 1985) found that when children aged 2-6 years old were asked to "read" a favorite storybook, they produced speech that could be categorized first as being an act of reading; that is, the speech was clearly differentiated prosodically, syntactically, and topically from the child's conversation surrounding the reading event. Second, these reading attempts could be placed into 11 subcategories in a classification scheme for emergent reading of favorite storybooks.

This scheme appeared to have developmental properties. There was a cross-sectional progression from younger to older children, with no 2-year-old attending to print as the source to be read from and many 5- and most 6-year-olds treating the print as the source of the story. The intermediate levels on the scale demonstrated the children's growing ability to distinguish between oral and written language. When data from these independent reenactments were analyzed longitudinally, developmental trends were evidenced, with individual children moving from (1) strategies of labeling and commenting on items in discrete pictures, to (2) weaving an oral recount over the pictures in order, to (3) creating a story with the prosody and wording of written language, to (4) the beginning to attend to, and finally decoding, the actual printed story. These reading attempts were dependent upon access. They were only produced from favorite storybooks, i.e. storybooks that had been read repeatedly to the children.

B. Mediation

Access to storybook readings, however, is not a simple issue. Family storybook reading is a socially created activity: situations in which there is access are normally accompanied by mediation. As a result a book read by the same parent-child pair can change over time, or the same book may be read differently in different families. The role of adult mediation therefore needs further examination because of its importance to literacy acquisition.

A parallel can be drawn to Wells' work on language acquisition (Wells, 1981). Acknowledging that young children's language learning is affected to some degree by sheer quantity of parent-child interaction, Wells detailed what he found to be important qualitative aspects of parent-child conversations. Some of these aspects—for example, modifying one's speech and making "rich interpretations"—were evidenced in all of the parents in his sample. But other strategies like checking and adopting the child's perspective so that the child's intended meaning could be extended, were accomplished differentially across parents. This led Wells to conclude that some parents were more effective than others in their role as a developer of the child's language. For storybook reading this implies that the effects of being read to are not merely a present/absent, or quantitative, issue. How the parent reads to the child— the ways in which the literate text is mediated for the child—is of great importance.

Research of the past decade has provided a number of detailed descriptions of the language and social interactional features of home storybook reading (e.g., Crago & Crago, 1983; Heath, 1982; Teale, 1984) and of storybook readings in classroom settings (Green & Harker, 1982; Dunning & Mason, 1984; Teale & Martinez, 1986). It is clear from these descriptions that there is considerable variation in the ways different adults mediate storybooks for the children they are reading to. Studies by Ninio (1980) and Heath (1982) suggest, furthermore, that some forms of mediation have more positive effects on children's vocabulary development and school achievement than do other forms of mediation. Examining vocabulary acquisition in the context of joint picture book reading for high-SES versus low-SES mother-infant dyads in Israel, Ninio (1980) found relationships between dyadic interaction styles and language development. During the readings, low-SES mothers were less skilled in eliciting words from their children. The "eliciting style" of reading (mother asks "what" questions; new information is provided in form of feedback utterances) used, predominantly by high-SES mothers, was positively associated with the development of productive vocabulary.

Heath's study of storybook reading was part of her ethnography of communication in Roadville, Trackton, and Maintown that was described earlier. Although Trackton parents did not read to their children (a case of no access), both Roadville and Maintown parents did. On the other hand, while mainstream Maintown parents immersed their children in book reading routines that helped the children learn the basic concepts of reading *and* linked book knowledge and experiences to other contexts in the children's lives, Roadville parents tended *not* to extend the information or skills of book reading beyond its original context. Heath concluded that this pattern of literacy socialization was linked to the children's future school achievement. Children from Roadville and Maintown both tended to do well in the early stages of reading in school. But once children reached the upper elementary school, and the curriculum proceeded beyond the basics of decoding and sight word recognition to higher-level comprehension skills, the achievement levels of Roadville children fell significantly behind those from mainstream families.

Heath's work suggests that it is not merely the presence or absence of storybook reading that affects the child's literacy development; both the Maintown and Roadville families read to their children. The ways in which Maintown parents actually mediated the book for their children—the language and social interaction surrounding the text —had a profound impact on the children's ultimate attainment of literacy.

Mediation by a novice storybook reader.

Other research by Heath (Heath & Thomas, 1984) serves as an interesting case study of the mediation of storybooks for a young child and also extends beyond the laboratory setting Ninio's (1980) findings concerning the differential success of various book reading styles. Subsequent to her studies in the Carolinas, Heath worked in a teacher-researcher relationship with a high school English teacher, Amanda Branscombe, in the deep South of the United States. One of the students in Branscombe's class, Charlene Thomas, a 16-year-old who had a 1-year-old son named De, dropped out of school 2 months into the academic year because she was expecting a second child. Charlene came from a community in which language and literacy patterns were much like those of Trackton: there was no cultural practice of storybook reading and adults "did not consciously model, demonstrate, or tutor reading and writing for their children" (Heath & Thomas, 1984, p. 53). In an effort to keep Charlene in touch with schooling, improve her literacy skills, and encourage her to obtain a high school diploma through night school, Heath and Branscombe attempted to maintain her involvement with the types of language and literacy activities that had been going on in the English classroom. Eventually they asked Charlene to read to De 10 minutes per day and tape-record the readings. In this respect access to storybook reading had been created for De. Heath's analyses of these readings provide a fascinating real-world example of the development of mediation strategies by the mother and the effects of storybook reading, in this case on the literacy of both mother and child.

In the initial sessions (when De was approximately 1 year, 8 months old) Charlene held books on her lap but did not talk about them. "Instead she asked De to name objects in the room and to call members of the family." Within two months the following routine had evolved:

> [The mother] began the reading by focusing on the objects in the alphabet book and saying, "Say___" After only several such directives, the requests shifted to people and objects. "Say mama, say daddy." After each request, she waited for De to repeat. Often he made no response; on other occasions he repeated the name, and at other times, his repetitions were indistinct in pronunciation but dearly imitative in rhythm and intonation. (Heath & Thomas, 1984, p. 59)

The mother often focused far less than a minute on the items in the book, moving instead to having the child label objects and persons in the environment. As Heath points out, "during the initial weeks of trying to read with De, [the mother] . . . seemed to equate reading with saying the names of things" (Heath & Thomas, 1984, p. 60).

Transcripts from readings 3 weeks later show that the mother still employed the "Say____" strategy with De when reading alphabet books. With stories she frequently stopped reading the text to focus on objects in the pictures, ask for repetitions, and make topic comments. Over the next 3 months the mother continued to read to De. Heath notes that although the pattern of their reading interactions never did approximate that of the mainstream parents (e.g. the content of books was not extended to real life) there were no extended dyadic conversations, Charlene had begun to use numerous literacy socialization strategies (knowing when and where to read with De, how to hold De and the book, how to focus De's attention, and others).

De went from no access to storybook reading to some access to storybook reading. The mediation that took place in the storybook reading was, however, not so effective as it might have been at helping the child develop the appropriate concepts of, and skills in, reading necessary for school success. At first the mother provided mediation that was tentative and reflective of her lack of experience with the activity. She and De developed in their storybook reading to the point where there were many positive features of the interaction. However, as Heath points out, the mother "will continue to need occasions for talking about what she and De have learned from their jointly achieved literacy, and she will need opportunities to see that this literacy can extend to institutions outside her home" (Heath & Thomas, 1984, p. 69).

Mediation for the transition from interactive to independent functioning.

As a contrast to the interactions of Charlene and De around storybooks, let us examine storybook reading for another mother-child dyad, Joyce and Hannah, in which the mother mediates books in a way that is likely to foster the child's easy transition into literacy. Hannah was the focal child in one of eight families observed for our longitudinal study of the language and social interaction of home storybook reading (Sulzby & Teale, 1987). In this study the parent audiotape-recorded one storybook reading session approximately every 4 weeks. As soon as possible after the recording a researcher reviewed the tape with the parent, asking the parent to interpret speech and behaviors and to indicate nonverbal actions that had occurred.

During the first month that Hannah was in the study, her mother read her *Counting* (Federico, 1969). The book had a distinctive pattern of a two-page spread for each numeral, 1 through 10. On the left page were the numeral and the number word, as well as a listing of items pictured on the right page. The right page contained an array of different items, with each item being represented according to the number displayed on the page (e.g., 3 buttons, 3 telephones, 3 trees, and so forth). All of these pictured items were contained within a large representation of the numeral.

At the time of the first recorded reading of this book, 31 December, 1983, Hannah was 1 year and 8 months old. The excerpt contained in Transcript 1 represents the character of the language and social interaction of this reading. A pattern was clearly visible in the interaction. First, the reading was a dialogically achieved one, much like the routine described by Ninio (1980). The mother (1) draws the child's attention to the item to be identified (001: M points to numeral 1) and (2) requests the label for the item (001: " . . . what's that?"). The child then (3) provides the label (or the mother supplies it if the child cannot), and finally (4) the mother gives feedback on the child's contribution (020-021: "Pinwheels. That's right."). Thus, the mother played a key role in mediating the book for the child.

001 M:	OK COCONUT, WHAT'S THAT? [pointing to numeral 1 on left page]
002 H:	/dʌ/
003 M:	ONE (thinking that H had said one and repeating it distinctly for her)
004 H:	Two. (picking up with the counting intonation, 1, 2 from M's previous utterance)
005 M:	NO, IS THIS [pointing to 1] a 1?
006 H:	One?
007 M:	ONE.
008	OKAY, WHAT'S THAT RIGHT THERE? [pointing to picture of lion]
009 H:	/tʊ:/
010 M:	WAIT A MINUTE.
011:	WHAT IS THAT?
012 H:	/mayn, layn/
013 M:	LI:ON.
014:	OKAY.
	[turning to pp. 3-4]
015:	WHAT'S THIS? [pointing to numeral 2]
016 H:	TWO.
017 M:	TWO.
018:	WHAT DO YOU SEE ON THIS PAGE? [pointing to bottom of p. 4]
019 H:	/dþ wiː wol/ [pointing to pinwheels]
020 M:	PINWHEELS, THAT'S RIGHT.
021 M:	AND WHAT IS THIS RIGHT HERE? [pointing to pumpkins]
022 H:	Punkins.
023 M:	PUMPKINS?
024	AND WHAT ARE THESE UP HERE? [pointing to kittens]
025 H:	Boats,
026:	Kitty,

027 M: WHA . . .
028   YEAH, KITTIES.
029 H: Boats
030 M: AN . . .
031   AND WHAT'S THIS RIGHT HERE? [pointing to turkey]
032 H: /kɪti/
033 M: TURKEY?
034 H: Turkey.
035 M: OKAY, DO YOU KNOW HOW MANY THERE ARE?
036   LET'S SEE IF WE CAN COUNT THEM.
          [M takes H's hand and points]
037   O:NE, TWO.
038   CAN YOU COUNT?
039 H: (softly) Two.
040 M: SAY, "ONE".
041 H: One.
042 M: TWO.
043 H: /tri/
044 M: NO, SAY, "TWO."
045 H: Two.
046 M: O-KAY.
047:      SAY, "O-NE."
048 H: One, /du/,   ⎰ /bʌ/
049 M: ⎱ GO:OD
050   NOW, LET'S COUNT THE PUPS.
051:      CAN YOU COUNT THE PUPS?

Transcript 1. Hannah and Mother reading *Counting Book* (31 December 1983)

The eliciting pattern was embedded within a larger framework for reading the book. In approaching the two-page spread for each numeral in the book the following tasks were interactionally accomplished: (a) identify the numeral on the left page, (b) identify the items pictured on the right page, and (c) count some or all of the items in each section of the numeral on the right page. Sometimes (b) and (c) alternated for each group of items pictured within the numeral, but consistently these three tasks were accomplished. Tasks (a) and (c) were usually played out through the eliciting pattern.

Note also that the reading of the book was selective. Some features of the graphic display were constantly ignored, such as the printed list of the items on the left page. Hannah and Joyce's reading of other books also exhibited selective use of the print. When reading a particularly complex book of fairy tales, for example, the mother would modify the language of the text considerably to create a story that would not lose Hannah's attention. In other books, parts of the text that were not critical to the story line were left out. As Hannah got older, and capable of attention to longer and more complex texts, the print would actually be read in its entirety. Thus, though Hannah and her mother's readings were truly an interactional accomplishment, the mother played a critical role in determining what, and in what manner, particular features were focused upon.

In the second recorded reading for this book, from March 1984, when Hannah was 1 year and 11 months old, the dialogic character of the reading was still present even in the beginning of the transcript, but at that point Hannah accomplished much more reading by herself and actually "short circuited" some of what previously would have taken place in exchanges between her and her mother. For instance, in utterances 008 and 009 she both requested a label and provided it. In utterances 011-015 she labeled five items without her mother's having to request each label. Her mother still provided certain parts of the routine (e.g. feedback in 016, 018, and 020) even when Hannah "read on her own." From utterance 022 on, the language and social interactional features of the episode closely resembled those of the December 1983 reading, but with Hannah still taking over more of what had previously been accomplished interactionally (see, for e.g., utterances 047-054).

001	H:	*Counting, Counting Book.*
		[Hannah has picked up *The Counting Book*]
002	M:	OH, YOUR *Counting Book*, now?
003		O.K.
004	H:	Hannah read it.
005	M:	OH, HANNAH READ IT.
006		O.K., HANNAH CAN READ IT. .
007	H:	[inaudible]
008		What's that?
009		One. [pointing to the numeral 1]
010	M:	ONE.
011	H:	Worm, [pointing to each item as she labels].
012		Lady bug,
013		L-Lion,
014		Safety Pin,
015	H:	Pencil,
016	M:	UH-HMM.
017	H:	Bus,
018	M:	VERY GOOD.
019	H:	Worm.
020	M:	VERY GOOD!
		[Hannah turns page]

021 H:	What's this . . . what's this, Mommy? [pointing to numeral 2]
022 M:	YOU TELL ME.
023	WHAT COMES AFTER ONE?
024 H:	Three.
025 M:	NO, NOT THREE.
026	WHAT COMES AFTER ONE?
027 H:	Hmm.
028 M:	ONE . . . (intonation suggests the beginning of a counting sequence)
029 H:	/t/ -
030 M:	THAT'S RIGHT!
031 H:	Two.
032 M:	GOOD.
033	VERY GOOD, HANNAH. (clapping)
34 H:	[inaudible]
035 M:	SO WHAT NUMBER IS THIS? [pointing to 2]
036 H:	That's a one.
037 M:	NO, THAT'S NOT A ONE.
038	WHAT COMES AFTER ONE?
039	WHAT NUMBER?
040 H:	Three.
041 M:	NO.
042	WHAT COMES AFTER ONE?
043	YOU SAID IT JUST A MINUTE AGO.
044	ONE . . . (counting intonation)
045 H:	Three.
046	Two.
047 M:	TWO.
048	THAT'S A TWO.
049 H:	That's two.
050	Five kitties, [pointing to each item as she labels]
051	Five boats,
052	Kitty,
053	Boats,
054	Five boats
055	Five turkeys,
056	Five pin wheel.
058 M:	NO, THOSE AREN'T FIVE.
059	THEY'RE TWO.

Transcript 2. Hannah and Mother reading *Counting Book* (March 1984)

In a third reading of the *Counting Book*, May 1984 (not reproduced here), Hannah continued the pattern of change evidenced from
December to March: (1) she accomplished the labeling of the pictures
much more independently and (2) she spent even more time at the
beginning of the reading trying to reverse roles with her mother, thereby exhibiting more control over the activity.

A fortuitous data collection from August 1984 (Hannah was 2
years and 4 months old) revealed the dramatic effects of the mother's
mediation of the text, and emphasized the shift that was taking place,
from interpsychological to intrapsychological functioning. Hannah was
given a doll by her grandfather. She named the doll Judy and that
afternoon propped Judy up to read her the *Counting Book*. Transcript 3
contains an excerpt from the tape.

005 H: (three unintelligible syllables) Ready? What's dat? [pointing to
         numeral 1]. (waits two seconds for Judy to answer) One? What's
         that? [pointing to picture of ladybug] This. [points again to same
         picture]
         What's that? (waits two seconds) Ladybug?

. . . .

012 H: [returning her attention to Judy] Ladybug? Okay. [pointing to lion]
         That's a lion. And what's dat? [pointing to pencil] Pencil and Safety
         pin? [turns page] Okay. And what number's dis? [pointing to 2]
         (waits one second) Two. What's dat?
013 M: HMM? THAT'S A TWO. (M interpreted the question as being directed
         to her, not because H didn't know the answer but because H was
         trying to involve her, M, in the reading. Therefore, M answered.)
014 H: Wh . . What's that? Two? What's that? [points to the appropriate
         picture as she labels each of the following items] /jæ-o-læncrnz/
         (jack-o-lanterns) and the cups and the . . . the pinwheels and cats
         an . . . and ships an' . . . an' turkeys . . . [turns page]

**Transcript 3. Hannah reading *Counting Book* to her doll (Independent
Reenactment, August, 11, 1984)**

The language and social interaction of the activity of reading
the *Counting Book* had become internalized to the point that Hannah
was able to conduct the activity independently. In this case she supplied both parts of the dialogue. The transcript represents a spontaneous instance (with a non-story text) of the researcher-induced emer-

gent readings of favorite storybooks described by Sulzby (1985), and also serves as evidence of the importance of the adult's mediation of the text: Hannah reproduced not the text itself, but the speech that was created by her mother and herself as the storybook reading.

The final reading of the *Counting Book*, tape-recorded November 1984 (when Hannah was 2 years and 7 months), showed further evidence of the importance of parent mediation in storybook reading. The initial segment of the reading saw Hannah accomplishing most of the task independently. The mother "nudged" Hannah three times (002, 004, 012) and gave positive evaluation feedback twice (011 and 016), but the remainder of the first 20 utterances consisted of Hannah's unassisted labeling of the items. Utterance 021 marked a significant turning point, one that was characteristic of the remainder of the reading. In earlier readings it was sufficient for Hannah to label and count the items. In this reading the mother "raised the ante" by, for example, requesting that Hannah also identify a characteristic of turkeys (023), extending the concept of boat with the discussion of the word *ship* (026-032) and later in the transcript having Hannah identify the colors of various objects. The mother also responded positively to Hannah's spontaneous linking of certain pictured objects with people in her world ("That one's daddy's car, that one's grandma's car . . ."). In these ways the mother initiated explorations of additional concepts, extended other concepts, and reinforced and encouraged Hannah's extensions of the text.

001 M: Okay, we're gonna read the *Counting Book*.
002:    Let's see if you can count.
        [opens to pp. 1-2 of book and points to numeral 1 on p. 1]
003:    One.
004 M: ONE . . . (rising intonation, waiting for H to continue)
005 H: [pauses 2 seconds, then begins pointing to objects] Ladybug.
006:    Lion.
007   Worm.
008:    A bus.
009:    Safety pin.
010:    A pencil.
011 M: VERY GO-O-OD!
        [turns page]
012:    OKAY. (uttered with an intonation indicating that H should continue)
        [points to numeral 2]
013 H: Two.
014:    [points to objects] A cat.
015:    And jack-o-lantern.
016 M: UH-HUH. (yes)

017 H: And cups.
018:     An . . . and pinwheels.
019:     Boats.
         [2 second pause]
020:     And . . . turkeys!
021 M: WHAT DO TURKEYS SAY?
022 H: What. (not said with question intonation)
023 M: WHAT DO TURKEYS SAY?
024 H: Gobble, gobble, gobble.
025 M: THAT'S RIGHT!
026 M: AND YOU KNOW, THOSE [pointing to boats], ARE GREAT BIG
         BOATS.
027:     AND YOU KNOW WHAT GREAT BIG BOATS ⎰ ARE KNOWN AS?
028 H: ⎱ Yes.
029 M: THEIR NAME ARE *ships*.
030 H: Oh, ships.
031 M: UH-HMM. (yes)
032 M: WHEN YOU SEE GREAT BIG BOATS, THEY'RE CALLED SHIPS.

Transcript 4. Hannah and Mother; Hannah reading *Counting Book* to her doll (8 November 1984)

We have been able, then, to identify characteristic patterns in the mother's mediation of the *Counting Book*. As the transcripts are examined over time there is evidence that Hannah has internalized many aspects of the interactional pattern and that, as she does so, new features become part of the interaction. The way in which Joyce mediated the *Counting Book* for Hannah serves as an example of Vygotsky's notion that teaching should always be in advance of development (Vygotsky, 1978). Joyce and Hannah engaged a mutually constitutive process, reading the *Counting Book*, but as Hannah demonstrated that she was gaining more and more control over the task, Joyce led her on to more sophisticated and elaborated readings. What Joyce and Hannah did in interaction strongly affected Hannah's subsequent strategies for, and attitudes toward dealing with, the *Counting Book* in particular and books in general.

There is one additional point to be made about Hannah's development that relates to her independent reenactment of the *Counting Book*. In her rereading Hannah engaged in labeling and commenting on items in the pictures. This strategy is representative of the lowest point on Sulzby's (1985) Classification Scheme for Emergent Reading of Favorite Storybooks, even though the *Counting Book* is not a *storybook*. As such, it may appear we have dwelt at too great length on a process that has relatively little payoff for Hannah's learning. However, it is critically important to keep in mind that the labeling and commenting is exactly the strategy Hannah's mother had used with her in interaction, and is common for 2-year-old children.

Hannah also produced spontaneous reenactments of storybooks. For example, the book *Are You My Mother?* (Eastman, 1960) was introduced into the home by the researchers. Joyce and Hannah engaged in repeated readings of the book, and at age 2 years, 10 months, Hannah read the book independently from cover to cover. Such behaviors increase the likelihood of Hannah's attending to print with appropriate literate expectations.

Hannah's sophistication with books has grown steadily over the more than 2 years of observation, and she is predictive of an easy transition into conventional literacy and school reading and writing instruction. In comparison, the slice of De's storybook reading that is presented by Heath looks as if it will not have a similar effect. The mediation patterns in the two families are quite different. Studies like those of Heath (1982) and Ninio (1980) suggest that more research work on the nature and significance of the language and social interaction of parent-child storybook reading continues. Access to storybook reading is a vitally important step: children who are not read to are less likely to learn to read easily and fluently than are children who are read to. But mediation—what actually goes on, what actually gets talked about in the interaction between parent and child—holds the key to the effects of storybook reading on children's acquisition of literacy.

IV. CONCLUSIONS

Literacy is a cultural practice. We have attempted to study the acquisition of literacy by examining one aspect of early childhood literacy experience: storybook reading. Recent research has led to a conceptualization of the first few years of life as a time when important literacy knowledge and skills are developed. The process of becoming literate is accomplished through the child's active construction, construction that internalizes social interaction and construction based on independent exploration of written language. Although storybook reading is most often an activity not engaged in for the express purpose of deliberately teaching young children to read, it plays a key role in the process of becoming literate.

Like literacy itself, storybook reading is also a cultural practice. As with any cultural practice, two general questions are of significance in the issue of learning: who engages in the practice (and who does not), and how is the practice actually accomplished? Who actually engages in storybook reading is important because, as correlational research indicates, being read to facilitates a child's learning to read. Storybook reading enables children to experience the reading act, and to perform before they are fully competent. Performance leads to the independent practice of reading through reenactments of familiar books, readings which mirror the parent child interaction of storybook reading but which are also creative in the sense that children are reading in a new, inventive way, nor merely mimicking or imitating interaction. Such reenactments play a significant role in literacy acquisition. Thus it is clear that access to (i.e. participation in) storybook reading is facilitative to literacy acquisition. But equally important is that the nature of parent-child interaction in storybook reading episodes has significant effects on children's knowledge about, strategies for, and attitudes toward reading. It is this issue which researchers have only begun to explore and which, because of its potential significance for helping parents and educators understand how to maximize the likelihood for children's transition into literacy, deserves increased attention in future studies.

ACKNOWLEDGEMENTS

Parts of this chapter were presented in a paper given at the 1986 American Education Research Association Annual Meeting, San Francisco. The research reported on in this chapter was supported by a grant from The Spencer Foundation.

REFERENCES

Brown, R. (1973). *A first language: The early stages*. Cambridge, MA: Harvard University Press.

Burroughs, M. (1972). *The stimulation of verbal behavior in culturally disadvantaged three-year-olds*. Unpublished doctoral dissertation, Michigan State University.

Clark, R. (1983). *Family life and school achievement*. Chicago: University of Chicago Press.

Crago, M., & Crago, H. (1983). *Prelude to literacy: A preschool child's encounter with picture and story*. Carbondale: Southern Illinois University Press.

Dunning, D., & Mason, J. (1984, November). *An investigation of kindergarten children's expressions of story characters' imitations*. Paper presented at the 34th Annual Meeting of the National Reading Conference, St. Petersburg, FL.

Eastman, P.D. (1960). *Are you my mother?* New York: Random House.

Federico, H. (1969). *Counting.* New York: Western Publishing Company.

Feitelson, D., & Goldstein, Z. (1986). Patterns of book ownership and reading to young children in Israeli school-oriented and non-school-oriented families. *The Reading Teacher, 39,* 924-933.

Feldman, D.H. (1980). *Beyond universals in cognitive development.* Norwood, NJ: Ablex.

Ferreiro, E., & Teberosky, A. (1982). *Literacy before schooling.* Exeter, NH: Heinemann.

Fodor, M. (1966). *The effect of systematic reading of stories on the language development of culturally deprived children.* Unpublished doctoral dissertation, Cornell University.

Goodman, Y.M. (1980). The roots of literacy. In M. P. Douglass (Ed.), *Claremont Reading Conference Forty-fourth Yearbook.* Claremont, CA: Claremont Reading Conference.

Green, J.L., & Harker, J.O. (1982). Reading to children: A communicative process. In J.A. Langer & M. T. Smith-Burke (Eds.), *Reader meets author/bridging the gap: A psycholinguistic and sociolinguistic perspective* (pp. 196-221). Newark, DE: International Reading Association.

Harste, J. C., Woodward, V.A., & Burke, C.L. (1984). *Language stories and literacy lessons* Portsmouth, NH: Heinemann.

Heath, S.B. (1982). What no bedtime story means: Narrative skills at home and school. *Language in Society, 11,* 49-76.

Heath, S.B. (1983). *Ways with words: Language, life and work in communities and classrooms.* Cambridge, MA: Cambridge University Press.

Heath, S.B. (1986). Separating "things of the imagination" from life: Learning to read and write. In W.H. Teale & E. Sulzby (Eds.), *Emergent literacy: Writing and reading.* Norwood, NJ: Ablex.

Heath, S.B., & Thomas, C. (1984). The achievement of preschool literacy for mother and child. In H. Goelman, A. Oberg, & F. Smith (Eds.), *Awakening to literacy.* Exeter, NH: Heinemann.

Holdaway, D. (1979). *The foundations of literacy.* Sydney: Ashton Scholastic.

Irwin, O. (1960). Infant speech: Effect of systematic reading of stories. *Journal of Speech and Hearing Research, 3,* 187-190.

Lock, A. (1980). *The guided reinvention of language.* London: Academic Press.

Moon, C., & Wells, C.G. (1979). The influence of the home on learning to read. *Journal of Research in Reading, 2,* 53-62.

Ninio, A. (1980). Picture-book reading in mother-infant dyads belonging to two subgroups in Israel. *Child Development, 51,* 587-590.

Scollon, R., & Scollon, S. B. K. (1981). *Narrative, literacy, and face in interethnic communications.* Norwood, NJ: Ablex.

Snow, C.E., & Goldfield, B.A. (1983). Turn the page, please: Situation-specific language acquisition. *Journal of Child Language, 10,* 535-549.

Snow, C., & Ninio, A. (1986). The contracts of literacy: What children learn from learning to read books. In W. H. Teale & E. Sulzby (Eds.), *Emergent literacy: Writing and reading*. Norwood, NJ: Ablex.

Sulzby, E. (1983). *Children's emergent abilities to read favorite storybooks* [Final report to The Spencer Foundation]. Evanston, IL: Northwestern University.

Sulzby, E. (1985). Children's emergent reading of favorite storybooks: A developmental study. *Reading Research Quarterly, 20*, 458-481.

Sulzby, E., & Teale, W.H. (1987). *Young children's storybook reading: Longitudinal study of parent-child interaction and children's independent functioning* [Final Report to the Spencer Foundation]. Ann Arbor: University of Michigan.

Sulzby, E. (1986). Writing and reading: Signs of oral and written language organization in the young child. In W.H. Teale & E. Sulzby (Eds.), *Emergent literacy: Writing and reading*. Norwood, NJ: Ablex.

Taylor, D. (1983). *Family literacy: Young children learning to read and write*. Exeter, NH: Heinemann.

Teale, W.H. (1982). Toward a theory of how children learn to read and write naturally. *Language Arts, 59*, 555-570.

Teale, W.H. (1984, November). *Learning to comprehend written language*. Paper presented at The National Council of Teachers of English 74th Annual Convention, Detroit, MI.

Teale, W.H. (1986). Home background and young children's literacy development. In W.H. Teale & E. Sulzby (Eds.), *Emergent literacy: Writing and reading*. Norwood, NJ: Ablex.

Teale, W.H., & Martinez, M. (1986). Teachers' storybook reading styles: Evidence and implications. *Reading Education in Texas, 2*.

Teale, W. H., & Sulzby, E. (1986). Emergent literacy as a perspective for examining how young children become writers and readers. In W.H. Teale & E. Sulzby (Eds.), *Emergent literacy: Writing and reading*. Norwood, NJ: Ablex.

Vygotsky, L.S. (1978). *Mind in society*. Cambridge, MA: Harvard University Press.

Vygotsky, L.S. (1981). The genesis of higher mental functions. In J.V. Wertsch (Ed.), *The concept of activity in Soviet psychology*. White Plains, NY: M. E. Sharpe.

Wells, G. (1981). *Learning through interaction: The study of language development*. Cambridge, MA: Cambridge University Press.

Wells, G. (1982). Story reading and the development of symbolic skills. *Australian Journal of Reading, 5*, 142-152.

Wells, G. (1985). Preschool literacy-related activities and success in school. In D.R. Olson, N. Torrance, & A. Hildyard (Eds.), *Literacy, language, and learning: The nature and consequences of reading and writing*. Cambridge, MA: Cambridge University Press.

10

Children's Problems in Learning to Read Chinese, Japanese, and English

Harold Stevenson
The University of Michigan

I. INTRODUCTION

Chinese, Japanese and English are written with three of the world's most diverse writing systems. Children learning to read these scripts would appear, therefore, to face very different types of problems. Written Chinese uses logographs (characters), hundreds and then thousands of which must be memorized singly and in combination. Written Japanese also uses Chinese logographs, but the reader of Japanese is required, in addition, to learn two syllabaries (symbols representing syllables). The alphabet of written English has no parallel in written Chinese or Japanese.

It is of interest, therefore, to compare the progress made, and the problems encountered, by young children who are learning to read these writing systems. Although much has been written about learning to read the writing systems used for different languages (e.g., Taylor & Taylor, 1983), little comparative research has been reported. The major obstacle to such research has been the lack of comparable reading materials in the different languages. When conclusions are reached, therefore, they are derived primarily from efforts to create conditions in one writing system that simulate those found in the other languages of interest. For example, English-speaking children have been asked to pair English words with Chinese characters (i.e. Rozin, Poritsky, & Sotsky, 1971) in an effort to see whether they could learn to read English pronunciations of characters more effectively than words written in an alphabet. Or words have been represented by drawings depicting syllables to create an English version of a syllabary to assess the ease with which children could learn to read this mode of representation of words (Rozin & Gleitman, 1974). The results of such studies give us little insight into the problems children face in their everyday efforts to learn to read.

Why should there be interest among readers of English in studying how children learn to read different writing systems? The answer is straightforward. To the degree that there are unique problems in learning to read a particular writing system, arguments can be made for attributing reading difficulties to the writing system and for attempting to modify the writing system to eliminate these problems. Such arguments have been suggested by numerous writers (see Kavanagh & Venezky, 1980).

This chapter is divided into two sections. The first section describes the reading scores of Chinese, Japanese and American children on a reading test developed especially for this research. The level of difficulty of the material is held constant by grade level in the Chinese, Japanese and American versions of the test. Comparisons are made of the performance of kindergarten, first- and fifth-graders to determine whether children learning to read make more rapid progress with one writing system than with another. These data help in evaluating the validity of the twin arguments that the holistic and distinctive nature of Chinese characters, and the perfect symbol-sound correspondence of the Japanese syllabary, result in more effective reading skills than does the use of an alphabet with irregular symbol-sound correspondence such as is used in English. To the degree that there is similar progress in learning to read with the three writing systems, the importance of the writing system as a source of problems for children is decreased. A second approach to exploring children's reading problems is discussed in the second section of the paper. Mothers and teachers of elementary school children in the three countries were asked to discuss problems they had observed among children learning to read. When members of the three countries mention different types of problems, evidence is obtained for the importance of different processes in learning to read. For example, if Chinese and Japanese mothers and teachers mention poor memory for words as a problem in learning to read Chinese and Japanese, but this factor is never mentioned by American mothers and teachers, an argument can be made for the different role of memory in learning to read the three writing systems. Similarly, if American children are described as having problems in learning to segment words into syllables, but Chinese and Japanese children are not described as having problems in segmenting strings of characters into words, the importance of this analytic skill would appear to differ in learning to read English, Chinese, and Japanese.

II. WRITTEN CHINESE AND JAPANESE

A brief introduction to reading in Chinese and Japanese is presented in the following paragraphs for readers who are unfamiliar with these languages. Examples of written Chinese and Japanese appear in Figure 10.1.

The major tasks in learning to read Chinese are to pronounce the characters correctly and to gain meaning from the characters. In Taiwan, *zhuyin fuhao*, a phonetic spelling system, is used to assist in the pronunciation of characters. *Zhuyin fuhao* is a set of 37 symbols for which there is consistent symbol-sound correspondence. The pronunciation of all Chinese characters can be represented by from one to three of these symbols. (In the People's Republic of China, *pinyin*, an alphabetic form of writing with consistent letter-sound correspondence, is used for this purpose.) *Zhuyin fuhao* notation continues to be printed alongside all characters in the reading text for the first several years of elementary school. After that it is used primarily for teaching new characters, but no longer appears printed alongside written texts. By the end of the elementary school the children have acquired approximately 3000 characters. A character is not equivalent to a word; most Chinese words are composed of combinations of two or more characters. Thus, by the end of elementary school children know many thousands of words formed from combinations of the 3000 characters.

Japanese children are first taught *hiragana*, a set of 46 symbols, each corresponding to a distinct syllable. The symbols are increased by 25 through the use of diacritic marks to yield a total of 71 *hiragana*. All words in Japanese can be constructed from these 71 *hiragana*. Shortly after *hiragana* are introduced the children are taught a second syllabary, *katakana*. The *katakana* provide an alternative way of writing Japanese syllables, and are used most frequently for foreign words introduced into the Japanese language. In addition, children are taught *kanji*, Chinese characters, which are used singly, in combination, or in combination with *hiragana* to represent words. By the end of the second half of the grade the Japanese child is presented sentences that include all three forms of writing—*hiragana, katakana,* and *kanji*. Nearly a thousand *kanji* are taught in elementary school. Finally, all Japanese children learn the English alphabet, *romaji*, so that they can understand scientific notation and other materials that rely on the use of letters.

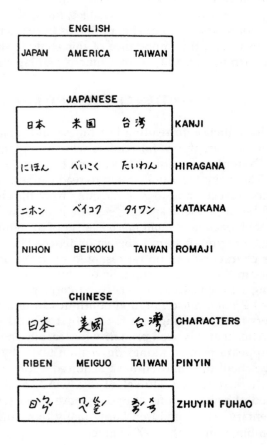

Figure 10.1. Examples of the forms of writing used in Chinese and Japanese. (the meaning of the words is written in English)

III. THE READING TEST

Before discussing the research it is necessary to describe the reading test on which the research was based. We sought to develop a test that would be administered individually to one child at a time in order to increase the test's reliability. The test contained three types of items: sight reading of vocabulary, reading of meaningful text material, and comprehension of text. Because of the close similarity in the results for all three types of items, only the results for reading vocabulary and comprehension are discussed in this chapter.

The test was developed after careful review of Chinese, Japanese and American elementary school textbooks. Two of the most popular text series in the United States and in Japan, and the single series used in Taiwan, were analyzed. All words, including transliterations into roman letters of Chinese in *pinyin* and of Japanese in *romaji*, were entered from each of the text series into the computer according to the grade and semester of the word's first appearance, the number of characters in Chinese and Japanese words, and the English translation. It turned out that the total of approximately 21,000 computer entries compiled from the three sets of textbooks was nearly evenly divided among the three languages. Analyses were also made of the time at which various grammatical forms were introduced, and of the topics discussed in the textbooks.

This information enabled us to include words, sentences and paragraphs that were comparable in difficulty and equivalent in grammatical complexity across the three languages. Items were constructed simultaneously in all three languages from the words appearing in the computer lists. This procedure insures greater comparability for all languages than the common practice of constructing items in one language and then translating them into the other languages of interest. In all cases decisions about the acceptability of items were made through group discussion by persons from each culture. Before an item was retained in the test there was a final review by professionals in each country to insure that the item was culturally appropriate and written in standard forms of the language. The test was composed of three parts arranged according to grade level:

1. *Kindergarten items.* The kindergarten test involved matching, naming and identifying letters in English (*zhuyin fuhao* in Chinese and *hiragana* in Japanese.) The choice of each letter or symbol was based on frequency counts of its appearance in first-grade readers. The number of items in the kindergarten test was increased when the test was given to kindergarten children in order to increase its reliability.

2. *Vocabulary.* Children were asked to read single, isolated words. Words were selected according to the grade and semester of their first appearance in the textbooks of the three countries. In grades one to three all words contained in the three versions of the test were common to all three languages. In grades four to six it was impossible to use words common to the three languages. Few new words are introduced at the same grade and semester levels in the textbooks of the three countries after the third grade. To insure comparability of the

three versions of the test after third grade, words were selected that were comparable to each other according to two criteria: (a) they appeared in the textbooks for the first time at the
same grade and semester, and (b) they had a similar frequency of usage as determined by reference to books containing
frequency counts of words and characters in the three languages.

3. *Reading comprehension.* Meaningful text was presented in
    clauses, sentences and paragraphs, and children were to
    respond to true-false and multiple-choice questions about
    what they read. As in the vocabulary test, words used in con-
    structing the items for the first three grade levels of the test
    were the same in all three languages, and were first intro-
    duced in the textbooks during the same grade and semester.
    From grades four to six comparable words were chosen from
    those appearing at the same grade and semester and having a
    similar frequency of usage in the three languages. Phrases or
    sentences described one of three pictures; key words omitted
    from sentences were listed; or alternative answers to questions
    about the paragraphs were read. In each case the child was to
    choose the correct answer from among the alternatives.

The test was administered individually to the elementary school children
approximately 4 months after the beginning of the fall term, and to the
kindergarten children near the middle of the winter term. The score for
each part of the test was the number of items answered correctly. Further
information about the test appears elsewhere (Stevenson et al., 1982).

IV. THE CHILDREN

The children included in the study were from public and private schools
in the metropolitan areas of Taipei (Taiwan), Sendai (Japan) and
Minneapolis. These cities were chosen because of their comparable size
and cultural characteristics within each country. Ten elementary schools
were randomly selected to represent the range of schools within each
metropolitan area. Within each school two first-grade and two fifth-
grade classrooms were randomly chosen for testing. A total of 24 kindergarten classrooms was chosen to constitute representative samples of
kindergarten classrooms in each city. Children classified as mentally
retarded were not included in the study.

The numbers and ages of the children to whom the reading test
was given appear in Table 10.1. All teachers were interviewed, but it

TABLE10.1. Mean Chronological Ages of the Children (in Years).

	USA		Taiwan		Japan	
	N	Mean	N	Mean	N	Mean
Kindergarten	288	6.1	286	5.9	280	6.1
Grade 1	410	6.8	912	6.7	789	6.8
Grade 5	453	10.9	956	10.8	775	10.9

was impossible to interview all of the mothers individually. Instead, interviews were conducted with the mothers of three boys and three girls randomly selected from each elementary school classroom, yielding a total of 240 first- and 240 fifth-grade mothers. The interview was wide-ranging, and included questions about many facets of the child's every-day experience at home and at school. Questions dealing only with read-ing will be discussed in this chapter.

V. READING SCORES

A score which is easily compared among countries and across age levels is a standard (z) score. The z-scores were computed in the following fashion. Scores on the vocabulary test for all kindergarten children were combined into a single distribution. The mean and standard deviation of this distribution were determined and a z-score for each child was com-puted. The z-scores were then recombined according to country, and the mean z-score for each of the distributions of scores was computed. This procedure was followed for the vocabulary and reading comprehension scores at each age level.

If children from all three countries performed equally well the mean z score for each country at each grade would be 0. Departures from 0 indicate the relative superiority or inferiority of the scores for the children from each country.

The results for reading vocabulary and reading comprehension are presented in Figures 10.2 and 10.3. Rather than finding marked supe-riority of any one group of children, the mean z-scores in all three coun-tries were remarkably similar at all three grade levels and clustered closely about a mean of 0. The small differences were, however, statisti-cally significant. Chinese children received significantly higher scores than the Japanese and American children on both vocabulary and com-prehension at each grade level. The American children received signifi-cantly higher scores than the Japanese children on vocabulary, $p < 0.01$.

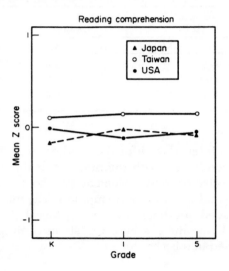

Figure 10.2. Mean reading vocabulary z-scores of children in kindergarten, first and fifth grades

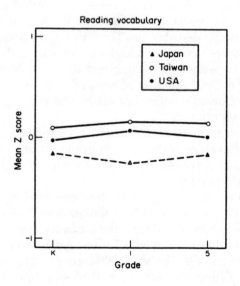

Figure 10.3. Mean reading comprehension z-scores of children in kindergarten, first and fifth grades

The percentage of children with severe reading problems was similar for the three countries. This is of special interest, for some writers have proposed that extremely low scores representing reading disabilities would not be found among Chinese and Japanese children of normal intelligence (e.g., Makita, 1968). Reading disability is commonly defined as a retardation of reading achievement of more than 2 years below grade level. Using this definition with the fifth-grade children, 3% of the American children, 2% of the Chinese children, and 8% of the Japanese children would be classified as reading-disabled; that is, they were unable to meet the criteria for successful reading of the materials at grade three on the test. Kindergarten children and first-graders are too young for reliable diagnosis of reading disabilities according to this definition.

Chinese characters, it appears, are not especially helpful to children learning to read. Both Chinese and Japanese children were required to read isolated Chinese characters in the vocabulary test. Yet children in Taipei received the highest scores on the vocabulary test and children in Sendai received the lowest scores. Nor does the use of an alphabet with its irregular symbol-sound relations appear to be especially detrimental. The American children's scores were midway between those of the Chinese and Japanese children.

It is likely that the lower average scores of Japanese children in learning how to read Chinese characters are related to the use of several systems of writing in Japanese. Learning to read *hiragana* is not difficult, but the multiplicity of homonyms in Japanese makes it necessary to use characters with increasing frequency as the material becomes more complex. Thus, while the Chinese children are learning characters and the American children are learning to read words, Japanese children are required to learn and integrate several different writing systems.

Reading comprehension was even more similar among the three countries than was the reading of vocabulary words. Again, Chinese children obtained the higher scores, but the Japanese children, presumably benefiting from the contextual cues provided by the combination of *hiragana* and *kanji* in the written text, attained a more favorable position in relation to the children in the other two countries than they had reached in the vocabulary test. By reading the parts of the clauses and sentences written in *hiragana*, it is often possible to deduce the meaning of the *kanji*. This is impossible, of course, when the *kanji* are presented alone, as they were in the vocabulary test.

The major conclusion from the results of the reading test is that the writing systems do not appear to lead to major differences in the rate at which children learn how to read. Although Chinese children consistently obtained significantly higher average scores from the kindergarten year onward, their superiority was relatively small—never as much as half a standard deviation. This superiority in performance does not necessarily indicate a superiority of the Chinese writing system. Other explanations are equally tenable. For example, their more rapid learning can be explained by the greater amounts of practice they receive through their homework and the greater amounts of instruction they receive during the school year. The Chinese children spent nearly twice as much time doing their weekday homework as either the American or Japanese children: an average of 114 minutes during the fifth grade versus 46 minutes for the American and 57 minutes for the Japanese children. In school, Chinese children were estimated to spend 40.4 hours a week involved in academic activities; the estimates for the Japanese and American children were 32.6 and 19.6 hours, respectively (Stevenson et al., 1986).

VI. MOTHERS' VIEWS

Another way of determining whether children experience different problems in learning to read different writing systems is to ask children's mothers and teachers about the problems the children had experienced. Even though children from different countries may emerge with similar levels of skill, the problems encountered in attaining these levels of performance may differ. To obtain this information, mothers and teachers were asked a series of questions about children's reading problems. Mothers were asked whether they believed their child had problems in reading, why they thought there had been problems, and what they had done about the problems.

Defining the Problems

The first question we asked the mothers was a very general one: "Has your child ever had problems in reading?" Most mothers did not believe their children had experienced any problems. Among mothers of fifth graders, 75% of the American mothers, 56% of the Chinese mothers and 82% of the Japanese mothers said their child had displayed no problems. These percentages seem large; however, more mothers believed their children had problems in reading than in arithmetic. In response to a parallel question about problems in arithmetic, 91% of all American mothers, 67% of the Chinese mothers and 86% of the Japanese mothers said their child did not have problems with arithmetic (see Table 10.2).

What mothers perceived as reading problems was often very different from the kinds of reading problems that are of concern to psy-

TABLE 10.2. Coincidence and Independence of Problems in Reading and Arithmetic at Grade 5 (Percentage of Children).

	USA	Taiwan	Japan
Reading and arithmetic	6	19	6
Reading only	19	25	12
Arithmetic only	3	14	8
No problems	72	42	74

chologists, teachers and reading specialists. To a greater degree than we expected, the mothers failed to describe problems relevant primarily to reading. Their responses fell into three categories, and only the first category contained problems explicitly related to reading. This category contained examples of poor reading skills. Mothers who made these types of responses said their child had difficulty in phonics or phonetics, did not know idioms, had a poor vocabulary, did not know grammar, was a "choppy" reader, reversed letters, or did not know Chinese characters. The other two categories of problem described by the mothers were much more general. One concerned cognitive abilities. In this case the mother said her child had a poor memory for words, had difficulty in concentrating, appeared to be a slow learner, or did not take initiative in reading. The third category of problems included difficult experiences related to reading that their child had encountered, such as being assigned a poor reading teacher, being given material that was too hard, or not getting training in basic reading skills. These three categories are referred to as Basic Skills, Cognitive Abilities, and Experiential Problems in Table 10.3.

Chinese, Japanese and American mothers emphasized different types of problems. American mothers emphasized problems related to cognitive abilities. Chinese mothers, on the other hand, rarely mentioned cognitive abilities, but described problems they believed to be derived from inadequate or inappropriate experiences. Japanese mothers gave still another pattern of responses. They mentioned cognitive abilities, but also were more likely than either American or Chinese mothers to describe deficiencies in their child's reading skills.

TABLE 10.3. Percentages of Mothers Mentioning Reading Problems in Various Categories (Percentage of Cases Where Reading Problems are Said to Exist).

Category	USA		Taiwan		Japan	
	Grade 1	Grade 5	Grade 1	Grade 5	Grade 1	Grade 5
Poor skills	30	29	22	28	50	64
Cognitive abilities	64	66	7	2	56	40
Experiential problems	15	26	77	71	8	4

Differences among countries in the patterns of response were highly significant at both grades, p <0.001.

Japanese mothers were better able to describe their children's problems in reading than were Chinese or American mothers. It is likely that they had more information about their children's reading problems because of their close daily supervision of their children's school work. Mothers in Japan are noted for the assiduous attention they give to their children's education. Chinese families are also dedicated to advancing their children's education, but it is primarily the family, rather than the mother, that assumes this task. The mothers in this study were asked about the relative contributions of the father and mother as sources of help to their children. It was "mostly" or "always" the mother 82% of the time in Sendai, 46% of the time in Taipei and 70% of the time in Minneapolis. The high percentage for American mothers does not mean that they actually spent a large amount of time working with their children. In fact, they estimated that someone in the family spent an average of only 14 minutes a day on such activities, compared to an average of 27 minutes for the Chinese families and 17 minutes for the Japanese families.

Severity

How serious did the mothers consider their children's problems to be? Among American mothers who thought their fifth-grader had reading problems, 77% thought their child's problems were "very serious" or "moderately serious." Chinese and Japanese parents were less worried. Only 30% of the mothers of the Chinese fifth-graders thought their child's problems were serious; 64% of the mothers of Japanese fifth-graders made this judgement. As would be expected, mothers of fifth-graders were more likely to judge their child's problems to be serious than were mothers of first-graders. The data are presented for each grade in Table 10.4.

TABLE 10.4. Mothers' Ratings of the Seriousness of Their Child's Reading Problems (Percentage of Mothers).

	USA	Taiwan	Japan
Grade 1			
Very serious	8	5	15
Moderately serious	46	20	27
Not serious	46	76	58
Grade 5			
Very serious	12	10	26
Moderately serious	65	20	40
Not serious	23	70	35

A direct means of evaluating the mothers' judgements is to look at the children's reading scores and ask whether the scores of children who were judged to have problems of various levels of severity differed from each other. A percentile score combining the scores from the three parts of the reading test was computed for each fifth-grader. The means of these scores, separated according to the mothers' judgement of the existence and severity of the reading problem, appear in Table 10.5. Children who were judged to have a reading problem obtained lower mean scores than did children who were judged not to have a reading problem. Thus, mothers made this differentiation reliably. There was not a close relation, however, between the mothers' judgements of the severity of the problem and the children's reading scores. For example, American children who were judged to have "very serious" reading problems actually made higher scores on the reading test than did the children whose mothers judged the problems-to be "not serious." Analyses of the data in Table 10.4 indicate significant differences among the means for Minneapolis and Sendai, $p < 0.01$, but not for Taipei, $p < 0.05$.

TABLE 10.5. Mean Percentile for Children's Reading Scores, Separated According to Mother's Rating of Severity of Child's Reading Problems.

Severity	USA	Taiwan	Japan
Very serious	36.3	32.4	28.0
Moderately serious	33.9	45.8	45.2
Not serious	30.6	43.8	34.2
No problem	58.9	52.2	52.4

Despite the fact that more American mothers believed their children had serious problems in reading than did Chinese or Japanese mothers, the reading scores of American children were not lower than those of Chinese and Japanese children in these categories (i.e. "serious," "very serious"). For example, the mean score on the vocabulary test for American children judged to have a "very serious" problem was 45.3, while it was 41.5 and 41.0, respectively, for the Chinese and Japanese children. The mean comprehension scores for the American, Chinese and Japanese children who were judged to have "very serious" problems were similar: 77.8, 79.7 and 77.6.

We conclude, therefore, that although mothers were reasonably effective in judging the presence or absence of problems, they were not able to make reliable judgements about the severity of problems. Mothers in the three countries did not appear to be equally effective in isolating reading problems from other academic problems their child might be experiencing. The cognitive problems described so frequently by the American mothers may represent the basis of problems in academic work, rather than being restricted to the area of reading. Similarly, the experiential problems frequently mentioned by the Chinese mothers may represent loose interpretations of what might be considered problems in reading. Most of the mothers appeared either not to know enough about their child's abilities to describe specific reading problems, or avoided discussing the child's problems by diverting the discussion to possible bases of the problems rather than discussing the problems themselves.

Causes

To what did the mothers attribute their children's reading problems? They were asked: "Why do you think your child had reading problems?" The most common belief held by mothers in all three countries was that reading problems were related to the types of earlier training and stimulation the child had received. This included factors such as not being taught properly, needing more supervision and needing more stimulation. Few mothers considered their child's problem to be derived from poor cognitive abilities or low motivation. Several other factors were mentioned, as can be seen in Figure 10.4, but they were all of much lower frequency than the answers related to training and stimulation.

For purposes of contrast the reasons why mothers believed their children had difficulties with arithmetic are presented in Figure 10.5. The pattern of responses was very different from that obtained when the mothers discussed reading. Training and stimulation were not such dominant reasons for children's difficulties in learning arithmetic. Cognitive and motivational factors were much more frequently mentioned. In short, mothers were much more likely to attribute difficulties in learning to read to external sources, such as the teacher and the school, but were more likely to attribute difficulties in learning arithmetic to factors within the child.

Solutions

In a final question the mothers were asked what they had done to help their child. Despite the mothers' beliefs that the major factor underlying their child's problems in reading was the teaching they received, few looked to the school as a source of help. Seeking assistance from the school was mentioned by 14% of the American mothers, and by 1% of the Chinese and Japanese mothers. American mothers frequently suggested they consulted a specialist such as a psychologist or physician, but

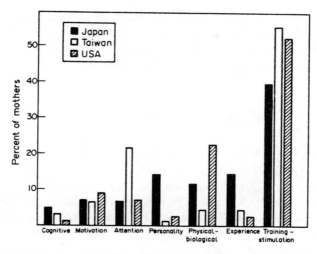

Figure 10.4. Mothers' explanations of the basis of children's problems in reading
mathematics

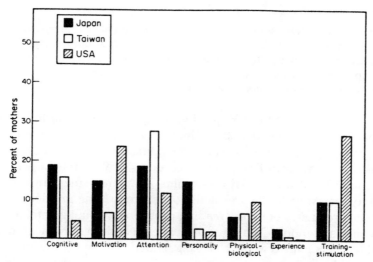

Figure 10.5. Mothers' explanations of the basis of children's problems in
mathematics

Chinese and Japanese mothers did not; the respective proportions were
30%, 9% and 6% of the mothers. The most frequently mentioned source of
help was in the home. Half (49%) of the American mothers, 58% of the
Chinese mothers, and 80% of the Japanese mothers said that they depended upon the family for helping their child with reading problems. Many
types of family help were mentioned, ranging from forcing the child to
study more, giving the child support and encouragement, working coop-

eratively with the child, seeking assistance from siblings or other family members, and altering their approach to interactions with their child. There were no notable differences among the three countries in the frequency with which these various types of family help were mentioned.

VII. TEACHERS' VIEWS

The children in each country were enrolled in 20 classrooms at each grade. Our sample of teachers consisted, therefore, of 40 first- and fifth-grade teachers in each country. This is not a large sample, but it is sufficient to obtain some ideas about how teachers evaluate children's reading problems. Most of the teachers had many years of experience. Teachers had taught an average of 15 years in Minneapolis, 17 years in Sendai and 17 years in Taipei.

The initial question we asked the fifth-grade teachers was phrased in the following manner:

> In some countries some children are seriously behind their classmates in reading ability. That is, the children are of normal intelligence but their ability to read words and understand what they read is approximately two grades behind that of their classmates. Do you have such children in your classroom?

In Minneapolis 90% of the fifth-grade teachers responded affirmatively, in Taipei 70% and in Sendai 60%. Children who met this criterion (two grades below grade placement) on the reading test were actually found in 65% of the American fifth-grade classrooms, 75% of the Taipei classrooms and 70% of the Sendai classrooms. Thus the American teachers tended to overestimate the prevalence of severe reading problems. Even though the frequency of severe reading problems was not greater among American than among Chinese and Japanese children, American mothers and teachers tended to have an exaggerated estimate of the incidence of such problems.

As expected, teachers generally had much clearer ideas about reading problems than the mothers. The most common problems mentioned by American teachers were poor comprehension (75%) and inaccurate pronunciation (65%). Japanese teachers were aware of the fact that children in their classes experienced some difficulty in reading Chinese characters; this was the problem they mentioned most frequently. Sixty percent of the Japanese teachers, but only 30% of the Chinese teachers mentioned this problem. The explanation of this difference probably lies in the fact that it is imperative that Chinese children learn to read Chinese characters, whereas Japanese children sometimes fail to master the learning of characters because they can deduce the meaning of sentences from the words represented in *hiragana*.

The teachers' ideas differed from those of parents in a second important way. Most parents, but few teachers, regarded problems in reading as an isolated characteristic. Only three American, two Japanese and no Chinese teachers said that children who had reading problems did not display difficulties in other subjects. The suggestion that children who have problems in reading also have problems in mathematics was made by half of the American teachers, 80% of the Chinese teachers and 78% of the Japanese teachers. In addition, Chinese and Japanese teachers—72% and 64%, respectively—suggested that children with reading problems also had difficulties in science. American teachers seldom mentioned science as a source of difficulty for children. Thus, according to these teachers, children with severe reading problems frequently have problems in other school subjects.

Causes

The teachers, like the parents, attributed most of children's reading problems to the children's everyday experiences (see Table 10.6). In contract to the parents, however, teachers pointed to factors in the children's homes rather than in the school as the basis of the problems. Seldom did the teachers attribute children's reading problems to inadequate teachers. Rather, they believed family influences, such as the lack of help given children by their parents, parents' lack of involvement in the children's reading and parents' failure to be good models for their children by not reading frequently, were the most common causes of reading problems. Such factors were less frequently mentioned by the Japanese teachers that by the American and Chinese teachers.

TABLE 10.6. Teachers' Explanations of Basis of Serious Reading Problems (Percentage of Teachers).

	USA	Taiwan	Japan
Family influence	54	54	28
Low motivation	32	43	44
Poor attention span	32	14	16
Do not read enough	17	50	44
Low ability	15	25	24
Physical-perceptual problems	12	4	0
Poor learning of basics	12	18	4
Inadequate teachers	2	4	0
Other	63	25	36

Teachers also mentioned children's lack of motivation and interest in reading as a source of children's reading problems. Although motivational problems were among the problems most frequently mentioned by teachers, few mothers attributed their children's problems to a lack of motivation or interest. Japanese and Chinese teachers also attributed children's reading problems to their failure to read frequently at home. Few teachers mentioned the possibility that there were medical or psychological problems that, if corrected, would remedy the children's difficulties in reading, a factor mentioned by over 20% of the American mothers.

Solutions

When asked how they would try to improve the reading skills of children, American teachers said they would attempt to increase their sensitivity to the children's reading levels so they would be able to supply proper materials, put the children in appropriate reading groups and give the children increased attention (see Table 10.7). Chinese and Japanese teachers were more likely to ask the children to read more. Chinese teachers, along with the American teachers, also thought they could encourage the children to build their self-confidence about reading, and that teachers could repeat training in basic skills.

TABLE 10.7. Teachers' Recommendations About How Teachers Can Help Children Improve Their Reading Skills (Percentage of Teachers).

	USA	Taiwan	Japan
Increase sensitivity to reading level	68	29	32
Encourage them	44	43	24
Repeat training in basic skills	34	25	12
Ask child to read more	24	54	48
Tutor, special class	17	0	0
Peer intervention	9	11	4
Other	59	25	56

Recommendations to the parents made by the teachers from the three countries were very similar (see Table 10.8). By far the most common suggestion for improving children's reading skills was that the parents should read more to their children. This suggestion is interesting in relation to the percentage of mothers in each country that reported reading to their children regularly. In Minneapolis 86% of the mothers said they read regularly to their child, yet 93% of the teachers believed they should read more to their children. While 63% of the Japanese mothers said they read to their child regularly, the predominant suggestion made by the Japanese teachers was that they should read more. In Taiwan, where only 53% of the mothers said they read regularly to their children,

TABLE 10.8. Teachers' Suggestions About Ways Parents Can Help to Improve Children's Reading Skills (Percentage of Teachers).

	USA	Taiwan	Japan
Read more to children	93	46	84
Review reading materials	49	25	0
Buy reading materials	15	58	5
Get consultation	5	4	0
Hire a tutor	0	4	0
Other	48	29	32

46% of the teachers thought the mothers should read more. Neither Chinese teachers nor mothers appeared to emphasize reading to the child as a means of improving the child's reading ability. Rather, the Chinese teachers appeared to believe in the value of children's reading by themselves; 58% suggested parents should buy more books for their children. Surprisingly few teachers mentioned the utility of parents' obtaining consultation from other professionals about children's reading problems.

VIII. CONCLUSIONS

The most salient aspects of the results are the pervasive similarities among the children of the three countries in children's average levels of achievement in reading and comprehension. In view of these results it is difficult to accept the hypothesis that problems in reading are closely linked to different writing systems. Rather than finding much better reading and comprehension among children learning to read highly patterned, distinctive Chinese characters or among children using a syllabary with perfectly predictable symbol-sound relations, as contrasted with American children who must read an alphabet, the levels of reading skill with the three writing systems were similar. Moreover, neither the mothers nor the teachers seemed to have observed highly distinctive problems in reading one writing system rather than another. Views about what constituted problems and their solution did differ, but they typically were related to experiences children have at school and at home, rather than to differential demands created by the writing systems.

The information we obtained from mothers was disappointing. Mothers were not good judges of their children's reading skill. Although children whose mothers said their child had a reading problem performed less well on the reading test than did children whose mothers denied their child had a problem, mothers were not accurate judges of the severity of their child's problem. American mothers were especially prone to overstate the frequency and severity of reading problems.

What we were looking for in asking mothers about reading problems were fundamental features of reading problems that might be described differently in the three countries. Rather than discover such differences from the mothers' descriptions, we mainly found emphases on different cultural factors the mothers believed to be associated with learning to read. Teachers were somewhat more informative, although their descriptions of the problems also revealed few basic differences in the problems faced by the children in the three countries. Perhaps the questions were not specific enough to pick up problems children were having. Or perhaps mothers and teachers were not skilled enough observers to discover these problems. However, if differences in the ways children learn to read these three writing systems exist, they did not emerge in questioning the nearly 1500 mothers and 120 teachers included in this study. It seems more likely that there are fundamental similarities in the tasks all children face in learning to read.

We can speculate what these similarities might be. Learning to read appears basically to involve learning how to decode strings of written symbols into words and how to organize these words into comprehensible units. Chinese children must learn to decode characters and to combine and segment sequences of characters into words and phrases. Japanese children face a similar task, except that interspersed among the Chinese characters are sequences of symbols representing syllables that also must be segmented into words and phrases. For the American child, words are more clearly distinguished than for the Chinese and Japanese child, but the reader of English must learn to segment the words into the phonemes that constitute the basic sounds of English. In all three writing systems, therefore, the reader faces the task of dividing strings of symbols into manageable segments and integrating the segments into meaningful units. This analytic procedure can be assumed to be the fundamental task shared by readers of all writing systems. Within every culture children differ in the rate at which they master this task, but the percentage of children who have serious difficulties in doing so does not appear to differ greatly among cultures—at least among the three cultures that we have studied.

ACKNOWLEDGEMENTS

This study has involved the collaboration of many persons, including Shin-ying Lee, James Stigler and William Lucker in the United States, Professor Seiro Kitamura in Japan and Professor C. C. Hsu in Taiwan. The research was supported by the National Institute of Mental Health (MH-30567).

REFERENCES

Kavanagh, J. F., & Venezky, R. L. (1980). *Orthography, reading, and dyslexia*. Baltimore: University Park Press.

Makita, K. (1968). The rarity of reading disability in Japanese children. *American Journal of Orthopsychiatry, 38*, 599-614.

Rozin, P., & Gleitman, L. (1974). *Syllabary: An introductory reading curriculum*. Washington, DC: Curriculum Development Associates.

Rozin, P., Poritsky, S., & Sotsky, R. (1971). American children with reading problems can easily learn to read English represented in Chinese characters. *Science, 171*, 1264-1267.

Stevenson, H.W., Stigler, J.W., Lucker, G.W., Lee, S.Y., Hsu, C.C., & Kitamura, S. (1982). Reading disabilities: The case of Chinese, Japanese, and English. *Child Development, 33*, 1164-1181.

Stevenson, H.W., Stigler, J.W., Lucker, G.W., Lee, S.Y., Hsu, C.C., & Kitamura, S. (1986). Classroom behavior and achievement of Japanese, Chinese, and American children. In R. Glaser (Ed.), *Advances in instructional psychology, 3*. Hillsdale, NJ: Erlbaum.

Taylor, I., & Taylor, M.M. (1983). *The psychology of reading*. New York: Academic Press.

IV

LITERACY IN MULTIETHNIC AND MULTILINGUAL CONTEXTS

11

Introduction

Bambi B. Schieffelin
New York University

There are a number of recurring scenarios in which literacy, an important linguistic resource, may be introduced and accepted into society. In multilingual and multiethnic contexts the problems and complexities multiply. The following chapters, which focus on literacy acquisition in three different societies—rural Morocco, Israel and Fiji—are examples of three different scenarios. In Morocco there is an established linguistic and cultural heterogeneity, with literacy in a standard language; Israel, also with a standard literate language, is experiencing sudden mass immigration from outside populations creating social and linguistic diversity; Fiji and much of the South Pacific, with considerable linguistic diversity, had no indigenous vernacular literacy. Literacy, along with other languages, was brought in as part of missionization. In all three scenarios certain common problems must be solved, problems of communication and education.

Understanding language use in multiethnic and multilingual speech communities is a complex task that requires the consideration of social, cultural, historical and psychological factors. These case studies demonstrate how information concerning each factor contributes a critical perspective toward understanding the organization, acquisition and processes of social change in the linguistic resources (of which literacy is one piece) in a given speech community. Critical in this approach to the study of language use is the recognition of the dimensions along which groups in contact may vary, for example, in terms of social class and educational backgrounds, geographical and economic conditions and the experience of outside religious or political influences. Furthermore, through an approach that considers social, psychological and historical dimensions in the study of language use, we can begin to understand how literacy and its acquisition comes to have different educational, religious, cultural and political consequences for members of different social groups (Schieffelin, 1986).

While the study of language use in any society is in itself a worthwhile endeavor, the study of the acquisition of literacy brings applied as well as theoretical issues into sharp focus. Before being able to make general claims about why and how particular groups of individuals are "successful" in this learning process, the different factors that contribute to this task must be teased out and examined separately. Each case study must be presented according to the salient features of the groups being documented. For example, the situation in rural Morocco is considered in terms of evaluating the effects of the language background of the young learner (Berber or Arabic) and the nature of the activities and experiences of the young learner (Quranic preschool or no preschool experience) prior to primary schooling which is carried out monolingually in Arabic. In spite of the high status of the language of literacy (Standard Arabic) with its deep ties to Islam, part of the cultural identity of both Berber and Arabic-speaking Moroccans, a substantial number of Berber children remain behind their Moroccan Arabic-speaking peers through the third year of primary school. The Morocco Literacy Project also reminds us that social, linguistic and political relationships in developing societies such as Morocco are not static, but in constant flux, and only that by seriously considering in-depth multidimensional research, as exemplified by this project, can policy-makers develop educational programs that will benefit children of all social and linguistic backgrounds.

In contrast to Morocco, where there has been a long tradition of stable heterogeneity, Israel presents another scenario, one in which recent mass immigration from diverse linguistic and cultural groups has caused major shifts in the composition of the population. The effects of this heterogeneity creates profound stresses on an educational system that has previously operated successfully along certain assumptions: parents can and will facilitate the literacy acquisition of their children by participating in reading and writing activities; parents are familiar with the expectations and values of the school context and support those beliefs. As the research in contemporary Israel shows, when parents lack necessary linguistic skills and educational levels to assist the child, the stress on the parent-child relationship as well as consequences of the child's learning are serious. In addition, this diversity taxes the teacher-student relationship, as well as the peer relations within the classroom. The case study from Israel emphasizes the importance of educating the parents about the education of their children in order to reduce the inevitable misunderstandings bound to arise in the situation.

In addition to sensitizing educators to these sociopsychological dimensions of linguistic, social and educational diversity, the case of Israel as presented considers the social as well as the cognitive factors that contribute to successful reading comprehension. Like the other chapters in this section, the role of early home literacy experiences is evaluated in terms of predicting later school success. The series of experiments carried out in Israeli primary schools demonstrate that exposure to, and experience with, books positively contributes to increased interest and skill in oral language and reading on the part of the young listeners. This finding is supported by the Fijian study, and no doubt other evidence can be found for this claim. What the Israeli study suggests is that the particular ethnic or cultural affiliation of the young learner was not a significant factor in the degree of success, but participation in literacy events was the key.

Another important point detailed in the Moroccan and Israeli studies is the nature of the differences in the language of the home and the language of literacy in terms of ease of multilingual acquisition. These differences, whether they are at the level of language, dialect or register variation, in written or spoken form, must be fully considered. In addition to the differences in linguistic forms themselves, genre conventions and narrative structures in written texts, as compared to other forms of language use, must also be taken into account as part of the knowledge that is acquired along with different vocabulary and syntactic structure. Furthermore, these differences in the organization and use of literate materials point out how different social groups organize and value the presentation and display of knowledge, also part of what the learner must master in becoming competent. In the case of linguistic minorities, or where there is no established tradition of early literacy socialization in the home, the school must fill in. What we see in several of these case studies is the importance not only of providing the experience, but understanding language- and orthography-specific problems that arise due to the particular languages and orthographies in contact. Finally, as both the Moroccan and Israeli studies demonstrate, educational policies can have profound effects not only on the speakers, but on the status of the languages themselves. In Morocco, due to policies of Arabization, the number of monolingual Berber speakers seems to be diminishing. Over time this can affect the language itself. In Israel the opposite has occurred; through the use of Hebrew in the classrooms this language is experiencing a revival.

The third case study from the South Pacific provides an example of yet another common scenario concerning a change and reorganization of linguistic resources, the introduction of literacy and formal schooling by foreign missionaries. Here we see how particular demographic, cultural and linguistic factors of each country affect the ways in which literacy is developed and achieved. The South Pacific provides many examples of different routes to, and success rates concerning, literacy acquisition. This case study focuses on multilingual and multiethnic Fiji, and examines the historical, social and educational factors that lead to literacy acquisition and use. One finding of this study was that schools with large libraries produced better readers than schools with small or no libraries. This led to an experiment (the Book Flood Project) in rural schools to evaluate the role of experience with high-interest books in the development of literacy skills. Consistent with other studies the Fijian experiment reports that receptive language skills are substantially improved, and that transfer to related language skills occurs. Critical to the positive results is the activation and encouragement of interest and enjoyment on the part of the learners. Here we see the importance of the ideology of reading and learning, as the traditional notion had been that reading for pleasure was time wasted in the learning process. Teachers must provide models of this type of activity, in addition to educational institutions providing the materials themselves.

The Fijian example raises an important point about the languages of literacy, that is the role of vernacular literacy as well as second-language literacy. Sociological as well as ideological issues are critical here, and will determine how each literacy will be assigned a different domain of use.

Yet another scenario which was not mentioned in these chapters concerns the introduction of literacy as one way to transform an essentially monolingual society into a multilingual one. When I first went to Papua New Guinea in 1967 the Kaluli (Mount Bosavi, Southern Highlands Province), like other cultures in that country, did not have traditional or indigenous literacy. They had no exposure to literacy, nor did they know anything about it. Over the years I have had the opportunity of studying the introduction of literacy in English, Tok Pisin and the vernacular through the mission into Kaluli society.

One of the results of observing the Kaluli was a realization of the necessity to take into account the ideological issues underlying introduced literacy, and how it fits with the native language ideology and the general role of language in that society. The Kaluli have an elaborate metalinguistic system and explicit theories of language acquisition and use. The effects of Kaluli beliefs on the acquisition of literacy were (when it was introduced in the early 1970s) profound. For example, the Kaluli said that labeling—just saying the names of objects—was an activity that had no purpose; and labeling is the essence of using the literacy materials available, a word and a picture. The reader is to say the name of the object and connect its orthographic and visual representation. Many Kaluli found the point of this activity incomprehensible and actively discouraged it, especially when their young children showed any interest in looking at books and saying the names of pictures. So, for Kaluli speakers, there is a conflict between traditional patterns of appropriate language use and introduced language use. This conflict, among others, contributed to the lack of interest and skill in literacy acquisition (Schieffelin & Cochran-Smith, 1984).

In addition to conflicts in linguistic ideology that may inhibit the acceptance of literacy, other conflicts may also be involved. One may be a conflict of interest in achieving literacy (Woolard & Schieffelin, 1994). Several of the chapters discussed the role played by religious institutions in introducing literacy. In certain cases there may be little interest on the part of the particular religious group to create a literate tradition that would serve a wide range of communicative and educational functions. The literacy program that is communicative and educational functions. The literacy program that is connected to missionization may have an agenda that is different from a literacy program that has been developed for a secular educational system. For example, in parts of Papua New Guinea there is a noticeably underdeveloped interest in writing. Literacy programs introduced through certain missions often focused only on reading. This may be due to the fact that literacy is considered as a way to take in new information, and not as a way to generate or communicate new information outside of the religious domain. Among the Kaluli, individuals had little access to writing materials, could not easily buy stamps to send out letters, and were not encouraged to write things down or to generate their own written materials. Literacy was about learning how to read the Bible and to talk about the Bible (Schieffelin, 1996).

This type of literacy experience is probably not restricted to the Pacific (see also Reder, and Bennett & Berry, this volume). As part of a conflict of interest in achieving literacy, especially where there is a religious organization in charge of literacy, which is the case in many developing countries, it is also important to consider the nature of vernacular literacy materials themselves. Even when the literacy materials are written in the vernacular the medium often carries a new message. Literacy materials may either ignore or "put down" traditional culture, portray people carrying out non-traditional activities and being successful in abandoning traditional ideology.

    People who were depicted in traditional ways of dressing, wear-
ing traditional hairstyles and living in traditional houses, were shown to
be missing out on the future. Those depicted in Western clothing, living
in Western-style houses with nuclear (rather than extended) family and
reading their literacy books were shown earning cash through employment in non-traditional activities outside of the area. Vernacular materials often introduced European words as well as European ways. This is
a conscious attempt to use literacy as a way of separating the old from
the new—part of different self-definition promised when new religious
doctrine is accepted. An implicit message communicated through these
literacy materials was "if you don't read, you're part of the old way."
What needs to be emphasized is the fact that literacy comes with strong
feelings and strong political ideology attached to it.

    An additional issue, drawing on the Fijian example, concerns
the question of what determines a literate form, ultimately a literary
form in a situation of developing literacy. This is an important issue for
people working on vernacular literacy materials to think about. There is
ample evidence from Papua New Guinea, that pidginization of the vernacular was engaged in by missionaries who created the literacy materials. The Bible was taken as the literate genre to be followed. Because of
the asymmetrical power relationship between foreign missionaries and
local people, it is quite easy to understand how native assistants might
be unable to criticize or correct the European authorities on literacy.

    Pidginization of the vernacular affects the way people think
about their language. Orthographies are often developed that are not
accurate. In the Bosavi situation four dialects lived very happily together
until the mission selected one as the basis of a written version of the language. Thus a consciousness of a standard was created when one previously did not exist. Of course, this made it easier for some speakers to
acquire literacy skills, in addition to introducing new bases of stratification into a linguistic situation where none previously existed. In the work
that Steven Feld and I have done towards creating Kaluli vernacular literacy, we have tried to maintain the oral performance style. In planning
these materials, and discussing them with Kaluli, we decided to provide
materials that were transcriptions of traditional stories the people were
interested in, and to provide a cassette that could go with the materials so
that people could actually hear the way tellers delivered these stories.
One literate Kaluli said, when he looked at the transcripts, "that's not
how we were told to write." We tried to introduce the idea that the
telling style was just as good as anything that anyone else would write
down and edit. It seems essential that outsiders introducing vernacular
literacy materials do not determine the shape or structure of native-
speakers' texts, but rather provide the opportunity and encouragement
for native-speakers to develop their own literacy and literary style.

In conclusion, in considering cross-cultural studies, especially in multilingual and multiethnic societies, one must carefully examine the agendas of any literacy program (Schieffelin & Doucet, 1994). There are political agendas and there are social agendas; there are agendas based on understanding and agendas that are based on not understanding. It is important to seriously consider the nature of these different agendas. This is critical if we are to understand why some literacies and some literates have a future, and why others do not.

REFERENCES

Schieffelin, B.B. (1986). Introduction. In B.B. Schieffelin & P. Gilmore (Eds.), *The acquisition of literacy: Ethnographic perspectives*. Norwood, NJ: Ablex.

Schieffelin, B.B. (1996). Creating evidence: Making sense of written words in Bosavi. In E. Ochs, E. Schegloff, & S. Thompson (Eds.), *Interaction and grammar*. Cambridge, MA: Cambridge University Press.

Schieffelin, B.B., & Cochran-Smith, M. (1984). Learning to read culturally. In H. Goelman, A. Oberg, & F. Smith (Eds.), *Awakening to literacy*. Exeter, NH: Heinemann.

Schieffelin, B.B., & Doucet R.C. (1994). The "real" Haitian Creole: Ideology, metalinguistics and orthographic choice. *American Ethnologists, 21*(1), 176-200.

Woolard, K., & Schieffelin, B.B. (1994). Language ideology. In W. Durham et al. (Eds.), *Annual review of anthropology 23*. Palo Alto, CA: Annual Review Inc.

12

Childhood Literacy Acquisition in Rural Morocco: Effects of Language Differences and Quranic Preschooling[1]

Abdelkader Ezzaki
Université Mohamed V, Morocco

Jennifer E. Spratt
Research Triangle Institute

Daniel A. Wagner
University of Pennsylvania

I. INTRODUCTION

While interest in reading and writing have always been important to researchers and educational policy-makers, multidisciplinary investigations of the acquisition of literacy are a relatively new enterprise. In the Arabic-speaking world, in particular, there have been relatively few

---

[1]This research is an outcome of a collaborative research project undertaken by the Faculte des Sciences de l'Education of the Universite Mohamed V (Rabat) and the Graduate School of Education of the University of Pennsylvania.

183

efforts to discover what kinds of literacy abilities the child brings to the classroom, and what kinds of home, preschool and language environments lead to various levels of literacy both in and out of school. The research described here presents data collected during the first 3 years of the Morocco Literacy Project, whose general aim has been to investigate the process of literacy acquisition and retention in Morocco (see Wagner, 1993). The present paper considers the effects of preschool experience and language background on a sample of primary school children in rural Morocco.

The first issue addressed is that of language background. Does learning to read in one's native language, as opposed to a second language, make a difference? More specifically, do Berber- and Arabic-speaking children achieve different levels of Arabic literacy skills during primary school? Do such differences persist in subsequent years of schooling? Do differential language skills affect particular literacy abilities, leading to a different patterning of skills? The second issue concerns that of organized preschool experiences. Does Quranic preschooling experience facilitate literacy acquisition among rural Moroccan children in primary school? Does any initial advantage carry over into later years of public schooling? Answers to these questions hold implications for Moroccan educational policy as well as for other multilingual and educationally diversified societies. As an understanding of context is essential to a discussion of the present results, brief descriptions of the language situation and of Quranic schooling in Morocco are provided later.

II. THE LANGUAGE SITUATION IN MOROCCO

Contemporary Moroccan society can be characterized as a multilingual community in which three primary languages are used: Arabic (in at least two varieties), Berber, and French.[2] The degree of multilingualism exhibited by any individual or group appears to be a function of the degree of urbanization, the geographical and ethnic origin of the speak-

Funding was provided, in part, by grants from the National Institute of Education (G-80-0182), National Institutes of Health (HD-14898) and the Spencer Foundation. Authors are listed in alphabetical order. The original version of this chapter was a preliminary report from the Morocco Literacy Project. The final and complete version of the data and findings are available in Wagner (1993).

[2]As a function of the Spanish colonial period in northern Morocco, Spanish is still spoken in that region, particularly among older adults. Its importance has decreased since Moroccan Independence.

er, and the level of his or her education. For example, in the large urban centers of Morocco, Arabic and French are widely used side by side, and code-switching is often engaged in by the more educated Moroccans. In contrast, French is rarely heard in rural areas, where Arabic and/or Berber dominate, depending on the region. The present study was undertaken in a rural location.

As pointed out by Ferguson (1959), spoken Arabic consists of at least two major varieties which stand in a diglossic relationship to each other: in the case of Morocco, these varieties are standard (or literary) Arabic (SA) and Moroccan Arabic (MA). The former is the official language of the country and therefore the language of the mass media, school instruction, and formal settings, hence Ferguson's reference to it as the "high" variety. It is the *lingua franca* of the Arab world, since it is the variety most intelligible across all Arab countries. It enjoys considerably more prestige than MA because it is associated with Islam and the written Quran, and is viewed as a symbol of unity in Arabic-speaking countries. SA is also the language of literacy, being the only variety of Arabic commonly used in written communication of any kind; for an overview, see Ezzaki and Wagner (1992).

MA, on the other hand, is the colloquial, unwritten variety acquired by most Moroccan children as their native tongue. Contrary to SA, MA is a regional variety which forms part of a continuum of varieties spoken across the Arab world, in which the level of resemblance and mutual intelligibility between varieties declines with physical and historical distance. Thus, MA is more intelligible to Arabic speakers of nearby Tunisia or Algeria than it would be, for example, in Iraq or Egypt. While SA is used in formal settings, MA is limited to home and everyday activities, hence fitting Ferguson's label of "low" variety. As such it is almost never used in formal writing or publishing, though it occasionally appears in personal letter writing when complete SA writing skills may not be available to the individual.

Along with Arabic/French bilingualism and SA/MA diglossia, an additional opposition exists: that of the Arabic and Berber languages. While Arabic is a Semitic language, Berber belongs to the Hamitic family of languages, and is the language of nomadic groups already settled in Morocco before its conquest by the Arabs in the 8th century A.D. The Berber language in Morocco exhibits three broad regional variations: *Tashelheit* spoken in the southwestern part of the country, including the city of Agadir; *Tamazight*, spoken in the Atlas Mountains; and *Ta'rifit*, spoken in the Rif mountains and northern plains. An ancient alphabetical writing system for the language exists (*Tifinagh*), however it is virtually unknown in present-day Morocco.

While official statistics on the number of native Berber-speakers in Morocco are not available, estimates range from about 30% to over 60% of the population (Moatassime, 1974). Most adult male Berber-speakers are at least partly bilingual or even trilingual (in Berber, Arabic, and French or Spanish), and schooling, media, and increased migration to urban areas in recent years has further promoted the "bilingualization" of Berbers, particularly among the younger generations. It is still possible, however, to find predominantly monolingual Berber-speaking individuals among the women and young children of certain rural areas. An example of such a place is the site selected for the study reported here, a small town in the Atlas foothills of central Morocco.

Although MA and Berber constitute the two predominant mother tongues for Moroccan children, neither language is used as a medium of instruction or literacy training in public government schools. Since the most recent enactment of an educational policy of Arabization, the official language of schooling and literacy at all stages is SA (Grandguillaume, 1983). Thus, both MA- and Berber-speaking students are obliged to learn their lessons in a language other than their mother tongue. However, it was hypothesized that MA-speaking children might have an advantage in literacy acquisition because of the relatively close kinship of their spoken language (MA) with the language of literacy (SA). This hypothesis was based on transfer theories, as discussed in James (1980) and Lado (1957). Similarly, Badry (1983) studied children's knowledge of linguistic rules operating in MA, and suggested that the transfer of SA syntactic rules, which are embedded in spoken MA, might benefit SA literacy acquisition in Moroccan children.

For both Arabic- and Berber-speaking children, then, direct exposure to the language of literacy occurs mainly in the school setting. This is especially the case in rural areas, where there is limited access to print media outside of the schools. For a good number of children of both MA and Berber language backgrounds, such literacy exposure begins in the preschool, and in most rural settings, the single type of preschooling available is the Quranic school. Another issue is that of exposure to spoken SA, available through the mass-media (radio and TV) and in various social contexts (e.g., with foreign SA-speaking visitors or in the Quranic preschool, discussed later). A general discussion of the relationship between language, literacy and context in Morocco is available in Wagner, Messick, and Spratt (1986).

III. THE RURAL QURANIC PRESCHOOL

Quranic schooling in Morocco was historically the first step in a Muslim boy's religious education; girls rarely frequented such schools until relatively recently. Through this experience the child was introduced to the Arabic writing system and literacy by laboriously memorizing and rote-reciting entire chapters from the Islamic holy book, the Quran—a work that challenges comprehension and interpretation even among the highly literate. Having undergone a decline in numbers and attendance during the French colonial period (1912-1956), Quranic schools were revitalized in 1968 following a royal declaration, and entrusted with the mission of preparing both boys and girls for entrance into public primary schools. Contemporary Quranic schools, whether urban or rural, now generally present a curriculum which includes explicit alphabet instruction, basic arithmetic, and non-Quranic vocabulary presentation, alongside the traditional activities of Quranic memorization and recitation, and training in the principles and practice of Islamic religion.

For both Arabic-speaking and Berber-speaking children, the Quranic school experience may begin as early as three years of age, and represents an important introduction to the language (Standard Arabic), learning activities, and strict discipline expected in formal school settings. For many Berber-speaking children coming to the town's Quranic school from outlying areas, it also provides a first opportunity for intensive exposure to MA as a language of peers. As such, the Quranic school can be viewed as an environment for the early development of bilingual skills.

The material culture of the Quranic school, most often a bare-walled room with mats or low benches for seating, is bland and austere when compared to the bright classrooms of the primary school, filled with desks, colorful learning aids, and students' artwork. Pencils, pens, paper and textbooks, required of every child in primary school, are lacking in the average Quranic school, where a single blackboard and the children's individual slates and chalk serve as the only material available for reading and writing practice.

For the rural Moroccan child, whose parents are likely to be illiterate, the Quranic preschool may well be the richest print-media and SA language environment yet encountered. It was hypothesized, therefore, that Quranic preschooling might foster early reading knowledge. While reasonable in light of the practice obtained in the preschool context, this hypothesis challenges the claims of some education specialists who have contended that Quranic school has a negative effect on cognition and literacy (cf. Moatassime, 1974; Zerdoumi, 1970). For more information on the contemporary Quranic school and discussions of its potential childhood consequences in Morocco, see Eickelman (1978, 1985), Wagner and Lotfi (1980), Spratt and Wagner (1986), and Wagner (1993).

IV. DESCRIPTION OF RESEARCH DESIGN AND METHOD

The sample of children on which this study is based was drawn from several first-grade classrooms of five primary schools located in the foothills of the Middle Atlas mountain range in central Morocco. Children were chosen to participate according to two criteria required by the research design shown in Table 12.1: (1) maternal language (Arabic or Berber); and (2) preschool experience (no preschool or Quranic preschool). Children were assigned to "Moroccan Arabic monolingual" and "Berber monolingual" groups on the basis of their own reports of parental mother tongues and family language use, and short conversational tests of Moroccan Arabic and Berber. These preliminary measures were subsequently validated by the results of a picture vocabulary test of Moroccan Arabic language ability. Children were 6-7 years of age and enrolled in the first grade when the study began, and were assessed over a 3 year period.[3]

TABLE 12.1.Description of the Children in the Sample.

	Main Contrasts			
I. Preschool	No Preschooling		Quranic Preschooled[a]	
II. Language	Berber	Arabic	Berber	Arabic
Subsample labels:	NB	NA	QB	QA
Subsample size				
Total N = 166)[b]	27	23	56	60
Gender:				
boys	13	11	30	29
girls	14	12	26	31
Mean years age				
in year 1:	7.4	7.4	7.4	7.4
Mean years of				
preschooling:	0.1	0.1	1.1	1.6

[a]Note abbreviations as follows:
NB = Non-preschooled Berber-speaking; NA = Non-preschooled Arabic-speaking; QB = Quranic preschooled Berber-speaking; QA = Quranic preschooled Arabic-speaking.

[b]As a longitudinal study there was attrition in the sample over the three year period of this study. Sample size in year 2 was 143; sample size in year 3 was 130.

---

[3]Due to the fact that many elementary school children repeat one or more grades, the number of years in school may not indicate the actual grade level achieved. Thus roughly half of the children in this study who completed 3 years of school were not, in fact, in grade three, but rather in grade two. The implications of school grade repeating (or retention) is an issue which we are currently examining.

Preschool attendance information was collected from the children themselves, and checked against school records (if available), with individual Quranic preschool teachers, and finally with the children's parents. The convergence of these four sources of information provided a reliable way of gathering such preschooling information, which can often be difficult to ascertain. The sample included roughly equal numbers of boys and girls, but since there were no gender-related differences in results these cells have been collapsed.

Four main comparison groups were created in this quasi-experimental design: Quranic preschooled Arabic-speaking (QA); Quranic preschooled Berber-speaking (QB); non-preschooled Arabic-speaking (NA); non-preschooled Berber-speaking (NB). The smaller sample sizes in the non-preschooled groups reflect the fact that most primary school children had received some Quranic schooling; also, as noted earlier, we selected for monolingual children only, which additionally reduced the number of children available for the study. A battery of experimental SA reading tests, constructed especially for the purposes of this project, was administered to the children in the Spring of their first year of primary school and again, (using separate forms) one and two years later. The results of these three tests measured beginning reading knowledge up through comprehension skills, and are briefly described later.

a. Letter Knowledge test. Administered in years 1 and 2, this test consisted of four subtests which measured the child's knowledge of Arabic orthography; from which a total score was calculated as the mean of z-scores of the subtests. These subtests are as follows: (i) Recognition of a written symbol, to be chosen among two foils (e.g., Which of these three letters is a *kaf*? Point to it please.); (ii) Recognition of two configurations of the same letter, as Arabic orthography requires different shapes of a letter according to its position in the word (e.g., Here are three letters. Which two have the same sound?); (iii) Identification of a given letter (e.g., Look at this letter; what is this letter?); (iv) Voicing of a written letter combined with a vocalizing diacritical mark (e.g., How do you read this?).

b. Word Picture Matching test. Administered in all three years, this test (modeled on the Gates-MacGinitie test, 1965) is similar to many standard reading tests, and requires the child to choose which written word, among 3 choices 4 choices in year 3), "names the picture". Thus, the Word Picture Matching test measured the child's ability to recognize and comprehend text at the single-word level.

c. Sentence Maze test. Administered in years 2 and 3 (since very few first grade children could accomplish this task), this test represents a popular measure of reading comprehension at the sentence level. It consists of a series of sentences with a single word missing. From an adjacent list of 3 (year 2) or 4 (year 3) possible choices, the child is asked to select the one word that best completes the sentence.

All tests were constructed based on words and Arabic syntactic structures selected from first through third grade Moroccan primary school primers, and were pretested on different children prior to use in this project. The three tasks were administered in alternate forms over the years of testing, which controlled for possible learning effects on specific measures. Tests were administered individually in years 1 and 2; in year three they were presented in a group testing format. The overlapping test design was necessitated by the wide range of ability exhibited by the children in this study. In addition to the reading tests discussed here, other reading and cognitive tests were administered to the same children, and home interviews were conducted with about 85% of the children's parents; more information on these measures are available in Wagner (1993).

V. RESULTS AND DISCUSSION

A. Effects of Moroccan Arabic vs. Berber as Mother Tongue

The data obtained were analyzed in a 2 x 2 ANOVA design (language background by preschool experience) repeated on the dependent measures of the first, second and third years (where tested). Because of the wide variety of tests used in the project, and because the three tests described here vary in content and length across the years of research, the subsample contrasts may be seen more clearly from standard or z-scores which were calculated on the sample for each separate task,[4] with ANOVA results are shown in Table 12.2.

In terms of language differences, Arabic-speaking children performed better than Berber-speaking children on both of the first-year reading measures (Letter Knowledge and Word Picture Matching). This

---

[4]Standard or z-scores basically provide each individual or group of individuals with the part of a standard deviation above or below the mean score for a single test for the entire sample in a given year.

TABLE 12.2. Summary Effects of Language and Quranic Preschool on Reading Tasks.[a]

	N	Quranic Preschool[b]		Language[c]		QS x Lang
MEASURES						
Year 1						
Letter Knowledge	(163)	1.677		1.838		.009
Word Pic Match	(166)	2.924[+]	QS > N	6.613**	A > B	.348
Year 2						
Letter Knowledge	(141)	.028		2.168		.028
Word Pic Match	(143)	.081		1.777		.037
Sentence Maze	(138)	.649		5.744*	A > B	.507
Year3						
Word Pic Match	(130)	1.275		3.677[+]	A > B	2.095
Sentence Maze	(130)	.667		.196		.000

[a]Note: [+]significant at .10 level; *significant at .05 level; **significant at .01 level.

[b]The Quranic preschool contrast compares QS (QA and QB) with N (NA and NB) .

[c]The Language contrast compares Arabic (A) speakers (QA and NA) with Berber (B) speakers (QB and NB); see further explanation in the text.

superiority of the Arabic-speaking group was generally maintained in the second and third years across the different tests; although the differences were not always statistically significant, the Arabic-speaking groups was superior to its Berber-speaking counterpart. In years 2 and 3, both tests of more advanced reading skills, the Word Picture Matching test and the Sentence Maze test, showed general superiority for the native Arabic-speaking children. The single large statistical interaction indicated that, on year 3 of the Word Picture Matching test, the Quranic-schooled Berber-speaking group (QB) had caught up with the Arabic-speaking samples, while the non-preschooled group (NB) remained behind.

The superiority of the Arabic-speaking children in these early stages of literacy acquisition is most likely explained by the greater similarity between their spoken language (MA) and the language of literacy (SA). This similarity provides a closer relationship of the phonological system of spoken MA with that of written SA, which makes the tasks of word decoding and the vocalization of letters, letter blends, and words easier for the Arabic-speaking group than for the Berber-speaking group. Similarly, the kinship between the lexico-semantic systems of the two varieties of Arabic gives an advantage to the Arabic-speaking group in terms of word recognition, decoding words, and reading comprehension.

The exact route by which language similarities existing between MA and SA operate to facilitate the acquisition of literacy for MA speakers is, however, not entirely clear. It may be direct, such that the phonological and lexical overlap is called into play independently of any formal instruction given in the early months of the first year of primary school. On the other hand the effects may be more indirect, such that the similarity between the two Arabic varieties facilitates the MA-speaking pupils' understanding of, and benefit from, the teacher's verbal instruction delivered (predominantly) in SA during the first year of school. The most probable explanation for the observed superiority of performance by Arabic-speaking children is a combination of both direct and indirect effects. Similar findings are well known in the literature on bilingualism and education (Downing, 1973, 1984; Saville & Troike, 1971; UNESCO, 1953; Weber, 1970).

The present findings demonstrate that Berber-speaking children begin the process of literacy acquisition with a significant disadvantage in Arabic language and literacy skills. It appears that this initial disadvantage was reduced over the years of the study, particularly for the Berber-speaking children who had attended Quranic preschool. However, while it is certainly the case that most Berber-speaking children are learning to read in Arabic, a disproportionate number of these children continue to exhibit literacy abilities below those of their Arabic-speaking classmates, even into the third year of the study. The effects of this delay may be serious in terms of promotion in elementary school, and in terms of later access into the secondary school system. Only later years of the study will permit a clearer picture of long-term consequences.[5]

Upon entering primary school the Berber-speaking children, originally monolinguals, make daily progress toward Berber/MA bilingualism; with time, it is reasonable to expect that their growing proficiency in MA will aid in the acquisition of SA literacy in more or less the same way as it does for the monolingual MA-speakers of the sample. In the course of this study, then, the monolingual Berber-speakers of this sample are becoming more and more bilingual; this fact is a methodological reminder that "linguistic category" cannot be treated as a constant trait variable where language communities are in constant interaction. Where this incipient Berber/MA bilingualism will permit the average Berber-speaking child to reach the level of Arabic-speaking children of the same age and school grade remains to be seen.

---

[5]At the time of the preparation of this paper, the Morocco Literacy Project had collected the first three years data of a five year longitudinal study of primary schooling. The MLP collected data on the group of primary school dropouts to study the retention of literacy among adolescents who left school at an early age, the results of which can be found also in Wagner (1993).

Another factor which distinguishes the Moroccan case from many other studies of bilingualism and reading acquisition is the fact that there is no competing literacy in Berber. For rural families and their children, SA literacy is the first key to school success. In addition, social factors such as motivation for learning a second language probably also play a role (cf. Gardner & Lambert, 1972; Lambert, 1967). As was pointed out earlier, the language of literacy for both groups is the language of Islam, and as such, enjoys as much acceptance and respect among Berbers as Arabs. Thus, it is reasonable to posit that, relative to other societal situations of bilingualism and biliteracy, rather minimal differences exist between the motivation of the two language groups toward learning to read in SA. In the United States, for example, a main issue in bilingual policy is whether Spanish literacy should be taught to Hispanic children before or alongside English literacy. In post-independence Morocco, Standard Arabic has replaced French as the official spoken and written language. Similarly, in spite of considerable discussion and debate concerning the maintenance of French as a partner in education, Arabic has become the predominant language of instruction and literacy in Moroccan schools, notably through the present Ministry of Education's "arabization" policy (see Souali & Merrouni,1981).

B. The Effects of Quranic Preschool vs. No Preschool Experience

With respect to Quranic preschool experience, the results indicated a pattern similar to that of language differences, with Quranic preschooled children exhibiting performance levels generally superior to those of children without Quranic preschooling. However, while paired comparisons often showed Quranic groups to be superior to their non-Quranic counterparts, statistical significance was reached only for Word Picture Matching in year 1. The largest inter-group differences appeared to be between the Berber-speaking samples who did or did not go to Quranic school, with the group NB performing generally least well on most measures over the three year period.

The analyses showed that, while Quranic preschool experience is helpful for both Berber- and Arabic-speaking children in the early stages of literacy acquisition, the effects are fairly small. We had originally speculated that such preschooling might be differentially more useful to the Berber-speaking children, since this experience would provide them with earlier access to SA. This expectation was partially confirmed by the large interaction in Word Picture Matching in year 3.

VI. CONCLUSIONS

> The young Berber-speaking pupil often finds himself, without any
> initial preparation, confronted with other national languages and
> foreign languages taught at the school. A conflictual psychological
> situation inevitably follows, effectively reducing the pedagogical
> effort. (Moatassime, 1974, p. 641)

> Quranic school imposes on [the child] a purely mechanical, monoto-
> nous form of study in which nothing is likely to arouse his interest.
> The school thus tends to curb his intellectual and moral activity at
> the precise moment when it should be developing rapidly.
> (Zerdoumi, 1970, p. 196)

The present study suggests that the situations depicted above are not as
grim as their authors, North African social scientists, would have us
believe. While there must be some truth to these portraits, language
background and preschool experience appear to have differential and
complex effects on literacy acquisition among rural Moroccan children
in the first three years of primary school. By the second year, some of
these effects where attenuated, while other effects carried on into the
third year of primary schooling. This matrix of results points out some
important aspects of linguistic and schooling factors in present-day
Morocco, and may be helpful in guiding educational policy.

Within the Berber-speaking population in Morocco, the language of literacy (SA) enjoys considerable prestige and acceptance as the
language of Islam, which is as central to Berber cultural identity as it is
to Arabic-speaking Moroccans. Thus, it is not surprising that most
Berber-speaking children rapidly begin to acquire MA and SA as soon as
they begin primary school, if not before. The gains in elementary reading abilities are a natural consequence of this advance towards bilingualism, as has been shown in other countries by Engle (1976). Nonetheless,
it is also the case that the majority of Berber children remain behind their
MA-speaking peers even through the third year of primary school. As in
other countries with complex and politically sensitive linguistic situations, Moroccan government authorities have opted for a national program of Arabization where Berber is completely absent from the primary and secondary school classroom. Government statistics provide very
little information concerning the consequences of this monolingual
Arabization policy for the monolingual Berber-speaking community,
though our impression is that the monolingual Berber-speaking community is rapidly decreasing relative to the overall population. The present
study has demonstrated a certain number of effects on a small sample
from one rural community. Further research using larger samples would
be needed to confirm the present findings.

As for the usefulness of the Quranic preschool experience for promoting reading skills, the data suggest that the reading advantages held by children who had attended the traditional preschool were modest but consistent over the first three years of primary school. This finding may seem to conflict with a World Bank report (Smilansky, 1979) on the lack of usefulness of typical Western preschool programs producing persistent IQ gains. Indeed, beyond its effects on literacy, Quranic schooling also plays a role as a socializing agent and as an institution for instruction in religious and cultural values and ethics. Though this additional role is sometimes in dispute depending on the values of the observer (cf. Zerdoumi, 1970, cited earlier), evidence from the present research project indicates that rural parents retain consistent and positive attitudes toward the Quranic schools, whether or not their own children have attended such schools.

In sum, the analyses reported here suggest that in rural Morocco, early experience (and especially home language) continues to exert some influence on literacy acquisition through a child's third year of modern school attendance. The findings also suggest, however, that Quranic and modern public school contribute to the reduction of initial disparities in literacy skills. As later analyses subsequently indicated (Wagner, 1993), these trends were substantiated over the remaining years of primary school for this sample of children, through further work in Morocco and other countries has yet to be undertaken.

In terms of policy implications it seems clear that primary school does not exacerbate entry differences between the groups of children selected within this research study. Nonetheless, one cannot claim that the uniformity of curriculum is having an early or complete effect of reducing such entry differences, particularly with respect to maternal speakers of Berber. While the differences in literacy ability due to such preschooling are not very large in magnitude, it would seem useful to maintain and improve such preschooling for as many children as possible in rural Morocco. While some specialists might prefer an emphasis on "modern" preschools based on the French model, there is little evidence that such schools are superior to traditional Quranic schools in Morocco,[6] and it is unrealistic to hope, in the near future, that modern

---

[6]Analyses indicate that, on both cognitive and reading measures, urban children who attended modern-style preschools were roughly equivalent in performance to children who had attended traditional Quranic preschools for about the same time period. On a number of reading measures, both preschooled groups generally outperformed another group of urban children who did not attend any preschool (Wagner & Spratt, 1987). Our ethnographic observations supported these findings in that much greater similarities were found between so-called "modern" and "traditional" preschools than originally anticipated. While more

preschools could come close to accomplishing the enormous service already being rendered by the network of widely dispersed Quranic schools; for a discussion of possible impact of Quranic preschools in other countries, see Wagner (1989). Finally, it should be clear to policy makers that only through in-depth research such as that described here can reasonable programs be developed which will offer the maximum opportunity for children of different social and language backgrounds.

The future of literacy in Morocco would appear to depend greatly not only on the government's educational institutions, but also on the developing linguistic and political situation. The contemporary linguistic situation is, as noted earlier, in constant flux, and it is possible that current language policy will result in such a reduction of the monolingual Berber-speaking community that the educational issues will be solved by the transformation of this group into a predominantly bilingual Berber/MA speaking community. The politics of Moroccan education are subject to change as well, and the future of Quranic schooling will necessarily depend on its political support vis-à-vis more modern preschools. Though Morocco has made substantial gains in reducing what was once an extremely high national illiteracy rate, its future success in teaching Arabic literacy will depend, as in other countries, on a complex and unique set of local cultural factors. The present research indicates that, within contemporary Moroccan society, maternal language and traditional preschooling continue to play important roles in determining how, and how much, literacy is acquired during the childhood years.

VII. POSTSCRIPT

A decade later the Quranic schools of Morocco have weathered well the test of modernization. Indeed, internal agencies, such as the World Bank and Unicef, have led efforts to reinforce and refurbish traditional Islamic schools in Morocco. Parents continue to see such schools as a reasonable provider of value-rich experiences for their young children. And, of course, these traditional schools have not stayed unchanged over time, with the new, younger, and better trained teachers continuing to replace the more traditional teachers of yesteryear. How the government, the public, and other agencies will view this holdover from centuries past is one of the more interesting questions in the education of children growing up in Muslim countries.

---

focused on religious learning than modern preschools, Quranic preschools also provided, as noted in the text, elementary instruction in reading and arithmetic. Conversely, the modern preschools offered some Quranic study and emphasized rote recitation and memorization to an extent greater than expected (cf. Wagner, Messick, & Spratt, 1986).

REFERENCES

Badry, F. (1983). *Acquisition of lexical derivational rules in Moroccan Arabic: Implications for the development of Standard Arabic as a second language through literacy.* Unpublished Ph.D. dissertation, University of California, Berkeley.

Downing, J. (1973). *Comparative reading.* New York: Macmillan.

Downing, J. (1984). A source of cognitive confusion for beginning readers: Learning in a second language. *The Reading Teacher,* January, 366-370.

Eickelman, D.F. (1978). The art of memory: Islamic education and its social reproduction. *Comparative Studies in Society and History, 20,* 485-516.

Eickelman, D.F. (1985). *Knowledge and power in Morocco.* Princeton, NJ: Princeton University Press.

Engle, P. L. (1976). The language debate: Education in first or second language? In P. Sanday (Ed.), *Anthropology and the public interest* (pp. 247-272). New York: Academic Press.

Ezzaki, A., & Wagner, D.A. (1992). Language and literacy in the Maghreb. *Annual Review of Applied Linguistics* (Special issue on Literacy), Vol. 7.

Ferguson, C.A. (1959). Diglossia. *Word, 15,* 325-340.

Gardner, R.C., & Lambert, W.E. (1972). *Attitudes and motivation in second-language learning.* Rowley, MA: Newbury House.

Gates, A.I., & MacGinitie, W.H. (1965). *Gates-MacGinitie reading tests: Primary A, primary B, primary C.* New York: Teachers College Press.

Grandguillaume, G. (1983). *Arabization et politique linguistique au Maghreb.* Paris: Maisonneuve.

James, C. (1980). *Contrastive analysis.* London: Longman.

Lado, R. (1959). *Linguistics across cultures.* Ann Arbor: University of Michigan Press.

Lambert, W.E. (1967). Social psychology of bilingualism. *Journal of Social Issues, 23,* 91-109.

Macnamara, J. (1966). *Bilingualism in primary education.* Edinburgh: Edinburgh University Press.

Macnamara, J. (Issue Editor). (1967). Problems of bilingualism. *Journal of Social Issues, 23*(2).

Moatassime, A. (1974). Le "bilinguisme sauvage:" Blocage linguistique; sous-developpement et cooperation hypotheque; l'exemple maghrebin; cas du Maroc. *Tiers Monde, 15,* 619-670

Saville, M.R., & Troike, R.C. (1971). *A handbook of bilingual education.* Washington, DC: Teachers of English to Speakers of Other Languages.

Smilansky, M. (1979). Priorities in education: Preschool; evidence and conclusions. *World Bank Working Paper,* No. 323, April.

Souali, M., & Merrouni, M. (1981). Question de l'enseignement au Maroc. *Bulletin Social et Economique du Maroc,* Nos. 143-146.

Spratt, J.E., & Wagner, D.A. (1986). The making of a fqih: The transformation of traditional Islamic teachers in modern times. In M. White & S. Pollack (Eds.), *The cultural transition: Human experience and social transformation in the Third World and Japan.* New York: Routledge and Kegan Paul.

UNESCO (1953). The use of vernacular languages in education. *Monograph on fundamental education,* No. 8. Paris: UNESCO.

Venezky, R.L. (1970) Nonstandard language and reading. *Elementary English, 47,* 334-345.

Wagner, D.A. (1982). Quranic pedagogy in modern Morocco. In L.L. Adler (Ed.), *Cross-cultural research at issue.* New York: Academic Press.

Wagner, D.A. (1989). In support of primary schooling in developing countries: A new look at traditional indigenous schools. *World Bank Background Paper Series,* Doc. No. PHREE/89/23. Washington, DC: World Bank.

Wagner, D.A. (1993). *Literacy, culture and development: Becoming literate in Morocco.* New York: Cambridge University Press.

Wagner, D.A., & Lotfi, A. (1980). Traditional Islamic education in Morocco: Sociohistorical and psychological perspectives. *Comparative Education Review, 24,* 238-251.

Wagner, D.A., Messick, B.M., & Spratt, J. (1986). Studying literacy in Morocco. In B.B. Schieffelin & P. Gilmore (Eds.), *The acquisition of literacy: Ethnographic perspectives.* Norwood, NJ: Ablex.

Wagner, D.A., & Spratt, J.E. (1987). The cognitive consequences of contrasting pedagogies: The effects of Quranic preschooling in Morocco. *Child Development, 58,* 1207-1209.

Weber, R.M. (1970). *Linguistics and reading.* Washington, DC: ERIC Clearinghouse in Linguistics.

Zerdoumi, N. (1970). *Enfants d'hier: L'education de l'enfant en milieu traditional algerien.* Paris: Maspero.

13

Reconsidering the Effects of School and Home for Literacy in a Multicultural Cross-Language Context: The Case of Israel

Dina Feitelson†
University of Haifa, Israel

I. INTRODUCTION

Many people consider Israel a technologically highly developed society, with a well-educated population. This view does not take into account demographic shifts that occurred as a consequence of mass immigration, when a society of less than a million absorbed many times its original numbers. Immigrants came from 107 different countries speaking 82 languages. Additional groups, like the recent wave of immigrants from drought-stricken Ethiopia, continue to come. One problem faced by many of the immigrants was that, like immigrants in other countries, they lacked a knowledge of the language that was the main medium of communication in their new country.

---

†Deceased

In the case of Israel the language problem was greatly compounded by the diversity of cultural backgrounds of oldtimers and newcomers. The majority of immigrants were refugees from Arab countries, where in many cases educational standards for the masses had been poor. These new immigrants found themselves in a society known for its exceptionally high level of educational aspirations, where music and knowledge quizzes were a national hobby that commanded prime time on the mass media. Today, about 70% of each year's first-grade population in Israeli schools are children or grandchildren of men who had only very few years of schooling, if any, and of women who in most cases were illiterate. What do these facts mean in terms of young children about to enter school?

Recent studies have described in detail how well-educated parents in mainstream cultures help their young children make the transition to literacy (Bissex, 1980; Chomsky, 1972; Heath, 1983; Snow, 1983; Teale & Sulzby, this volume). In modern societies children are exposed in their daily lives to a variety of written messages. Educated adults tend to take the time and trouble to interpret these messages, in addition to providing detailed information on the technicalities of encoding and decoding processes, adjusted to children's developmental stage and level of prior knowledge (Mason, 1980; Goodman, 1984). Thus, children receive continuous direct aid in inferring and acquiring the graphic code which represents spoken language. School-oriented homes also typically provide role models and first-hand experiences which socialize young and even very young children to intensive book usage and to linking book-centered activities with pleasure and enjoyment.

On reaching school-entering age, children who grew up in homes of this kind will be well prepared for the learning tasks they face. Many of them will already have considerable understanding for the way spoken and written language are related to each other, or be able to decode texts on their own. Others, though perhaps less advanced, will still have acquired some important preparatory skills.

The proliferation of studies which deal with the role of home-related factors in the acquisition of literacy may have some unforeseen side effects. Texts for teachers and teachers-in-training that describe these studies may, without intending to, lead teachers to expect that children will acquire reading mainly by being exposed to books. Teachers may also come to overestimate the part that non-school related factors as opposed to school factors play in successful learning of all children.

In multicultural societies teachers will frequently deal with students whose home conditions are entirely different from those familiar to them. Feitelson (1954), Heath (1982, 1983), Schieffelin (this volume) and others have provided descriptions of children growing up in communities where parents do not habitually engage their children in book-linked experiences. Living in a multicultural society means among other things that the experiences children have in school may be very different from those their parents had when they were young. Expecting parents to provide background knowledge and ongoing help for children's learning may therefore be unrealistic. Even if parents were aware of the school's expectations, and willing to comply, they might frequently lack language knowledge and other necessary skills in order to undertake tutoring tasks effectively.

Another factor to keep in mind is that persons experiencing transitional processes in a multicultural society may be exposed to considerable stress. Having to learn to cope with new demands and strange situations exerts a price. Short tempers and strained interpersonal relations may be more prevalent than in former, more tranquil times, when individual members of the society usually had more adequate support systems to fall back upon. Having one's children exposed to an environment and requirements one has not experienced oneself, and knowing that one will be unable to assist them in any way, is undoubtedly threatening. Burdening parents under these conditions with responsibilities that they have no way of fulfilling satisfactorily, may not lead to the hoped-for results. Worse still, pressures of this kind may in fact lead to a deterioration of parent-child relationships and/or to a possible breach between school and home.

This means that in multicultural societies the formal school establishment may find that it has to take on tasks which teachers in highly industrialized stable communities expect the home to perform. Thus what is needed is a reassessment of the roles of teachers and parents in relation to each other, and of the responsibilities each side bears for providing a basis for children developing into happy, fully functioning members of their society. The following sections will present examples of some of the outcomes of such a reassessment in the area of beginning reading.

In order to prevent misunderstandings it may be best to emphasize that a reassessment of respective responsibilities should not be taken to mean that parents can or should be excluded from their child's school life, or cut off from fully participating in as many aspects of it as possible. However, what is suggested is that success in learning tasks and vicarious participation in all other experiences offered in modern schools cannot be allowed to depend only on parents' ability to prepare their children for these tasks and experiences.

Experience in Israel has shown that parents from a wide variety of backgrounds can become acknowledged partners in school decision-making, as well as in many school activities and events (Fridman, 1984). Today, parental help and active involvement is solicited in many schools, and every effort is made to keep parents informed about curriculum, instructional approaches and about their own child's performance. However, interpreting school-home cooperation to mean that, in a multicultural society, the onus for corrective action in cases of school problems can or should be transferred to parents, would clearly be a mistake. Whenever it is in the best interest of children and their success in learning tasks schools will have to fall back on their own resources and undertake the necessary steps in order to help individual children progress satisfactorily.

Let us now examine two examples of how schools can provide successful learning experiences for beginning readers, who enter school with little preparation for school tasks and cannot look forward to help in their homes.

II. LAYING THE FOUNDATIONS FOR COMPREHENSION PROCESSES

During the past decade the main interest of reading researchers has shifted from the area of decoding to that of reading comprehension (Pearson & Samuels, 1980). Presently major research efforts are underway that aim at providing an understanding of the many complex skills that are activated in reading comprehension.

Over the years a great number of studies have shown that children growing up in middle-class school-oriented homes generally do well in reading (Chall & Snow, 1982; Marjoribanks, 1974). What is it then that happens in school-oriented homes which is not duplicated in homes where children have difficulties? Studies of early readers and good readers have consistently shown that these children tended to have access to books from an early age on, and were read to extensively by members of their families (i.e., Durkin, 1966; Chomsky, 1972; Clark, 1976; Wells, 1981).

Though minority groups in multicultural modern societies may use written language in a variety of ways, this fact does not necessarily mean that reading to young children has become accepted practice (Heath, 1982, 1983; Schieffelin & Cochran-Smith, 1984). Comparing the book environments of 51 kindergartners whose middle-class parents originated from Europe with that of kindergartners whose working-class parents originated from Near Eastern and North African countries, Feitelson and Goldstein (1986) found that children in the first group, on average, personally owned 54.6 books, and except for two, whose mothers knew little Hebrew, were read to daily for extended periods of time.

On the other hand more than 60% of the children in the second group did not own any books, and only about 15% were read to more or less regularly. Also, in about half of the homes in the first group, regular reading had started before children were 2 years old, and joint looking at picture books had started considerably earlier. On the other hand, many parents in the second group maintained that there was no point in providing children with books before they were able to read them by themselves. They also considered buying books for children so young a waste, because they were sure to tear their books up.

A series of related experimental studies investigated the effects of reading to kindergartners and first-graders in formal school settings (Feitelson, Kita, & Goldstein, 1986). In most of the studies the experimental intervention consisted of whole classes which were read to collectively between three and six times a week for 4-5 months. In several of the studies, children in control groups were exposed to other kinds of interventions, such as a cognitive enrichment program or teacher-led group games. Except for one study where intervention had lasted only 3 months, experimental children in all the studies significantly outperformed their controls on measures of reading (for kindergartners, listening comprehension). When asked to tell a story according to a picture sequence, children in the experimental groups used longer sentences than their controls. In many of the studies children who had been read to also had significantly higher scores on number of different words used, and measures of story structure and causality. Furthermore, teachers reported that experimental children often used typical "book words" and phrases when interacting with each other. First-graders in an immigrant neighborhood, who had been read to from a many-volumed series story, induced their families to buy them additional volumes in the series, and read them on their own. This happened despite the fact that a great number of families in that neighborhood are social welfare recipients, and did not normally have financial resources to spare, despite the exceedingly high price of children's books in Israel.

These studies show that adults who read to 5- and 6-year-olds in formal school settings can indeed impart some of the skills that children in school-oriented homes acquire when being read to at earlier ages by members of their families. In addition such findings support a causal relationship between reading to children from storybooks and children's emergent reading/listening comprehension and additional language and cognitive skills. Let us now try to understand in what way reading to young children may lead to such positive results.

In many languages the difference between daily speech directed at young children and literary language is much greater than in English. This is not only a matter of vocabulary, which tends to be more precise and richer. In literary Hebrew, for example, sentences are long and complex and do not open with the subject. In addition both nouns and verbs are invariably conjugated even in children's books, a usage which has been discarded in daily speech. As a result a highly familiar word like *Aba* (father, dad) turns into *Avi, Avicha, Avotehem* and additional variations for "my father," "your father," "their fathers" and the like. Being read to massively from early childhood on means that children will be immersed in this written kind of language, with the persons reading to them simplifying and clarifying as they go along (Cochran-Smith, 1984; Feitelson & Goldstein, 1986). Thus, upon attaining the ability to decode, children will pick up books to read on their own, and "book language" will not be an obstacle; they can make the transition to becoming active readers unhindered. However, children who had no prior experiences with literary language may encounter an unforeseen setback when, at the same stage, they turn expectantly to books. Though they are able to decode, what they read may fail to make sense.

Being read to prepares the ground for subsequent reading comprehension in additional ways. Children's books provide information beyond a child's immediate here and now. Adults in school-oriented families who read to children tend to mediate between their children and this new information by elaborating, expanding, scaffolding and calling to mind past experiences and stories (Anderson & Pearson, 1984; Heath, 1982; Stein, 1979). These activities are considerably enhanced when, as is often the case, reading adults are intimately acquainted with the children to whom they read so that they can draw on their personal experiences. As a causal relationship between background knowledge and reading comprehension has by now been firmly established (Beebe, 1984; Tierney & Cunningham,1984), there is reason to believe that the large amounts of information children acquire in this way will be of considerable help in their later unmediated encounters with text.

Providing children with what Gates (1947) called a "story sense", and today's researchers refer to as story schemas, namely a feeling for the structural elements of narratives, is a further way in which early reading to children seems to prepare them informally for reading on their own. The stories children told in response to a picture sequence were rated on whether there was a plot with a clearly discernible beginning and end, or on whether children talked about the contents of each picture separately without combining them into a sequential happening. First-graders who had been read to regularly for 6 months outperformed their controls on this measure (Feitelson, Kita, & Goldstein, 1986). This result supports the view that listening to stories develops familiarity with story schemas.

Our studies show that, even when children are read to in formal primary school settings at somewhat older ages, such regular reading over 5-6 months has beneficial results. By emulating what parents in school- oriented homes do naturally, namely read to their children, teachers in multicultural societies can upgrade pupils' reading/listening comprehension.

Our second example deals with the respective roles of teachers and parents in the area of decoding. As we shall see the issue of possible cultural differences between school and home is compounded by problems related to the nature of the written language children are acquiring.

III. ASSUMING RESPONSIBILITY FOR MASTERING DECODING SKILLS

Languages differ from each other in the way speech is translated to symbolic graphic codes. It is now generally accepted that the process of acquiring written language is partly influenced by the specific characteristics of the writing system that is being learned (Kavanagh & Venezky, 1980). In the same vein, the model of middle-class youngsters acquiring the rudiments of reading English informally, with the help of their parents, may be misleading with regard to preschoolers learning to read other languages in entirely different circumstances.

The advent of mass immigration to Israel was accompanied by extensive failure in first-grade reading, with up to 50% of first-graders in many schools unable to continue to second grade (Dror, 1963; Enoch, 1950). Until that time, reading had been taught, seemingly very success fully, by a whole-word approach. This approach originated in Great Britain and the United States, where most leading educators were trained in the days before Israel became independent. An examination of the suitability of this approach to the idiosyncrasies of written Hebrew led to the tentative conclusion that most of the tenets of this approach would not apply in Hebrew (Feitelson, 1973). Indeed, when, under the auspices of the Israeli Ministry of Education, alternative approaches bases on the characteristics of the Hebrew language and orthography were developed and disseminated, the problem of first-grade failure in immigrant areas ceased to exist (Adiel, 1968; Adler & Peleg, 1976). There remained an intriguing question, however: How could a teaching approach that had evidently been particularly unsuited to language circumstances be successful for nearly 30 years? Interviews with parents of children who had learned to read successfully by the former approach revealed that in many cases these parents had considerably augmented whatever teaching their children had received in class (Feitelson, 1973). When newly immigrated parents, who were themselves unschooled, where unable to provide similar help the approach failed.

Beginners' texts in English usually contain numerous repetitions of distinct unchanging words. In inflected languages like Finnish, Arabic or Hebrew, words are conjugated according to gender, tense, mode, number, etc. Even beginners will thus be exposed to different forms of the same word as unchanging words are simply not available. There may be added difficulties like excessively long words in Finnish, or vowels that are represented by diacritical marks instead of full sized letters in Arabic and Hebrew. As the Israeli example showed, helping learners to cope with intricacies of this kind required instructional strategies that had been specifically adapted to particular language contingencies. This is a further reason why, when teaching decoding insights, teachers who are knowledgeable about the rationale of language-linked strategies, and have experience in using them, may play an increased role in literacy acquisition.

Let us now progress to examples of what is meant by instructional strategies that are adapted to language specifications. This also leads to the question of whether adapting instructional strategies to language idiosyncrasies means that pedagogical insights about beginning reading cannot be transferred across languages?

Among alphabetic languages, even languages that have entirely different origins or orthographies may share characteristics that translate into similar learning problems. With respect to learning to decode, the more characteristics two orthographies have in common, the more it seems possible to make use of strategies that have been shown to be effective in one orthography also in the second (Feitelson, 1966, 1967, 1973, 1976). Furthermore, results of basic research which investigated particular contingencies within one orthography seem to be applicable whenever the same contingencies recur.

For example, Carnine (1976, 1980, 1981) found that when young children are taught to recognize symbols that are visually similar, like English "b" and "d" or "p" and "q", children's confusions can be significantly reduced by introducing the symbols that tend to be confused in conjunction with symbols that are visually distinct rather than in conjunction with each other. The same holds true for auditorily confusable items.

Educators in several countries seem to have been led by classroom experiences to the same conclusions, and to have acted accordingly. In respective statements about beginning reading instruction in Austria (Schenk-Danziger, 1967) and Finland (Kyöstiö, 1980), both authors refer to the fact that the sequential order in which letters are learned is influenced by their properties, and that it is well known what letters are "easy" or "difficult". In Hebrew, where auditory and visual confusability of letters is a special problem (Shimron, 1984) consistent efforts at spacing similar letters as far away from each other as possible have proved effective (Feitelson, 1965, 1973, 1980). Subsequently similar strategies were adopted also for Arabic (Chazan, Marsha, & Charadan, 1982), where visual and auditory confusability of letters is even greater (Chazan, 1979; Marsha, 1980).

In many languages in which symbol-sound correspondences are consistent, educators have developed synthetic (phoneme-grapheme correspondences are taught directly and combined to form words) approaches for introducing children to written language. Finland and the. Soviet Union are among the better-known examples. In those countries, program designers found that it was optimal to sequence letter introduction in such a way that the first two letters children learn can be quickly combined into a meaningful word, and every added letter leads to further functional words and phrases. Research has shown that preschoolers discriminate, match and learn single-letter symbols significantly better than letter strings and words (Calfee, Chapman, & Venezky, 1972; Feitelson & Razel, 1984; Samuels, LaBerge, & Bremer, 1978). These results seem to indicate that a synthetic approach, where graphemes are learned one by one, may indeed be easier for school beginners than an analytic (whole words are learned first, and letter-sound correspondences are inferred from them) approach.

Current reading theory holds that learning to read is a cognitive process in the course of which the learner discovers the connection between the technical aspects of reading and meaningful reading acts (Gibson & Levin, 1975; Mason, 1980). In functional synthetic approaches, where the very first letters learned are immediately combined into meaningful messages, this discovery occurs in the initial stage of learning: Furthermore, by carefully structuring the learning situation, teachers actively lead students step by step to the necessary insights. On the other hand, in most whole-word approaches currently in use, learners have to infer the crucial connections on their own, as a result of a relatively large amount of pertinent information amassed over weeks and months of learning (Feitelson, 1988; Gibson & Levin, 1975). It would seem, therefore, that functional synthetic approaches may be especially suited for school beginners in multicultural societies, who often lack preparation for school, and help at home while learning. On the other hand the method of instruction per se might make less difference for children from school- oriented families, who seem to acquire the rudiments of reading largely at home.

IV. A LOOK INTO THE FUTURE

Characteristics of multicultural societies are not a unique outcome of recent mass migration, such as in Israel. In demographically stable societies there may be significant linguistic, cultural and ethnic differences among subgroups who sometimes live in close proximity to each other, such as in the United States. Today's school establishments in many countries, Israel included, are keenly aware of the need to help children preserve the cultural tradition of their families. However, working actively towards this end does not mean that schools can forgo their responsibility for equipping children with all they need in order to have access to the full opportunities of the wider society.

Compared to other countries, progress towards this end in Israel has been particularly rapid. The percentage of university students and persons in political office and leading positions whose families originated from Third World countries is remarkable and steadily increasing. There is no question that these achievements are largely due to the way schools have adapted to the necessity to play a critical role in ensuring children's learning.

REFERENCES

Adiel, S. (1968). Reading ability of culturally deprived first graders. *Megamot, 15,* 345-356. (in Hebrew)

Adler, C., & Peleg, R. (1976). *Evaluating the results of studies and experiments in compensatory education.* Jerusalem: Hebrew University, School of Education. (in Hebrew)

Anderson, R.C., & Pearson, P.D. (1984). A schema-theoretic view of basic processes in reading comprehension. In P.D. Pearson, R. Barr, M.L. Kamil, & P. Mosenthal (Eds.), *Handbook of reading research.* New York: Longman.

Beebe, M.J. (1984). *The integration of psycholinguistic and discourse processing theories of reading comprehension.* Paper presented at the 29th annual convention of the International Reading Association, Atlanta, Georgia.

Bissex, G.L. (1980). *Gnys at work: A child learns to write and read.* Cambridge, MA: Harvard University Press.

Calfee, R.C., Chapman, R., & Venezky, R. (1972). How a child needs to think to learn to read. In L.W. Gregg (Ed.), *Cognition and learning in memory.* New York: Wiley.

Carnine, D.W. (1976). Similar sound separation and cumulative introduction in learning letter-sound correspondences. *Journal of Educational Research, 69,* 368-372.

Carnine, D.W. (1980). Two letter discrimination sequences: High-confusion-alternatives first versus low-confusion-alternatives first. *Journal of Reading Behavior, 12*, 41-47.

Carnine, D.W. (1981). Reducing training problems associated with visually and auditory similar correspondences. *Journal of Learning Disabilities, 14*, 276-279.

Chall, J.S. (1983). *Learning to read: The great debate.* Updated edition. New York: McGraw-Hill.

Chall, J.S., & Snow, C.E. (1982). *Families and literacy: The contribution of out-of-school experiences to children's acquisition of literacy.* Final Report to the National Institute of Education.

Chazan, H. (1979). *Developing and field-testing a program for teaching beginning reading to native speakers of Arabic.* Unpublished Masters thesis, University of Haifa. (in Hebrew)

Chazan, H., Marsha, S., & Charadan, S. (1982). *I read.* Haifa, Gestilit. (in Arabic)

Cochran-Smith, M. (1984). *The making of a reader.* Norwood, NJ: Ablex.

Chomsky, C. (1972). Stages in language development and reading exposure. *Harvard Educational Review, 42*, 1-33.

Clark, M.M. (1976). *Young fluent readers.* London: Heinemann.

Dror, R. (1963). Educational research in Israel. In A.M. Dushkin & C. Frankenstein (Eds.), *Studies in education, Scripta Hierosolymitana.* Jerusalem: Magnes.

Durkin, D. (1966). *Children who read early.* New York: Teachers College Press.

Enoch, H. (1950). Dropouts and students who continue in the municipal schools of Tel Aviv. *Megamot, 2*, 34-51. (in Hebrew)

Feitelson, D. (1954). Childrearing practices in the Kurdish community. *Megamot, 5*, 95-109. (in Hebrew)

Feitelson, D. (1965). Structuring the teaching of reading according to major features of the language and its script. *Elementary English, 42*, 870-877.

Feitelson, D. (1966). The alphabetic principle in Hebrew and German contrasted with the alphabetic principle in English. In P. Tyler (Ed.), *Linguistics and reading.* Newark, DE: International Reading Association.

Feitelson, D. (1967). The relationship between systems of writing and the teaching of reading. In M. Jenkinson (Ed.), *Reading instruction: International forum.* Newark, DE: International Reading Association.

Feitelson, D. (1973). Israel. In J. Downing (Ed.), *Comparative reading.* New York: Macmillan

Feitelson, D. (1976). Sequence and structure in a writing system with consistent symbol-sound correspondence. In J. Merritt (Ed.), *New horizons in reading.* Newark, DE: International Reading Association.

Feitelson, D. (1980). Relating instructional strategies to language idiosyncrasies in Hebrew. In J. F. Kavanagh & R.L. Venezky (Eds.), *Orthography, reading and dyslexia.* Baltimore: University Park Press.

Feitelson, D. (1988). *Facts and fads in beginning reading: A cross language perspective*. Norwood, NJ: Ablex.

Feitelson, D., & Goldstein, Z. (1986). Patterns of book ownership and reading to young children in Israeli school-oriented and non-school-oriented families. *Reading Teacher, 39*, 924-930.

Feitelson, D., Kita, B., & Goldstein, Z. (1986). Effects of listening to series-stories on first graders' comprehension and use of language. *Research in the Teaching of English, 39*, 924-930.

Feitelson, D., & Razel, M. (1984). Word superiority and word shape effects in beginning readers. *International Journal of Behavioural Development, 7*, 359-370.

Fridman, I. (1984). *School, home and community in Israel*. Jerusalem: Henrietta Szold Institute.

Gates, A.L. (1947). *The improvement of reading*. New York: Macmillan.

Gibson, E.J., & Levin, H. (1975). *The psychology of reading*. Cambridge, MA: MIT Press.

Goodman, Y. (1984). The development of initial literacy. In H. Goelman, A.A. Oberg, & F. Smith (Eds.), *Awakening to literacy*. Exeter, NH: Heinemann.

Heath, S.B. (1982). What no bedtime story means: Narrative skills at home and school. *Language in Society, 11*, 49-76.

Heath, S.B. (1983). *Ways with words: Language, life and work in communities and classroom*. London: Cambridge University Press.

Kavanagh, J.F., & Venezky, R.L. (Eds.). (1980). *Orthography, reading and dyslexia*. Baltimore: University Park Press.

Kyöstiö, O.K. (1980). Is learning to read easy in a language in which the grapheme-phoneme correspondence is regular? In J.F. Kavanagh & R. L. Venezky (Eds.), *Orthography, reading and dyslexia*. Baltimore: University Park Press.

Marjoribanks, K. (Ed.). (1974). *Environments for learning*. London: National Foundation for Educational Research.

Marsha, S. (1980). *Linguistic considerations in teaching reading to native speakers of Arabic*. Unpublished Master's thesis, University of Haifa. (in Hebrew)

Mason, J.M. (1980). When do children begin to read: An exploration of four year old children's letter and word reading competencies. *Reading Research Quarterly, 15*, 203-227.

Pearson, P.D., & Samuels, S.J. (1980). Why comprehension? *Reading Research Quarterly, 15*, 181-182.

Samuels, S.J., LaBerge, D., & Bremer, C.D. (1978). Units of word recognition: Evidence for developmental changes. *Journal of Verbal Learning and Verbal Behavior, 17*, 715-720.

Schenk-Danziger, L. (1967). The concept of reading readiness in Austria. In M.D. Jenkinson (Ed.), *Reading instruction: An international forum*. Newark, DE: International Reading Association.

Schieffelin, B.B., & Cochran-Smith, M. (1984). Learning to read culturally: Literacy before schooling. In H. Goelman, A.A. Oberg, & F. Smith (Eds.), *Awakening to literacy*. Exeter, NH: Heinemann.

Shimron, J. (1984). The psychology of reading Hebrew: Letter perception. *Studies in Education, 40,* 21-48. (in Hebrew)

Snow, C.E. (1983). Literacy and language: Relationships during the preschool years. *Harvard Educational Review, 53,* 165-189.

Stein, N.L. (1979). How children understand stories: A developmental analysis. In L.G. Katz (Ed.), *Current topics in early childhood education, 2.* Norwood, NJ: Ablex.

Teale, W.H. (1984). Reading to young children: Its significance for literacy development. In H. Goelman, A. A. Oberg, & F. Smith (Eds.), *Awakening to literacy*. Exeter, NH: Heinemann.

Tierney, R.J., & Cunningham, J.M. (1984). In P.D. Pearson (Ed.). *Handbook of reading research*. New York: Longman.

Wells, G. (1981). *Learning through interaction: The study of language development*. Cambridge: Cambridge University Press.

14

Literacy in the South Pacific: Some Multilingual and Multiethnic Issues

Francis Mangubhai
University of Southern Queensland, Australia

I. INTRODUCTION

The development of literacy in the vernacular languages in the South Pacific is due almost entirely to the efforts of the missionaries who first came to the region in the nineteenth century. They saw the need to translate the Bible stories into the language of the people they were attempting to convert and to teach them to read those stories. The result has been, at least in the eastern part of the South Pacific, a very high rate of literacy in comparison to many developing countries in other parts of the world. Biliteracy was introduced when formal schooling became established, particularly, as it happened in many countries in the South Pacific, when the colonial government began to take a greater interest in the education of the people they were governing.

Literacy in the vernacular in the monolingual parts of the South Pacific took root quite quickly. It was, however, a different matter in those countries that were multilingual, where the development of literacy in the vernacular was held back because of the multiplicity of lan-

213

guages, the small number of speakers for many of the languages, and the lack of orthography for many of them. The development of literacy in these countries began largely in a language of wider communication like English or French in a formal school environment.

In this chapter, after touching briefly on literacy in the South Pacific, a sketch of language and education in multilingual and multiethnic Fiji will be presented as a background to the Book Flood Project, designed to improve the reading skills of elementary children in schools in Fiji. The Project will be described, and implications for literacy, particularly the enhancement of literacy skills in educational contexts, will be discussed. Finally, it will be suggested that literacy practices in the South Pacific develop along different domains for different languages, and that the people of the South Pacific are becoming biliterate, in some cases literate first in the mother-tongue and then a language of wider communication, and vice-versa in other cases.

II. LITERACY IN THE SOUTH PACIFIC

Literacy in the South Pacific, particularly in the eastern part, has a common historical origin: the movement from a completely nonliterate state to becoming literate, initially, for the prime purpose of reading the Bible and other religious writings. Fiji, regarded as the meeting place of Melanesia and Polynesia, saw its first missionaries in 1835. Their mission was to convert Fijians to Christianity and one of their major weapons towards this end was literacy. They were specifically charged to "draw up a comprehensive statement respecting the character of the language, and the difference between it and other Polynesian dialects, the principles on which you have settled its grammatical form, and the rules by which you have been guided in translating into it the word of God" (Cargill letters, 18 June 1839, quoted in Schutz, 1972, p. 2). The first missionaries in fact arrived from the neighboring island Kingdom of Tonga where Christianity and its concomitant literacy (in the Tongan language) had been introduced some few years earlier. Literacy practices of one type or another have therefore existed in countries such as Fiji, Tonga and Western Samoa for over 150 years.

By contrast, literacy in the western part of the South Pacific, in Vanuatu and Solomon Islands, is considerably less universal. The reasons for this are both historical and linguistic. The missionary activities in Solomon Islands, for example, took a different turn from that in the eastern part of the Pacific for at least three reasons: the diversity of languages, the climate and the indigenous Melanesian social structure which was more fragmented and egalitarian (Whiteman, 1983). Historically, therefore, these two countries have not had the same sort of educational opportunities prior to their independence. In Solomon Islands, for example, until recently less than half the children of school age went to an elementary school. While Vanuatu is a good deal more fortunate in that respect, there is nevertheless a high dropout rate and the paucity of junior high schools ensures that for many children education terminates after the elementary school.[1] Linguistically, these two countries are quite diverse. In Solomon Islands there are 62 distinct languages while Vanuatu with its even smaller population has 104 distinct languages (Lynch, 1984). The number of speakers varies a great deal across those languages and for many of these languages an orthography has yet to be devised. In the light of such linguistic diversity and their past political history, development of a more universal literacy has been limited.

In this chapter it will be argued that a more widespread literacy in mother-tongue and/or a second language is potentially easier to achieve in small island states than in those countries with larger populations and land masses. However, in those small island states that have a multiplicity of languages, many of which have a comparatively small number of speakers, more widespread literacy will occur in a language other than the vernacular languages, in an international language or in a lingua franca (e.g., pidgin) if that is encouraged by official government policy. The main agency for the spread of literacy in these countries will initially be the churches, but at some stage the governmental educational system will take over this function. The literate use of language for *critical, aesthetic, organizational* and *recreational* purposes (Heath, 1980; Swain, 1981) is likely to be confined for the near future to the four walls of the classroom for the greater part of the school population. Outside the institutional setting, uses or practices of literacy will be dependent largely on the social institutions which foster such practices and in which they become embedded (cf. Street, 1984, 1993). The uses of the mother-tongue literacy and the second language literacy will increasingly occur in different spheres of activities with normally little overlap. The situation can be regarded as a form of diglossia (see Ferguson, 1959) without one language necessarily being regarded as superior to the other, but rather more appropriate in one domain than in another (cf. Scribner & Cole, 1981; and Ferguson, 1978).[2]

---

[1]Seventy-five percent of the children according to the 1984 World Bank Report on Vanuatu, and only a small percent of the remaining 25% finish grade 12. Tyron (1988) cites 1987-1988 figures for Solomon Islands which shows that only 40% of a cohort reach grade 7, 13% go on to secondary education and only 0.6% of that cohort completes grade 12.

[2]The determination of different literacies in different languages (or dialects) can be aided by asking ourselves, along the lines of Hymes (1972) did for speaking: who writes to or for whom, when, for what purposes, in which manner, and in which language or dialect?

In order to explore the role of the educational system in the development of literacy, and particularly school-related literacy (as support for this type of literacy is currently generally lacking in the societies of the South Pacific), it is necessary to briefly outline the educational developments that have taken place in one of the South Pacific countries, Fiji, since the introduction of reading and writing. Parallel developments have taken place in countries such as Tonga and Western Samoa in the eastern part of the South Pacific, but with one major difference: neither of these countries is multilingual or multiethnic.

III. LANGUAGE AND EDUCATION IN FIJI

With the arrival of missionaries in Fiji in 1835, formal schooling was introduced into a society where learning previously had been integrated into the everyday life of the people and where particular types of learning were the prerogative of particular groups within a tribe. One learned to become a fisherman by going fishing with other fishermen and learning from the actual practice of fishing. One learned to be a canoe builder by working with the canoe builders. In short, traditional education was "practical, vocational and was concerned largely in maintaining the status quo" (Bole, 1972, p. 1). The initial educational emphasis was on the teaching of reading in the Fijian language for which a romanized alphabet had been devised, to which later some teaching of elementary numeracy was added. The prime focus remained the teaching of reading in order to read the Bible and other religious writing (see Mangubhai, 1984, 1994 for further details).

However, there was not just one variety of Fijian language throughout the group of islands, and as the missionaries spread to other major islands the economics of printing forced a choice of one of the Fijian languages (or communalects) as the main literary medium (Geraghty, 1984). The choice was most judicious on the part of the missionaries. The seat of the most powerful "state" at that time was the small island of Bau, so the Bauan dialect was chosen.[3] Moreover, this language was similar to the "Standard Fijian" which was the existing language of diplomacy. Hence the Bauan Language was "objectified"; the written form became a standard against which language could be judged as correct or incorrect. It became an objective yardstick.

---

[3]Geraghty (1984) has in fact argued that it was not quite the Bauan language but the missionaries chose to call it that, a tactical foresight that served their purpose well.

However, this very process of objectification of one of the Fijian dialects is not without an irony that springs from the way the written word is viewed by a society that has moved into a literate state (cf. the attitude of educated English in the nineteenth century to the English used in the James II version of the Bible). This language, which subsequently appeared in books and became the literary standard for the Fijian society, was, according to linguist Geraghty (1984, p. 35), different

> in a number of ways from the actual language of Bau. . . . What had become the literary Fijian was, quite simply Fijian as the missionaries spoke it; and they seem to have spoken it rather poorly for a number of reasons. Paramount among these is that they were under pressure, both from their superiors and from Fijian converts, to learn the language and produce translations quickly.

This particular codification of a spoken language into a written form still has a powerful influence over the Fijian people with regard to what is acceptable or not acceptable in print.[4]

The Wesleyan Methodist Church, to which the first missionaries belonged, soon established village schools run by pastor-teachers who underwent a rudimentary form of teacher training. By the time Fiji was ceded to Great Britain in 1874 and became a crown colony, reading was widespread enough for the first Governor of Fiji in 1874 to comment upon it. Over 50 years later, Mann (1935, p. 13) was to say that due "almost entirely to the efforts of the missions, most adult Fijians can read and write their own language." For 50 years after Fiji had become a British crown colony the churches, Methodist and Catholic, the latter having arrived in Fiji a decade later than the former, continued to play a leading role in the education of the Fijian people. The Methodist Church emphasized the use of the Fijian language in their schools but the Catholic schools, as far back as the 1890s, had begun to teach some English. The introduction of some English into the school curriculum, and the colonial government's policies after 1916 when it established a Department of Education, was to change the emphasis of language used in educational settings dramatically in the 1900s.

---

[4]In the early 1970s, for example, a collection of short stories written in a more colloquial Fijian was published, but it received a very cool reception from the leaders of opinion in the Fijian society because amongst other reasons it did not use the "literary" Fijian, the language of the Fijian Bible. Racule (personal communication, 1994), the Director of Curriculum Development Unit in the Ministry of Education, suggests that there is beginning to be a change in the type of language that is regarded as "legitimate" in print, especially in books. The Fijian attitude is undergoing a change and more colloquial, modern Fijian is beginning to be acceptable in printed books and printed stories.

After 1879 the racial composition of the country also underwent a dramatic change. The colonial government brought in Indians from the subcontinent of India to work on the sugar cane plantations. By the time this indentured labor system was abolished in 1920, over 60,000 *indentured* laborers had been brought to Fiji, many of whom elected not to return to India, (Lal, 1983, 1994). With natural increase and some further migration from India, the country rapidly became multiethnic and multilingual, with the present composition being about half Fijians and just under half Indo-Fijians.[5]

By the middle of 1930s the Methodist Church had relinquished control of most of the elementary schools to the government. The use of Fijian as the medium of instruction thereafter became less widespread; a new policy was implemented whereby the medium of instruction for the first three years was to be the vernacular language, Fijian or Hindi, but thereafter to be replaced by English.[6] This ensured the predominance of English in the education system right to the present time, even after political independence in 1970.

This remains true even now 7 years after two military coups that Fijianized (indigenized) the government and changed the constitution to ensure that political power remained in the hands of the indigenous Fijians. There is, however, now a greater emphasis placed upon the development of literacy in the vernacular languages (Fijian, Hindi and Urdu) right up to grade 12, and not just grade 10 which was the case until the mid-1980s. The regional university, the University of the South Pacific, is introducing the study of Fijian and Hindi from the beginning of 1995, with Tongan and Samoan to be introduced at a later date.

IV. LITERACY FOR WHAT?

It is obvious from this very brief sketch of the development of the educational system in Fiji that the initial emphasis in education was on literacy in the vernacular language. However, the colonial government's policy, promulgated from 1916 onwards, of financially aiding those schools that taught some English, and the concurrent vocal demand of the Indian population after 1920 for more English, gradually changed the emphasis

---

[5]Prior to 1987 when the elected government was overthrown in a military coup, the proportions of population for the major ethnic groups were reversed.

[6]Such a policy was facilitated by the monoracial character of most of the elementary schools, a situation that has historical, political, sociological and geographical roots, and these largely separate school systems have continued to the present day.

and tilted it in favor of English. By then certain types of uses of literacy in the Fijian language had been established and had become socially accepted forms of behavior: reading the Bible and other religious writing; reading the government monthly paper in Fijian, government notices and such like; and probably some letter writing.[7] That letter writing for a variety of purposes was not embedded in the Fijian social institutions in the nineteenth century is evidenced by the following:

> While he [a chief] might offend the qase [the older folks, those in traditional authority] in Natewa bay (sic) by sending for their youths to build houses for him at Somosomo by letter in the *European fashion*, not by word of the accredited matanivanua [diplomat] as etiquette dictated. . . . (Blythe to Colonial Secretary, 23 September 1881, FCSO 81/1913, quoted in Scarr, 1980, p. 96, emphasis added)

With increased emphasis on education since World War II and the increased emphasis on the English language within the educational system, co-occurring with the development of towns and cities, the range of uses of literacy has also increased, including some reading of fiction, magazines and comics in English, political flyers and administrative notices in English, Fijian and Hindi.[8] These developments have been uneven, resulting in marked differences between the urban and rural areas. The former are served by newspapers, two dailies in the English language and two weeklies in Fijian and one in Hindi.[9] The population on the smaller islands of the country do not have regular access to such

---

[7]See also Clammer, 1976, pp. 146-173 for a discussion, somewhat tentative in nature, of the uses of literacy in the Fijian society by the end of the nineteenth century.

[8]There is, it seems, considerable interest in reading in the Fijian language in villages. The mobile library on the main island if Fiji is constantly asked as it visits villages whether there are any new publications in the Fijian language, and are disappointed when told "No" (Chief Librarian of Fiji, personal communication).

[9]In the late 1950s, there were one English daily, one English/Fijian weekly, three other Fijian publications appearing, weekly, fortnightly and monthly, five Hindi weeklies and one Tamil (a south Indian language) monthly (Lal, 1994, p. 158). Many of these publications were polemic and represented interests and viewpoints of segments of society or different interest groups within the one ethnic society. It highlights the role that literacy played in awakening political consciousness amongst the urban Indo-Fijians, particularly. Articles dealing with the local political scene were read and discussed or information derived from them was passed on to others. Each segment of the society interpreted the situation according to their own perspective and these newspapers served as a vehicle for propounding partisan viewpoints.

media. Important differences between the two groups, the Fijians and the Indo-Fijians, in regard to the literacy practices and the languages involved, have also become evident. For example, a study of newspaper circulation in 1984 showed that while two English dailies each published 25,000 and 22,000 copies every day, the two weekly papers in the Fijian language had a circulation of 17,000 and 8,000 compared to only 7,000 circulation for the Hindi paper (Geraghty, 1984). These differences are interesting when considered in the light of the fact that the Indo-Fijian population is concentrated in or around the coastal towns and cities of the two larger islands of the country and therefore has greater access to media mentioned earlier. It suggests that either the practice of reading newspapers in the vernacular language is not as widespread as in the Fijian community, or that a shift in language use is occurring within the Indo-Fijian society. The latter is more likely to be the case (see Moag, 1982, pp. 281-282).

While there has been no systematic study of the kind or types of uses of literacy in Fiji, or in any of the other island states in the South Pacific,[10] the amount of print available in the environment, the availability of electricity, working patterns of farmers in the rural areas, the transportation facilities, social institutions and values allow one to infer the range of literacy in the societies. People in urban areas are surrounded by print, mostly in English: notices, signs, advertisements, newspapers, magazines, books and so forth. By contrast the rural dwellers, particularly on the smaller islands, are in a relatively print-free environment, except for materials such as posters, government notices, the occasional advertisement or two in the local store and whatever books they may have at home. The latter are more likely to be religious, and written generally in the vernacular languages. Movement of the Fijian people from smaller islands to the larger ones for job purposes has necessitated some letter writing, but this occurs when there is a very definite purpose and not just for the purpose of "keeping in touch," which is much more likely to occur through regular monthly money orders and special trips on the occasion of a birth, marriage or death. However, a lively letters-to-the-editor column in one of the Fijian newspapers, and an equally lively one in the English newspapers, suggests a definite change in one of the uses of literacy (Geraghty, 1984). A sampling of the two English newspapers currently published shows lively letters on political topics, a phenomenon which would not have been seen 30 years ago. Prior to independence, a few non-

---

[10]A notable exception being Clammer's study, cited above. See also Spolsky et al. (1983), who have suggested that in the monolingual Kingdom of Tonga there was a more varied use of literacy because, amongst other reasons, it "was found to be useful by traditionally influential members of the community, that is to say, by the King and the nobles he chose to help him govern".

Europeans (non-Anglos) wrote to the newspapers. This then is a new phenomenon and suggests that, over time, new uses of literacy may develop into other areas also, like writing short stories,[11] poems, plays and more expository type of writing for polemical purposes.

By contrast the Indo-Fijian, with basic cultural and linguistic roots in India and Pakistan, has to a limited extent used the Hindi newspapers as an outlet for creative writing; but it has not been widespread, nor has there been a reading public large enough to foster the establishment of a regular literary magazine. One of the obstacles to the development of more creative writing in Hindi is that newspapers only accept writing in standard Hindi, whereas the language commonly spoken by people, referred to as *Fiji Baat*, is different in many ways from the standard form.

The question of the real extent of literacy in Fiji is a matter of some debate. The census in 1976 did not ask any questions related to language use but, if the same criterion that was employed in the 1966 census were to be used on the 1976 figures, a rough indication of the number of literate people in the country could be derived."[12] The 1966 census considered a person literate if he or she had 4 years of formal education. Using this definition the 1976 census indicated that over two-thirds of the population was literate in a mother-tongue, Fijian or Hindi (Mangubhai, 1977).

The question remains as to the nature and extent of this literacy, in either the vernacular languages or in English (which is generally taught in grade 2; in grade 1, only oral English is taught). Just how literate was a person who had a grade 4, 5 or 6 education? To answer this question a group of educators set out in 1977 to determine the level of achievement in English reading across the country.

V. READING SURVEY

A standardized test of reading comprehension was administered to 1,234 grade 6 children in a random sample of 54 schools which were selected to reflect the ethnic and linguistic composition of the country, the rural/urban dichotomy, and the variety of agencies that are involved

---

[11]It is interesting to note that while some Fijian short stories are written for publication in the Fijian newspaper, national short story writing contests conducted in all three languages, Fijian, Hindi and English, produce very few entries in the vernacular languages but a substantial number in the English language. This may be because the contests are advertised mainly through the English-language newspapers. Most of the writers in English are Fijian and Indo-Fijians. A small body of local literature in the English language is therefore available in a more permanent book or magazine form than is possible in a newspaper.

[12]See Graff, 1978, pp. 8-10 for a discussion on the problems of both a definition of a literate person as well as the measurement of the extent of literacy.

in running elementary schools in Fiji. The reading test consisted of a series of short passages in English, increasing in difficulty, each followed by some multiple-choice questions.[13] A questionnaire was administered to the teachers of the grade 6 classes used in the study (Elley & Mangubhai, 1979).

While the mean score on the reading test was 51%, over one-quarter of the sample had a mark that was low enough to suggest that they were merely guessing the answers. One pupil out of every four was unable to read simple short stories in English of about 100 words with understanding by the time he or she had reached the end of elementary school, after 6 years of English.[14] In the light of this finding it would seem that the use of education up to grade 4 as a benchmark for literacy is inappropriate, or at best a very crude measure. As no equivalent testing has been done in the vernacular, it is difficult to make a more categorical statement on this matter.[15]

The survey also showed that urban pupils did better than rural children, a not too unusual a finding (cf. Ladefoged, Glick, & Criper, 1968; Williams, 1981). Children in urban areas tended to come from a more advantaged family background, were more exposed to English and print around them and were generally taught by better-educated teachers. One of the interesting findings in this survey was that schools with libraries[16] of over 400 books produced much better readers than schools with smaller libraries or schools with no libraries. Educationally,

---

[13]The split-level reliability of the test was 0.92. The marks ranged from 3 (8%) to 37 (100%) with the mean of 19 (51%). The test also correlated highly with other measures of reading comprehension. When a cloze test of reading was administered to a sample of 100 pupils involved in the survey, from four schools, the correlation obtained was 0.79. The correlation with the English marks from the Fiji Intermediate Examination on 100 pupils was 0.77. The correlation with a New Zealand test (Progressive Achievement Test Reading Comprehension) for 38 pupils from two schools, after a break of 6 months, was 0.74.

[14]Compare Elley and Achal, 1981, who also found a similar pattern for English reading comprehension in their work on the production of standardized tests of achievement for Fiji. By contrast, only 12% of the pupils of grade 6 scored below chance level in English listening comprehension.

[15]Work done by Elley and Achal on standardized tests of achievement in vernacular languages, but not reported in the 1981 publication, has suggested that achievement in reading at grade 5 in Fijian is quite good; in Hindi less so and in Urdu quite poor, resulting in the abandonment of standardized tests of achievement in Urdu (Elley, personal communication).

[16]The term "libraries" as used here does not necessarily imply a special room set apart in the school. More frequently libraries in Fiji are storerooms or the principal's office from which books are taken to the classrooms.

this was an important indicator since, while little can be done directly and immediately to change the home factors, provision for a greater quantity of reading materials in schools can be effected in a relatively short time. The question would then be whether the provision of books by itself would make any difference in reading achievement in schools when the practice of *recreational* reading, either in schools or in the society at large, was very limited. The experiment described in the following section was designed to answer this question.

VI. BOOK FLOOD PROJECT

In order to evaluate the effects of putting high-interest, well-illustrated story and non-fiction books into classrooms, a carefully controlled experiment, referred to as the Book Flood Project, was set up in Fiji. In the choice of books the emphasis was on interest and good illustrations in order to give maximum pleasure to the readers in a way that children from homes where bedtime reading is a regular feature derive pleasure from such an activity (Holdaway, 1979). Fifteen predominantly rural schools were chosen for pre-testing because the pupils would be exposed to English in the school environment only, and were likely to be in contact only minimally with either spoken or written English once outside the school compound. To be considered for the experiment the schools also had to have few children's storybooks in the school so that reading for pleasure was not likely to be a school practice. In these respects they were typical of most primary schools in the rural areas.

Twelve schools (614 pupils together) were identified for the Book Flood Project. Eight of the schools received books and did daily reading for 25-30 minutes. This was in lieu of some other activity carried out during the English lesson. The remaining four schools received no books but were to carry on their normal English lesson. The time set apart for English lessons was constant across schools in keeping with the directives from the Ministry of Education. Thus there was no difference in the amount of time devoted to English by the experimental or control group. The groups were similar in English reading ability and ethnic distribution. The eight schools selected for the book flood were divided into two similar groups of four, so that an additional comparison could be made between two methods of using the books with the pupils: shared book reading and uninterrupted sustained silent reading. In each school a class of grade 4 and grade 5 were chosen since: (1) it was expected that pupils in grade 4 would be reading in English; and (2) it was thought that books in English at that level (grades 4 and 5) might be easier to obtain. The choice of English allowed for both Fijian and Indo-Fijian pupils to be tested, and because there are so few books in the vernacular languages suitable for that level. If there were to be a book "flood," it would be necessary to go to a source that would allow such a flooding.

Table 14.1 gives the design of the project as it was originally conceived. In addition to providing a comparison between two methods of reading it seemed that shared book approach to reading would suit the Fijian children better, as it reflected the social ethos of that culture in which socially cooperative behavior is the more acceptable norm. By contrast, reading silently by oneself is a form of behavior that does not have social approbation built into the culture of the Fijian society[17] except in the case of reading the Bible or some other religious writing. Yet it was obvious in this study that children, Fijian and Indo-Fijian, did sit down quietly and read books. It was an acceptable behavior within the "school culture," even if it might not be completely acceptable outside the confines of the school. In both the Fijian and Indo-Fijian communities the practice of reading for recreation or for increasing one's general knowledge store is uncommon outside the context of formal schooling.

TABLE 14.1. Design of Book Flood Project, 1980.

	February	March	April-October	November
Shared book experience group	Pretests	3-day workshop	250 books supplied to groups 4 and 5	Posttests
Silent reading	Pretests	No workshop	250 books supplied to grades 4 and 5	Posttests
Control group	Pretests	1-day workshop	Usual program; no extra books	Posttests

A. TEACHING PROCEDURES

1. Shared book experience method

Holdaway (1979) developed the shared book experience method in New Zealand primary schools, where it is now used extensively by European and Polynesian children. The teacher chooses a high-interest story with appropriate language and illustrations, and introduces it to the pupils in a "sharing experience," similar to that of a bedtime story. Discussion is

---

[17]Cf. Heath, 1980, who makes a similar observation about a black community in south eastern United States. See also, Reder (this volume).

encouraged about the pictures, the likely contents, and a few new words. The teacher then reads all or some of the story to the class. To ensure that all of the group can see the text and illustrations, the book is frequently "blown-up" or rewritten in the form of a giant book, with suitably sized illustrations.

During the second or third reading, on subsequent days, children are encouraged to join in and read easier sections with the teacher, who continues to encourage discussion about the contents of the book. Emphasis is placed on prediction and confirmation of events in the story, so that children are constantly striving for meaning. If children enjoy the experience they will want to read it often, in the class group, in small groups, in pairs, or as individuals.

Follow-up activities include role-playing, word study, art work, and writing activities. The origin of these activities is always determined by the story, not by any pre-ordained system of the proper sequence of structures and vocabulary to follow.

2. Silent reading method

The eight teachers who used the silent reading method were given no special workshop. They were advised by the experimenters to display the books attractively, to read them aloud to the class occasionally and to let their pupils spend 20-30 minutes each day in sustained silent reading (cf. McCracken, 1971). The rationale is that children best learn to read by reading as often as possible. A definite period is set aside every day for reading, during which time the teachers must set a good example by reading also. No book reports are required and no written exercises are set. The children read for enjoyment.

3. Control group

The eight teachers in the control group were advised to follow their normal curriculum in English, which was a structural audiolingual program. Children have two 15-minute oral English lessons each day in which new structures are systematically introduced, in appropriate classroom situations, with repeated drills, variations, substitution tables, and so forth. Reading is taught through carefully graded readers, and activities are provided primarily for practice in order to consolidate the structures and vocabulary taught in the oral lessons.

B. RESULTS AFTER ONE YEAR

Eight months later, in November, all the classes were tested again. Grade 4 was given tests of reading comprehension, English structures,[18] word recognition and oral sentence repetition. Grade 5 had tests in reading and listening comprehension, English structures and composition writing. The results showed that the two book flood groups performed considerably better than the control group in all four of the posttests. For grade 4 (see Table 14.2), however, only the differences in reading comprehension and English structures were significant.[19] The other two tests, word recognition and oral sentence repetition, were administered orally to smaller number of pupils and the differences were not large enough to be significant (for further details see Elley & Mangubhai, 1981a). Similarly, grade 5 results showed that the book flood groups, together and separately, did better than the control group in all tests, though the differences were significant for two tests only, reading and listening comprehension, but not for English structures and a writing task.[20] (See Table 14.3.)

TABLE 14.2. Residual Gain Scores for Grade 4 (1980).

	Shared Book		Silent reading		Control		F
	N	M	N	M	N	M	
Reading comprehension	75	0.59	84	1.21	106	-1.40	9.30*
English structures	71	0.99	84	0.63	106	-0.95	10.90*

*$p<0.001$.

[18]Basically a test of English syntax where subjects are required to complete sentences.

[19]The results reported here are based on regression estimates, in which all pupils were retained in all groups. Using the pretest as a predictor, each pupil's score was estimated, and subtracted from the actual score, and analysis of variance were performed on these residual gain (or loss) scores. An additional analysis based on raw scores, matched precisely by omitting 40 cases from the grade 4 control group, produced almost identical findings to those reported here.

[20]At grade 4 level there were no significant differences between the shared book and silent reading groups, $F(1,258 = 0.81$; at grade 5 level there were significant differences between the shared book group and the silent reading group on reading and listening comprehension tests, and $F(1,267) = 9.87$, $p<0.01$, $F(1,266) = 5.19$, $p<0.05$ respectively. In both tests the book flood groups were significantly better than the control group, as shown in the table.

TABLE 14.3. Residual Gain Scores for Grade 5 (1980).

	Shared Book		Silent reading		Control		F
	N	M	N	M	N	M	
STAF† reading comprehension	91	2.08	88	-0.14	91	-1.82	21.07*
STAF† listening comprehension	91	2.18	87	0.63	91	-2.13	35.74*
English structures	91	0.12	87	0.24	91	-0.33	NS
Written composition	91	0.05	87	0.16	91	-0.07	NS

*$p<0.001$
†Standardized Tests of Achievement for Fiji

C. SECOND YEAR EFFECTS OF THE PROJECT

An interesting and disturbing finding was that after 5 years of study of oral and written English, a large number of fifth-grade pupils in all three groups were unable to write a simple story of about half a page. Yet these pupils were reaching a stage in their elementary schooling where there would be increasing demands placed upon them to produce longer and longer pieces of connected prose, in addition to reading increasingly more complex prose. It was also clear that after 8 months of a reading program the writing skills of the two groups undergoing these programs had not been affected in any perceptible way. The Project was therefore continued with the same three groups of pupils for another year, for two main reasons: (1) to determine whether the significant differences found at the end of the first year would persist into the second year; and (2) to see whether writing skills would be positively affected.[21] The three experimental groups received the same treatment as in the previous year.

The significant gains that the book flood groups made over the control group were maintained as evidenced by the results at the end of the second year (for details, see Elley & Mangubhai 1981b, 1983). Grade 5 (previously grade 4) students were given three tests (reading and listening comprehension, and structures) and grade 6 (previously grade 5) students were given four tests (reading comprehension, word knowledge, structures and written composition). At both grade levels the book

---

[21]It was also thought that any Hawthorne effect would be much reduced in the second year.

flood groups scored significantly better than the control group in all the tests (see Tables 14.4 and 14.5). However, no significant differences were found between the shared book group and the silent reading group at either grade 5 or grade 6.

TABLE 14.4. Residual Gain Scores for Grade 5 (1981).

	Shared Book		Silent reading		Control		F
	N	M	N	M	N	M	
Reading comprehension	66	2.13	70	2.67	91	-3.60	58.14*
Listening comprehension	66	1.10	70	0.81	91	-1.45	28.73*
English structures	66	0.81	70	1.28	91	-1.55	27.49*

*$p<0.001$

TABLE 14.5. Residual Gain Scores for Grade 6 (1981).

	Shared Book		Silent reading		Control		F
	N	M	N	M	N	M	
Reading comprehension	81	1.27	64	1.40	87	-2.22	24.66*
Word knowledge	81	0.92	64	1.62	87	-2.02	30.17*
English structures	81	1.65	64	1.22	87	-2.46	24.73*
Written composition	81	0.52	64	0.66	87	-0.99	25.00*

*$p<0.001$.

While, at the end of the first year, no effects on writing ability were perceived, by the end of the second year it was evident that the effects of improved reading skill had a positive effect on the writing skill of the two experimental groups. The modal score given in the shared book group, for example, was 9 out of 10. By contrast, the modal mark in the control group was 2. Sample openings of stories which were given these marks indicate the difference in the quality of the writing of the two groups.

From the shared book group:

One morning when Luke's mother was washing, and the men were drinking yaqona, Luke was boiling the water.

One day, Tomasi's mother was washing, the clothes beside the river, Tomasi's father was drinking yaqona under a shady tree, Tomasi was cooking the food beside their house, and his brother was carrying buckets of water.

The next three are examples from the control group:

Is ther was the women in the tree. mothe sitg in the tree there was a looking at hes mother . . .

One day there boy Seru is make the tea to drinking his morth was the colth . . .

One day morning their were a house any village by the sea . . .

One other finding is based on the results of the Fiji Intermediate Examination taken by Fijian pupils, but not Indo-Fijians, towards the end of the second term of grade 6. This examination is used for selection purposes, for entry into the better-established, more prestigious secondary schools whose intake is mostly Fijian pupils. In all subjects taken in this examination—English, General Studies (Science and Social Studies combined), Mathematics, and the Fijian Language—the book flood groups performed well above the typical performance of rural schools. The advantages shown by the book flood pupils was greatest, as expected, in the case of English and General Studies. but there was also an unexpected spread of effect to Mathematics and a similar but less marked tendency in the Fijian language examination. The positive effect on the performance in Fijian suggests that there might have been a transfer of second language reading skills to the first language, or the transfer of more abstract cognitive abilities developed through reading in the second language, or perhaps both. There may also have been a general increase in motivation for school work arising out of the activity of reading.

D. DISCUSSION AND IMPLICATIONS OF THE BOOK FLOOD PROJECT

This Project had set out to investigate the effects of the provision of a rich variety of high-interest, well-illustrated books in classrooms where the norm has generally been to have only instructional readers and very little other reading materials around the pupils. The findings clearly suggest that the receptive skills in a language, that is, reading and listening comprehension, are substantially improved by such a provision of reading materials, and apparently transfer to other related language skills. The superior performance in General Studies and Mathematics of the Fijian pupils from the experimental groups, seemingly through the improvement of literacy in an educational context, lends support to the view that language, particularly "school language," is a very important factor in educational achievement (Cummins, 1984; Stubbs, 1976).

The Project also set out to test the hypothesis that greater gains would be made by that group using the shared book approach to reading compared to the group which only read silently; however, the data supported this only in the first year analysis at grade 5 level on the receptive skill tests.

In the classrooms, time spent on reading for pleasure has traditionally been regarded as a waste of valuable time that could have been devoted to "learning," by which is generally meant that which has been decided in the school curriculum to be worth learning. This has been true of classrooms in both the developed and developing countries, including the small island states. Gradually this has been changing in the more developed countries, especially at the early stages of formal education, but it seems to be still a very strong feature of education in developing countries. It is an attitude that gets reinforced in small island states through the lack of provision of reading matter, either in the mother-tongue or in the typically international second language, which is quite expensive.

The Project showed that children enjoy the experience of reading when high-interest, well-illustrated books are provided. Classroom observation, discussion with teachers and head-teachers all suggested that the pupils were enjoying the experience of reading for pleasure. For many pupils it seemed that this was the first time they had sat down to read something in the classroom without worrying about questions the teacher might ask. Individual teachers had remarked how children would remind them that it was time for reading if the teacher had become too engrossed in normal curriculum of the school. It appears therefore that children can be "hooked on to the reading habit" even if the background they come from does not provide much opportunity for reading, or does not place high value on reading for pleasure, or where the background has a great paucity of printed matter (see also Wells, 1981).

Whether 250 books per classroom are necessary for the results achieved in this Project is debatable. It was obvious that many of the books provided in the Project were rarely used, evidence being their almost pristine condition at the end of the Project. By contrast, the most popular ones showed good evidence of wear and tear. They were the traditional favorite stories of Western children like *Jack and the Beanstalk*, *Cinderella*, and *The Three Pigs*. Resources for books in all the countries of the South Pacific are limited, and it seems that a smaller number, perhaps 150 well-chosen books, would have a similar effect. If a judicious choice is combined with a little organization the books could probably be used over 2 grades. It should be apparent that the provision of books has not been suggested in the context of a school library, which does not mean that the latter is unimportant. However, it is the author's experience that many school administrators use the lack of a facility called a "library" as a pretext for not attempting to provide reading materials apart from the instructional.

The development of reading in educational context is most likely to be successful if schools begin with the concept of *class* libraries— even if there is a central library in a school—so that interesting books are prominent in the classroom environment. Provision of books by itself achieves very little; they must be read. The Book Flood Project in Fiji suggests a way that pupils can be led to reading by schools providing a period between 20 and 30 minutes long for reading in each day's timetable. The importance of reading cannot be conveyed by words alone; teachers have to be seen reading and seen to be enjoying it (McCracken, 1971). Thus, one creates a particular type of literate environment within a school when such an environment is generally not available to the pupil outside the classroom.

With respect to language issues, most children in Fiji begin to learn to read in their mother-tongue and later begin to read in English. In an unpublished survey that the author conducted in 1977 to determine the language of instruction in the country, it was found that 94% of the elementary schools, out of a total of 691, used a vernacular language as medium of instruction until the beginning of grade 4; 6% of the schools used English as the medium of instruction from grade 1 or grade 2. However, as mentioned earlier, the amount of suitable material available for reading in the Fijian language is tiny: there has been no tradition of writing in Fijian for the purposes of "entertainment" (Clammer, 1976). For the Hindi-speakers, books from India can be and are imported so that the provision of reading materials for early grades is possible, but in practice it is rarely done in schools. The result is that the use of vernacular literacy in educational contexts is severely curtailed by the lack of books. This is a problem not restricted to Fiji only, but also found in other island states in the South Pacific. As awareness grows, some governments are beginning to make efforts at developing more writing in the mother-tongue for use at elementary schools.

In a multilingual and multiethnic country such as Fiji, government support for the development of local writing would have to encompass at least the two main vernacular languages. Writers would have to be found from both the language groups to do the writing. This is not an impossible task if the government were to provide funds to writers and potential writers to enable them to take leave from their normal occupation and devote themselves full time to writing. However, there is not this sort of institutional support (a system of patronage, as it were) available to encourage the development of local writing. In addition, there is the problem of publication, and unless there is government subsidy the cost of a book is so much higher than similar types of imported books that sales suffer. Many small island states do not have populations large enough to make publication of writing in vernacular languages profitable unless it is prescribed as a compulsory text by the Ministry of Education or one of the churches, in which case there is a guarantee of a more sizeable market.

An interesting project that indicates the direction that the smaller island states in the South Pacific might take is currently being conducted in Tuvalu with the help of the Institute of Education at the University of the South Pacific. It developed children's books in the Tuvaluan language. The thrust of this work is to motivate the teachers of the country to write the stories, printed by hand, illustrate it themselves and thus produce reading materials for their classes. As teachers become more comfortable with this process of producing reading materials, the next phase of the project will be put into operation: the production of little stories by pupils themselves so that their reading materials are of their own creation. In the light of the work of Graves (1983) and others, this method of producing books will not only help provide reading materials in the vernacular, but will also aid in the process of the development of the children's competence in the Tuvaluan language.

There is obviously a need to produce local writing in the vernacular languages and in English for children. The acquisition of the reading process is likely to be easier and faster if local stories are used (Downing, 1978; Goodman & Goodman, 1979). Naturally an additional impact of local writing is that it can balance prolonged exposure to reading materials produced for Western readers, often middle-class, which affects self-perception and the perception of one's culture in comparison to Western culture (Dixon, 1977).

VII. SOME RECENT DEVELOPMENTS IN LITERACY

The Book Flood Project provided an impetus to a greater discussion about literacy not only in Fiji but also in other countries in the South Pacific. This impetus was aided by the setting up of a Reading Center (later re-named Literacy Center) in the Institute of Education at the University of the South Pacific. It worked around the South Pacific encouraging more whole language approach to the introduction of literacy in both the vernacular and in the English language. With funding from the New Zealand government, the Center began pilot projects in reading at Grade 2 in Vanuatu, Kiribati, and Fiji, using selected readers from the New Zealand Ready-to-Read Series. In 1990, the program expanded into Grade 3 and there is, according to a Report on South Pacific Literacy Project, Phase I (1990), "growing and serious interest in wider implementation" (p. 6).

In 1990, the Australian Reading Association working closely with the New Zealand Reading Association, the International Reading Association and its International Development in Oceania Committee secured funds from the Australian Government through its International Literacy Year Program and commenced the South Pacific Literacy Project. The main goals of this project were to:

1. identify Key Literacy Workers in Pacific nations who will form a network of informants about literacy needs and priorities in their respective countries and create a team of local people with whom to work on future teacher development course in literacy education;

2. identify and assess the literacy professional development needs of teachers and Key Literacy Workers in Pacific Nations;

3. evaluate existing teaching initiatives to identify principles and practices to inform a teacher development course in literacy education; and

4. plan a pilot teacher development course in literacy education to meet the specific literacy teaching needs of Pacific Nation teachers and Key Literacy Workers.

As a result of the success of Phase I (to a considerable extent due to the efforts of the Project Director, Barbara Moore), funding was secured for Phase II of the project. The goals of this phase were to maintain and develop the Key Literacy Worker Network, to develop an integrated literacy program, negotiate with the Pacific governments support for trials of the integrated literacy program in their countries, and to carry out at least two pilot projects using the integrated literacy program developed in Phase I (aim 4). In an external evaluation of the Phase II Walker and Elley, (1991), made a number of suggestions for improvement to the integrated literacy program and concluded that "Phase II of this project has undoubtedly been successful" (p. 9).

Succeeding phases of this South Pacific Literacy Project have now been subsumed under a larger UNESCO-funded project in which Principals of schools will also be involved in the training of teachers in schools in providing a more integrated and whole language literacy program in schools.

This development through the 1990s will change the way literacy is taught in schools and will undoubtedly produce better readers and writers in the school system. A parallel development has also occurred in the production of vernacular materials, especially in the eastern part of the South Pacific. Once again, the Literacy Center at the Institute of Education at the University of the South Pacific has been at the forefront of this development and has been aided by grants from UNESCO for the production of books. The Ministries of Education in Tonga and Fiji have both encouraged vernacular story production but progress is slow because funds for this activity are limited. And there is not the culture of children's story (or other book) writing in the South Pacific so that there is a limited pool of writers to draw upon—most of whom hold full-time employment and do any writing in their spare time. Despite this, at the recent 4th South Pacific Conference on Reading held in January 1995 at the University of the South Pacific, a Fiji Ministry of Education participant was able to present some 30 titles in English, Fijian, and Hindi languages, very attractively illustrated and presented. Fiji, at any rate, seems to be on the verge of take off in terms of producing locally written and illustrated children's stories.

VIII. THE FUTURE OF LITERACY

The emphasis on developing greater literacy in the South Pacific island states will continue, but such developments will be seen primarily within educational contexts. In the multilingual small island states, literacy will continue to be developed in English (and in French also in the case of Vanuatu) for the foreseeable future. In the report of a conference entitled "Pacific Languages: Directions for the Future" held in Vila, Vanuatu in August 1984, the Solomon Island representative at the conference stated that:

> while the government recognizes Pijin [local name for the pidgin language used in the Solomon Islands] there is no policy of promoting it with respect to literacy or in any other way. The government also needs to look at the state of vernaculars, as there is no development of literacy in these languages either. (p. 11)

In the same report, Vanuatu's representative stated that local languages in education is not a high priority at present, but would be considered when the dual educational system, (British and French). a legacy to their country from their colonial past, was unified under one system. It seems that in these two countries literacy will be achieved in English (or French) first and then transferred to Pijin or Bislama

(Vanuatu pidgin) (cf. Lambert & Tucker, 1972, and Modiano, 1973). Literacy practices in such international languages as English and French are likely to be restricted to the educational and government bureaucratic contexts, while practices in pidgin literacy are likely to have more social and pragmatic foundations—for example, reading signs, posters, advertisement materials, newspapers and political flyers.

In the monolingual countries of the South Pacific, the use of the vernacular languages will grow so that literacy practices in them will be maintained and in many cases expanded. There is certainly much more effort now to produce reading materials for children in the vernacular, which is the language in which most of the population of countries like Tonga and Western Somoa would like to read. Whether more adult reading matter, especially in book form, will be produced will depend upon the economies of scale. Established international publishers are not likely to produce them because of the small size of the buying market. However, with the easy availability of desktop publishing packages, some enterprising Pacific Islander may begin publishing books in the vernacular and still have a profitable venture in spite of the small market. For this to happen there has to be a slight change in the psychology of people—the perception of what constitutes books. Currently, it appears that books are regarded as having glossy covers and objects that generally come from the developed countries or alternatively are developed by the Ministry of Education, generally with external financial aid. If this perception changes and the local products begins to be valued more, then there can arise in the next twenty-five years, a thriving publication of books in the vernacular.

In Fiji, the Fijian language is going to grow, fed by nationalism and the expanded study of it at the senior high school level (available for study in grade 13 from 1995), and its availability from 1995 for study at the University of the South Pacific. Concomitant with this will be an expanded use of it in a variety of domains. Already, there is a growing recognition of the importance of the vernacular languages though the strength of this demand is not the same for the Indo-Fijian community. This community has shown less concern about their vernacular languages than about being successful in the English-based school system as judged by passing the national examinations at grade 10, 12, and 13 (Moag & Moag, 1977). Since the military coups of 1987, many Indo-Fijians have worried about their long-term prospects in the country and this uncertainty is likely to lead parents to emphasize the learning of English for their children. Parents want to ensure that their children are more literate in the English language to that they could migrate to an English-speaking country. The Indo-Fijian parent emphasizes higher literacy in the English language because it is the language of education, and education has been seen, since the 1920s as a means of social mobility and better employment. At the same time there is concern that lack of proficiency in Hindi might hasten the process of assimilation into the host society.

The development of higher levels of literacy in Hindi poses another problem, for this development so far has occurred in standard Hindi which is not commonly used by people in their personal interactions with one another. The Fiji Hindi, or *Fiji Baat* as it is also called, is regarded by purists as socially inferior and while the language is used for personal interactions in the community, there is resistance to its use in printed form or over the national radio service. For any literature in Hindi to development, it has to develop in the dialect of the people, but there is little evidence of a change in this direction.

The situation studied by Siegel (1973, cited in Moag & Moag, 1977) is still prevalent today. Siegel surveyed the Indo-Fijian speech community around Nadi, an urban area where the international airport is situated, and found that *Fiji Baat* was maintained for use in informal situations, but in formal situations there was a shift from standard Hindi to English (see also Moag, 1982). It seems therefore that the Indo-Fijian may become literate primarily in the English language, but will continue to use *Fiji Baat* for interpersonal communication, particularly in communal contexts.

English will continue to be a second language in a multilingual, multiethnic country such as Fiji where there is no other contending "lingua franca." The first Prime Minister of Fiji called it a "buffer language" between the two ethnic groups. Literacy in this language within the educational context will remain quite important.

In the monolingual, monoethnic countries of the South Pacific, such as Tonga and Western Samoa, it appears that literacy practices in both the mother-tongue and English will be maintained, with the latter confined much more to academic contexts and international settings. If the present emphasis on vernacular development in educational contexts continues, literacy practices in the vernacular may encompass an ever wider domain. Literacy for more technical reading materials is likely to be only in English, as the cost of translation, both in terms of manpower and money, will be too prohibitive for both these countries.

The question of literacy in which language, and for what purposes, will continue to be a matter of development, with sociological factors being the more important catalysts. The present indication is that this development will reflect the situation that obtains in bilingual or multilingual countries where each language is generally used in clearly defined domains. Similarly, there will be domains in which literacy in mother-tongue is used and in other domains, largely related to educational contexts, trade, and bureaucracy, literacy in an international language will be used—a type of "specialization of function" for the two languages (Ferguson, 1959). Naturally, the domains may not be restricted to a single form of literacy; there will be preferred languages for different domains but such preference will give way to pragmatic considerations in situations where interlingual or inter-ethnic communication takes place.

There is an added factor that is likely to increase its influence in the 1990s and into the new millennium: the introduction of television in the South Pacific. Reading for pleasure is not a practice that has been established in any of the Pacific societies. With the advent of television the development of such practice may be further retarded and reading practices confined to academic contests, newspapers, and the like. The television in Fiji, for example, plays programs beamed from New Zealand, largely entertainment, much of it "low brow". It is certainly a more popular mass medium and will have far reaching effects upon not only the literacy activities of the South Pacific peoples but ultimately also upon their social structures and practices.

ACKNOWLEDGMENTS

I am grateful to Rejiele Racule for providing me with some current data with which to update this chapter.

REFERENCES

Bole, F. (1972). *The possible conflicts which may arise as a result of individual expectations and communal demands.* Occasional Paper No. 8. Suva: School of Education, University of the South Pacific.

Clammer, J.R. (1976). *Literacy and social change: A case study of Fiji.* Leiden: E.J. Brill.

Cummins, J. (1984). *Bilingualism and special education: Issues in assessment and pedagogy.* Clevedon: Multilingual Matters Ltd.

Dixon, B. (1977). All things white and beautiful. In M. Hoyles (Ed.), *The politics of literacy.* London: Writers and Readers Publishing Cooperative.

Downing, J. (1978). General principles of comparative reading. In D. Feitelson (Ed.), *Cross-cultural perspectives on reading and reading research* (pp. 129-132). Newark, DE: International Reading Association.

Elley, W.B., & Achal, S. (1981). *Standardized Tests of Achievement (STAF) in Fiji.* Studies in South Pacific Education Series No. 2. Wellington: New Zealand Council for Educational Research and Institute of Education at the University of the South Pacific.

Elley, W.B., & Mangubhai, F. (1981a). *The impact of book flood in Fiji primary schools.* Studies in South Pacific Education Series No. 1. Wellington: New Zealand Council for Educational Research and Institute of Education at the University of the South Pacific.

Elley, W.B., & Mangubhai, F. (1979). Research project on reading in Fiji. *Fiji English Teachers' Journal, 15,* 1-7.

Elley, W.B., & Mangubhai, F. (1981b). The long-term effects of a book flood on children's language growth. *Directions, 7,* 15-24.

Elley, W.B., & Mangubhai, F. (1983). The impact of reading on second language learning. *Reading Research Quarterly, 19,* 53-67.

Ferguson, C.A. (1959). Diglossia. *Word, 15,* 325-340. (Reprinted in P.P. Giglioli (Ed.), *Language and social context.* Harmondsworth: Penguin Education).

Ferguson, C.A. (1978). Patterns of literacy in multilingual situations. In J.E. Alatis (Ed.), *Georgetown University round table on languages and linguistics 1978.* Washington, DC: Georgetown University Press.

Geraghty, P. (1984). Language policy in Fiji and Rotuma. In *Duivosavosa: Fiji's languages-their use and their future* (pp. 32-84). Fiji Museum Bulletin No. 8. Suva: Fiji Museum.

Goodman K., & Goodman, Y. (1979). *Reading in the bilingual classroom: Literacy and biliteracy.* Virginia: National Clearinghouse for Bilingual Education.

Graff, H.J. (1978). Literacy past and present: Critical approaches in literacy/society relationship. *Interchange, 9,* 1-21.

Graves, D. (1983). *Writing.* Exeter, NH: Heinemann.

Heath, S.B. (1980). The functions and uses of literacy. *Journal of Communications, 30,* 123-133.

Holdaway, D. (1979). *The foundations of literacy.* Sydney: Aston-Scholastic.

Hymes, D. (1972). On communicative competence. In J.B. Pride & J. Holmes (Eds.), *Sociolinguistics* (pp. 269-293). Harmondsworth: Penguin.

Kidston, P.G., & Moore, B. (1990). *South Pacific literacy project: Phase I report.* Australian Reading Association.

Ladefoged, P., Glick, R., & Criper, C. (1968). *Language in Uganda.* Nairobi, London: Oxford University Press.

Lal, B.V. (1983). *Girmityas: The origins of Fiji Indians.* Canberra: Australian National University.

Lal, B.V. (1992). *Broken waves: A history of the Fiji Islands in the twentieth century.* Honolulu: University of Hawaii Press.

Lambert, W.E., & Tucker, G.R. (1972). *Bilingual education of children: The St. Lambert Experiment.* Rowley, MA: Newbury House.

Lynch, J. (1984, August). Melanesia. Background paper presented at the conference on Pacific Languages: Directions for the Future. Vila, Vanuatu.

Mangubhai, F. (1977). Literacy in a multiracial society. *Fiji Library Association Newsletter, 4*(6), 184-191.

Mangubhai, F. (1984). Fiji. In R.M. Thomas & T.N. Postlethwaite (Eds.), *Schooling in the Pacific Islands* (pp. 167-201). Oxford: Pergamon Press.

Mann, C.W. (1935). *Education in Fiji*. Melbourne: University Press.

McCracken, R.A. (1971). Initiating "sustained silent reading". *Journal of Reading*, 14, 521-529.

Moag, R. (1982). The life cycle of non-native Englishes: A case study. In B. Kachru (Ed.), *The other tongue: English across cultures* (pp. 270-288). Oxford: Pergamon Press.

Moag, R., & Moag, Y. (1977) English in Fiji: Some perspectives and the need for language planning. *Fiji English Teachers' Journal*, 13, 2-26.

Modiano, N. (1973). *Indian education in the Chiapas Highlands*. New York: Holt, Rinehart and Winston.

Scarr, D. (1980). *Viceroy of the Pacific: The majesty of colour*. Canberra: Australian National University.

Schutz, A.J. (1972). *The languages of Fiji*. Oxford: Oxford University Press.

Scribner, S., & Cole, M. (1981). *The psychology of literacy*. Cambridge, MA: Harvard University Press.

Spolsky, B., Englebrecht, G., & Ostiz, L. (1983). Religious, political and educational factors in the development of biliteracy in the Kingdom of Tonga. *Journal of Multilingual and Multicultural Development*, 4, 459-469.

Street, B. (1984). *Literacy in theory and practice*. Cambridge: Cambridge University Press.

Stubbs, M. (1976). *Language, schools and classrooms*. London: Methuen.

Swain, M. (1981). Time and timing in bilingual education. *Language Learning*, 31, 1-15.

Tyron, D.T. (1988). *Illiteracy in Melanesia: A preliminary report*. Canberra: Australian Advisory Council on Language and Multicultural Education.

Walker, R., & Elley, W.B. (1991). South Pacific literacy education course: Evaluation report on phase II. Unpublished manuscript.

Wells, G. (1981). Language, literacy and education. In G. Wells (Ed.), *Learning through interaction: The study of language development* (pp. 240-276). Cambridge: Cambridge University Press.

Whiteman, D. (1983). *Melanesians and missionaries*. Pasadena, CA: William Carey Library.

Williams, D. (1981). Factors related to performance in reading English as a second language. *Language Learning*, 31, 31-50.

V

ADULT LITERACY IN CULTURAL CONTEXT

15

Introduction

Susan L. Lytle and Jacqueline Landau
University of Pennsylvania

The acquisition and development of literacy in adults has long been a prominent concern of policy-makers and educators in the Third World, and more recently the focus of considerable attention in industrialized countries as well. The majority of studies of adult literacy, however, have been concerned either with evaluating the results of large-scale literacy campaigns or with the effects of programs on individuals' levels of competence, while relatively little research has addressed the broader sociocultural contexts of adult literacy learning. The studies in this section by Purves, by Bennett and Berry, and by Reder thus mark an important new trend in the study of adult literacy: the description and analysis of adult literacy practices as they occur in natural settings. To suggest the significance of this direction for adult literacy research and education, we need first to examine briefly some of the assumptions, values, and attitudes of those currently working in the field.

A common but often implicit assumption about adult learning and the teaching of adults is that adults who lack reading and writing skills are somehow "deficient." In industrialized countries, in the era of compulsory schooling, these adults represent the failures of the system, those for whom schooling has been inadequate or somehow unsuccessful. It is important to note that this assumption of "deficit" or "deficiency" contrasts markedly with the way we typically think about literacy acquisition of school-age (and even preschool) children for whom literacy learning is seen as a natural, developmental process. For adults, the

243

lack of acquired reading and writing skills is sometimes taken to mean a more generalized lack of competence, so that adult non-readers are judged to be intellectually, culturally and even morally inferior to others (cf. Fingeret, 1984).

Congruent with this assumption, then, many literacy programs for adults approach their task as one of elevating learners from a difficult and dreary existence. A small number of compelling studies suggest, however, that these same adults are often productive members of their communities, and that in spite of a lack of formal training many have educated themselves through their life experiences (Sisco, 1983). Fingeret (1984) argues that "illiterate adults should be seen as members of oral subcultures with their own set of values and beliefs, rather than as failing members of the dominant literate culture." Her own studies of adults reveal that "illiterate adults see themselves, often, as interdependent, rather than dependent, sharing their skills and knowledge with members of their social networks in return for access to the reading and writing skills of friends, neighbors, and relatives" (p. 14). These studies and others (e.g., Heath, 1980; Horsman, 1990) indicate that, in many cases, educators have apparently misperceived the nature of the adult learner's environment, thereby undervaluing the prior experiences and social and cultural resources that adult learners bring to the tasks of reading and writing. In addition, Hunter and Harman (1979) suggest that we should distinguish between external standards that programs impose and internal goals that people set for themselves. Program standards may reflect an ideology of "cultural reproduction" (Bourdieu & Passeron, 1977) rather than the learners' own views of the situations, interests and needs. Some argue that educationally disadvantaged adults will continue to drop out or drop behind unless more community-based educational alternatives are developed that reflect these adults' perceptions of the world.

The critical need to examine our underlying assumptions about adult literacy is further strengthened by a less than encouraging picture of program success. One source of problems may be the discrepancy between what adults bring to programs and what they are typically taught. Although usually seeking instruction related to their particular purpose or set of purposes (e.g., passing a driver's test, reading the Bible, helping children with homework), adults are often given a program of instruction based on a single hierarchy of skills which can be uniformly applied across sociocultural contexts. The contrast between literacy as a neutral or objective set of skills and literacy as cultural and social practice is reflected in Street's (1984 and this volume) distinction between "autonomous" and "ideological" models. In the autonomous view, literacy skills exist independent of any specific social context or ideology. In contrast to this, we know from ethnographies of literacy that the functions and uses of literacy vary from community to community (Heath, 1980; Scribner & Cole, 1981). We also know that "learners frequently possess and display in out-of-school contexts skills relevant to using literacy which are not exploited in school learning environments" (Heath, 1980, p. 132; Taylor & Dorsey-Gaines, 1988). For example, the literacy practices Heath describes in a South Carolina working-class community reveal a wide array of functions and uses quite different from those emphasized in schools. Examining notions of "schooled literacy" implicit in many current adult literacy campaigns and programs, and developing concepts more appropriate to the social fabric of adult practice (both inside and outside of educational settings) seem to be critical needs.

Each of the chapters in this section explores the relationship between sociocultural context and adult literacy development; thus, the section as a whole suggests some important directions in adult literacy research and practice. Some of the central topics addressed are: the relationship between literacy practices and formal education or schooling; the social functions served by reading and writing for adults in different cultural contexts; the ways in which knowledge of literacy is learned in practice-specific ways; the perceptions and meanings of literacy brought to learning; and the processes by which adults actually learn to read and write, in and out of educational contexts. After considering some of the particular concerns of each chapter we will explore some links with other work in progress as well as directions for the future.

In "Literacy, culture and community," Purves draws on data from two cross-national studies of reading and writing conducted in more than a dozen countries over the past 15 years. Although the learners surveyed are adolescents, whose presence in secondary schools would suggest that most are not likely to appear later in statistics about adult illiteracy, Purves' work invites us to examine schooling as a cultural context and the effects of formal schooling as one dimension of literacy as practice. By demonstrating cultural differences in different interpretive communities, Purves shows that readers' preferred responses to literature in schools are shaped by the values prevailing in their community, and that these responses more consistently reflect the community's norms (as reflected in the responses preferred by teachers) as the students mature in the schooling process. In his current study of written composition, Purves and other researchers are looking at the extent to which students are taught to be members of rhetorical communities. Results suggest that student writing differs systematically by culture of origin along a number of continua which Purves details in his chapter. It is clear that learning literacy is not merely a matter of developing a set of skills, but of acquiring considerable cultural knowledge about and procedures for comprehending and composing written text. In a recent essay Cook-Gumperz (1986) has argued that assumptions about what constitutes valid knowledge are created by society's ideology of learning and teaching, so that literacy skills in present day schooling reflect implicit and explicit theories about knowledge itself.

Purves' inquiry into the responses of readers and writers reveals cross-cultural contrasts in the ideology of reading and writing, in the nature of literacy texts, and how people "take [them] to mean" (Heath, 1982). His work shows that students in school are clearly expected to learn the preferences and practices of a larger cultural community as well as the specialized conventions of particular academic communities. Purves points out that the policy implications of these findings may differ for industrialized and Third World countries, although his assumption that the distinction between teaching "formal school literacy" and "literacy for everyday life" applies primarily to developing nations should perhaps be questioned. We need to think about how these findings relate to Heath's observations (see above) about the disjunction between practices in and out of school, and to what the subsequent chapters in this section tell us about spontaneous acquisition of literacy and collaboration outside of formal school contexts.

In "The future of Cree syllabic literacy in Northern Canada", Bennett and Berry examine the functions and uses of the Cree syllabic script in Northern Ontario, Canada, and its changing role in four communities. In a sociohistorical analysis using documents, community surveys and tests (the latter are not reported in this chapter), the authors contrast traditional and contemporary Cree culture to show the effects of schooling, the frequency and different uses of syllabic and alphabetic scripts (in communication, religion and record-keeping), the norms and attitudes which surround literacy, and the relationship between Cree syllabic literacy and Indian identity. They describe how English and new technology (e.g., the telephone) have affected dramatically the communicative functions that the Cree language previously played. One might expect that the Cree script would eventually disappear, but this does not seem likely to happen. Although the primary communication function of the Cree script has not been retained (i.e., the passing of information from one community member to another), the script has acquired an important cultural role in the preservation of Cree identity. The example of the Cree documents the close relationship between literacy and cultural values, and suggests that even when literacy serves no essential communication function, there may be a strong motivation for acquisition of literacy in community contexts outside of school when it serves important cultural functions.

    In "Comparative aspects of functional literacy development: three ethnic American communities", Reder describes the effects of increasing environmental demands for the use of written material in daily life as evidenced in three ethnic American communities: an Eskimo fishing village; a Hmong community on the west coast; and a partially migrant, partially settled Hispanic community in the Pacific northwest. Reder compares these communities in terms of the major contextual features impacting on literacy development, including different sociohistorical and sociolinguistic aspects of literacy, as well as the ways in which literacy skills are socially organized in the community and their resulting social meanings. In each site, ethnographic research methods formed the core of the study, and literacy practice itself (and not the measured level of an individual's reading or writing skill) was used as the primary unit of observation and analysis.

    Reder's findings point to the importance of literacy as collaborative practice in which reading and writing tasks are done collectively. In these group contexts, literacy is both used and transmitted from one person to another. Reder shows how individuals engage in literacy practices with different modes of engagement (i.e., some actually handle the materials while others provide knowledge or expertise or are engaged in the activity from a social perspective). Adults acquire different types of knowledge about literacy from these practices, with each type being learned in practice-specific ways. They also acquire considerable literacy skill without participating in any formally constituted literacy education classes. Extrapolating from these findings and others, Reder draws implications for literacy education, urging that planners take a broader view of literacy development and thus encourage adults to learn literacy through participation in practices beyond those available in formal educational settings. More research into the ways that participants collectively accomplish literacy activities, and the social arrangements supporting such development, is called for. His comprehensive analysis of literacy practices in all three sites argues eloquently for the importance of cultural factors in understanding adult literacy development in different contexts. Program planners, Reder explains, must take into account the values inherent in situations and the social meanings of particular practices so that literacy will be regarded positively by those for whom instructional programs are being designed.

    Taken together, these three different approaches help to clarify the concept of adult literacy in cultural context. Furthermore, when they are linked to other research in progress, some significant questions and directions for educational research emerge. We know very little, for example, about the conditions that lead people in different cultural settings to seek literacy instruction, or about the actual uses of literacy by adults living in the "literate environments" of cities. In our own research on the reading and writing of adults in Philadelphia (Lytle, 1991; Lytle, Marmor, & Penner, 1986), we used a sociocultural or ideological perspective on literacy acquisition and development to design alternative assessment procedures for use in adult literacy programs. Assessment provided the opportunity for systematic study of what literacy means to different learners, what counts as literacy to different groups and individuals within the society, as well as what strategies adult learners bring to their interactions with print. These evaluation procedures make the assumption that adults bring to a literacy program considerable resources and life experiences, and that, in turn, the experience of reading and writing will affect their modes of participation in social networks and their community. To document these experiences from the perspective of the participants, the study used a series of one-to-one planning conferences conducted at intervals over time and reflecting the specific needs and interests of each individual. This direction in assessment stands in contrast to the development of standardized tests which are widely used to evaluate individual growth and the effectiveness of particular instructional programs. Decontextualized examinations of reading and writing assume literacy to be an autonomous and technical set of skills, and not the culturally learned and embedded sets of practices that the three studies in this section and others would indicate. As we have shown above, one might conclude from community and cross-cultural studies that individuals can be expected to vary greatly in their purposes for reading and writing, in the texts they choose to read and write, as well as in the contexts for performance of reading and writing abilities. Literacy abilities cannot then be simply ranked along a continuum from the unskilled to the highly proficient, illiterate to literate, because of the many possible interactions of reader/writer, text, purpose and context. Elsewhere (Lytle et al., 1986) we have suggested that an individual's literacy profile might be better conceptualized as a patchwork, a quilt in process, whose configuration is closely linked to settings which are in turn characterized by specific opportunities and constraints. An individual's literacy profile may be profoundly influenced by participation in particular literacy programs wherein the cultures of teaching and assessment define the possibilities and limitiations on what counts as literacy and learning (Lytle, Belzer, & Reumann, 1993).

Following this line of reasoning, we would argue that taking into account the cultural contexts of adult learners may be more difficult in some settings or types of adult education programs than in others. Fingeret (1984) has distinguished between two types of literacy programs: individually oriented and community-oriented. Individually oriented programs focus primarily on literacy and aim to meet the complex, interrelated needs of individuals, while community programs focus more broadly on social and political issues identified as problems by members of a community, and on providing a combination of services to help persons and groups take more control over their lives. Though both types of programs aim to empower individuals, community-oriented programs advocate collective action in order to improve the conditions in the entire community.

Literacy education also varies depending on service providers' underlying assumptions about the nature of literacy or literacies, such that literacy may be treated primarily as discrete skills, as sets of functional tasks, as social and cultural practices, or as critical reflection and action (Lankshear & McLaren, 1993; Lytle & Wolfe, 1989) Programs may be more or less oriented to a banking model of education (Freire, 1970) or to more learner-centered and participatory approaches to teaching and learning (Fingeret, 1992). Program designers may need to consider the social functions served and potentially served by reading and writing by different groups of adults, as well as what Reder has called the "value systems in situations and the social meanings assigned to particular practices." Above all, it seems that finding out what adults already know and need to know, what literacy (or illiteracy) means to the learners' themselves, constitute a necessary beginning.

To make instruction more culturally appropriate for adult learners in diverse situations will require that educators take an active role in assimilating and using the information gained from studies such as those included in this section. An even more promising direction would be the design of research in which service providers, community-based educators and adult learners would join with university researchers to address some of these critical issues through collaborative projects centered in, and informed by, the adult learner's own voice and view of the world.

REFERENCES

Bourdieu, P., & Passeron, J. C. (1977). *Reproduction in education, society and culture.* London: Sage Publications.

Cook-Gumperz, J. (1986). Literacy and schooling: An unchanging equation? In J. Cook-Gumperz (Ed.), *The social construction of literacy.* Cambridge: Cambridge University Press.

Fingeret, A. (1984). *Adult literacy education: Current and future directions.* Columbus, OH: ERIC Clearinghouse on Adult Career and Vocational Education, Ohio State University.

Freire, P. (1970). *Pedagogy of the oppressed.* New York: Seabury Press.

Graff, J. H. (1982). The legacies of literacy. *Journal of Communication,* 32(1), 12-26.

Heath, S. B. (1980). The functions and uses of literacy. *Journal of Communication*, Winter, 123-133.

Heath, S. B. (1982). Questioning at home and at school: A comparative study. In G. Spindler (Ed.), *Doing the ethnography of schooling: Educational anthropology in action*. New York: Holt, Rinehart, & Winston.

Horsman, J. (1990). *Something on my mind besides the everyday: Women and literacy*. Toronto: Women's Press.

Lankshear, C., & McLaren, P. (Eds.). (1993). *Critical literacy: Politics, praxis and the postmodern*. Albany: State University of New York Press.

Lytle, S.L. (1991). Living literacy: Rethinking development in adulthood. *Linguistics in Education, 3*, 109-138.

Lytle, S., Belzer, A., & Reumann, R. (1993). *Initiating practitioner inquiry: Adult literacy teachers, tutors, and administrators research their practice* (Tech. Rep. TR93-11). Philadelphia: University of Pennsylvania, National Center on Adult Literacy.

Lytle, S., Marmor, T., & Penner, F. (1986). *Literacy theory in practice: Assessing reading and writing of low-literate adults*. Paper presented at the annual meeting of the American Educational Research Association, San Francisco.

Lytle, S., & Wolfe, M. (1989). *Adult literacy education: Program evaluation and learner assessment*. Columbus: ERIC Clearinghouse on Adult, Career and Vocational Education, The Ohio State University.

Scribner, S., & Cole, M. (1981). Unpacking literacy. In M. F. Whiteman (Ed.), *Writing: The nature, development, and teaching of written communication, 1*. Hillsdale,NJ: Erlbaum.

Sisco B. (1983). The undereducated; Myth or reality? *Lifelong Learning: The Adult Years, 6*, 14-15.

Street, B. V. (1984). *Literacy in theory and practice*. Cambridge: Cambridge University Press.

Taylor, D., & Dorsey-Gaines, C. (1988). *Growing up literate*. Portsmouth, NH: Heinemann.

16

Literacy, Culture and Community

Alan C. Purves[†]
State University of New York, Albany

I. INTRODUCTION

Literacy has increasingly held the attention of scholars and policy-makers. The former group has come to see literacy as a complex phenomenon related to the nature of texts and how they are viewed in a particular society, especially as the society is affected by technological shifts. The latter group, policy-makers, tend to view literacy in simpler statistical terms such as census figures, school enrollments, and comparisons of group with group or country with country.

Many of those concerned with the measurement of educational performance try to bridge the world of the scholar and the policy-maker by seeking to make the complex a bit more simple or at least easier to understand, and simultaneously work to avoid oversimplification of educational issues and their solutions. From the perspective of the evaluator, literacy—both as reading and writing—involves not a simple score on a test, but a relatively clear set of performances which are judged according to criteria that are culturally appropriate. The basis for making this assertion can be found in previous and present work on achievement in reading, literature, and writing undertaken in a number of developed and developing countries under the auspices of the International Association

[†]Deceased.

for the Evaluation of Educational Achievement, or IEA. Two of those studies in particular, the literature study and the writing study, suggest that one aspect of becoming literate is that a person joins a literate "community" and subscribes to its norms. This chapter will present a brief definition of community first, then the findings that support the definition, and next suggest a theory to account for those findings together with some implications for educational policy.

The term "community" comes from the metaphor that Stanley Fish (1980) used so effectively to explain why there are consensual interpretations of literary texts. He referred to classrooms as the seedbeds of "interpretive communities," groups of individuals bound together by the way they perceived and interpreted literary texts. Fish makes the point that the interpretation of a text is bound by the norms and conventions of the community that an individual inhabits, and that these communities are bound by language and particularly by a common semantic space, including common denotations, connotations and idioms. Fish's point is not novel; it extends to literature that has been a commonplace of linguistics since de Saussure (1916), and later Gumperz and Hymes (1974), with their depiction of speech communities and how people learn to be members of them. In applying the idea of community to the reading of a text, Fish follows upon the earlier work of Richards (1929), who observed of his subjects that many of them exhibited what he called "stock responses" to the texts they read, which responses came from the reader and did not appear to be derived from the text. Examples in literary criticism might include the Marxist or Freudian or "new critical" readings that people give to the poems, novels, and other literary texts that they read, and that they extend to all sorts of written texts as well as to other events. As we shall see, interpretive communities may be large or small; they may persist over a long period of time; and they appear to perpetuate themselves primarily through formal educational systems such as schools (although there are informal means of perpetuation as well—such as the literary journal or review). One should not restrict interpretive communities to literate societies; in oral cultures the ways by which story-telling and story-listening are performed suggest that interpretive communities exist there as well. Such oral interpretive communities have been masterfully delineated by Heath (1983) in her description of families and churches in the southeastern United States.

II. THE IEA STUDY OF LITERATURE

The IEA Study of Literature (Purves, 1973) was conducted in the early 1970s; in part it explored the nature of interpretive communities as national or regional phenomena by examining the preferred responses of students to literary texts (e.g., what the students indicated was important to write about) in secondary schools in ten educational systems: Flemish-speaking and French-speaking Belgium; Chile, England, Finland, Iran, Italy, New Zealand, Sweden, and the United States. On the basis of a content analysis of each sentence in compositions written by over 1000 students and teachers in response to a variety of short stories and poems (Purves & Rippere, 1968), there emerged 20 core issues concerning literary texts, each of which could be framed as a question. In any one country students appeared to select certain questions from that core. The questions could be classified according to the object of concern (e.g., character, language, theme) and according to the illocutionary force of the statement (personal-reactive, analytic, classificatory, interpretive, or evaluative). These 20 core questions were used as a measure that asked a larger sample of students in each country to select the five questions they thought most important to raise in writing or talking about a short story. Each student responded to the measure three times (following the reading of each of two stories and in a general questionnaire with respect to fiction in general), so that one could derive a picture of what a student saw as important in the abstract and after reading each of two stories. The questions were rated by their teachers and of a group of experts on literature and its pedagogy in each country.

The result of this exercise showed that, as students progressed through secondary school, they became more consistent in their responses across texts and thus came to approach all the fiction that they read with a single perspective. Students in any one country tended to have increasingly similar responses as they progressed through school. This is not to say that the different stories had no effect on the students' responses, but that in each of the systems of education studied the effect of the text was less strong on the older students than it was on the younger ones.

In terms of national differences the results showed that there were both an international interpretive community and national communities. Students in all countries generally rejected the question "Is this a proper subject for a story?" and "Is anyone in this story like the people I know?" They generally found attractive the questions "Has anything in this story a hidden meaning?" and "What happens in the story?" Aside from these general rejections and predilections, students in different countries exhibit sharply different profiles of response. Two sets of questions form the coordinates on which one could plot the major differences between countries (Figure 16.1). The first coordinate could be said to be a "personal-impersonal" continuum, and the second a "form-content" continuum. Belgium and Italy are countries whose students emphasize the impersonal and the formal; Chile, England, and Iran emphasize the personal and the content-oriented response; and United States Students are concerned with content but not from a personal point of view.

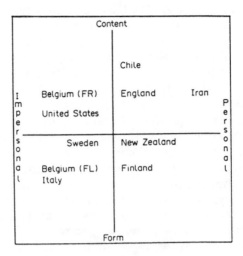

Figure 16.1. Position of countries relative to continua of personal-impersonal and form-content responses (from Purves, 1973)

Responses to what one reads, then, which form an important aspect of literacy, are partially dependent on the particular text read, but appear more crucially dependent on the culture of the reader, the reader's membership in a community of readers. Such dependency increases as people progress further through the educational system; students' responses become increasingly like the responses preferred by teachers, and to a lesser extent, experts (critics, curriculum-makers, and teacher trainers whom we polled). For the younger students in the IEA Literature Study (age 14) the average rank-order correlation between the question preferred by student and teacher was 0.35; for the older students (in the pre-university year) that correlation was 0.54. It would seem that the teacher serves as a major force in influencing how students respond to a text, and thereby serves as the individual who inducts students into the interpretive community of a particular society.

From these results one should infer that a part of literacy learning in a society is learning to be a member of the interpretive community that helps bind that society together. During the course of learning to read an individual learns also how to respond to what is read, and to form a pattern of discourse about what is read, both of which are shaped by a culture and its conventions and traditions with respect to how the reader should act towards the text. Such appears to be true of both a broad spectrum of readers in secondary school language classes and the more specialized readers in particular disciplines, as Fish (1980) suggests.

III. THE IEA STUDY OF WRITTEN COMPOSITION

The question then arises as to what other communal patterns of performance are learned as an individual becomes a literate member of a society. The IEA Study of Written Composition is currently exploring that issue. The study is looking at the writing of students in Chile, England, The Federal Republic of Germany, Finland, Hungary, Indonesia, Italy, Netherlands, Nigeria, New Zealand, Sweden, Thailand, the United States, and Wales. One aspect of the study is exploring the extent to which students are taught to be members of rhetorical communities. The hypothesis underlying this exploration is that, in schools, students learn to write according to certain conventions, many of which have little to do with the structure of the language and more to do with the literary and cultural heritage of the society. That is to say that many aspects of texts are not bound by the morphology and grammar of a particular language but by custom and convention.

This hypothesis is based in part on the fact that, in many academic disciplines, as well as in certain professions that demand a great deal of writing, individuals learn to write according to certain explicit and implicit conventions that affect patterns of organization, syntax and phrasing, and even the selection from the lexicon. It is apparent that the scholarly article in a given academic discipline has properties demanded by the history of that discipline. In the humanities, references to previous research on the topic comes at the beginning of an article, or are sprinkled throughout the text when needed; in psychology they always occupy the second of five sections of the article; and in the biological sciences they occur in separate articles from the report of a particular piece of research. In addition to structural conventions, disciplines differ in the degree to which they allow the writer to use the first person,[1] the degree to which the passive is tolerated, and the degree to which interpretation or inference is permitted, to name but three instances. If such differences divide academic disciplines, and even permeate these disciplines to the extent that the conventions obtain regardless of the language in which the article is written, it would seem reasonable to expect

---

[1]An earlier draft of this chapter was written in part for an audience of English teachers, and the use of "I" and "we" and the active voice permeated the paper. The editor of this volume, a psychologist, requested that those pronouns be removed and thus the passive voice emerged, another example of stylistic preferences.

that similar kinds of differences separate cultures and societies. Such is the line of reasoning behind *contrastive rhetoric*.

Earlier studies in the field of contrastive rhetoric have concentrated primarily on people writing in a common second language, or on literary styles as they change across linguistic or temporal boundaries. The IEA Study of Written Composition intends to provide a way of examining the possibility of such differences by looking at a systematically drawn sample of writing in a number of rhetorical modes by an average school population writing in the language of instruction. It is also examining the criteria used by teachers of writing in each of the countries, in order to see if there are systematic differences that might help define rhetorical communities.

The first problem to be dealt with, as in the Literature Study, was that of creating a standardized set of neutral descriptors so as to portray these possible differences. There needed to be two sets of descriptors: one for the compositions themselves and one for the criteria used to judge the writing. The first of these will receive most attention in this section.

As an initial step there were gathered a number of compositions written by small samples of students (approximately 100) at or near the end of secondary school in several of the countries in the study and three countries no longer in the study (Australia, Japan, and Israel). The compositions were on the topics "My native town" and "What is a friend?" both thought to be relatively neutral topics that would not force a particular kind of pattern of organization or style on the students. If the compositions were not in English they were translated by a literary translator and checked by bilingual teachers for their fidelity to the original. A team of three researchers then examined the whole group of compositions and found that they could place them into piles according to certain common characteristics (not including the content) and that the piles coincided with the country of origin. They then proceeded to see if we could define the characteristics that led to our selection. We found that the compositions tended to differ systematically by culture of origin along a number of continua, some of which matched those of earlier researchers, particularly Carroll (1960), Glenn and Glenn (1981), Hofstede (1981) and Kaplan (1966). The continua that emerged were the following:

Personal-impersonal: this continuum depends primarily on the frequency of references in the text to the writer's thoughts and feelings about the subject.

Ornamental-plain: this continuum may also be defined as "figurative-literal" and depends on the frequency of use of metaphor, imagery, and other figures of speech.

Abstract-concrete: this continuum is defined in terms of the amount of specific information and detailed references in the text, as well as to the general level of abstraction.

Single-multiple: this continuum refers to whether the text focuses on one selected aspect of the subject or tries to cover a large number of aspects of the subject.

Propositional-appositional: this continuum, which is similar to Glenn and Glenn's abstractive-associative and some of Kaplan's diagrams, refers to the types of connectives that hold the text together, and whether there appears to be a clear order that follows one of a number of "standard" types of development (e.g., comparison-contrast); such a composition would be propositional. An appositional composition would use few connectives besides *and* or *but*, and often omits cohesive ties other than idioms and repetitions.

These characteristics appear to distinguish the writing of students in different cultures; from the initial research it appears that the characteristics form some of the dimensions by which the models of text are delimited in certain cultures (see Figure 16.2). The differences noted in Figure 16.2 are not inherent in the language, but result from some form of cultural learning, because the differences occur between students writing in the same language (such as English) but living in different cultures.

It is clear so far that the compositions of students in various countries can be classified according to the criteria that have been developed, although other differences may emerge given other sorts of compositions (e.g., narratives or letters). If the compositions by students from a particular country were consistently classified according to a certain set of dimensions (e.g., personal, figurative, single, appositional) one might proceed to ask whether such a style is desired by the educational system of that country. It is here that one turns to the question of criteria. In the pilot phase of the study a number of these compositions were given to a group of teachers from the countries in the study, and they were asked to both rate and comment on the compositions. From a content analysis of the comments followed by a factor analysis four factors emerged (apart from mechanics, spelling, and handwriting): (1) content, (2) organization and structure, (3) style and tone, and (4) personal response to the writer and the content (Purves, 1984a). These "general merit factors" of judgement appeared in all countries, but the relative emphasis and interpretation varied systematically.

In order to check the teachers' criteria, students were asked to write a letter of advice to people younger than they who were about to attend the student-writers' schools. The letter was to suggest ways to succeed in school writing, and a content analysis of the resulting compo-

| | Dimension | | | | |
Country	Personal	Ornamental	Abstract	Single	Appositional
Australia	High	High	Low	High	High
England	Medium	Low	Low	Low	High
Fed. Rep. Germany	High	Low	Low	Low	High
Finland	Low	Low	Low	Low	High
Israel	High	Medium	Low	High	Low
Italy	High	High	High	High	Low
Ivory Coast	Medium	Low	Low	Low	High
Japan	High	Low	High	High	Medium
Netherlands	High	Low	Low	Low	High
New Zealand	Low	Low	Medium	Low	High
Nigeria	Low	Low	Low	Low	High
Scotland	Low	Low	Low	Low	High
Thailand	High	High	Medium	Medium	High
United States	Low	Low	Low	Medium	Low

Figure 16.2. Dimensions of writing across cultures (from Purves & Takala, 1982)

sitions proved most revealing, although not necessarily complimentary to the schools. Students in all the countries noted that spelling, handwriting, grammar, and neatness were of paramount importance. Yet there were other differences that appear from even a cursory look at the responses (the full analysis is still going on). Students in one culture suggested that originality is most important; in another students claimed that a "fancy style" is what counts; and in yet another a simple style was said to prevent a student from "getting into trouble."

Each of the three aspects of the Study of Written Composition (the examination of actual compositions, of the teacher questionnaires concerning criteria, and of the letter of advice) suggests that students in a particular educational system do indeed learn to become members of a rhetorical community, that they learn not only how to write but also what aspects of their writing are valued in their society. At times there is direct instruction, at times it is implicit, but in either case the students learn that being able to write is being able to produce texts that match certain models, and that these models serve as criteria for student and teacher criteria. If one puts these findings together with the findings of the literature study we can see that learning literacy in a society is not merely a matter of acquiring a set of skills.

IV. TOWARDS A THEORY OF LITERATE KNOWLEDGE AND LITERATE COMMUNITIES

The two IEA studies tend to support the idea that a great part of learning to be literate is learning the conventions of a particular literate community, and thus becoming a part of that community. Recent cognitive psychology has tended to support this view in suggesting that literacy involves the acquisition of schemata, or *chunks* of content, as well as linguistic structures and rhetorical structures (Anderson, Spiro, & Montague, 1977; Scardamalia & Paris, 1984). Schemata should be broadened to include models of various types of discourse in certain situations, such as those appropriate in a social, academic. or commercial context as well as models of the pragmatics of reading and writing, and particularly as models of how to proceed in the activity of reading or writing.

In her recent history of writing, Gaur (1985) begins by saying that all writing is information storage. She shows how from the earliest invention of writing the main function of the text was to store information, usually commercial but also governmental and later religious information, so that it could be retrieved by the writer or by some other person at a later date. In early civilizations writing was done by scribes, who perfected the system and made advances in the technology of writing such as shifting from the stylus to the brush or pen. The scribes also set forth standards for penmanship, conventions of writing such as word boundaries and sentence boundaries, and even text structures and matters of morphology, grammar and syntax for the written language. Some of the conventions they set were for efficiency, and some were for elegance.

As a result of the major technological shift to movable type and the availability of cheap paper, the scribal world opened up during the seventeenth and eighteenth centuries, and simultaneously or consequently more and more people became literate. The kinds of information stored increased to include the literary arts and popular literature, as well as the news of the day and advertising. Changes in the structures and forms of written language came slower, and in most societies the scribal tradition of setting forth standards for words, syntax, and text structures has continued but has been modified as different groups took on scribal responsibilities, and different fields of knowledge took on their own scribal functions. In addition, there arose standards as to how texts should be read; to some extent these standards arose from religious practices such as a reverence for the exact wording of the text as opposed to a tolerance for individual interpretation and the piling of commentary upon commentary, but scribal practices in the reading of lay texts, such as in the reading of law in England or the *explication de texte* in France, also had their influences.

These standards and traditions have persisted in all societies, and they form a part of that which defines a society. Scribner and Cole (1984) have shown how the development of Vai script in Liberia has brought with it a set of conventions about language, text forms, and the ways in which texts are to be read and written. Vai texts are for communal reading and writing. These conventions with respect to Vai exist parallel to the conventions used for reading the Quran, which is also communal but sacramental, and for reading English, which is a solitary affair.

As a person becomes literate that person gathers and assimilates a great deal of this cultural knowledge about text forms, text pragmatics, and procedures for reading and writing texts, much of which is represented within schemata. There is knowledge of the lexicon, both oral and in print; there is knowledge of syntactic structures and of generative rules; there is knowledge of text structures such as how stories begin and end or what a paragraph looks like; there is knowledge of appropriate phrases and other locutions to be used in certain contexts; and there is knowledge of when and under what circumstances it is appropriate to write a particular kind of text or respond to a written text in a particular fashion. These kinds of knowledge, in addition to the knowledge about the world at large, are stored in the mind and are brought into play in different situations where reading and writing are called for. Being literate therefore involves activities that bring various storehouses of knowledge into action when the situation calls for them. Figure 16.3 presents a general psychological model of literacy behaviors when culture is taken into consideration.

The knowledge bases serve as models in the individual's head as the individual reads or writes, and signal when a particular text that is being written or read meets the demands of the situation in which a literate act is called for. In addition, a literate reader knows when certain texts are to be read and when certain texts are superfluous (such as the information printed on the inside flap of a cardboard milk carton in the United States or a ticket in the Metro in Paris), as well as when particular

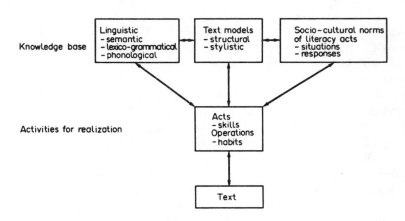

Figure 16.3. A graphic depiction of literacy

written forms are called for or when particular procedures with regard to texts are called for (when it is important to make a written record, and when it is important to check surface features or to revise, or when one should respond to a text with more than a word or a phrase).

Given this complex array of knowledge a literate individual engages in the activity of reading and writing, thus producing or comprehending and responding to a text. Such activities constitute the manifestations of literacy, which call into use cultural knowledge concerning literacy within a given context. Successful performance depends both upon the knowledge that an individual has and the adeptness in deploying that knowledge. Literacy, then, is not simply a matter of skill, or a set of habits, but is the use of such skills and habits in a culturally appropriate manner that indicates that one is a member of a particular literate community, whether the narrow community of members of a discipline or a field of endeavor, or the broader community of a particular society. Literacy is a communal affair involving conventions at many levels, and those who work to promote literacy should be aware of the fact that they are not simply purveyors of a skill but conservators and imparters of a set of communal standards.

V. FORMAL EDUCATION AND LITERACY

Much of the evidence from the IEA studies comes from an examination of the reading and writing of students in secondary schools. There seem to be some differences between what goes on with respect to literacy training within these institutions as opposed to what goes on outside of them (Heath, 1983; Scribner & Cole, 1981). In exploring these differences one may elaborate this first approximation of a model and see what constitutes the twin domains of school reading and school writing. Kádár-Fülop (1987) describes three major functions of the language curriculum in school, basing her argument on a survey of writing curricular goals and aims in the countries in the IEA Study of Written Composition (see also Weinreich, 1963). The first of these functions is the promotion of *cultural communication* so as to enable the individual to communicate with a wider circle than the home, the peers, or the village. Such a function clearly calls for the individual to learn the cultural norms of semantics, morphology, syntax, text structures, and pragmatics, as well as procedural routines so as to operate within those norms and be understood. The second function is the promotion of *cultural loyalty* or the acceptance and valuing of those norms and the inculcation of a desire to have them remain. A culturally loyal literate would have certain expectations about how texts are to be written or to be read, as well as what they should look like, and would expect others in the culture to follow those same norms. Because Americans had a loyalty to certain norms in the 1960s, for example, they reacted strongly when a cigarette advertisement substituted "like" for "as", and one suspects the advertiser was fully conscious of this loyalty.

The third function of literacy education is the development of *individuality*. Once one has learned to communicate within the culture and developed a loyalty to it, then one is able to become independent of it. Before then, deviation from those norms and values is seen as naive, illiterate, or childish (Markova, 1979; Vygotsky, 1956). For example, teachers of English in the United States will accept a sentence fragment in a student's composition only when they know that the student is fully aware of the rules and the effect of breaking them. In some societies, particularly those of emerging nations, individuality in reading and writing does not form any part of the curriculum; in "romantic" post-industrial societies it is given great lip service but not really tolerated except in a select few.

Already in the IEA Study of Written Composition we have seen that secondary school students are aware of many of the norms and standards, such as the importance of handwriting, spelling, and neatness as well as many other norms concerning style, organization, and content. In some cases, perhaps in many, they share these cultural values concerning writing, just as the students in the Literature Study shared the values of appropriate response to a text. Whether they could live up to these norms and standards when asked to write a composition or criticize a text was another matter. Probably many could, some could not, and some chose not to. The important bond they share is a general understanding and acceptance of those norms and standards. Students, by and large, *know* and accept as valued more than they might have the skill to do. They know they should "watch their language," even if they make the most egregious errors.

As formal educational institutions, then, schools set out to make literacy learning serve both broad societal purposes and purposes specific to the subculture of schooling and the academy. School reading, to take up one side of the coin of literacy, differs from out-of-school reading in many respects. To make the distinction clear, an individual outside of school may purchase or borrow a novel, read it, and put it down. There is no demand to do anything outside of the activity of reading the text. In school, reading a novel is a complex activity of which the act of perusing the text is but one constituent. Other acts include various demonstrations to a skeptical audience that one has read the text with something called comprehension, or appreciation, or understanding. The individual must be prepared to answer oral or written questions about the content, structure, or style of the text, must be prepared to produce some sort of reenactment of the text, or must be expected to commit part of the text to memory. In school the individual must also be prepared to read different types of text on demand, to shift subject matter and form as well as response style every hour on demand, to have the reading interrupted, and be prepared to read texts that may be opaque or downright incomprehensible. I remember observing a secondary-school language class where I was told by the teacher that two students in the back could not read. The class was reading and discussing an obscure modern poem; the two girls in the back were reading a magazine about film stars and discussing it intelligently. They could read but they could not—or would not—do school reading.

For most cultures the domain of school reading and the relationship of those two girls to it may be represented graphically (Figure 16.4) (Purves, 1984b), which sees achievement in school reading as involving two main aspects: reading competence and reading preference—what students can do and what they "should" choose to do. The distinction is based primarily on the criteria used to assess these two forms of achievement. Competence is usually associated with a set of standards of performance upon which there is some consensus. Preference is usually seen as a set of desired behaviors, upon which there is less consensus as to the criteria. The preferences do not usually appear as stated outcomes, although they may appear in some printed curricula (Purves, 1971, 1984b); as Heath (1983) observes, preference may indeed be the most important aspect of the reading and writing curriculum.

Parallel to this sort of domain statement for reading, there is one for writing (based on Takala, 1983) which appears as Figure 16.5. Again it can be seen as consisting of competence and preference, and can be subdivided into a number of discrete parts. Like reading, writing builds upon a substratum of knowledge. In some instances these units of knowledge are the same. Like school reading, school writing asks of the individual: (1) articulateness according to certain conventions, (2) fluency, (3) flexibility in moving from genre to genre, and (4) appropriateness, suiting what is done to the norms of the genre and the situation. The competence aspect includes two sorts of competence: one relating to the motor acts in producing text, the other relating to the acts involved in discourse production. Again, schools focus a great deal of attention on writing preferences; not all writing activities are approved in schools (e.g., graffiti, love notes), despite the various sorts of ingenuity with language they might display. Writing in school must follow particular conventions, and the conventions appropriate in one subject are not always those in another. Students must be apprenticed to five or six rhetorical communities *seriatim* during the day or the week.

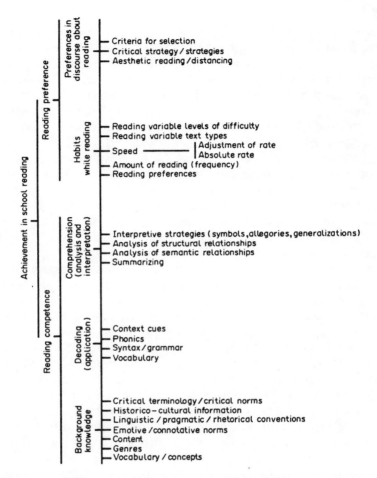

Figure 16.4. The domain of school reading (reproduced from the _American Journal of Education_, vol. 93, no. 1 [1984] with permission from the University of Chicago Press)

In both school reading and school writing, then, we can see that students are expected to learn not only the practices and preferences of a larger cultural community of readers and writers, but also those of several specialized academic communities. As they progress through the academic world to the university they will learn the even more specialized practices and preferences of various scholarly communities. As they go into various occupations they will learn the conventions of literate behavior in the various institutions that make up a complex society.

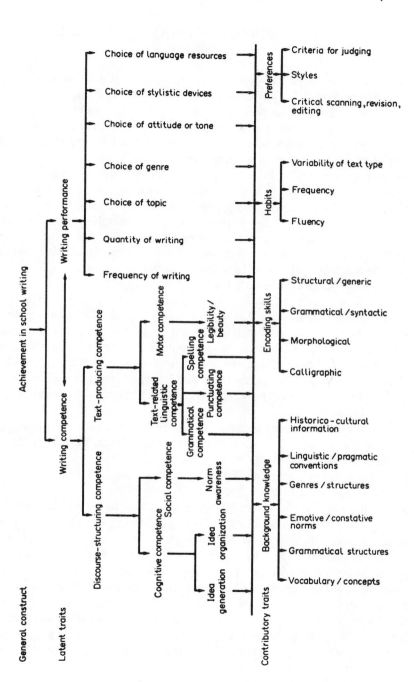

Figure 16.5. The domain of school writing (adapted from Takala, 1983)

VI. IMPLICATIONS FOR LITERACY POLICY AND THE FUTURE OF LITERACY

Literacy, then, must be seen as a complex of various forms of cultural knowledge, which individuals must acquire and put into practice when they read and write. As people become literate they join a larger cultural community as well as specialized communities. Such communities exist throughout the world; many communities have become trans-national and trans-lingual; many communities are highly specialized; and many have strict barriers to keep people out, and the barriers are often conceived in terms of reading and writing (Törnebohm, 1973). Such is true of many of the scholarly and professional communities. In the *developed* nations much of literacy learning within schools and universities involves learning the literate activities of various of these inquiring systems. Literacy does not liberate the individual from constraint; it merely introduces the individual to a different set of constraints from those which exist in the non-literate state.

The issue the developed nations need to face in planning for the future is whether there will emerge a double standard of literacy: one for those who work at the forefront of the various specialist communities and one for those who perform the routine service in the economy (see the chapter by Sticht in this volume). The ideal of educational equality is clearly not met in most of the developed nations, as those who are highly literate appear to be moving farther and farther away from the marginally literate.

In the *developing* nations a major problem is that of bringing people into the broader literate community of a cultural group. In many of those countries which are in the post-colonial phase, one aspect of the problem concerns whether literacy training should be in a non-native language (such as English, French, Spanish, or Arabic) or in an indigenous language. If the former, a question arises as to whether students should learn the cultural norms of the colonizing group that brought the language, or whether local norms should be developed, which might change literate behavior in that particular society although it has a language in common with other societies. To a certain extent such a development will happen regardless of policy as Kachru (1982) has shown, but the policy-maker must decide whether to impede or retard the development of indigenous morphemes, syntax, text structures, or patterns of response to written text. If policy-makers choose a native language which has no history of literate norms and models, then they must be developed.

Another issue facing these policy-makers is whether to emphasize literacy instruction that is accompanied by a high degree of abstraction, and that is apart from everyday life in a subsistence rural economy such as exists in many parts of Third World countries. That is the sort of literacy that typifies technologically oriented schooling in the industrialized world. An alternative to this sort of schooling is a literacy instruction that is indistinguishable from the activities of everyday life in the village, and makes it somewhat easier for people to store and retrieve information (Cole, 1985; Scribner & Cole, 1981). This latter kind of literacy is not tied to major technological and economic transformations of the society; "formal" school literacy appears to be clearly tied to the modern economy and may even be what makes it possible (Goody, 1977). It may be, however, that the latter is a necessary mediating step in national literacy programs even though it does not pay off international debts.

Such are but some of the decisions concerning literacy that policy-makers must face—or turn away from. But they must indeed face the fact that when they deal with issues of literacy they are dealing with issues that involve more than a simple skill. Becoming literate involves becoming a member of a literate community which involves learning of a complex body of knowledge about texts, language, pragmatics, and procedures for reading and writing, and which involves subscribing to its standards, whether they be the standards of some sort of *ancient regime* or the standards of a "new" liberated society. Both sets of standards are complex, and whatever set of standards a society selects it must be aware of both the complexities of literacy and the con sequences of decisions about standards for literacy.

POSTSCRIPT

In the ten years since this paper was originally written, the IEA Written Composition Study has been completed (Purves, 1992) and the IEA has also completed a study of Reading Literacy (Elley et al., 1994). Those two studies have done little to change the conclusions reached in this paper; in fact, the Written Composition Study results show clearly how the standards of good writing are bound by culture; the Reading Literacy Study also showed cultural patterns of achievement across the domains of narrative, exposition, and graphs and charts.

It is clear from other studies, notably those of Daniel Wagner in Morocco (1993) and David Olson (1994), that literacy and schooled literacy have long been culturally embedded practices (probably since the invention of the technology and the training of the first scribal class, Purves, 1991). To think of reading or writing or literacy as a universal construct is indeed a mistake. By extension it is also probably a mistake to think of education or the educated person as culturally neutral. The ways in which we are taught to think of the acts of reading and writing and to think of the texts that surround us are deeply imbued with cultural and community values. It was so in the medieval monastery, in the rabbinical school, in the renaissance court, the Chinese civil service, and the variety of educational and social institutions that today abound to teach these so-called skills, Despite the advances in technology, the intertwining of literacy and culture will remain.

REFERENCES

Anderson, R. C., Spiro, R. J., & Montague, W. E. (1977). *Schooling and the acquisition of knowledge*. Hillsdale, NJ: Erlbaum.

Carroll, J. (1960). Vectors of prose style. In T. A. Sebeok (Ed.), *Style in language*. Cambridge, MA and New York: Technology Press and Wiley.

Cole, M. (1985). Education and the third world: A critical discussion and some experimental data. In E. Bok, J. P. P. Haanen, & M. A. Walters (Eds.), *Education for cognitive development*. The Hague: SVO/SCO.

Elley, W. E. (1994). *The IEA study of reading literacy: Achievement and instruction in thirty-two school systems*. Oxford: Pergamon Press.

Fish, S. (1980). *Is there a text in this class? The authority of interpretive communities*. Cambridge, MA: Harvard University Press.

Gaur, A. (1985). *A history of writing*. New York: Scribner's.

Glenn, E. S., & Glenn, C. G. (1981). *Man and mankind: Conflict and communication between cultures*. Norwood, NJ: Ablex.

Goody, J. (1977). *The domestication of the savage mind*. Cambridge: Cambridge University Press.

Gumperz, J. J., & Hymes, D. (1974). *Directions in sociolinguistics: The ethnography of communication*. New York: Holt, Rinehart & Winston.

Heath, S. B. (1983). *Ways with words*. New York: Cambridge University Press.

Hofstede, G. (1981). *Culture's consequences*. Berkeley, CA: Sage.

Kachru, B. (1982). *The other tongue: English across cultures*. Urbana, IL: University of Illinois Press.

Kádár-Fülop, J. (1987). Culture and education in written composition. In A. C. Purves (Ed.), *Contrastive rhetoric*. Beverly Hills, CA: Sage.

Kaplan, R. B. (1966). Cultural thought patterns in intercultural education. *Language Learning, 16*, 1-20.

Markova, A. K. (1979). *The teaching and mastery of language*. London: Croom Helm.

Olson, D. (1994). *The world on paper: The conceptual and cognitive implications of writing and reading*. Cambridge: Cambridge University Press.

Purves, A. C. (1971). Evaluation of learning in literature. In B. S. Bloom, J. T. Hastings, & G. Madaus (Eds.), *Handbook of formative and summative evaluation of student learning.* New York: McGraw-Hill.

Purves, A. C. (1973). *Literature education in ten countries: An empirical study. International studies in evaluation.* Stockholm: Almqvist & Wiksell.

Purves A. C. (1984a). In search of an internationally-valid scheme for scoring compositions. *College Composition and Communication, 35,* 426-438.

Purves, A. C. (1984b). The potential and real achievement of U.S. students in school reading. *American Journal of Education, 93,* 82-106.

Purves, A. C. (1991). *The scribal society: An essay on literacy in the technological age.* White Plains, NY: Longman.

Purves, A. C. (Ed.). (1992). *The IEA study of written composition II: Education and performance in fourteen countries.* Oxford: Pergamon Press.

Purves, A., & Rippere, V. (1968). *The elements of writing about a literary work.* Research Monograph No. 10. Champaign, IL: National Council of Teachers of English.

Purves, A., & Takala, S. (Eds.). (1982). *An international perspective on the evaluation of written composition: Evaluation in education: An international review series, 5(3).* Oxford: Pergamon Press.

Richards, I. A. (1929). *Practical criticism.* New York: Harcourt Brace.

Rosenblatt, L. M. (1978). *The reader, the text and the poem: The transactional theory of the literary work.* Carbondale: Southern Illinois University.

de Saussure, F. (1916). *Cours de linguistique général.* Lausanne: Payot.

Scardamalia, M., & Paris, P. (1984). *The function of explicit discourse knowledge in the development of text representation and composing strategies* (Occasional Paper No. 5). Centre for Applied Cognitive Science. Toronto: Ontario Institute for Studies in Education.

Scribner, S., & Cole, M. (1981). *The psychology of literacy.* Cambridge, MA: Harvard University Press.

Takala, S. (1983). Achievement in written composition. Unpublished manuscript. Urbana, IL: IEA Study of Written Composition.

Törnebohm, H. (1973). *Perspectives on inquiring systems.* Department of Theory of Science, University of Gothenburg, Report No. 53.

Vygotsky, L. S. (1956). *Izbrannye psikhologicheskie isseldovaniia.* Moscow: RSFR Academy of Pedagogical Sciences.

Wagner, D. A. (1993). *Literacy, culture, and development: Becoming literate in Morocco.* Cambridge: Cambridge University Press.

Weinreich, U. (1963). *Languages in contact: Findings and problems.* The Hague: Mouton.

17

The Future of Cree Syllabic Literacy in Northern Canada

J. A. H. Bennett and J. W. Berry
Queens University, Canada

I. INTRODUCTION

At the turn of the century the Cree-speaking people of northern Canada had what was arguably one of the highest literacy rates in the world. They read and wrote their own language in a syllabic script which had been devised for them in the late 1830s by a Methodist minister in northern Manitoba. The success of this script, its rapid transmission and nearly total penetration of the Cree-speaking population, took place without any of the pedagogical tools so familiar to us: there were no schools, no teachers in the specialized sense of the word, no standard writing materials, and very little printed (or written) matter to read. Moreover, older Cree people affirm that there was little time or energy to expend upon matters not pertaining to immediate survival. Yet it appears from work in progress that nearly all Cree over the age of 40 are capable users of the syllabic script, and nearly all of these state that their parents were literate as well. Most, in fact, say it was their parents who taught them to read and write.

In general, older Cree syllabic literates learned their script from a relative, most often a parent, on a one-to-one basis. The script was studied whenever there was "time" and this meant anywhere from several times a day to once a week. Again, the syllabic script might have been studied for a period varying from a couple of minutes to several hours at a stretch. Teaching methods and procedures varied tremendously, as did writing materials. Traditional writing materials consisted of nearly all flat surfaces available in the environment and any objects capable of leaving marks on these. People wrote with stones, knives, axes, bones, sticks, feathers, charcoal and fingers on materials as diverse as wood, stone, bark, hide, dirt, snow and later, of course, paper. They carved their characters into the writing material, or traced them, or used "inks" made from charcoal, crushed stone, plants, animal blood or gunpowder

Around 40 years ago this unusual situation with respect to literacy began to change. Its demise was marked by the introduction of schools into native communities. Although instruction in literacy skills was—and is—one of the avowed aims of schools, syllabic literacy in the Cree native tongue was suppressed within school walls, as was the use of the Cree language itself. Instead, Cree children were taught to read and write only in English, using only the Roman alphabet. By the 1970s government policy had partially reversed itself in this respect, and schools began to provide instruction in syllabic reading and writing, albeit in rudimentary fashion. There were no real guidelines for this kind of instruction and, in each community, syllabics instructors (who were for linguistic reasons necessarily drawn from the local area) were left more or less on their own to invent a curriculum for children of various ages and at various stages of syllabic expertise, as well as to try to divine the principles of pedagogy in an institution utterly antithetical to the values of Cree society. A major exception to this otherwise bleak picture has been the innovative and highly popular summer program at Lakehead University designed specifically for native syllabics instructors working in government schools.

Not surprisingly, the teaching of syllabic literacy in school has not been a resounding success. There are many reasons for this, among them the perceived necessity for fluency in the competing English script, and access to increasingly sophisticated means of communication over long distances, i.e. telephone, communication satellites carrying English TV and radio broadcasts, as well as things like "bush" radios for use on the trapline. These factors hinge around a major change in the role of syllabic literacy over the past 40 years, which is itself a reflection of broader patterns of acculturation (Berry, 1980, 1985).

This chapter reviews the changing fortunes of the Cree syllabic script in northern Ontario, and shows how these changes are reflected in the numbers of people who actually become literate in the script. It looks at the role of syllabic writing in both traditional and contemporary Cree society, noting that many of the uses to which the syllabic script was traditionally put have been usurped not so much by another script but by other means of communication. In addition, although new functions for literacy have arisen as a result of increased interaction with Euro-Canadian individuals and agencies (government and otherwise), these functions are filled only by literacy in English. By contrast, the viability of syllabic literacy appears to be increasingly linked to its association with native identity. This association may make the teaching of syllabics in Euro-Canadian schools somewhat problematic.

We have been engaged in a study of Cree syllabic literacy for the past 2 years, limiting ourselves to an investigation of the script as it is used in four communities in northern Ontario: the Cree-speaking communities of Fort Albany and Attawapiskat on the James Bay Coast (denoted as West Main Cree in Helm, 1979), and the (self-denoted) Oji-Cree speaking communities of Big Trout Lake and Kasabonika in northwestern Ontario. These latter are referred to as "Northern Ojibway" by Helm in the *Handbook of North American Indians* but the appellation is by no means universally accepted (see, e.g., Rogers, 1983; Rogers & Taylor, 1979). When speaking English the "Northern Ojibway" usually refer to themselves as "Cree" (also noted by Rogers, 1983, p. 86). The present study combines the research methods and analytical techniques appropriate to the disciplines of anthropology and psychology, namely participant observation, community surveys, and individual testing. In each of the four communities trained native assistants[1] have carried out the major part of the survey data collection as well as assisting with psychological testing (not reported on here).

Although there are significant social and linguistic differences between the Cree of the James Bay Coast and the inland Northern Ojibway (or Oji-Cree) of northwestern Ontario, it is possible, at least for present purposes, to consider the two groups as similar in a broad and general way. For the sake of convenience, both groups will be denoted here as "Cree."

Native language remains strong in the areas in which we worked. It is still the predominant language in each of the four communities and no-one could partake of full community life without a good command of the local dialect. Nearly all conversation takes place in Cree, and nearly all internal community business. Most church services

---

[1]In some cases the same assistants were involved in several phases of the project; in other communities they were not. We worked with a total of thirteen assistants in the four communities but special mention should be given here to Evelyn Nanokeesic of Big Trout Lake and to Elizabeth Gull of Attawapiskat, who assisted with survey data collection and psychological testing, as well as seeing to our physical well-being and providing invaluable community introductions.

are conducted in Cree. Euro-Canadian clergy from the two "established" Christian churches (Anglican and Roman Catholic) are invariably fluent speakers and writers of Cree, as are two of the three Hudson Bay Company managers. English, on the other hand, is used primarily for communicating with the "outside," or with outsiders within the community. Most people over 40 speak, in any case, only a smattering of English. Young people who have attended school display varying abilities with the English language. According to their elders young people display the same variation in connection with their mother-tongue. Old folk frequently lament the deterioration of Cree linguistic ability among the younger generations. They say the young ones do not know how to speak Cree properly. This appears to be a combination of underdeveloped vocabulary and confusion with regard to certain fine points of grammar. Young people speak Cree far more than they speak English, although their Cree speech is sprinkled with occasional English nouns and phrases. Small children typically arrive in school knowing little or no English but having an improved ear for the phonetics as a result of watching TV. In summary, the domains of Cree and English speech are sharply marked in northern Ontario and correspond directly to perceptions of what is internal and external to the community (or to a "neighborhood" of local communities).

II. GENERAL BACKGROUND

Until recently the Cree have been nomadic, following a foraging existence in the boreal forests of northern Canada. They have also been crucially involved in the Canadian fur trade for several hundred years. Traditionally, there were annual cycles of movement (Rogers, 1962; Hallowell, 1949; Dunning, 1959; and Honigman, 1956) which led to a dispersal of people into the bush in late summer/early fall and a regrouping in late spring/early summer at customary locations, which were often also the locus of a Hudson Bay Company trading post, a church, or both. Over time many of these summering spots developed into year round communities. These communities eventually became the focus for the designation of various Indian "bands"—each Band associated with a different geographical community and surrounding territory. (The use of the word "band" to—officially—describe groups of native people is in itself an attribution of marginality. Only consider what other sorts of people are linguistically grouped into "bands": gypsies, thieves, assassins, thugs, outlaws, Robin Hood's merry men and, of course, rock musicians.)

Until approximately 40 years ago, community or settlement life was, for most people, a matter of a few hot, communal, summer weeks when friends and relatives gathered together to visit with one another, collect their treaty money, trade at the Hudson Bay post and celebrate the backlog of weddings, confirmations and baptisms that had built up over the previous year. The brief collective life of summer was followed by 10 or so months in the bush. Here people lived isolated from each other in small hunting groups which tended to be abbreviated forms of the extended family, often centering on parent-child or sibling bonds, with attendant spouses and children. Within this group, nuclear family units usually had their own dwellings (Dunning, 1959; Bishop, 1974; but see Honigman, 1956). Once out in the forest, families often divided further, women and children remaining more or less stationary around a kind of "base camp" while the men, either alone or in pairs, made excursions further afield. Such excursions had game and/or furs as their object and might last anywhere from an afternoon to a fortnight. The relative scarcity of game in a severe environment necessitated a thin dispersal of human beings over the landscape (Steegman, Hurlich, & Winterhalder, 1983; Rogers, 1969). Although cooperation and inheritance were enjoined upon the wider family (with, possibly, a slight patrilineal emphasis), it was impossible for large family groups to live together for any extended period of time. Today, when most people live year-round in permanent settlements, the older pattern of domestic grouping still persists; that is, households made up of the nuclear family plus an occasional extra relative or other dependent, most often the widowed parent of one of the spouses (Honigman, 1953). Such a pattern fits nicely with Euro-Canadian ideas about household composition, and has probably been fostered (consciously or otherwise) by official housing policies.

Incursions of Euro-Canadian culture into the communities of northern Ontario have occurred at an ever-accelerating pace. As a general rule such incursions came earlier to coastal communities than to those inland. The Hudson Bay Company, for example, has had a presence on the James Bay Coast for over 300 years, inland for under 200. The treaty signed by all four communities with the Canadian government dates back 56 years. Federally funded schools came within the last 25-35 years. Religious schools of various sorts had been available on a haphazard basis for considerably longer, but were usually attended for only a few weeks during the summer. (The exception here is Fort Albany, which has had a permanent school of some sort since the turn of the century.) Weekly scheduled air flights have been available for 10-30 years depending on the community. Telephone service came in the 1970s. Community-wide electric power arrived within the past decade. Along with electric power came the inevitable flood of TV sets: few households are without one. Three channels are normally available and many peo-

ple run their sets 10-15 hours per day, often playing them simultaneously with cassette recorders and/or radios and/or phonographs—a practice alarmingly cacophonous to the Euro-Canadian ear.

Concurrent with these developments, the economic base of the
communities has shifted from subsistence hunting, trapping, and fishing, to a predominantly sedentary existence in small settlements (400 to
900 people) which are now inhabited year-round, and in which the
majority of the people are dependent upon government monies of various sorts for their support—either directly through such payments as
unemployment benefits and family allowance or indirectly through
employment with the band or with various federally funded activities:
education, housing, health services, transportation, and equipment
maintenance. Fur trapping, once the economic centerpiece of the north,
now contributes only a minimal amount to the income of these communities. (In one settlement the Hudson Bay Company store manager
claimed it amounted to less than 5% of his annual turnover). Income
here refers, of course, to monetary income. The important contributions
made to family "income," not to mention morale and well-being, by
hunting and fishing are easily overlooked, no doubt because they are
difficult to measure. Nevertheless, although not every family hunts or
fishes, fish and game comprise a significant portion of the diet in many
households and many family freezers are full to bursting with trout,
moose and goose (unplucked). As among Euro-Canadians, self-provid-
ed or self-produced food is far more likely to be informally shared than
is food bought at a store.

Changing communications and changing economies have
brought about increased exposure to Euro-Canadian culture.
Knowledge of English, a superfluity 50 years ago, is now perceived by
most Cree as "necessary for survival in the white man's world." There is
an implicit admission here that the once foreign world of southern
Canada is now standing on the doorstep.

III. THE SYLLABIC SCRIPT

The Cree syllabic script was composed in the 1830s in Norway House,
Manitoba by the Methodist missionary, James Evans (Murdoch, 1981).
The use of the script spread extremely rapidly by a process of person-to-
person instruction, so that by the 1850s it was in wide use throughout
much of northern Canada. The script is said to have derived from
Pitman shorthand (Murdoch, 1981). However, other influences also
seem plausible, among them: the Cherokee syllabic script devised by
Chief Sequoia in 1820 (Murdoch, 1981; Walker, 1969; White, 1962); the
pre-syllabic system of trail signs (cf. Skinner, 1911); traditional Cree

embroidery and beadwork patterns (Murdoch, personal communication); a possible influence of Ojibway midewewin hieroglyphs (cf. for example, Landes, 1938 and Johnston, 1976. In this connection it is worth noting that John Evans spent many years among the Ojibway prior to working with the Cree).

The script is unusual in that it relies on a minimal number of characters, usually between ten and thirteen depending on the dialect. Each character is associated with the sound of a single consonant: "t," "p," "m," and so forth. In addition, each of the characters can be rotated into one of four orientations—corresponding to our own conventional representations of "north," "south," "east" or "west." The orientation of the character gives the vowel quality of the syllable (see Figure 17.1). The script is thus extremely economical when compared with other syllabic scripts, or even with alphabets. The Cherokee syllabic script, for example, contained some 85 characters (Walker, 1969). West African scripts may include over 200 (Scribner & Cole, 1981).

Although some information is available on the historic and linguistic aspects of Cree syllabic writing (see, for example, Murdoch, 1981; Burnaby & MacKenzie, n.d.; Burnaby, Nichols, & Toohey, 1980; Darnell & Vanek, 1973), information on the actual distribution and practice of syllabic literacy skills in native communities has been minimal and largely anecdotal. In order to obtain such information we administered a community survey in each of the four communities in which we worked. Over 440 people above the age of 16 have been interviewed so far, representing approximately 30% of the population over that age. The survey, now in the initial stages of analysis, was meant to provide concrete information on the uses to which both the syllabic and the alphabetic scripts were put, the frequency of use, and in a general way the norms and attitudes which surround literacy. Work to date has underlined several significant factors:

1. The distribution of English and Cree syllabic literacy differs markedly by age across the population, and to some extent parallels linguistic distribution.
2. Literacy in syllabics is nearly universal among people over 40 years of age. People of this age have little, if any, familiarity with English literacy and a limited comprehension of spoken English.
3. Literacy in English is nearly universal among people under the age of 35, nearly all of whom have attended school.
4. Programs of instruction in syllabic literacy are in place in all four communities (and have been for 10 to 15 years- depending on the community). Nevertheless, there is strong evidence to support Native people's observations that, despite daily

syllabic lessons in school, children are not acquiring the proficiency in their own script that their parents and grandparents acquired outside school.

5.   Because there was a period in each community when syllabics were not taught in the schools, there is, in each of the four communities, a "missing generation" of people who are not literate in the syllabic script. The age of this "generation" varies from community to community but always falls somewhere between 25 and 40.

6.   This "missing generation" of syllabic literates contains a sizeable group of very able people, many of whom are now actively involved in running their communities.

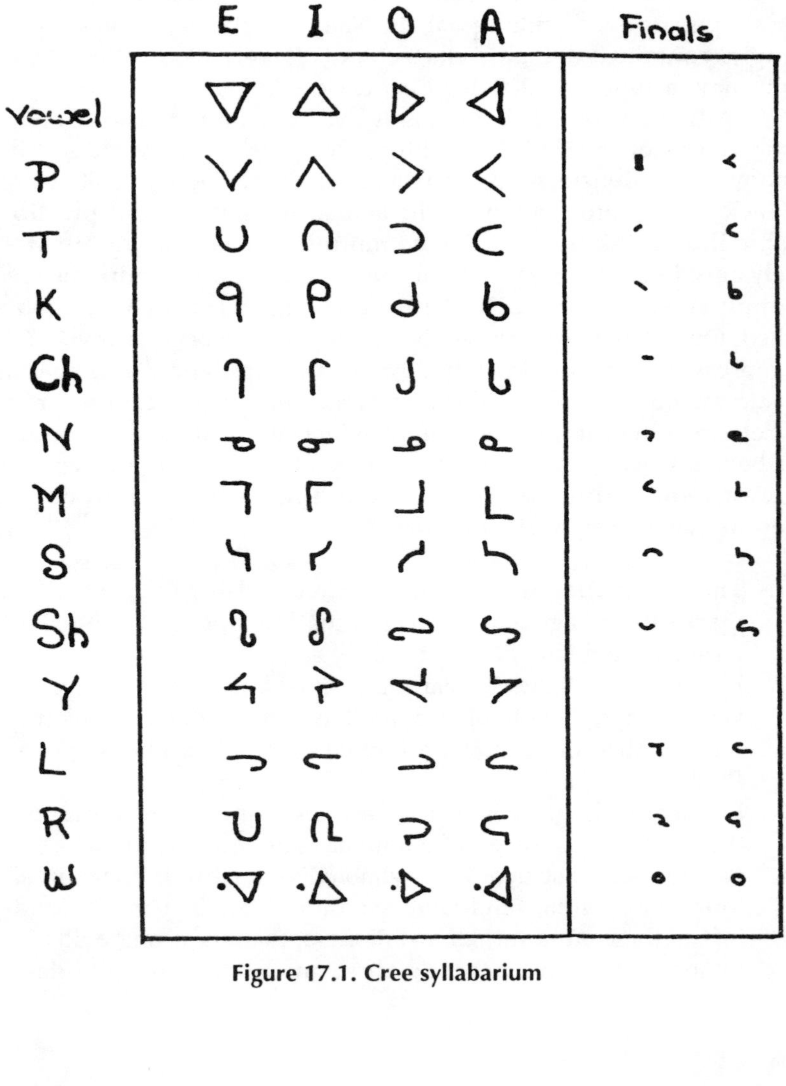

Figure 17.1. Cree syllabarium

IV. SYLLABICS THEN AND NOW

A. Communication

The biggest changes in the role of the syllabic script in northern Ontario have come about in the area of communications. Traditionally the syllabic script was the only means of direct long-distance communication—with the possible exception of magic. Today the script is hardly ever used for this purpose.

It is possible, of course, to hypothesize about long ago, about isolation experienced by small family groups spread out over the forbidding winter landscape, almost completely out of touch with all other human beings. But it is hard if not impossible to get a real glimpse into that past. That the desire for communication was great we may surmise from the existence of an ancient system of "trail signs" by which people travelling in the forest could leave behind information concerning the size, health and travel intentions of themselves or their group. Traditionally, too, dreams and divination were considered to be sources of information about events happening at a distance, though usually this had to do with hunting (Rogers, 1962; Honigman, 1956). However, we heard at least one report of a "shaking tent" being used as a kind of supernatural telegraph, a wizard's wireless by means of which the practitioner could discover events happening to far-away relatives.

With the advent of the syllabic script it became possible to send letters to relatives and friends. These letters, originally written on birchbark, usually contained important family news (mainly births, illnesses, deaths, and marriages) and would be sent along with a friend or a stranger who was travelling in the right direction. Letters were also regularly sent and received by native people living in the south: men working in the mines, children sent off reserve to school, people receiving long-term care in southern hospitals. A number of people said they only learned syllabics on the occasion of being sent off to boarding school—in order to communicate with loved ones left behind.

Shorter letters in the syllabic script were also sent between persons living in the same settlement. Such letters appear to have been more in the nature of what we think of as notes: reminders of appointments, requests for food, for fire, for services (babysitting, for example), lovers' assignations, etc. Such notes were carried by children or sometimes (as in the case of love-notes) deposited surreptitiously into the recipient's hand.

Today, the preferred mode of communication with far-flung friends and relatives is the telephone. In northwestern Ontario, in particular, people have taken to the telephone and made it into something very much their own, endlessly chattering into the receiver right through meals, TV movies, changing baby diapers, and community bingo games—that is, just about anything that can be done while remaining stationary. Most calls are local but many families run up bills of several hundred dollars a month calling long distance, which in northern Ontario means anywhere off the reserve. Some of these telephone conversations, particularly those with people not regularly spoken to, appear to reproduce the form of the old syllabic letters. In our own phone contacts with native field assistants, people invariably begin the conversation by relating compelling family or community news (recent deaths, severe illnesses, changes of residence, births or chieftancy elections), and only then go on to matters of minor import such as our research.

For families or individuals staying in locations not served by the telephone, i.e., traplines, winter camps, etc., bush radios are a popular, if expensive, item, allowing the comfort of contact with "home" as well as the security of a quick rescue should illness or other calamity strike. Within the community, note-passing, too, has been replaced with modern telecommunications technology. Besides the ubiquitous and much loved telephone system, each community also has its own local radio station which functions as a combination of news and information center, bulletin board, political platform, bingo parlour, soap box, and training ground for would-be disc jockeys. The institution of local radio is delightfully informal. For example, people who are looking for someone frequently use the radio to "page" the person they are looking for. Fire alarms and other requests for immediate help are often sent out over radio. And mishaps, such as drifting boats, are reported there. The community of Attawapiskat has, in addition, a television station which at the present time serves mainly as a vehicle for local community information. Broadcasts from all these community stations are extremely limited in range and can be picked up only by local residents. The language of transmission is Cree. If an outsider is invited to come on air (as we were—to appeal for community acceptance), his or her message is translated into Cree afterwards.

For both long-distance and across-the-settlement communication, the use of the syllabic script has largely been replaced by technologically augmented verbal communication. The Cree are quite conscious of this and many individuals explicitly connect the appearance of electronic media with the growing lack of importance of the syllabic script. "A long time ago we didn't have telephones so it [the syllabic script] was the only way to communicate." "There was no other way to communicate, no radio, no phone. Writing letters was the only way to be in touch with people in other communities."[2]

---

[2]These were individual responses to an earlier version of the community survey which we were able to test in the field of 1983 thanks to a pilot grant from the Queen's University Advisory Research Council (1983). The quotes are from two older men in Big Trout Lake, aged 51 and 69 respectively.

B. Religion

The use of the syllabic script has always had a strong religious association. The script was developed by a missionary whose first printing effort was a Cree hymnal (Murdoch, 1984). Bibles, hymnals, prayer books and catechisms were, for over a hundred years, nearly the only items printed in the script. (The sole exceptions were books such as dictionaries or syllabariums.) It is important to note, however, that such publications followed the spread of syllabic literacy; they did not precede it, nor were they responsible for it (Murdoch, 1984). The Cree tended to adopt whichever brand of Christianity proselytized among them. In general this was Roman Catholic on the coast and Anglican inland. Religious books proliferated in native communities and were often the first and most insistent demand of native people when they encountered traveling missionaries. "They [the people of Big Trout Lake] were very much pleased to have a visit from the Archdeacon of the district. . . . Books were in great demand as no books had come for three or four years, and the few books brought by the Archdeacon went quickly" (Faries, 1921; see also Murdoch, 1981).

The syllabic script continues to be a mainstay of both the Roman Catholic and Anglican churches in the four communities. Most services in these churches are conducted in Cree, with liturgical books in the syllabic script bountifully available in the church pews. Recently, however, English services have also been introduced. They are fewer in number, and are aimed specifically at the young people. One cleric said this was necessary because young people can no longer read religious material in syllabics. Pentecostal and fundamentalist churches, which have appeared in all four communities within the past decade, conduct their services in English almost without exception, and make no use of the syllabic script whatsoever.

Although, in the traditional context, only the syllabic script was used for religious purposes, the Roman alphabet has made and continues to make significant inroads upon this once exclusive domain. Greater accommodations are constantly being made to the use of English and the English script in both religious services and religious literature. The reason given for this is that it is not possible to reach the young people using syllabics. The increasing use of English in the religious sphere must, therefore, be considered a response rather than an innovation. It is following literacy and linguistic changes in other domains.

C. Syllabics and Record-Keeping

The Cree used their syllabic script for many of the same purposes as Europeans and their descendants have used the roman script. People kept diaries, wrote histories, noted family births, deaths, etc. They recorded "business" information, made notes at meetings and decorated their houses with favorite proverbs. The Cree, however, generally did not use their script for amusement—to while away long leisure hours. There was no body of literature available for this purpose and, in any case, few hours of leisure.

Today, older people continue to use their script as they have always done, although a few new items may be noted in their collections, among them: lists of frequently called telephone numbers taped on the wall above the telephone receiver, or instructions (printed by Bell Canada) on how to make long-distance calls (sic). For people under 40, however, the main functions of literacy have been co-opted by English literacy. The list of these functions has also been greatly expanded. For example, reading for leisure has become a well-established practice. Newspapers and magazines abound in many houses, and there is a small but dedicated number of confirmed novel readers. More importantly, knowledge of English and the roman script has become necessary for the continued survival of the community. For bands located in Ontario, relations with all levels of the Canadian government are ultimately conducted in English. In addition, the bands have to cope with a progressively expanding volume of paperwork concerned with government regulations, and with the transfer of monies to the bands either as corporate entities, or to individual band members or to local projects (housing, sewage, road-building, etc.). Fluency in the English language and script is therefore a prerequisite for native leaders or their immediate advisors. It is no accident that band offices in northern Ontario are currently staffed almost exclusively by people in their 20s and 30s whose command of English is excellent. In fact, on two of the four reserves we worked in, a Euro-Canadian is working as a full-time and fully acknowledged member of the band office staff. Individual band councillors and/or chiefs do not necessarily know English themselves, but the band office as a writing entity is far more dependent on English than on Cree. Even local community notices tend to be written in English first and then translated into Cree afterwards. Some find this situation regrettable, even deplorable. At least one old gentleman went so far as to suggest that Cree, as an aboriginal tongue, ought to be allowed equal billing with English and French as an "official language" of Canada. Although this seems unlikely to happen, it is possible that with the increased control of their own government promised to them in the near future, the Cree-speaking constituencies of the First Nations of Canada may be able to reverse the trend of deepening dependency upon English and its alphabetical script.

In the domain of record-keeping and personal writing there is a division between generations which echoes that already noted in the religious context. Older people continue to rely upon the syllabic script. Younger ones use English. For English literates, however, the number of uses to which literacy is put has been vastly expanded. In sum, the uses for the older, syllabic, script are shrinking, while those for the more recently introduced alphabetical script are growing rapidly.

In this situation there would appear to be little incentive for children to learn the older script and many parents do, in fact, complain of their children's overall indifference noting that syllabics homework is invariably finished last—if it is done at all. Nevertheless the future of the syllabic script in northern Ontario is not necessarily so bleak. As the utilitarian functions of the syllabic script have disappeared, it has paradoxically begun to acquire some significance as a carrier of native cultural identity.

D. "Indian Identity"

Cree society is marked by a decided lack of formality and a corresponding emphasis upon the paramount importance of the individual's autonomy and independence. This has been noted by many researchers. According to Preston, among the Cree "explicit formal rules are few and covert" (Preston, 1971). Landes commented on the "ruthless individualism" of the neighboring Ojibway and suggested that the Cree were similar (Landes, 1937, 1938). Honigman (1968) discussed the same phenomenon under the rubric of "atomism."

For example, Cree society does not specify what behavior "should" be in situations which most other societies structure very highly. Among the Cree there is a near-total absence of greetings and greeting formulas; there is a corresponding lack of "respectful" terms of address and the widespread use of first names to designate everyone from the chief to grandchildren; comings and goings are likewise unmarked—arrivals and departures are casual even after long absence (no exclamations of reunion, no lingering farewells); and meals—as distinct from food preparation—are frequently formless to the point of nonexistence. In a related vein, Cree child-rearing practices appear (to most Euro-Canadians) to be permissive in the extreme. Cree children are seldom interrupted in their activities unless their behavior is life-threatening, and even this stricture is interpreted leniently.

In general the Cree have a distaste for giving/receiving orders, for making commands or demands on others—in short, a distaste for anything which looks like an exercise of power by one person over another. For most purposes the Cree have no "proper" or "best" method of proceeding. If they have a preference at all, it is a preference for avoiding rule-bound situations and rule-making people, a preference for flexibility and economy, a preference for what works adequately with the least amount of effort and fuss (both social and physical). Transmission of Cree syllabic literacy under traditional modes of instruction adhered admirably to Cree values. In typical Cree fashion, only the goal was specified—learning to read. The means of arriving at it were left to the ingenuity and inventiveness of particular individuals in particular circumstances. This helps to explain the incredible diversity of learning experiences reported by older syllabic literates (see above, Introduction). This diversity applied right across the board—to every aspect of learning: to methods of instruction, to the person of the instructor, to the writing materials used, to the frequency and duration of "lessons" and to the uses of literacy afterwards. It is interesting to note that the traditional writing materials named by older Cree literates were all familiar objects, part of their environment, and this may have helped to reinforce the notion of the syllabic script as something essentially Indian—as would the informal, unstructured nature of the "lessons." In fact, many syllabic literatures (and non-literates) remain unaware of the true origins of the syllabic script and regard it instead as something intrinsic to their own culture. We collected at least one pseudo-mythological version of the script's origins which tells of two native people struck by a great light while out in the bush, and then learning the script in a kind of spirit world.

The Cree are proud of their script and possessive of its future. They also regard it to a great extent as synonymous with their language. When questioning people about the future of their script, researchers found it almost impossible to prevent a simultaneous discussion of the future fate of the Cree language. People typically stated that they thought it would be a bad thing if they lost the ability to write the syllabic script because then they would lose their language, forget their culture and lose their Indian heritage. The confusion of language and script may rest to an extent upon usage in the Cree language itself. "He speaks" is *"ayamihew"* (literally, "he addresses him"). "He reads" is *"ayamihtaw"* (literally, "he addresses it"). Moreover, the two scripts (alphabetic and syllabic) are commonly referred to by the name of the language they are used to represent—that is, "English-writing" and "Cree-writing"—and are not distinguished from each other by the nature of their symbolic characters or "letters." The confusion goes deeper, however, than a semantic identity between language and script. Despite our persistent efforts to disentangle the two strands of script and speech, people would still "forget," and tell us that it was important to learn to read the syllabic script "because it's the language [sic] for the Indian people, the same as whites have to learn their language." And the link with culture explicit, "It [syllabics] is part of the culture and it is part of a person's responsibility to keep his culture alive."[3]

One cannot, of course, be sure from where the force of the identification derives, but it seems likely that for a nomadic people living in a stringent environment with a necessarily limited material culture and an unelaborated ritual/ceremonial system, the main embodiments of culture would have been language and knowledge of survival skills. The latter of these two has lessened in importance as a result of the increasing urbanization of the Cree. We should therefore expect that language would remain the single most important symbol of Cree identity. And, to the extent that cultural identity is perceived to be closely tied to language, it will also be bound up with the syllabic script—because of the strong linkage between the two.

Thus we should not be surprised to find the Cree syllabic script endowed with considerable symbolic value. This may help to explain the tenacity of the script in the face of official indifference or persecution. It might also help to explain the continuing efforts of the Cree people to maintain and expand educational programs for teaching the syllabic script to their children. In the process of acculturation certain aspects of culture may be relinquished while others are maintained. Syllabics would appear to be a cultural element that native people would like to preserve. In this light it is interesting to note that no efforts are being made on any of the reserves in question to write the Cree language using the roman alphabet. When people are questioned as to whether or not they thought this might be a good idea they often looked rather bewildered—at least initially. Here again we see the strength of the linkage between language and script.

V. SYLLABIC LITERACY AND COGNITION

In recent extensions of the work reported so far, we have been examining the nature of cognitive competence among the Cree, and how this might be related to syllabic literacy. An overall notion guiding this work is that both competence and literacy may be adaptive to ecological context.

With respect to perceptual and cognitive abilities, the ecological and cultural adaptations of northern Aboriginal peoples appear to have encouraged the development of a set of skills that enable success as hunters and trappers. These include high levels of visual discrimination,

---

[3]Quotations again taken from responses to the pilot survey data (see footnote 2).

disembedding and spatial abilities (Berry, 1976) combined with a well-developed sense of personal independence and non-interference in the lives of others. This particular pattern has been plausibly linked to the notion of the field-independent cognitive style (Berry, 1976), and extended to include a preference for a visual learning style as well. In the Canadian North (to which this generalization is limited), there is thus a documented set of abilities that underpin a whole range of practical activities in the technological sphere. In essence, the long-term ecological and cultural adaptations of norther Aboriginal peoples appear to have prepared them well, at least cognitively, to participate in the technological world of southern Eurocanadian society.

The central question that was addressed in the cognitive abilities portion of this study concerned the relative effects of schooling and syllabic literacy on cognitive test performance (Berry & Bennett, 1989, 1991, 1994). Results indicate that schooling has a major influence on English language tests, with a lesser influence on perceptual and cognitive tests (Spatial, Rotation, Raven's Matrices) and on Cree Language Tests. In contrast, Syllabics Reading was unrelated to schooling, once age is taken into account. Thus, there is a clearly stronger relative degree of influence of schooling, over syllabic literacy, in controlling test performance.

A second question was whether the relatively high level of spatial (and related abilities) reported in the literature for northern Aboriginal peoples (McShane & Berry, 1988) might be a consequence of the widespread syllabic literacy found in the population, rather than to ecocultural adaptation (as proposed by Berry, 1976). It is evident that the influence of syllabic literacy on cognitive test performance is minimal. Hence, the conclusion that there is an important role for ecological and cultural factors in the cognitive development of northern Aboriginal peoples appears to stand.

With respect to the goals of cognitive development, a recent study (Berry & Bennett, 1992) used both ethnographic and psychometric procedures to uncover what the Cree understand by notions such as "intelligent", "smart", "clever", "able", and "competent". The first stage was to work with a small set of key informants to elicit Cree concepts for these and similar terms, and to seek both linguistic and contextual elaborations of them. We collected a list of twenty words dealing with cognitive competence through a series of a very loosely structured interviews conducted with Cree speakers in northern Ontario.

The twenty words were written out in the Cree syllabic script on cards. The cards were given to participants, all of whom were able to read syllabics. We asked them to put the cards into piles on the basis of similarity of meaning. Multidimensional scaling revealed two dimensions. The horizontal dimension ranges from negative to positive evaluation, with the possible inclusion of moral and social aspects as well. That is to say, the negative words are not only disliked, ("stupidity" and "craziness" are not positively valued) but they are probably considered to be morally reprehensible as well (e.g., "cunning" and "backwards knowledge", a Cree concept referring to wisdom that is turned to the service of disruption and disharmony).

The vertical dimension is more difficult to label, but may be one of toughminded versus tenderminded. At one extreme there are two words for "mentally tough" in the sense of being brave, and of having courage or fortitude. At the other extreme are "religious" and "understands new things". This dimension may have something to do with openness or sensitivity.

There is one main cluster of words on the right side and slightly above center (i.e., both sensitive and morally good) containing the words we have rendered in English as "wise", "respect", "respectful", "listens", "pays attention", "thinks hard", and "thinks carefully". This cluster, we suggest, constitutes the core meaning of "thinking well among the Cree". It is interesting to note that the word most directly opposite the core cluster, the word which is therefore most distant from it on both dimensions (i.e., insensitive and morally bad) has been rendered as "lives like a white", in the sense of behaving, thinking and comporting oneself like a white person. It would be tempting to regard this as something like a Cree version of being a "klutz" (particularly since clumsy boorishness features in so many stories of white men in the bush), and has some quite derogatory overtones. Its very position on the diagram should alert us to look for meanings and negative moral content and insensitivity. Its closeness to words like "cunning", "stupid", "crazy", and "backwards knowledge" underlines this view.

VI. CONCLUSION

On the basis of the studies presented here, syllabic literacy among the Cree faces an uncertain future. However, it has great symbolic import, and appears to be cognitively adaptive to their traditional ecological context. These observations suggest that syllabic literacy may continue for some time as an important way of expressing their "Creeness" to the rest of the world. And while their ecological engagement has changed dramatically in the past few decades, there are signs that with the advent of Aboriginal self-government, and the evident desire for cultural reaffirmation on the part of many, these trends may reverse. Acculturation is not a one way street (Berry, 1990), and cultural recovery is well-known. As long a syllabic literacy retains some place in Cree life, there is the possibility, indeed the probability, that syllabic literacy will be with us for a long time to come.

REFERENCES

Berry, J. W. (1976). *Human ecology and cognitive style: Comparative studies in cultural and psychological adaptation.* New York: Sage/Halsted.

Berry, J. W. (1980). Native peoples and the larger society. In R. Gardner & R. Kalin (Eds.), *A Canadian social psychology of ethnic relations.* Toronto: Methuen.

Berry, J. W. (1985). *Multiculturalism and psychology in plural societies.* Paper presented to IACCP Conference on Ethnic Minorities, Malmo, Sweden, June.

Berry, J. W. (1990). Psychology of acculturation. In J. Berman (Ed.), *Cross-cultural perspectives: Nebraska symposium on motivation, 37* (pp. 201-234). Lincoln: University of Nebraska Press.

Berry J. W., & Bennett, J. (1989). Syllabic literacy and cognitive performance among the Cree. *International Journal of Psychology, 24,* 429-450.

Berry, J. W., & Bennett, J. A. (1991). *Cree syllabic literacy: Cultural context and psychological consequences.* Tilburg University Monographs in Cross-Cultural Psychology. Tilburg: Tilburg University Press.

Berry, J. W., & Bennett, J. A. (1992). Cree conceptions of cognitive competence. *International Journal of Psychology, 27,* 73-88.

Berry, J. W., & Bennett, J. A. (1994). Syllabic literacy and cognitive performance among the Cree and Ojibwe people of northern Canada. In D. Olson & I. Taylor (Eds.), *Scripts and literacy: East and west* (pp. 341-357). Amsterdam: Kluwer Academic Publishers.

Berry, J. W., Poortinga, Y. H., Segall, M. H., & Dasen, P. R. (1992). *Cross-cultural psychology: Research and applications.* New York: Cambridge University Press.

Bishop, C. A. (1974). *The Northern Ojibwa and the fur trade: An historical and ecological study.* Toronto: Holt, Rinehart & Winston of Canada Ltd.

Burnaby, B., & MacKenzie, M. (n.d.). *Native functions of literacy: Who reads what in Rupert House.* Ontario Institute for Studies in Education.

Burnaby, B., Nichols, J., & Toohey, K. (1980). Northern Native Languages Project. Ontario Institute for Studies in Education. Unpublished report.

Darnell, R., & Vanek, A. L. (1973). The psychological reality of Cree syllabics. In R. Darnell, (Ed.), *Canadian languages in their social context.* Edmonton: University of Alberta Press.

Dunning, R. W. (1959). *Social change among the northern Ojibway.* Toronto: University of Toronto Press.

Faries, R., (Archdeacon) (1921). *Early history of mission at Big Trout Lake.* Unpublished record now on display in the vestibule of the

Anglican church at Big Trout Lake. Alleged to have been copied from the original Baptismal Book now preserved in the Keewatin Diocese, Synod Office in Kenora, Ontario.

Hallowell, A. I. (1949). The size of Algonkian hunting territories: A function of ecological adjustment. *American Anthropologist, 51*, 35-45.

Helm, J. (Ed.). (1979). *Handbook of North American Indians.* Washington, DC: Smithsonian Institution.

Honigman, J. J. (1953). Social organization of the Attawapiskat Cree Indians. *Anthropos, 48*, 809-816.

Honigman, J. J. (1956). The Attawapiskat Swampy Cree—an ethnographic reconstruction. *Anthropological Papers of the University of Alaska, 5*(1), 23-82.

Honigman, J. J. (1968). Interpersonal relations in atomistic communities. *Human Organization, 27*, 220-229.

Johnston, B. (1976). *Ojibway heritage.* Toronto: McClelland & Stewart.

Landes, R. (1937). *Ojibwa sociology.* New York: Columbia University Press.

Landes, R. (1938). *The Ojibwa woman.* New York: W. W. Norton.

McShane, D., & Berry, J. W. (1988). The abilities of Native North Americans. In S. H. Irvine & J. W. Berry (Eds.), *Human abilities in cultural context* (pp. 385-426). New York: Cambridge University Press.

Murdoch, J. (1981). Syllabics: A successful educational innovation. Unpublished master's thesis, University of Manitoba.

Murdoch, J. (1984). *A bibliography of Algonquian syllabic texts in Canadian repositories.* Project ASTIC. Quebec: Gouvernement du Quebec, Ministères des Affaires culturelles, Direction regionale du Nouveau Quebec et service aux autochtones.

Preston, R. (1971). Cree narration: An expression of the personal meanings of events. Unpublished PhD. thesis, University of North Carolina at Chapel Hill.

Rogers, E. S. (1962). *The Round Lake Ojibwa.* Toronto: The Royal Ontario Museum.

Rogers E. S. (1969). Natural environment—social organization—witchcraft: Cree versus Ojibwa—a test case. In D. Damas (Ed.), *Contributions to anthropology: Ecological essays* (pp. 24-39). Ottawa: National Museum of Canada, Bulletin, No. 230.

Rogers, E. S. (1983). Cultural adaptations the northern Ojibwa. In A. T. Steegman, Jr. (Ed.), *Boreal forest adaptations: The northern Algonkians.* New York: Plenum Press.

Rogers, E. S., & Taylor, G. (1979). Northern Ojibwa. In J. Helm (Ed.), *Handbook of North American Indians.* Washington: Smithsonian Institution.

Scribner, S., & Cole, M. (1981). *The psychology of literacy.* Cambridge, MA: Harvard University Press.

Skinner, A. (1911). Notes on the Eastern Cree and Northern Saulteaux. *Anthropological Papers American Museum of Natural History, IX*, part 1.

Steegman, A. T., Jr., Hurlich, M. G., & Winterhalder, B. (1983). Challenges of the boreal forest. In A. T. Steegman, Jr. (Ed.), *Boreal forest adaptations: The northern Algonkians*. New York: Plenum Press.

Walker, W. (1969). Notes on native writing systems and the design of native literacy programs. *Anthropological Linguistics, 11*, 148-166.

White, J. K. (1962). On the revival of printing in the Cherokee language. *Current Anthropology, 3*, 511-514.

18

Comparative Aspects of Functional Literacy Development: Three Ethnic American Communities

Stephen M. Reder
Portland State University

I. INTRODUCTION

The diversity of situations described in this volume indicates that both the theory of literacy development and the practice of literacy education throughout the world can benefit from systematic, comparative studies of literacy development in diverse historical and societal contexts. In the past, comparative work has tended to focus primarily on the material aspects of literacy development, matters of orthography and technologies of producing script and print. But other aspects of literacy must also be considered in comparative treatments. Such work must also focus on the social functions served by writing, and the forms or genres of writing used in particular cultural contexts. Brian Street's eloquent critique of the "autonomous" model of literacy development (this volume) reminds us that comparative analyses must not limit their coverage to only these aspects, either; the ideological dimensions of literacy development, often bound up with the spread of particular religious, political or economic orders, must also be carefully examined and systematically described in accounts of variations in literacy development. The relationship between formal schooling—an instrument through which many societies enculturate their social, political, economic, and religious beliefs—and literacy development is particularly noteworthy and problematic in this regard.

What little comparative perspective on literacy does exist today has emerged gradually in piecemeal fashion, as an increasing body of descriptions of individual cases has been accumulated. Few studies have examined in depth several developmental contexts in parallel. Most have looked in depth at a particular society or cultural context, such as Scribner and Cole's (1981) contemporary work with the Vai in West Africa, or Goody and Watt's (1963) speculative analysis of Western literacy traditions deriving from the case of classical Greece. Heath's (1983) comparison of two rural communities in the southeastern United States represents a major advance in comparative analysis, in terms of both the specific results of her study and of her persuasive demonstration of the power of the comparative method for literacy research. In this chapter a comparative study of literacy development that Karen Reed (Green) Wikelund and I conducted is briefly described.

II. A COMPARATIVE STUDY

The focus of the study was on the relationship between sociocultural context and adult literacy development. Three communities within the United States were selected for comparative study: an Eskimo fishing village in south-central Alaska, a community of Hmong immigrants from the highlands of Laos now living on the West Coast, and a partially migrant, partially settled Hispanic community in the migrant stream in the Pacific Northwest. Despite the many obvious surface differences among these communities, they offer systematic features for comparison and contrast with respect to adult literacy development. All three communities share what was felt to be an important feature for literacy development: each community has recently encountered rapidly increasing demands for literacy in everyday life. Major contrasts exist among the sociohistorical contexts in which these new environmental demands for literacy are being experienced. Table 18.1 compares these communities in terms of major contextual features impacting literacy development.

In Seal Bay, a pseudonym for the Eskimo village, contact with literacy has come as part of a broad, gradually increasing penetration of

TABLE 18.1. Comparative Features of Adult Literacy.

Aspects of literacy	Site 1 Seal Bay* (Eskimo)	Site 3 Pleasantville* (Hispanic)	Site 2 Newton* (Hmong)
Sociohistorical aspects of literacy development	Literacy originally imposed from outside; no displacement of population from traditional environment and work roles	Partial displacement of population from traditional environment and economy; Spanish language literacy sometimes acquired informally (self-taught or via friends or family)	Immigrated into literate society, displacement of population from its traditional environment and economy; exposure to literacy only within past 20 years; native literacy often self-taught (through primer)
Sociolinguistic aspects of literacy	Change to use of English nearly complete; expanding literacy in English; little or no literacy remains in native language (bilingual ↔ monolingual in English with very limited previous literacy in another language)	Exclusive use of English literacy for some; some Spanish and English biliteracy (English predominant); some recent migrants learning English; many monolingual Spanish speakers with some literacy, some illiterate	Change to use of English just beginning; little literacy in English; little in native language, (primarily monolingual ↔ bilingual, though some previous bilingualism in Hmong and Lao, with small educated group literate in another language)
Social organization of literacy skills within the community Distribution of skills	Literacy skills (in English) concentrated among persons under 40	Literacy skills concentrated among education residents; limited skills in English or Spanish among recent migrants; occasional cases of spontaneous acquisition of Spanish literacy	Literacy skills heavily concentrated among wealthier, better educated first wave immigrants and the young; limited skills in Hmong, Lao, or English among recent arrivals; continuing spontaneous acquisition of native language literacy

TABLE 18.1. Comparative Features of Adult Literacy (con't).

Literacy Use in Domains of Activity	Site 1	Site 3	Site 2
Literacy skills as role markers	Use of literacy specialists (though skills becoming more widely distributed)	Mixed distribution—use of English literacy specialists among many community members; use of Spanish literacy specialists among some community members	Use of literacy specialists—heavy reliance on specialists
Resulting social meanings	Conflicting social meanings attached to literacy activities (developed from historical context)	Multiple social meanings dependent on context of literacy use and intra-group relations	Multiple social meanings—generally positive
Economic activity			
Traditional work roles	Literacy incorporated into existing economic roles	Relatively little use of literacy in traditional economic roles	Little possibility of incorporation into existing economy (and no use in traditional economic roles)
New work roles	A few new vocational opportunities for literacy specialists	Some new vocational opportunities for literates	Extensive new vocational opportunities for literates
Perception of welfare system with regard to economic independence	Welfare seen as competing with economic independence	Intermediate case with varied perceptions	Welfare seen as a temporary aid to adult literacy education and eventual economic independence
Entrenchment of welfare system in community	Relatively high (though a secondary source of support)	Intermediate (language and legal status are variables)	Low in time depth, but high in terms of current impact (major source of economic support)
Educational activity			
Past exposure to formal schooling	School in community for over 50 years; high dropout rate	Wide range of exposures, from none to graduate degrees; some schooling in Mexico; high dropout rate	Limited previous exposure to schooling—73% no schooling, 86% 3 years or less; high dropout rate

TABLE 18.1. Comparative Features of Adult Literacy (con't.).

Literacy Use in Domains of Activity	Site 1	Site 3	Site 2
Felt need for adult literacy training	Relatively low—main interest GED (for employment, and/or as valued credential); low participation in formal programs	Intermediate—main interest ESL/vocational training; uneven participation in formal programs	Relatively high—main interest ESL/vocational training; high participation in formal programs
Religious activity			
Role in introduction of literacy	Literacy originally introduced by Russian Orthodox Church in Slavonic and Alutiiq; lay reader (specialist) highly esteemed; some teaching of literacy to children	Value of literacy perhaps introduced by the Catholic Church though in Latin; participation limited to priests (specialists)	Literacy in Hmong introduced by missionaries (several different scripts) only 20 years ago; continuing efforts of missionaries in U.S. to provide literacy training
Present use of literacy	Literacy in English used in church activities; particularly among the young; reliance on specialists	Spanish literacy used in church activities, some English literacy; participation in literacy activities uneven; reliance on specialists	Limited use of Hmong literacy (self-taught); some use of hymn books and Bibles in Hmong; reliance on specialists
Governance	Recent rapid increase in need to use literacy; development of native specialists	Heavy reliance on outsiders; gradual development of expertise (bilingual); situation complicated by illegal status of many residents	Extremely rapid increase in need for use of literacy; rapid development of native specialists (bilingual)

*Pseudonym

village life by the outside world (first by Russians in the early nineteenth century and later by the United States). Both the initial contact with writing and much of the subsequent development of literacy in this community has occurred without displacement from its traditional environment or economy. In recent years a series of political and economic events has radically altered the relationships between the village and external governmental agencies, as well as accelerating the transition of villagers from subsistence fishermen to commercial fishermen. These changes have placed new demands for literacy skills on adults in Seal Bay.

In Newton, a pseudonym for the immigrant Hmong community, the introduction and development of literacy has occurred in a dramatically different sociohistorical context. Rather than being surrounded and increasingly penetrated by the literate, English-speaking world, as happened in Seal Bay, Hmong settlers in Newton were transplanted from their traditional environment and economy in Southeast Asia into radically different ones, fraught with incremental demands for new language and literacy skills (the Hmong were by and large a preliterate group prior to moving to the United States).

In Pleasantville, a pseudonym for the Hispanic community studied in the project, literacy development has taken place in a third context, in many ways, intermediate between those of Seal Bay and Newton. The community in Pleasantville is partially migrant (like the Hmong of Newton) and partially settled (like the Eskimo of Seal Bay). Some adults in the community encountered and developed literacy in a previous environment in Mexico, whereas others are becoming literate in the new environment. Economic roles in Pleasantville overlap partially with the traditional roles many held in Mexico.

The three sites contrast in many important ways, but were carefully selected to share an essential property: recent literacy development is primarily a response to changing environmental demands for use of written materials in everyday life. The sociohistorical context in which the three communities encountered these incremental demands for literacy radically differed, and we have seen how the distinctive character of each context has profoundly influenced the development of literacy. The differences among the communities studied offer some perspective on how changes in various aspects of a community's environment—such as in its patterns of language use, its economic opportunities or its physical setting, for example—are related to literacy use and development.

Ethnographic research forms the core of study in each community. Reports of some aspects of this research have appeared elsewhere (Green & Reder, 1986; Reder & Green, 1983; Reder & Wikelund, 1993). In each of these studies, fieldwork was composed of a variety of research activities and had several topical foci, including ethnohistorical inquiry into the development of literacy in the community, as well as the myriad uses and formats of written materials evident in contemporary life. Where possible, individuals' skills and attitudes regarding the use of written materials in their lives were systematically assessed.

III. SOME FINDINGS FROM THE FIELD

In each community, close observation of the actual uses of literacy concurs with what Scribner and Cole (1981) found with the Vai in Liberia and Heath (1983) found in the Roadville and Trackton communities in the United States: literacy is manifested as a set of culturally patterned practices. The predominant literacy practices vary from site to site, as do such specifics of particular literacy practices as the structure of their participant groups, the nature and extent of the knowledge and values associated with the practice, and the language and script utilized in the practice (Reder, 1993, 1994a).

The critical point here is taking the literacy practice itself, rather than the inferred level of an individual's reading or writing skill, to be the primary unit of observation and analysis. With the focus on the socially patterned use of writing in a given activity or practice, questions are asked about aspects of the social organization of the given literacy practice, including the distinct social roles evident among its participants, the social status and other characteristics of the individuals who fill those roles, the specialized knowledge (including that pertaining to reading and writing) associated with those roles, the ways in which written materials are used in the practice, the impact which various degrees of skill at working with those materials has upon the performance of the practice, and how practice specific knowledge is socialized among participants.

A. Literacy as Collaborative Practice

A literacy practice is said to be collaborative when it regularly occurs in the social context of more than one person. There are important distinctions among the ways in which a literacy practice may be termed collaborative. Literacy practices are often collaborative in nature. Heath (1983), Reder (1992), Reder and Green (1983), Shuman (1983) and Fingeret (1983) have described a variety of collaborative literacy practices. A literacy practice may be collaborative in the sense that two or more interactants utilize written materials, as when members of a religious congregation read aloud as part of a responsive reading or family members alternately read cards aloud from a board game being played. Alternatively, a collaborative literacy practice may involve a single participant who reads or writes in the performance of the task, but other members of the participant group nevertheless actively manipulate the information associated with that reading or writing. Many familiar forms of oral reading offer examples of collaborative literacy practices in which the reading skills of one participant are utilized to accomplish a group task. One member of a group reads material aloud (e.g., a newspaper article, a personal letter, or part of a storybook) for the group to hear and possibly discuss. In some participant groups it is always the same person whose literacy skills are used, whereas in other participant groups or in other literacy practices this may vary or rotate (e.g., when parents alternate reading stories to their children).

Other social architectures of collaborative literacy practices are "scribal" in nature. The specialized knowledge or status of one participant combines with the writing skill, knowledge or status of another (the "scribe") to accomplish a task such as writing a letter or completing a form. Many variations of such collaborative practices were observed in the three communities studied, involving a wide range of tasks, topical knowledge, and literacy expertise.

In many cases the collaborative nature of literacy practices, in which a group of individuals pool their knowledge and literacy skills to accomplish a mutual task, cannot be well accounted for in terms of the different levels of reading and writing proficiency among the individuals involved. Although in some cases the individual who functions as the "scribe" may have better literacy skills than other participants, in other cases the scribe fills this role not because of the uniqueness of his or her skills, but because members of the participant group have different statuses. As an example, consider the collaborative literacy practice of dictating a letter in a modern office setting. The "boss" (one social role in this literacy practice) dictates the letter to the "secretary" (another social role in the practice). The fact that the secretary rather than the boss is doing the actual writing (i.e., functions as the "scribe") may or may not reflect the distribution of specialized literacy skills between the two; more likely it reflects their relative statuses within the organization in which they work. Similarly, when an individual asks an accountant or tax-preparer (another professional "scribe") for assistance in filling out income tax forms, it may or may not in a given instance reflect a specialization of knowledge or skills—it could merely represent a desire to spend one's time doing things other than filling out tax forms. An important implication of this is that if social factors strongly influence individuals' access to participant roles that have specialized responsibilities for reading and writing, and if experience in those roles is closely linked to developing a particular body of knowledge and skills, then those same social factors will influence the social distribution of skills and knowledge within the participant community. Increasing individuals' comfort with, or access to, roles having specialized responsibilities for reading or writing may stimulate the development of the requisite skills and knowledge.

In all of the settings studied, literacy development has been heralded by the emergence of collaborative literacy practices, in which reading and writing tasks are accomplished collectively. Individuals routinely share literacy skills and knowledge in order to perform particular tasks, much as they share other types of skills, such as carpentry, babysitting, and small engine repair. In Pleasantville, letters between distant family members are written and read in this collaborative fashion. In Seal Bay, churchgoers take on roles in the religious services that draw on their literacy skills, assisting each other as necessary to conduct the service in the absence of a priest. In Newton, family members sit together to sort through the day's mail, struggling to discern the unfamiliar categories of mail in the United States. An impressive array of literacy skills and knowledge are on display as the group collectively manages to discard junk mail but retain critical utility bills, personal correspondence, and form letters from government agencies. Each piece of mail is carefully inspected and sorted into an appropriate pile, with one pile of mail of undetermined status designated for inspection and assistance from a more knowledgeable relative not present in the group.

There are, of course, many literacy activities that take place in social isolation. Individuals often read and write as solitary activities. But the extent of such solitary literacy activity need not distort our view of the essentially collaborative nature of many literacy practices. As discussed below, many solitary literacy activities derive from collaborative practices. We need only think of the parental admonition "read to yourself" to remind ourselves of the social origins of such activity. The perspective adopted here of viewing literacy practices as being fundamentally collaborative social activities is not intended to downplay the significance of solitary literate activity—it is, after all, a highly valued type of activity in schools and many other institutions of Western societies. But the results of the research reported here indicate that emphasizing the solitary aspects of literacy seriously misrepresents the significant group contexts in which literacy so often develops, is frequently used and—as discussed below—is typically transmitted from one person to another.

B. Modes of Engagement in Literacy Practices

Individuals participate in these collaborative literacy practices in varied ways. Some persons directly manipulate written materials, reading and/or writing as part of performing the task at hand—these individuals are here said to be *technologically engaged* in the literacy practice. The term technologically engaged refers to the particular technology of writing involved in the practice. Other individuals may not be technologically engaged in the practice but nevertheless interact closely in performing the task with others who are technologically engaged—these individuals are said to be *functionally engaged* in the collaborative literacy practice. They may provide specialized knowledge and expertise as vital to the performance of the collaborative practice as the literacy skills deployed by the technologically engaged participants. Other individuals may be neither technologically nor functionally engaged in the practice, but nevertheless have knowledge of the nature of the practice and its implications for the life of the community, and must routinely take others' technological and functional engagement into account. Individuals in such positions are here said to be *socially engaged* in the practice.

These modes of engagement are not mutually exclusive, of course. They frequently overlap in the sense that given individuals' engagement in a literacy practice may encompass several of these modes. But they are nevertheless distinct participatory modes. Individuals may be functionally engaged in a literacy practice without being technologically engaged. One participant in a collaborative literacy practice may provide the technological skills needed for encoding or decoding written messages, whereas another may provide information needed for the joint accomplishment of the literacy task. Collaboration based on socially distributed modes of engagement within the participant group was observed regularly in literacy practices in each of the sites.

Individuals may also be technologically engaged in performing a literacy practice without being functionally engaged, although this pattern does not seem to occur as frequently. For example, an individual may sign a contract (at the request of another individual) without understanding the functional implications of his/her signature. Among Hmong immigrants it was not uncommon to find adults who could sign their name (as a technological act) but did not understand the implications of affixing their signature to various types of documents. Often they would collaborate with friends or relatives who could explain the significance of the document and of signing their name to it. In some circumstances, individuals refuse to sign their name once they understand the legal implications of doing so.

Sometimes the necessary aggregation of technological skills and functional knowledge is pooled across several participants as happened, for example, in a town meeting in Seal Bay in which several resources were combined in a literacy event that had great significance for the village: (1) the technological expertise of one individual at writing formal letters; (2) the political savvy of another individual who could not by himself write formal letters but understood how to use a letter to the editor (of a regional newspaper) as a tool for advancing the village's political interests; and (3) the historical knowledge and community support of village elders, who provided relevant background information for the letter and approved its tactical use.

This example illustrates the contrast among the three modes of engagement. One Seal Bayite, well educated and possessed of "academic" literacy skills, was technologically engaged in this particular literacy event, serving as the "scribe" in implementing the political approach and ideas generated by another village resident, whose political savvy and in-depth understanding of how print media, in general, and letters to the editor, in particular, could be utilized for social purposes. This latter individual was functionally engaged in the literacy task of preparing the letter. The elder villagers, who approved the tactic of using the letter to the editor, participated from a further remove: they had neither the specific technological capabilities nor the understanding of how media can be used for political purposes, but nevertheless took into account the skills and knowledge that others had, and made important and ultimately effective decisions in the matter. They were socially engaged in the literacy event. This collaborative literacy event established a common pattern for sharing socially distributed knowledge, reading and writing skills and native values for dealing with outside agencies through the written word—in short, a new collaborative literacy practice.

The three modes of engagement thus correspond in a general way to distinct levels of remove from the personal deployment of script in performance of a group task. The individual who is technologically engaged encounters written information directly. The individual who is functionally engaged (but not technologically engaged) encounters written information at one remove, mediated through the technological skills of others. Similarly, the individual who is socially engaged (but neither technologically nor functionally engaged) encounters the written materials used in a literacy practice at two removes.

C. Cognitive Aspects of Participatory Modes

An important set of findings from the field studies concerns the analysis of what it is that adults learn about literacy practices as their engagement proceeds. Three components of their acquisition identified are *technological knowledge*, *functional knowledge*, and knowledge of the *social meanings* of literacy. Each of these three types of knowledge is learned in a practice specific way, such as for writing personal correspondence or for filling out various types of applications.

Technological engagement in a specific literacy practice entails knowledge of a particular technology of reading or writing, and how to apply that knowledge to utilize the materials in the given literacy practice. Such technological knowledge usually includes, in the case of alphabetic orthographies, mastery of the correspondence between the phonological system of the spoken language and the graphic elements of the writing system, as well as knowledge of how to use the media involved in the particular practice (e.g., paper and pencil, a keyboard, etc.).

Functional knowledge of how writing is used for social purposes, and the impact its use or non-use has on task outcomes, is also an essential component of literacy. Functional knowledge about a specific literacy practice specifies the kind and sources of information (including sources of technological knowledge) needed to perform the task—much of this functional knowledge is necessary for the smooth coordination of a group collectively accomplishing a literacy practice.

Although technological and functional knowledge often overlap (in so far as many individuals often possess both types of knowledge about given literacy practices), it is important to distinguish between them. One may have functional knowledge about a given literacy practice without having its requisite technological knowledge, as when Hmong immigrants learn about American practices of sending greeting cards for special occasions such as weddings and Christmas without being able to sign their name or add the customary brief message or address the envelope. Many nevertheless participate in this literacy practice with their American friends and associates by using someone else's technological skills to perform those aspects of the practice. Related examples involving those having more sophisticated literacy skills in English are not hard to find. Consider the widespread use of various "literacy specialists" such as lawyers or tax preparers for assistance with particular types of written documents; we may have functional knowledge of how such documents are used in our society for various administrative purposes without having all the requisite technical knowledge—we may understand the significance of completing the document and what types of specialized literacy skills are needed from others to complete the task, we may understand the consequences of filling out or not filling out the form, of making mistakes in the document, etc. But we nevertheless rely on the technological skills and knowledge of others to accomplish particular instances of a literacy practice.

Conversely, one may have the necessary technological knowledge without having useful functional knowledge. Such a pattern occurs frequently among individuals who have technological skills but limited experience with their application in society, including many of the adult immigrants in the Newton and Pleasantville communities. A simple example of this may be seen in adults who have the technological skill to sign their name but do not understand the consequences of doing so on particular kinds of documents (e.g., contracts of various types). Schoolchildren, too, often develop considerable technological skill before acquiring the functional knowledge of how literacy practices are used in daily life (e.g. how written contracts are used, how to search for written information).

A third type of knowledge, shared by all who are socially engaged in a literacy practice, is what may be termed its *social meaning*. This term, used regularly by sociolinguists to describe the social motivations underlying individuals' choices and preferences for using particular languages in multilingual contexts (e.g., Fishman, 1972), has recently been applied to literacy (Reder & Green, 1983; Reder, Green, & Sweeney, 1983; Stubbs, 1980; and Szwed, 1981). Previous use of the term in regard to literacy has not been systematic. Reder and Green (1983) noted its significance for the development of literacy in Seal Bay in describing the different sets of values and norms which villagers in Seal Bay associated with use of different written languages (Slavonic, Alutiiq, English). A major finding in Seal Bay was that long after domain-specific distinctions in using the three scripts have been leveled by the ascendancy of literacy in English, sharp distinctions of values persisted regarding the use of writing in those same domains (Reder & Green, 1983). To systematize these "social meanings" within the theoretical framework being elaborated here, it may be helpful to review how the concept of social meaning has been used in sociolinguistic theory to account for interactants' choices and alternations among multiple languages, speech registers, verbal styles, and so forth.

In a bilingual setting, for example, individuals may use or even alternate between one or another language, depending on the situation, topic, and other contextual features. Their preferences and choices can be related to motivations to display greater or lesser affinities for different social groups in which use of one or the other language is preferred. In communicative situations in which participants have multiple statuses as members of social groups in which different languages are normally used or clearly preferred, a language choice situation arises. The interactants' choice of language reflects their definition of the situation (as to which of their multiple statuses is most pertinent or appropriate). Shifts between languages used reflect changes in their definition of the situation (which, in terms of the terminology introduced above, represent distinct communicative events). The social meaning of using a particular language in the situation, then, is tied to the social implications of the participants' recognizing one set of their multiple statuses rather than another.

It is important to emphasize that in this formulation the social meaning of using a particular language (or dialect, style, etc.) is not a feature of the particular language (or dialect, style, etc.) but rather of the interlocutors' choice of that language (or dialect, style, etc.) in situations where other communicative options are available. In Pleasantville the social meaning of a group of bilingual men speaking English in a given situation derives from their having the option of speaking Spanish to each other. If all interactants did not speak Spanish, then speaking English in that situation would not convey the same social meaning that would be carried if that choice were made among bilingual speakers.

The extension of this construct of social meaning to variations in use of written languages or writing systems seems to be consistent with developing a sociolinguistic approach to the study of literacy, an enterprise that Stubbs (1980), Spolsky (1981), and Fishman (1982), among others, are attempting. The application of the concept of social meaning to literacy practices, however, must keep several important points clearly in view. To begin with, it was noted above that social meaning is carried by a participant group's use of a variant in a choice situation; that is, one in which alternative means of conducting the communication were available. The situation-specific use of particular written languages in biliterate populations, for example, can be coherently analyzed in terms of social meanings, as was demonstrated for the use of multiple literacies in Seal Bay (Reder & Green, 1983) and the use of written Navajo and English on an Indian reservation in the Southwest (Spolsky, 1981). Such analyses can also be applied to the choices that Hmong youth and young adults frequently make between using written Hmong or written English (when both scripts are known to the participants) for various tasks: personal correspondence, recording traditional stories, composing lyrics for new songs, or exchanging love letters. In Pleasantville, systems of social meanings also govern the choice of written languages for particular purposes and in particular contexts among those who are biliterate. The decision to use Spanish for writing comments on the blackboard during a senior citizens' committee meeting, when all members of the committee were biliterate although not all were Hispanic, could be interpreted as making a social statement about the origin and character of the organization, for example. A Mexican mother who leaves notes in English for her literate children is making a choice based on social meanings associated with Spanish and English uses. This much seems straightforward and analogous to the construct of social meaning that sociolinguists have applied to the situation-specific choice of oral languages in multilingual settings.

But the situations in which social meanings govern the use of writing in everyday life are not limited to ones in which biliterates choose among alternative writing systems. In Seal Bay, systems of social meanings develop for the use of writing *per se* in particular social events, situations and domains of activity, even when there is no choice to be made among multiple written languages. Social meanings may be carried by participants' decision to use writing as one (of several alternative) means of communication. The Seal Bay study showed how the use of writing is embedded within a broad, abstract structure of social meanings villagers associate with a wide range of social situations and domains of activity in everyday life. Some of the social meanings associated with literacy in Seal Bay carry positive connotations for villagers, whereas others have negative implications. The interaction between these positive and negative social meanings varies across domains of activity, social situations and communicative events. In contexts where positive meanings prevail, literacy is more likely to be used and its specialized skills and knowledge are more likely to be socialized; in contexts where negative meanings prevail, literacy is less likely to be used and socialized.

The social meanings of literacy are carried in part by the impact of the use of written materials on the activity of the participant group. These social meanings, in a given practice, are closely related to the effect that use of the written materials has on participants' perception and definition of the situation. In Seal Bay, for example, the use of literacy in situations in which "outsiders" have historically exercised control over village affairs remains problematic. Negative social meanings are still present in many situations in which "outsiders" are part of the participant group (as happens in face-to-face contact between villagers and representatives of government agencies). In such contexts, use of written materials is rarely selected by villagers in the participant group; when selected by an outsider it tends to have a deadening effect on interactions among villagers present. When a representative of a local educational agency visited the village to convene a town meeting to discuss educational needs in the village and the village school program, a lively wide-open public discussion took place in which villagers freely and articulately expressed their views. As part of a literacy practice well established among "outsiders" in the setting of such meetings, the agency representative wrote down the suggestions of the participants on large sheets of paper mounted on a free-standing easel. This had no noticeable impact on the meeting. When the agent then tried to use another well-established "outside" literacy practice, however, it had a very different result. The agent requested that the assembled villagers break up into small groups, each of which was to appoint a "secretary" who would facilitate and record their discussion of the ideas that previously had been suggested and written down. Although such a procedure is effective in large group meetings held in many other settings in the United States, its attempted utilization in the Seal Bay meeting was met with silence and inaction, a spontaneous rejection of what was perceived as an in appropriate intrusion of an "outside" literacy practice into intra-village relationships. Use of literacy within villagers' participant groups is not appropriate in some contexts, particularly ones in which outsiders attempt (often inadvertently, as in this instance) to impose the use of literacy in a way that challenges, rather than fits comfortably with, established social groupings and modes of interaction. Knowledge of the individuals involved in this meeting and their reading and writing capabilities made it clear that it was the conflicting social meaning rather than any lack of understanding of the task or necessary skills that brought the proceedings to a halt. It was the attempted use of *literacy* in the small groups that was problematic here, as it carried the negative social meanings associated with village-outside conflict. In many other situations the same villagers spontaneously use the literacy skills required for the agent's task to accomplish their own objectives.

In the collaborative accomplishment of a literacy practice a particular set of the participants' statuses is usually reflected in the choice to utilize written materials (where there are, in fact, alternatives available), just as there are when bilinguals choose to use one language rather than another. The social implications of various modes of engagement in the literacy event must also be considered. Not all participants are equally engaged in a collaborative literacy task. Some may be technologically engaged; others may be only functionally engaged; others may be only socially engaged. In some contexts, who is technologically engaged may have considerable significance precisely because it carries so much social meaning. The example of the boss dictating a letter to the secretary reminds us of this. In another context the same individual who is "boss" in one context may choose in a group brainstorming meeting attended by his or her peers to be the recorder of their suggestions. The social meaning of being technologically engaged in literacy thus is tied to particular social contexts. In some situations, being functionally engaged may in itself carry considerable social meaning, as when one individual tries to gain (or avoid) functional knowledge of others' reading and writing activities. In still other settings an individual may be stigmatized by lack of technological engagement.

D. Spontaneous Acquisition of Literacy

Another significant finding in the field studies is that adults often acquire literacy spontaneously in response to new perceived needs for literacy in their lives. Although the term "spontaneous acquisition" may sound redundant, it is used here for emphasis, since one so often thinks of adult literacy development as the unique outcome of formal education or training. In all three of the communities studied here, many adults develop literacy skills—that is, become skilled participants in various literacy practices—without participating in formal literacy education classes. The evidence for this is change over time in individuals' skills in relation to their participation in training. Although formal adult literacy training is positively associated with literacy development, many adults show gains without participating at all, and overall participation in literacy training is a much weaker predictor of learning than other factors such as age or literacy in the native language.

From one perspective, of course, it should come as no great surprise that literacy develops spontaneously among adults in response to perceived needs for new literacy capabilities. After all, there is a great deal of evidence that many children learn to read and write without formal instruction. Durkin's (1966) study of early-reading children, as well as the contemporary studies of Teale and Sulzby (this volume), point to the often secondary role which schooling plays in children's literacy development. There has been surprisingly little research on this topic among adults, but there are several well known cases of adult literacy development taking place outside of institutional contexts for training. Scribner and Cole (1981) describe informal acquisition of literacy by the Vai in their native language. Walker (1981) describes a nearly universal literacy among the Cherokee in the nineteenth century that developed without benefit of formal schooling. Bennett and Berry (this volume) describe an incipient native language literacy among the Cree in northern Canada, who are exhibiting what is being termed here as spontaneous literacy development. Still another example can be seen among the numerous Hmong adolescents and young adults who have learned to read and write in their native language in recent years without going to school, in response to new needs for keeping in touch with friends and family separated by the aftermath of the war in Southeast Asia.

E. Distinct Socialization Processes for Literacy

In each site, distinct social distributions were observed for the three types of knowledge individuals have about literacy practices—the technological, functional and social meaning. The differential distributions of these types of knowledge appear to be the result of distinct socialization processes. A strong case can be made that participation in collaborative literacy practices is generally the vehicle for socialization of literacy practices. This includes, of course, not only participation in the literacy practices constituting academic training, but also the myriad other collaborative literacy practices encountered in everyday life. The mode of individuals' engagement in collaborative literacy practices has a strong influence on the type of knowledge socialized through their participation. Social engagement, as defined above, transmits knowledge of the social meanings of using writing in the particular practice; functional engagement is linked to the diffusion of functional knowledge about the literacy practice; and technological engagement is linked to the socialization of technological skills and knowledge.

Of course, the nature of individuals' participation in many collaborative literacy practices often entails two or three of these modes of engagement, so that multiple types of knowledge are socialized through participation in the collaborative practice. The fact that the socialization processes may frequently be active simultaneously should not obscure the fact that they are distinct processes. Many examples were seen in the three sites of individuals acquiring functional knowledge of literacy practices before (or without ever) developing related technological skills and knowledge. Young children learning about story books, that they have pages to be turned, beginnings and endings, pictures and "stories," and may be useful tools for soliciting parental attention, are but a few pieces of the complex functional knowledge children acquire in advance of the technological skills and knowledge required to read the story. The young children in Seal Bay who accompany their parents to the post office to get the mail flown in daily from the outside world, and help them sort through the mail, talk about it, and even prepare letters to be sent outside from the post office, often acquired functional knowledge of letter-writing practices long before they mastered the technological components of those practices. This knowledge was displayed in the games the children played in which they were "writing letters" and "going to the post office." The make-believe letters went into make-believe envelopes on which were squiggled rudimentary address and return address information.

Adults in the Newton and Pleasantville communities also displayed vast stores of functional knowledge about literacy practices that many were familiar with, but relatively few had the technological skills to perform directly. Such knowledge was required to utilize the technological skills of others collaboratively for accomplishing tasks such as letter-writing, filling out forms, reading the newspaper, etc. In the longitudinal study in the Hmong site, quantitative data strongly suggest that many individuals acquire such functional knowledge independently of technological knowledge. Although identifying the actual "location" where such knowledge is acquired is as difficult to do in these data as it is to pin down anywhere, there is the strong likelihood that it stems from collaborative participation in literacy practices.

In this regard it is interesting to contrast (a) literacy practices and domains in which individuals' technological knowledge develops in advance of their functional knowledge with (b) practices and domains in which functional knowledge develops in advance of technological capabilities. One of the hallmarks of literacy training in Western schools has been its decontextualized pedagogy—or insistence on teaching technological literacy skills in one context before students have an opportunity to apply them in other contexts. By contrast, in the fishing domain in Seal Bay, individuals acquire functional knowledge (and often the accompanying social meanings) about the literacy practices increasingly utilized in their work: the forms and licenses and agreements used to regulate their commercial fishing activities and relationships with the canneries; the repair manuals for small engines and other equipment; and the instructions for operating and interpreting increasingly sophisticated high-technology instrumentation used on commercial fishing boats. Fishermen report that they typically learn about these written materials and the associated literacy practices before (or in many cases without ever) learning to use the materials themselves. Typically they observe other village fishermen utilizing the materials first. Many never learn to read the manuals or fill out the forms themselves, but all learn who can help them with the written materials when necessary, and all are functional in terms of being able to collaborate with others' literacy skills to achieve their own ends.

IV. CONCLUSIONS

The foregoing conclusions have some strong implications for literacy education, particularly in contexts in which populations experience increasing environmental demands for literacy. The widespread phenomena of spontaneous acquisition of literacy in many contexts—that is, development without formal training—should encourage program planners to take a broader view of literacy development and the role that instructional programs can play. While there remains little doubt that formal literacy training has a major impact on adults' literacy development, encouraging adults to learn through participating in literacy practices other than formal education may also stimulate development. Based on results of the three field studies described here, the nature of what is learned through participation in particular literacy practices may depend on the individual's mode of engagement or participation in the practice. Designed carefully, it may be possible for literacy programs to facilitate broader participation in a wide variety of literacy practices— participation which may in turn stimulate adult literacy development. Examples of the effectiveness of programs having this design have been reported in welfare-to-work programs (Reder & Wikelund, 1994; Wikelund, 1993) and in the workplace (Reder, 1994b).

To develop such an approach, planners and policy-makers must pay attention to both the macro- and micro-level characteristics of the situations and practices involved in the efforts. At the micro-level, questions arise about how the fine structure of the socialization process is linked to details of how participants collectively accomplish literacy activities. Properties of the social interactions among participants may differentially facilitate acquisition of different types of knowledge. Participant structures that provide opportunities for individuals to be functionally engaged in the practice before they have the requisite technological knowledge and skills may be very successful means of socializing functional knowledge and knowledge of social meanings essential to accomplishment of the practice, stimulating individuals' acquisition of literacy even as they may be just learning basic technological skills.

The idea that features of the microstructure of collaboration in literacy practices are related to the extent and nature of the ensuing literacy socialization and development raises an important issue. Different modes of engagement have been hypothesized on the basis of preliminary results from the three sites studied to produce different types of knowledge about literacy practices. What is it, then, about the social arrangements under lying such collaboration that promotes development and acquisition (cf. Greenfield & Lave, 1982)? Careful, developmentally oriented microstudies of collaborative literacy activities are needed to address these issues directly. But a promising direction would be to extend the concept of "scaffolding" (Wood, Bruner, & Ross, 1976) from adult-child interactions to collaboration among adults. Scaffolding is a means of providing a learner or novice at some activity with the necessary support for constructing and performing the task jointly with the expert or teacher. Parents tend to do this with their children as a matter of course. So, it can be guessed, do effective teachers do this with their students. When effective scaffolding is present, there is a balance between observation on the part of the novice (learner) while the expert (teacher) performs the task and attempts of the novice to perform the task under guidance of the expert. This balance is mutually negotiated by participants/collaborators jointly accomplishing a literacy task.

But analysis of the microstructure of collaboration cannot alone account for some of the major findings of the study, and cannot alone be an adequate basis for program development. The overwhelming impact of the system of social meanings on the use and development of literacy in all three sites is a crucial phenomenon. The domain specific interaction of positive and negative social meanings in Seal Bay produced a complex map of literacy use and non-use, and of literacy development and non-development in daily life. Negative social meanings associated with formal adult education generally kept villagers from supporting the program. In sharp contrast, the generally positive social meanings Hmong attach to use of writing in most situations seem to facilitate their still incipient but rapidly increasing levels of literacy use. The Pleasantville site presents a case of conflicting social meanings about literacy acquisition and use. The divergent backgrounds and social standings of the various subgroups within the ranks of Hispanics in Pleasantville create highly complex patterns of participation in or avoidance of domain-specific literacy practices. These socially motivated behaviors directly affect individual group members' opportunities for acquiring new literacy skills and using them. On balance, although positive attitudes are voiced about learning to read and write, especially in English, the social contexts of literacy use in this community tend to inhibit the development of adult literacy in either language.

Many cultural factors must thus be considered in understanding adult literacy development in particular contexts. In these three studies we have seen that a complex array of cultural and historical variables shapes the ways adults work together with written materials. These patterns of collaboration in turn structure the ways in which the technological, functional, and social meaning dimensions of literacy practices are socialized in that particular cultural niche. Sometimes these socially organized patterns of collaboration—often with attendant inequities of technological and functional knowledge—remain stable over long periods of time. Educational programs, both schools and adult literacy programs, can be planned to intervene and stimulate new means for literacy to develop. Program planners must carefully consider, however, the value systems present in the situation and the social meanings assigned to particular literacy practices. Instruction must be carefully designed so that positive rather than negative social meanings become attached to the acquisition and use of literacy.

ACKNOWLEDGEMENTS

The author is pleased to acknowledge the support of this research by contracts from the U.S. Department of Education and the U.S. Department of Health and Human Services (Office of Refugee Resettlement). No official endorsement of the contents of this paper by these agencies should be inferred.

These comparative studies were conducted collaboratively with my long time colleague and friend, Karen Reed (Green) Wikelund. This paper is dedicated to Karen's memory and to her progressive vision of literacy and community. Mike Sweeney and Mary Cohn also assisted with the fieldwork in the Hmong community. The ideas presented here have benefited enormously over the years from stimulating discussions with Karen Reed Wikelund, Sylvia Scribner. Shirley Brice Heath, William Griffith and Nancy Faires Conklin.

REFERENCES

Durkin, D. (1966). *Children who read early*. New York: Teachers College Press.
Ferguson, C. (1979). Patterns of literacy in multilingual situations. *Georgetown University Roundtable on Languages and Linguistics* (pp. 582-590). Washington, DC: Georgetown University Press.
Fingeret, A. (1983). Social network: A new perspective on independence and illiterate adults. *Adult Education Quarterly, 33*(3), 133-146.
Fishman, J. A. (1982). Domains and the relationship between micro- and macrosociolinguistics. In J. J. Gumperz & D. Hymes (Eds.), *Directions in sociolinguistics*. New York: Holt, Rinehart & Winston.
Goody, J. (1968). Introduction. In J. Goody (Ed.), *Literacy in traditional societies*. Cambridge: Cambridge University Press.
Goody, J., & Watt, I. (1963). The consequences of literacy. *Comparative Studies in Society and History, 5,* 27-68.
Green, K. R., & Reder, S. (1986). Factors in individual acquisition of English: A longitudinal study of Hmong adults. In G. L. Hendricks (Ed.), *The Hmong in transition*. Minneapolis and New York: Jointly published by Center for Urban and Regional Affairs, University of Minnesota, and Center for Immigration Studies, New York.
Greenfield, P. G., & Lave, J. (1982). Cognitive aspects of informal education. In D. A. Wagner & H. W. Stevenson (Eds.), *Cultural perspectives in child development*. San Francisco: Freeman.
Heath, S. B. (1983). *Ways with words: Language, life, and work in communities and classrooms*. Cambridge: Cambridge University Press.
Reder, S. (1992). Getting the message across: Cultural factors in the intergenerational transfer of cognitive skills. In T. Sticht, B. McDonald, & M. Beeler (Eds.), *The intergenerational transfer of cognitive skills*. Newark, DE: International Reading Association.
Reder, S. (1994a). Practice engagement theory: A sociocultural approach to literacy across languages and cultures. In R. M. Weber, B. Ferdman, & A. Ramirez (Eds.), *Literacy across languages and cultures*. Albany: State University of New York Press.
Reder, S. (1994b). *Learning to earn: Direct incentives for work-based literacy learning*. Philadelphia: National Center on Adult Literacy, University of Pennsylvania.
Reder, S., & Green, K. R. (1983). Contrasting patterns of literacy in an Alaska fishing village. *International Journal of the Sociology of Language, 42,* 9-39.

Reder, S. M., & Green, K. R. (1985). *Giving literacy away: An alternative strategy for increasing adult literacy development*. Portland, OR: Northwest Regional Educational Laboratory.

Reder, S., Green, K. R., & Sweeney, M. (1983). *Acquisition and use of literacy in the Hmong community of Newton* (Annual Report of the Functional Literacy Project). Portland, OR: Northwest Regional Educational Laboratory.

Reder, S., & Wikelund, K. R. (1993). Literacy development and cultural identity: An Alaskan example. In B. Street (Ed.), *Cross-cultural approaches to literacy*. Cambridge: Cambridge University Press.

Reder, S., & Wikelund, K. R. (1994). *Steps to success: Literacy development in a welfare-to-work program*. Washington, DC: National Institute for Literacy.

Scribner, S., & Cole, M. (1981). *The psychology of literacy*. Cambridge, MA: Harvard University Press.

Shuman, A. (1983). Collaborative literacy in an urban multiethnic neighborhood. *International Journal of the Sociology of Language, 42*, 69-81.

Spolsky, B. (1981). Bilingualism and biliteracy. *The Canadian Modern Language Review, 37*, 475-485.

Stubbs, M. (1980). *The sociolinguistics of reading and writing*. London: Routledge & Kegan Paul.

Sulzby, E. (1983). *Beginning readers' developing knowledge about written language* (Project No. G-80-0176). Washington, DC: National Institute of Education.

Szwed, J. (1981). The ethnography of literacy. In M. F. Whiteman (Ed.), *Variation in writing: Functional and linguistic-cultural differences*. Hillsdale, NJ: Erlbaum.

Teale, W. H. (1984). Reading to young children: Its significance for literacy development. In H. Coleman, A. Ober, & F. Smith (Eds.), *Awakening to literacy*. Exeter, NH: Heinemann.

Vygotsky, L. S. (1978). The prehistory of written speech. In L. S. Vygotsky, *Mind in society: The development of higher psychological processes* (M. Cole, V. John-Steiner, S. Scribner, & E. Souberman, Eds.). Cambridge, MA: Harvard University Press.

Walker, W. (1981). Native American writing systems. In C. A. Ferguson & S. B. Heath (Eds.), *Language in the U.S.A.* Cambridge: Cambridge University Press.

Wood, B., Bruner, J. S., & Ross, G. (1976). The role of tutoring in problem solving. *Journal of Child Psychology and Psychiatry, 17*, 89-100.

VI

LITERACY, TECHNOLOGY AND ECONOMIC DEVELOPMENT

19

Introduction

Manzoor Ahmed
UNICEF, Japan

THE ISSUE OF DEFINITION

Far too often in discussion of literacy, a particular definition of literacy is taken for granted without stating it explicitly. Frequently, more than one definition or concept are used interchangeably in the same discourse. Commonly used concepts of literacy, some of which are overlapping include:

1. literacy equated to a self-sufficient educational program for adults,
2. literacy as a proxy for the level of general education acquired from schooling,
3. literacy as a self-contained non-formal basic education program conducted outside the formal school,
4. literacy as an essential element of primary education for children, and
5. literacy as an element of basic education or skill training programs for youth and adults.

Various Articles in this Section Illustrate the Point

Arthur Gillette revisits the experience and lessons of the Experimental World Literacy Programme (1967-1974) which attempted to promote functional literacy linked to productive skills for adults. Belying its ambitious aim of paving the way for "the eventual execution of a world campaign in this field," EWLP defined and emphasized functionality of literacy in terms of acquiring occupational skills. Roger Iredale equates literacy with education programs for adults and deplores a "disparity of investment" in the post-Jomtien era that favors formal primary education and works against adult literacy programs.

Stephen Anzalone presents literacy and numeracy as essential learning skills that children in primary schools have to acquire and describes experiments in Lesotho and Belize to facilitate language and mathematics drills with the use of a low-cost, hand-held electronic tool.

Bruce Fuller et al., revisiting the debate about justifying educational programs by their contribution to economic growth, attempts to identify the effects of literacy per se; but then seems to use the terms literacy and general basic eduction interchangeably or lump them together, for example, in the reference to growth of output and employment in Mexico "from rising levels of literacy and schooling" (p. 327). In one section under the heading "literacy versus schooling effects," the authors make three important points: that historically literacy preceded formal schooling; that literacy prior to the spread of public schools was more unevenly distributed favoring the wealthier and the elite groups, and that literacy today is largely a product of schooling and the level of achievement in learning rather than number of years of schooling is more strongly related to later economic benefits. Despite the heading of the section, understandably not much is said about literacy *versus* schooling effects in practical terms.

The question of definition is more than semantics. Clarity of concepts regarding the scope of literacy programs and how literacy fits into the effort to meet the basic learning needs of all is essential for developing effective programs for this purpose and for maximizing the social and economic benefits of education.

LITERACY AND BASIC EDUCATION

The 1990 Jomtien World Conference on Education for All—sponsored by the organizations most active in international education cooperation and preceded by an extensive preparatory process involving countries, professional bodies and nongovernmental organizations—represented a summation of experience of past decades and lessons for future priorities and strategies. The Declaration and Framework for Action of Jomtien articulated an "expanded vision" of basic education that meets the learning needs of children, youth, and adults. The literacy effort is viewed as a component of the total basic education effort encompassing early child-hood education, primary education, literacy for youth and adults, expanded opportunities to skills training, and increased access to knowl-edge and information for the whole population. Set in this larger context of basic education and learning needs of people, literacy as the means of "learning to learn" cannot but be an essential element of basic education programs, be it primary schools for children, "second chance" basic edu-cation for youth, or programs for basic education for adults. By the same token, it is futile to agonize over the separate social and economic effects of literacy versus those of schooling and non-formal basic education.

When the developmental benefits of literacy is discussed, litera-cy is generally meant to represent the learning outcome of schooling or non-formal basic education programs which are also often labeled as lit-eracy programs. Attempts to isolate the effects of literacy per se, distinct from those of schooling or non-formal programs amounts to academic hair-splitting and has little practical value. When Fuller et al. assert that their study of Mexico looked at the economic effects of "the spread of lit-eracy, *not* formal schooling," they really mean that they are looking at literacy as an outcome of schooling as well as other educational efforts that historically preceded the spread of schooling and continued later along with the school system.

The emphasis on the broad vision of basic education and meet-ing the learning needs of people expounded by Jomtien also call for a perspective of demography, state of development of education in the country including capacities and resources, and a time horizon for plan-ning and setting priorities in national "education for all" programs including achievement of the goal of eliminating illiteracy. From a pure-ly demographic perspective, in countries with half of the primary school age children failing to complete a full cycle of primary education, which is the case for countries with roughly half of the population of the devel-opment world, the most cost-effective literacy effort over a 10-year time horizon will be a program to retain most of the children in school to the end of the primary cycle.

Literacy and Economic Development

Whether literacy contributed to economic development of a nation and how much this contribution is—the principle concern of the human cap-ital theorists in the 1960s but which continues to surface repeatedly—are not particularly useful questions for two reasons. First, it is evident from what has been learned from experience and studies about education and economic development that the relationship between the two is an inter-active one rather than one of linear causation. The predictive model of investigation of physical sciences applied to the social phenomenon of how literacy interacts with other aspects of social change does not necessarily enhance knowledge and understanding. Expansion of education or launching of a literacy effort is not independent of other forces of social change. Secondly, societies fortunately do not take decisions on such questions as investment in basic education which impinge on their basic values and goals on the basis of rates of return. It is not a matter of debate that the value to society and from a longer term perspective, are about combinations of physical and human components rather than one or the other.

The pertinent questions are somewhat more complex: In my view, how does one promote a beneficial interaction in order to maximize the developmental benefits of educational programs? What content, methodology and organization would maximize the payoff in a particular socioeconomic context? The questions are clearly based on the premise of a general acceptance of the value of access to basic education opportunities for all citizens.

The burden of the effort to maximize the benefits of education, however, should not lie on the education sector alone. There have to be simultaneous changes in economic development policies and priorities so that the conditions are created for effective use of the human capital. These changes may occur through the working of the market forces or by deliberate policy choices of societies and governments, preferably through a combination, since the limitations of the "hidden hand" of the market can hardly be denied. As the authors of the Mexico case study put it, "The claims of true believers in literacy will be realised only under certain conditions".

CONCLUSIONS

The four chapters in this section individually would leave the reader uncertain about the policy implications and priorities in the future. Taken together, and read in the context of the recent developments including the Jomtien goals and strategies in basic education, they suggest at least three conclusions:

1. Literacy has multiple functionalities—ranging from a tool for access to knowledge and information to individuals; a means for religious, political, and cultural induction of groups of people; to a prerequisite for acquiring modern productive skills.

2. The multiple functionalities of literacy are realized, and the social and economic benefits are maximized, when literacy efforts are adapted to different contexts of the participants with their diverse characteristics and needs and are carried out as an essential element of meeting their different basic learning needs.

3. Pragmatically, where basic education is relatively undeveloped and the literacy level of the population is low, the optimal use of resources requires a focus on primary education for children and a targeted approach in literacy concentrating on basic education for adolescents and youth who have missed primary education; empirical evidence from experience on adult literacy programs also supports such a priority in societies with high illiteracy rates, rather than short-duration mass literacy campaigns.

20

Assisting Literacy with Technology in Lesotho and Belize

Stephen Anzalone
Education Development Center, Washington, DC

I. INTRODUCTION

Since the 1990 World Conference on Education for All in Jomtien, Thailand, the international community has recommitted itself to expanding opportunities for those persons whole educational needs are going unmet and to finding new ways to deliver education more effectively. Rich and poor countries alike find that young people leave school having achieved levels of literacy that leave them unprepared for the challenges they face in the expanding global information society.

While the new information technologies are not only a source of challenges for education, they are increasingly providing the means to deliver education more broadly and effectively—in programs both in and out of school. For many, the process of becoming literate is now tied to experiences with computers and related technology. Both for children and adults, computers serve as powerful motivators and tutors. In developed countries, the reach of computers into schools and programs of adult education has grown steadily since the advent of the personal computer. This has not been true in developing countries. There are numerous obstacles to introducing computers into education in developing countries, but the most important one is the cost. Especially for children in classrooms that still are without an adequate supply of textbooks, learning with computers in the classroom seems a distant dream—and the information superhighway something that will bypass their communities for a long time to come.

Interest in the potential of technology to improve education in developing countries prompted staff members at the Center for International Education at the University of Massachusetts to spend a year exploring the advisability of, and interest in, supplementing primary school instruction in developing countries by the use of one form of microprocessor technology—hand-held electronic learning aids. Informal testing and an exchange of views took place with educators from developing countries and with Texas Instruments, Inc., which manufactures some widely used electronic aids.

The dialogue resulted in a proposal to the U.S. Agency for International Development for a field experiment with electronic learning aids in schools in a developing country. The proposal called for developing and testing a prototype literacy aid that would combine the features of the Texas Instruments Speak & Read and Speak & Math (described later) in a local language, A grant from AID and a donation of equipment made possible an experiment with electronic learning aids in five primary schools in the Kingdom of Lesotho However, funds available at that time were not sufficient to permit the proposed adaptation of the learning aids to the local language. Sesotho; therefore, existing English language models of the Speak & Read and Speak & Math were used.

The experiment was conducted with the collaboration of the Lesotho Distance Teaching Centre and the National Curriculum Development Centre. It lasted for a period of 12 weeks between August and December 1983. Some 509 children participated in the test, either by using the aids or serving as control subjects. Pupils worked with aids in groups of four for 1 hour a day, two to five times per week during the appropriate classroom time for English or arithmetic.[1]

Purpose of the Experiment

The purpose of the Lesotho experiment was three-fold: to determine whether the use of existing models of electronic learning aids is feasible in primary schools in a developing country like Lesotho, to understand how the aids might fit into the structure and process of the classroom, and to discover whether pupils' mastery of English and arithmetic is strengthened by using the aids.

---

[1]A detailed discussion of the experiment and much of the data used in the present chapter is contained in Anzalone and McLaughlin (1984).

By exploring the usefulness of existing models of the Speak & Read and Speak & Math, it was hoped that the experiment might also suggest modifications required to make these aids more appropriate or effective in a developing country.

The Learning Aids

The Lesotho experiment made use of two "talking" electronic aids manufactured by Texas Instruments, Inc., the Speak & Read and Speak & Math. These devices provide drill and practice in English and arithmetic. The aids contain a three-chip system for synthesizing human speech. Consisting of a speech synthesizer, read-only memory, and controller, the system is based upon a voice-compression technique called linear predictive coding. The synthetic speech is linked to an eight-digit alphanumeric fluorescent display and keyboard. The aids weigh just over 1 pound and operate on four "C" cells. The aids cost about $30-40 in retail stores in the United States, although it is estimated that they can be produced at a cost for labor and materials of about $5.

The Speak & Read provides practice in phonics, sight vocabulary, and reading comprehension at levels of difficulty up to the U.S. third grade level. This aid gives practice with about 250 of the most basic English words. There are six different game routines and three levels of difficulty for some of the routines. The instruction provided by the device is expandable by insertion of one of eight available plug-in modules, each containing about 200 new words.

Speak & Math offers arithmetic drill through five different instructional routines at levels of difficulty ranging from first to sixth grade. The Speak & Math provides up to 100,000 different problems, generated randomly, at three levels of difficulty.

The Setting

Independent since 1966, the mountainous Kingdom of Lesotho lies entirely surrounded by the Republic of South Africa. With a population of just over one million people, Lesotho's economy is based upon agriculture and income received by Basotho miners working in South Africa.

In 1980, about 85% of the girls and 60% of the boys age 6-12 were enrolled in the country's more than 1000 primary schools. Classes tend to be large: the overall ratio of pupils to teachers was about 48:1 in 1981. The large size of classes the poor quality of school facilities, and the number of undertrained teachers working in the system are typical of conditions found in other developing countries.

Participating Schools and Children

Five schools took part in the experiment with electronic learning aids. Two of the schools were located in the capital, two were in rural areas, and one was in a small town. Practical considerations and the recommendations of the Ministry of Education weighed heavily in the selection of the sample.

The children using the arithmetic aid were in Standard 6 (11-13 years old). Those using the literacy aid were in Standards 3 and 4 (8-10 years old).

The Instructional Supplement

The objective of the experiment was to determine the effects of electronic learning aids when used as a supplement of regular school instruction. The supplement consisted of drill and practice with the aids in basic skills essential for proficiency in English (which pupils begin to learn early in school) or arithmetic. The aids were not intended to replace parts of the curriculum or the teacher.

Teachers were asked to use the aids, as circumstances permitted, for 1 hour per day during the appropriate time for English or arithmetic. Pupils were organized to use the aids in groups of four. Groups were expected to operate cooperatively with pupils helping one another and each member having opportunity to manipulate the aid.

A supplement of interactive drill with electronic learning aids such as was tried in Lesotho approaches the realm of practicability and affordability for primary schools in many developing countries. If the aids are rotated among grades and schools, if they are used in groups of four, and if they last for the normal 720 hours before needing replacement, this would result in a per pupil cost of U.S. $0.94 for a 60-hour supplement. The cost of batteries is additional and has not been estimated, since battery cost would be dependent on the feasibility of such possibilities as solar recharging of batteries, and it was not possible to test this possibility.

II. KEY ISSUES

The feasibility study conducted in Lesotho was believed to be the first of its kind. It was by necessity exploratory. Feasibility, for the purpose of the study, was taken to mean that the aids could be introduced into the classroom without undue resistance. cost, or time; that the keyboard,

visual display, voice, and instructional routines could be readily understood by the pupils; that the aids would not be easily broken or lost from
schools; that teachers and pupils would find them useful; and that the
learning benefits would appear to be positive. The study was divided
into three areas of investigation:

A. *Technical feasibility.* The variables that were measured were the
number of devices that broke during the course of the study,
the average length of time before batteries needed replacement, the number of devices that were lost from schools, and
the observed and reported difficulty of understanding the
speech, visual display, and other features of the learning aids.
B. *Human use effects.* This part of the study sought to understand
what happens in the classroom when electronic learning aids
are introduced. The study examined the reactions of pupils,
teachers, and administrators, and looked in some detail at the
actual behavior of pupils working with the aids through the
course of the experiment.
C. *Learning effects.* Although it was impossible to anticipate from
previous empirical work the range and magnitude of learning
effects that might accompany using electronic learning aids,
the study sought to examine the effects of the aids on two
measures of achievement. This is discussed later.

Looking at Learning Effects

The investigation into the learning effects associated with the use of electronic learning aids tried to answer two questions:

1. Does an electronic learning aid like the Speak & Read help to
improve a pupil's ability to recognize English words?
2. Does an electronic learning aid like the Speak & Math help
improve a pupil's ability to solve addition, subtraction, multiplication, and division problems?

Four classes used the Speak & Read: one for 12 weeks, one for 8 weeks,
and two for 4 weeks. These classes, and one class not using the aids,
were tested weekly on English word recognition. Two classes used the
Speak & Math: one for 12 weeks and one for 8 weeks. These classes and
a class that had the opportunity of using the language aids, but not the
arithmetic aid, were tested weekly on arithmetic.

True experimental designs require the random assignment of
subjects to control and treatment conditions, and the establishment of

control groups that are like treatment groups in every way except that they do not receive the treatment of interest. This was not possible in Lesotho, so the decision was made to use a "quasi-experimental" design to evaluate the hypothesis that the learning aids would positively affect the reading and arithmetic performance of the pupils who used them. The design that was chosen is a variant of a time series design (Campbell & Stanley, 1963).

Since subjects used the aids for varying lengths of time, and were tested at regular intervals during the course of the experiment, evidence for the positive impact of the learning aids would be present if test performance began to improve at the point where pupils began to use the aids. Given that performance did increase in accordance with the introduction of the learning aids, any explanation other than positive impact would be extremely implausible.

Measures of Learning Effects

Pupils using the Speak & Read and the control group were given a 20 minute test (50 items) each week on English word recognition. The test administrator said a word aloud and pupils marked an "x" on their answer sheets indicating "yes" or "no" whether the spoken word was the same as a written word on the answer sheet. Half of the words were words instructed by the Speak & Read (I), and half were non-instructed (NI).

The set of instructed words was compiled from a set of 100 words selected from the 112 words from the Dolch Basic Sight Vocabulary List that are contained in the Speak & Read. The non-instructed words were drawn from a list of 100 words of comparable difficulty not contained in the Speak & Read. These included 30 words from the Dolch Basic Sight Vocabulary List (preprimer, primer, and first grade levels) and 70 words from the Revised A and P Sight Word List (second, third, and fourth sets of 50 most frequently occurring words). The A and P list was used in addition to the Dolch list because the Speak & Read uses up most of the Dolch words at the preprimer to first grade levels.

The pupils using the Speak & Math and the control group took a 15 minute (32-item) test each week. The tests contained an identical mix of addition, subtraction, multiplication, and division problems and mixes of one-, two-, or three-digit number problems. Pupils solved problems on the backs of their answer sheets and entered responses on the fronts.

III. RESULTS AND DISCUSSION

The results of the experiment in Lesotho demonstrated the feasibility of using electronic aids to support school instruction in developing countries. Specific results in the three main areas of investigation included the following.

A. Technical Feasibility

The experiment showed that electronic learning aids can be introduced into primary schools in a developing country without great cost and preparation. The aids were used on average between 1 hour 20 minutes and 3 hours per week. Batteries lasted on average about 17 hours before needing replacement. Of the 62 learning aids allocated to schools, three needed to be replaced because of malfunctioning. None of the aids was lost or stolen during the experiment. Observation of classrooms found pupils to be adept in adjusting to the electronic voice and visual display. In the generally noisy atmosphere of the classroom, pupils would often put their ear right against the aid in order to hear it. In interviews with 23 children selected randomly, only two mentioned having difficulty with the pronunciation or the loudness of the electronic voice.

B. Human Use Effects

Interviews conducted with teachers, administrators, and pupils indicated a widespread belief that the aids were useful. Five out of six teachers interviewed praised the capacity of the aids to motivate pupils and engage them in learning tasks. Teachers indicated a desire to have more flexibility in the instructional routines that would permit a better fit with the school syllabus.

Pupil reaction to the aids was, not surprisingly, overwhelmingly positive. The enthusiasm expressed during interviews was confirmed by observation of classroom behavior. During the final 4 weeks of the experiment, this took the form of a structured exercise to determine the extent that pupils were actually engaged in the learning tasks provided by the aids, and how this might change as the novelty effect wore off.

A male and a female pupil were selected randomly in five of the experimental classes. Their behavior was sampled every minute for a 10-minute period that would begin after class activity was well under way. Their behavior at the beginning of each minute was observed and indicated on a list of different categories of behavior. For the purposes of the final analysis, the behaviors were collapsed into two categories: engaged (manipulating the aid or attending to another pupil's action with it) and not engaged (not paying attention to the aid, doing other tasks, or removing oneself from the lesson). The total number of engaged behaviors observed was 324 (81%). Some 76 (19%) not-engaged behaviors were observed. This would appear to be indicative of a high degree of pupil engagement in the instruction provided by the aids.

The time series designed of the experiment made it possible to compare behavior of groups that used the aids for different lengths of time. At the time that the structured observations began, two classes had been using the aids for 8 weeks, two for 4 weeks, and one had just begun. The behaviors of the five experimental groups are summarized in Table 20.1, which suggests some decline in pupil engagement with the learning aids when used over longer periods of time. However, the decline in engagement is not large and does not support suspicion of a large novelty effect that wears off quickly.

TABLE 20.1. Type of Observed Pupil Behavior by Length of Treatment.

Length of treatment	Behaviors		Total
	Engaged	Not-engaged	
8-12 weeks	117 (73%)	43 (27%)	160
4-8 weeks	138 (86%)	22 (14%)	160
0-4 weeks	69 (86%)	11 (14%)	80

C. Learning Effects

Pupils in the language classes (experimental and control) took eleven tests throughout the experiment. The tests measured pupils' ability to recognize English words, both words instructed by the Speak & Read and words not instructed (see Table 20.1). As a summary of test performance, weekly gains (in standard deviation units) have been averaged for users and non-users (at the time of the test) on instructed and non-instructed words. These gains are contained in Table 20.2, and shown graphically in Figure 20.1.

In Figure 20.1 curves approximating the trends in improvement of scores have been fitted to the data. The curve-smoothing is subjective. The graph suggests that use of the Speak & Read is associated with greater improvement in English word recognition. Specifically, the graph indicates: (a) greater differences between scores on instructed and non-instructed words for groups using the aids and the reverse for the control group: (b) greater improvement of scores on instructed words for groups using the aids than that of the control group; (c) greater improvement of scores on non instructed words for groups using the aids, suggesting transfer of learning.

TABLE 20.2. Weekly Improvement of Test Scores of Groups Using the Language Aids Compared to Groups not Using the Aids.

Test	Instructed	Non-instructed
Groups using aids		
2	0.27	0.24
3	0.53	0.68
4	0.33	0.48
5	0.93	0.32
6	0.13	0.48
7	0.70	0.03
8	0.49	0.87
9	1.44	1.16
10	1.56	0.83
11	1.58	1.31
Groups not using aids		
2	0.95	0.62
3	0.87	1.00
4	0.41	0.45
5	0.50	0.31
6	-0.21	0.93
7	0.39	-0.51
8	0.51	0.73
9	0.30	0.58
10	—	—
11	0.42	0.54

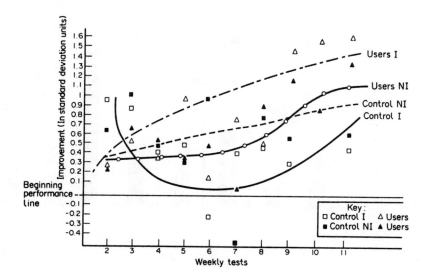

Figure 20.1. Weekly improvement of math scores of groups using the language aids compared to groups not using aids

Figure 20.2 compares the average gains made by each class before and after introduction of the learning aids. The two classes using the aids for 4 weeks showed more improvement after introduction of the aids. For reasons unknown, the class using the aids for 8 weeks averaged more improvement prior to introduction of the aids.

For the arithmetic classes, the weekly gains in test scores (expressed in standard deviation units) have been averaged for classes using aids and not using them (at the time of the test). This information is presented in Table 20.3 and depicted graphically in Figure 20.3. These suggest that pupils using the Speak & Math made greater improvement in arithmetic scores than pupils not using the devices. The difference, however, did not show up until after the eighth test. Figure 20.4 compares the average gains made by each class before and after introduction of the aids. The class using the aids for 8 weeks showed the biggest improvement following introduction of the aids, which further suggests the positive impact of the aids.

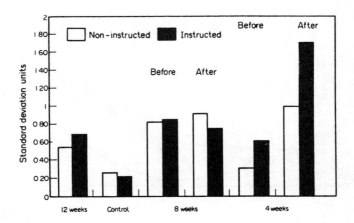

Figure 20.2. Average weekly improvement in language scores between and after introduction of aids

TABLE 20.3. Weekly Improvement of Math Scores of Groups Using the Arithmetic Aids Compared to Groups Not Using the Aids.

Test	Improvement
Groups using aids	
2	-0.29
3	0.43
4	0.67
5	0.05
6	-0.04
7	0.24
8	0.64
9	0.99
10	1.27
11	0.92
Groups not using aids	
2	-0.05
3	0.72
4	0.67
5	-0.06
6	-0.29
7	0.26
8	0.65
9	0.48
10	0.83
11	0.67

IV. CONCLUSIONS FROM LESOTHO

The data suggest that effects of using electronic learning aids on achievement in English word recognition and arithmetic were positive. Other analysis of the data found no significant differences in achievement between boys and girls, and showed that the aids had a greater impact on learning among the less able pupils.

There remains a suspicion, however, that the better test performance by pupils using the aids resulted from a large Hawthorne effect. Two things tend to discount this possibility. First, the control class for arithmetic had the opportunity of using the language aid. Consequently this class was exposed to an almost identical change of routine and heightened interest from outsiders as were the experimental classes. Second, the novelty of the aids seems likely to have been dampened by the lack of enthusiasm that often accompanied having to take "another test" each week.

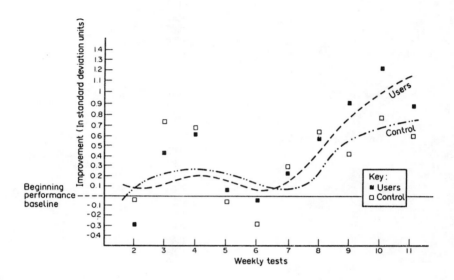

Figure 20.3. Weekly improvement of math scores of groups using the arithmetic aids compared to groups not using aids

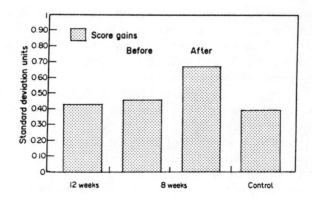

Figure 20.4. Average weekly improvement in arithmetic scores

Although the experiment in Lesotho points to the feasibility of using learning aids as an instructional supplement in a developing country, it would be premature to recommend electronic aids as a cost-effective addition to primary school instruction. The use of the aids must be studied over a longer period of time, and in other countries. There also needs to be a more careful examination of the range and magnitude of the learning effects likely to be fostered by the aids, and how they compare to other forms of instruction. Similarly, adaptability of the aids to different languages and more effective instructional routines must also be studied.

V. CONFIRMING EVIDENCE FROM BELIZE

There has been one known attempt to look at the use of electronic learning aids in another developing country. The A.I.D. Learning Technologies Project (1984-1991) undertook a collaborative program of activity with educators in the Central American nation of Belize in testing applications of educational technology that showed promise for improving educational quality in developing countries. During the course of this collaboration, it was decided to conduct a study of the use electronic learning aids as a means to improve student performance in mathematics.

The study compared, after one school year (1989-1990), student achievement in mathematics in classrooms receiving conventional instruction supplemented with drill and practice provided by the Speak & Math with students in control classrooms receiving only conventional instruction. The design consisted of a pre-post comparison of quasi-equivalent groups of students in standards 1, 2, and 3 (comparable to grades 3, 4, and 5 in the United States).

Eight schools took part in the study. They were selected on the basis of similarity in student performance on the 1988 Belize National Selection Examination (taken upon completion of primary school) and their proximity for monitoring visits from Belize City. These schools were then paired on closeness of score and whether it was located in an urban (Belize City) or rural area. Schools from each pair were then randomly divided into two groups of four schools, a group that would receive conventional mathematics instruction supplemented by drill and practice provided by learning aids and a group that would receive conventional instruction alone. The sample selected provided some 636 students for whom both pretest and posttest scores were available.

To keep costs to a minimum, teachers were asked to have students work in groups of three; students were directed to take turns operating the machine—an arrangement that had been successful in Lesotho.

The plan called for the two non-operators to use paper and pencils alongside the operator, seeing and hearing the feedback. Teachers were asked to review students' papers to identify any difficulties for additional remediation. Remediation was conducted according to each teacher's observations and judgment. Group formations varied according to what teachers thought was appropriate. Sometimes there were enough Speak and Math units available for two students to use one machine, and sometimes there was one machine for each student. All of the teachers reported that their students got equivalent amounts of machine time, even though some of them felt that slower students needed to spend more time with the learning aids.

Schools were visited on a bi-weekly basis. During these visits, students were observed using the learning aids, exercise books logs were checked, and assistance was provided to teachers. Batteries were supplied to the schools during these visits. The aids were used three to five times per week for periods of between twenty to thirty minutes.

Measures of Learning

Students were tested on skills in computation and numeration. The tests were developed by Friend Dialogues, Inc., a company with long experience in mathematics education in developing countries. The standard 1 test contained 25 items, and the tests for the other two standards contained 35 items. An evaluation of the pretest results suggested that it might not be suitable to use these tests as posttests at the end of the school year. It seemed that the tests might be too easy after a full year of school instruction. Posttests were developed by one of the Belizean investigators. The posttests were similar in content and style to the pretests. The posttest for standard 1 contained 35 items. The posttests for standards 2 and 3 contained 40 items.

Results: Pretests

The selection of schools was made on the basis of performance on the pretests. This was done by taking average scores across three grades. A breakdown of pretest scores by grade and treatment is shown in Table 20.4. For each standard, the difference in means between the learning aids group and the control group is small, except for standard 1 where there was a difference of nearly 10% in favor of the learning aids group. Analysis of variance showed that this difference was significant, $F(1,211) = 7.696$, $p < .006$. For the other two grades, the differences between treatments were not significant; for standard 2, $F(1,241) = .209$, $p < .648$ and for standard 3, $F(1,177) = .046$, $p < .831$.

TABLE 20.4. Means and Standard Deviations of Pretest Scores.

	Mean	Standard Deviation
Standard 1		
Learning Aids	71.14	17.15
Control	61.97	22.44
Standard 2		
Learning Aids	74.30	17.06
Control	75.47	16.47
Standard 3		
Learning Aids	60.92	12.80
Control	61.40	14.14

Source: Anzalone, Arunyakanon, Thompson, and Pelayo (1991)

Results: Posttests

The results of the posttests by grade and treatment are shown in Table 20.5. For all three grades, students using learning aids group outperformed control students.

To determine the significance of these differences, an analysis of covariance, using pretest scores as a covariate, was performed on posttest scores. The use of electronic learning aids proved to have a significant impact on mathematics achievement. Treatment had a significant main effect on posttest performance, $F(1,636) = 23.583, p < .0001$.

Not surprisingly, the Belize study showed that students' socioeconomic status also had a significant impact on achievement. Students who were ranked by teachers as bringing more advantages from home to school outperformed those bringer fewer advantages. This variable had a significant main effect on posttest performance, $F(4,636) = 6.316, p < .0001$.

The Belize study also looked at the effect of gender on mathematics achievement in the three grades studied. Gender did not have a significant main effect on posttest performance, $F(1,636) = .117, p < .733$.

Effect Sizes

The Belize study looked at the impact on achievement in terms of effect sizes. An effect size is the difference between the means of an experimental and control group divided by the standard deviation of the control group (Glass, 1977; Glass, McGaw, & Smith, 1981). Effect sizes permit comparison across tests, contexts, subjects, and other characteristics of studies (Walberg, 1984). The effect size for each grade was as follows:

TABLE 20.5. Means and Standard Deviations of Posttest Scores.

	Mean	Standard Deviation
Standard 1		
Learning Aids	68.53	29.82
Control	56.77	22.56
Standard 2		
Learning Aids	76.98	14.58
Control	70.09	14.38
Standard 3		
Learning Aids	73.26	17.74
Control	64.40	22.39

Source: Anzalone, Arunyakanon, Thompson, and Pelayo (1991)

standard 1, .52; standard 2, .48; standard 3, .40. The average effect size across the three grades was .47. This suggests a strong impact on achievement. An effect size of .45, for example, is "considered large and exceeds about 84% of those typically found in educational research" (Walberg, 1984, p. 23).

Effect sizes may be interpreted as an indication of where a student in the learning aids group would have performed had he or she not had the intervention and been in the control group. This can be expressed in terms of percentiles. In the Belize study, a student at the mean in the learning aids group would have scored at the 68th percentile had the student been in the control group.

VI. CONCLUSION

The studies in Lesotho and Belize suggest the potential of using high technology contained in small devices to assist in improving literacy and numeracy. In both cases, educational benefits were achieved with an off-the-shelf product and without making investment in new curriculum or materials development. The technology, when used in groups, is relatively affordable—an important consideration in most developing countries where the cost of more powerful personal computers prohibits their use in schools. Electronic learning aids are manufactured and sold as toys. Not surprisingly, students find them an enjoyable way to learn. Since the time that the studies in Lesotho and Belize were undertaken, there has appeared a growing diversity in the market of small devices to assist learning. Many are aimed at younger children and look to offer "pre-computer" experience. Whether the newer devices are educationally effective and culturally acceptable in developing countries has not been tested. Perhaps it is feasible to develop customized but affordable learning aids that would be better suited to the tasks of literacy acquisition in developing countries. But the potential of high technology in small devices to assist in improving literacy has remained largely overlooked.

REFERENCES

Anzalone, S. (1987). *Using instructional hardware for primary education in developing countries: A review of the literature* (Preliminary Draft). Project BRIDGES, Harvard University, Cambridge, MA.

Anzalone, S., Arunyakanon, P., Thompson, C., & Pelayo, V. (1991). *Boosting mathematics achievement with electronic learning aids: The experience of Belize.* Arlington, VA: Institute for International Research.

Anzalone, S., & McLaughlin, S. (1984). *Electronic aids in a developing country: Improving basic skills in Lesotho.* Amherst, MA: Center for International Education.

Campbell, D. T., & Stanley, J. C. (1963). Experimental and quasi-experimental designs for research on teaching. In N. L. Gage (Ed.), *Handbook of research on teaching.* Chicago: Rand McNally.

Glass, G. V. (1977). Integrating findings: The meta-analysis of research. *Review of Research in Education, 5,* 351-379.

Glass, G. V., McGaw, B., & Smith, M. L. (1981). *Meta-analysis in social research.* Beverly Hills, CA: Sage.

Walberg, H. J. (1984). Improving the productivity of America's schools. *Educational Leadership, 41,* 19-30.

21

Literacy and the Perils of Economics

Roger Iredale
University of Manchester

Despite everything that has been said about the importance of adult literacy, and particularly its advantages for women, their health, their productivity, and the well-being of their families, literacy development in the years since 1990 has been neglected in favor of a major concentration on the improvement of formal education systems, especially at the primary level. There are several reasons for this, and they arise mainly from the influence of donor agencies, especially the World Bank, on governments and in particular ministries dealing with activities in the social sectors. During the present period of financial stringency in many countries, particularly in Africa, donor methodologies, policies, and finances have a significant and powerful influence on national policies; in the scramble to support basic education in the past five years donors' views about priority areas for investment appear to have had a major impact on the thinking of ministers both individually and collectively.

Literacy was identified at the World Conference on Education for All in 1990 as a major element in the thrust towards providing education for all. The first phase of article 1 (meeting basic learning needs) emphasizes that "every person—*child, youth and adult*—shall be able to benefit from educational opportunities" (p. 1). Article 5 focuses specifically on youth and adults with a affirmation that "literacy programmes are indispensable because literacy is a necessary skill in itself and the

341

foundation of other life skills" (p. 5). Hence, literacy for adults was clearly established as one of the major goals of the 1990s.

While much of the Framework for Action appended to the World Declaration focuses on formal education systems, or generalizes about the broader area of basic education, within which literacy and adult education are subsumed, the documents published with the final report contain many explicit references to the need to develop adult literacy programs. The third volume of Roundtable Themes published after the Conference reflects that there are 950 million illiterate adults in the world today, the vast majority in developing countries and two thirds women (UNESCO, 1992).

The first volume of the Roundtable Themes focuses on literacy issues and emphasizes that "any global strategy for universal literacy and basic education that relies on the primary school alone, in the absence of complementary measures, is likely to be wasteful and inefficient" (p. 21). The importance of the message that literacy development among adults is of the highest importance is emphasized by the prefatory words of the Director General of UNESCO, Federico Mayor:

> The real question that is being asked is whether we can reach the goal of full literacy by the year 2000. My answer is "yes," if we all . . . decide to do so: if we exercise the political will to change priorities from military expenditure to expenditures on education, nutrition and health. (p. 21)

The ensuing paragraph suggests that there are three major conditions required for the successful implementation of a campaign: strong political commitment, centralized formulation of policy coupled with decentralized organization, and the assigning of political priority to literacy within a broad national strategy (UNESCO, 1992). The point is subsequently made that literacy opportunities will rapidly fade if they are not supported by constant practice and opportunities to develop skills acquired even further, a point already well established as relating to the concept of wastage, both of effort and of economic resources (Wagner, 1987; see also this volume).

Condition 2, however, presents considerable complexities since a form of decentralized organization and implementation by local authorities does not readily lend itself to combination with centralized policy formulation. Literacy acquisition by adults does not generally develop from a simple top-down approach in which the center radiates messages out to the periphery without the involvement of local organizations; on the other hand, the involvement of local organizations in a centralized strategy requires some considerable vision, sensitivity, and organization. If the actual provision of adult literacy is essentially a matter for local initiatives, the adaptation of materials and teaching methods to local conditions, and the follow-up process generated by the community through its own actions, then the role of the centralized authority has to be very carefully defined, thought through, and modulated. The fact is that the provision of adult literacy is, from a central organizer's point of view, both messy and labor-intensive.

If this is true of governments, it is all the more significant for aid donors, whose manpower resources are generally highly constrained, and who normally have to operate at distances of several thousand miles from the site of the ongoing work. Donors need to be able to define what they perceive as "projects" (which are not necessarily discrete projects from the recipient's point of view, since they frequently form only part of a much larger national effort involving several other donors as well) via a formula that will be readily acceptable to the donor's policy and executive groups as a recognizable way of structuring, monitoring, and measuring the operation once it has been approved.

There is therefore a fundamental barrier to donor involvement in literacy programs: There is rarely a unified "system" that will allow an education adviser to fly in from 10,000 miles away, readily enter into dialogue with a single minister or permanent secretary, undertake a simple analysis of managerial/physical needs across a complete country or region, negotiate sums of money and systems for spending the money, and fly back to base seven to ten days later. This is where the provision of literacy to adults is fundamentally different from that of developing a schools systems, where clear hierarchies of administration and management can be identified and their shortcomings addressed.

There is a further complication. Literacy is frequently not the prerogative of ministries of education for it is frequently not they who are responsible for the provision of literacy programs: with variations of nomenclature, it is variously the Ministry of Social Welfare, the Ministry for Women's Affairs, or the Ministry of Rural Development that has responsibility for this area of human resource development. This is not surprising, given the multidisciplinary nature of the activity, as well as the perceived value of its outcomes across a wise range of economic and social areas, including the alleviation of poverty (UNESCO, 1992).

Literacy programs will, therefore, only work if there are vary disparate organizations operating at the grass roots level. This presents any would-be donor with an immediate organizational problem: It means that they have to approach nongovernmental organizations, negotiate with them, ensure government agreement to their doing so, and see that throughout all this process there is some degree of accountability that is compatible with the aid donor's disbursement system. It means going to rural areas, preferably some of the most deprived and remote, often involving arduous journeys off tarmac roads, or even across lakes in coracles, or down rivers in longboats, and it means the defining of methods for listening to, assessing, and meeting locally expressed needs. This is not only physically arduous and frequently perceived as uncomfortable even though it may be highly informative, but it does not lie within the scope of a visitor appearing from a Club 10,000-mile flight in a Business Class cabin and seeking to return to 30,000 feet in the same relative luxury no more than a week later.

Hence the problems for aid donors are:

1. Organizational; it is simply not ready to identify and appraise projects that involve diversity and long distances and poor communications;
2. Financial; accountability is far more difficult when decision-making and action are decentralized and accounting systems are not therefore standard;
3. Political; many governments are not enthusiastic about allowing foreign donors access to grass roots movements frequently of a political character, where some of the literacy message may well not be supportive of the ethos of the regime at the center;
4. Methodological; it will inevitably require considerable effort, knowledge and research accurately to appraise local needs in a way that is authentic and meets communities' expectations.

But there is another major constraint: the economic argument. The reasons frequently given for investment in adult literacy programs are strong: It is well known that literacy has an impact on health, and any number of studies provide evidence of a clear correlation (Bown, 1990).[1] A recent study performed by the University of Liverpool indicates that in Nicaragua during the 1980s child morality was 18% higher among the offspring of illiterate women than among those who had undergone adult education, while the risk of low arm circumference for age was 59% higher and the risk of low weight for age was 85% higher (Sandiford, Cassel, Montenegro, & Sanchez, 1989). The significance of this particular study is that the women within the cohort all came from a

---

[1] A research project in South Africa discovered a correlation between women's literacy and immunization. Only just over 60% of women living in the surrounding neighborhoods brought their children to the center for immunization and the researchers identified four factors that made women less likely to bring their children, one of these was poor literacy.

similar cultural and social background but some had recently attained literacy through adult classes in refugee camps, while others had not. The authors claim that the study indicates that child health is not related to sociocultural factors with which literacy coincides, such as a strong family tradition of maintaining child care or the passing on of wealth. While there is much anecdotal evidence of the impact of literacy, questions still need to be answered relating to the effect of women's literacy on infant mortality rates, child nutrition, fertility patterns, life expectancy of mothers, education of the succeeding generation, women's involvement in production, their capacity to mobilize credit and savings, their capacity to establish and operate various types of economic organizations, their readiness to engage as individuals in business enterprise, and their spending patterns (Bown, 1990).

But it is not the fact that many of these questions remain unanswered that itself impedes the development of literacy, since many similar questions remain unanswered about formal education and such fundamental matters as its effects of morality, social behavior, and involvement in the labor market. A much greater obstacle to the development of literacy is its unquantifiability in logistical and economic terms. It is significant, for example, that one of the most important papers presented to the World Conference on Education for All, and hence one of the more significant books to arise from it, examines the costs and benefits of expansions within school systems, particularly at primary level (Colclough, 1993). Colclough is able to provide a detailed economic analysis of the cost of increasing primary schooling to the universal level by the year 2000, together with strategies (with detailed financial figures attached to them) for quantifiable savings and expenditures arising from various defined strategies. As has been indicated above, this is feasible where one is dealing with school systems, but it cannot be coped with where one is looking at an amorphous, grass-roots movement involving the unpredictable activities of adults attending classes on a voluntary basis for unspecifiable lengths of time and to unquantifiable levels of attainment.

The complexity of dealing with the economics of literacy is borne out by the relative paucity of reference to it as a component of "Education for All" in subsequent follow-up to the Conference. There has not been the same kind of follow-up to Jomtien in the literacy field as there has in relation to formal education as exemplified by the recently published work by Little, Hoppers, and Gardner (1994) which focuses on primary education since 1990 and suggests further research and implementation agendas. It is true that at the Education for All Summit which took place in New Delhi in December 1993 involving the education ministers of nine high population countries, there are ample references to adult education and literacy, but a more careful scrutiny of the text indicates that the emphasis is almost invariably on formal education rather than on nonformal or adult programs:

> With a majority of children still without benefit of a complete primary education in five of the nine countries, and programs of quality and equity evidence in all countries, primary education must, therefore, remain the top priority. (UNESCO, 1994, p. 57)

Despite references to the importance of literacy much of the rest of the Conference report concentrates on the quality of primary education, with the emphasis on the child and on teacher training and school curricula.

But most important of all, economic cost-benefit analysis is an additional important constraint. Kenneth King (1991) has already pointed out that one of the difficulties for donors is the absence of "literacy bricks and mortar" (p. 148). As King points out "literacy investment must be one of the only fields where at the end of a successful campaign or sustained period of external investment there is literally nothing physical to show for it." The Roundtable I paper from the World Conference on Education for All pauses for a moment to look at the assumed relationship between functional literacy as an investment in human capital and its effect on productivity and indirectly on human welfare. The paper has to conclude that the evidence for assuming such a linkage (however obvious it may be to do so) is meager, despite attempts to establish the relationship (UNESCO, 1991).

This is underlined by a more sinister barrier in the form of educational cost-benefit analysis, the process by which economists measure the return on investment to various types and levels of educational intervention. While educational cost-benefit analysis is a widely accepted technique used to assess the profitability of investment in education and while educational rate-of-return studies have been carried out in most developed countries and many developing countries there are nevertheless serious doubts about a number of aspects of the methodology. Hough's (1993) monograph dealing with cost-benefit analysis commissioned by the Overseas Development Administration suggests that the technique should be used only as a means of comparing alternative uses of resources in order to identify the most cost-effective.

However, this is not the way in which cost-benefit analysis has been used widely by the World Bank and other development agencies where economic analysis is a major factor in decision making. Many studies quantify the social and private rates of return to education at various level, and form one of the cornerstones of World Bank thinking about primary education in recent years. The Bank's policy paper *Primary Education*, (1990) opens with a justification for investment at this level of education based on increased productivity. It cites a study demonstrating that four years of education increases small-farm productivity by 7% across thirteen developing countries. Similar thinking from the Bank is exposed in its very recent book on higher education, where it attempts to quantify the social returns on higher education in economic cost-benefit terms, concluding that investment at lower levels within education systems are likely to produce a higher return (World Bank, 1994).[2]

Possibly the absence of data on the economic rate of return to literacy underlies the absence of any significant discussion of adult education and literacy itself in the draft World Bank paper on education currently circulating among donors and others prior to its proposed publication during the first part of 1995. The paper, provisionally entitled *Priorities and Strategies for Education* purports to present a case for Bank investment in education throughout developing countries as well as those in Eastern and Central Europe, but focuses entirely on formal education (World Bank, 1994). The paper contains ample reference to cost-benefit analysis and to private and social returns to education in various contexts and at various levels, however, its exclusive focus on school, college, and university education echoes the emphasis noted earlier at the Education for All Summit.

Similarly, the draft education and training policy of the European Community currently circulating among donors in draft form makes virtually no reference whatsoever to adult literacy programs, concentrating almost exclusively on formal education. By "basic" the authors clearly read "primary" and the other references to the support of women's education focus on primary schooling and teacher training.[3] The slimness of the document (24 pages) precludes any conscious elimination of adult education from European education policy on the basis of economic rate of return, however, the fact that the focus is apparently entirely on formal systems clearly derives from the approaches set by the Bank and others.

Whatever the demerits or merits of educational cost-benefit analysis and whatever its general conclusions where the methodology is accepted, we face the difficulty that there is probably no method for quantifying the effects of adult literacy education in economic terms. For the reasons stated earlier—the voluntary nature of attendance, the

---

[2]The book suggests that although higher education is important, many donors will not wish to invest in that level because of its relatively low rates of return; see pages 3 and 25.

[3]On coordination between the Community and the Member States on education and training schemes in developing countries (Commission of the European Communities, COM, 1994, 399 final, Brussels, 26.09.1994). Communication from the Commission to the Council and the European Parliament, mimeograph, page 15.

unquantifiable learning outputs, the difficulty of collecting standardized data—it is not possible for donors to justify adult literacy in the kind of hard number terms that appeal to their economists. Yet it is a requirement of project proposals in most donor agencies that there should be an economic cost benefit figure attached to any particular project, coupled with an indication of its likely rate of return.

That this aspect of literacy has been perceived by writers as not particularly significant is easily deduced from a random survey of works on literacy, where the emphasis is on such important matters as definition, policy, the needs of learners, the context, culture, language, technology, work, the community, curriculum, teaching methods, sustainability, integration, but rarely if ever on economic benefit (Jennings, 1990; Mace, 1992; Street, 1985). Lind and Johnson (1989) list the various research agendas for literacy and sponsorship, but make no reference whatsoever to the economics of adult literacy training. The nearest we get is Manzoor Ahmed's (1987; see also this volume) dismissal of the question whether literacy has contributed to economic development: Societies, he said "fortunately do not take decisions on such questions as investment in basic education which impinge on their basic values and goals on the basis of rates of return" (p. 274).

Ahmed was without doubt right to believe that an excessive concern with the rates of return to literacy would no influence governments in their decisions whether or not to mount literacy campaigns. Literacy activities are par excellence either political or philanthropic in their genesis and require no economic justification to persuade ministers of their importance. However, Ahmed had reckoned without the growing concentration over the past seven years amounting almost to obsession on the part of donors with needing to demonstrate economic return.

Such an approach is typified by the World Development Report of 1993 which concentrated on health issues, and where knowledge of the cost effectiveness of a health intervention "can be extremely useful for both public and private decisions." The report, not surprisingly since it emanates from a bank, reads like that of an accountant dealing with a commodity: Governments, we are told, can supply information about the outcomes and costs of different health interventions to consumers, providers, and insurers, "and this knowledge can increase the value per health dollar spent in the private sector" (p. 59). It is not difficult to imagine how similar questions can be raised about the relative payoff between investment in formal primary education and in adult literacy.

Exactly such questions were raised at the Tunis Literacy Forum organized by the Universities of Pennsylvania, Tunis, Botswana, and Ibadan in February 1994. The debates which the Conference prompted are unrecorded, however, they were conducted with considerable fervor. The underlying question was, "Should we continue to invest in primary education until such time as every potential pupil is enrolled, or is there a cut-off point where diminishing returns do not justify the sums involved?" The related debate, equally fiercely proposed and answered, revolved around the question, "Do you not secure a better return on your investment by committing it to primary education rather than to the largely unquantifiable adult literacy program—unquantifiable, that is, in its economic return on investment?"

The fact that donors can and do raise such issues argues strongly for research into rates of return on literacy programs for adults. The methodology would not be simple and certainly nowhere as straightforward as for formal education, where the uniformity and size of the sample provides data that are readily analyzable. Research into the costs and benefits of literacy would be far more controversial and less susceptible to generalization. Yet, if it does not take place, there is a real danger that literacy work will remain very much the poor relation of formal education for the rest of the decade.

However nugatory educationalists such as Manzoor Ahmed may still feel economic cost-benefit research is, a failure at least to try to get to grips with it may leave literacy as very much a low priority area for investment on the part of most donors. It certainly reduces the likelihood that large development banks of a multilateral character will find it easy to support, though bilateral donors are more likely to do so through their individual provision of assistance to nongovernmental organizations. The Overseas Development Administration, for example, makes little of its literacy work, even though it provides very substantial sums of money every year for nongovernmental organizations under its Joint Funding Scheme. The ActionAid study of ODA support for women's literacy work referred to earlier produced in 1990 a total of 44 supported projects from countries as far apart as Bangladesh and Belize, Cambodia and Zimbabwe (Bown, 1990).

Other donor agencies similarly support NGOs through other forms of scheme where the emphasis is always on supporting the initiative taken by a particular NGO, rather than providing direction to the NGO to go in a certain direction. This ensures that this particular kind of support is focused at grass-roots level and that projects are initiated by communities in consultation with local NGOs who in turn are supported by external NGO agencies. This is entirely the right way to approach adult literacy training, even where it is not supported by the kind of national campaign promoted in the UNESCO documents referred to earlier. However, it is, by its very nature, likely to involve only relatively modest funding compared with the gigantic sums of money poured into primary and other levels of formal education. Indeed, donors who want to invest a lot of money and effort may well find that there is a problem over absorptive capacity.

It is difficult to see how to get over this disparity of investment. In one sense, much more can be achieved by adult literacy classes working from the grass-roots level per pound or dollar spent than can be achieved in the bricks-and-mortar situation of the primary school with salaried staff and a large and expensive administrative infrastructure to support it. However, we should not be lulled by this comforting thought, since the total sums of money invested in primary education on the one hand, and adult literacy on the other, are so disproportionate. Moreover, there is the in-built resistance of ministries of education to the encouragement of grass-roots development which run counter to official concepts of centralized control and management. Personal experience suggests that even the most enlightened of educators can prove resistant to the idea that adult literacy can be organized from the bottom upwards; even they need to look over their shoulders at political masters for who educational ideologies spell danger.

Donors and governments alike must therefore continue to be persuaded and lobbied to support the emphasis on nongovernmental organizations in the World Declaration on Education for All. They should be exhorted to provide funds for further research into the impact of literacy on people, employment, population trends, family stability, and the environment. They should be encouraged to promulgate the results of those researches through all available channels. They should be encouraged to provide small sums of money for imaginative schemes aimed at following up literacy through appropriate reading materials written and produced by community groups themselves (dangerous as they may appear to some of them!) Most important, they should be reminded that the needs of the most vulnerable cannot be assessed from air conditioned vehicles on tarmacadamized roads twenty miles from capitals.

REFERENCES

Ahmed, A. (1987). Introduction. In D.A. Wagner (Ed.), *The future of literacy in a changing world* (Vol. 1, p. 274). New York: Pergamon Press.

Bown, L. (1990). *Preparing the future—Women, literacy and development.* London: ActionAid.

Colclough, C. (1993). *Educating all the children.* Oxford: Oxford University Press.

Commission of the European Communities. (1994, September 26). *On coordination between the community and the member states on education and training schemes in developing countries.* (Mimeograph, 399 final). Brussels: COM 94.

Hough, J.R. (1993). *Educational cost-benefit analysis.* London: Overseas Development Administration.

Jennings, J. (1990). *Adult literacy: Master or servant?* Dhaka: Dhaka University Press.

King, K. (1991). *Aid and education in the developing world.* London: Longman.

Lind, A., & Johnston, A. (1989). *Adult literacy in the third world.* Stockholm: Swedish International Development Authority.

Little, A., Hoppers, W., & Gardner, R. (1994). *Beyond Jomtien: Implementing primary education for all.* London: Macmillan.

Mace, J. (1992). *Talking about literacy.* London: Routledge.

Sandiford, P., Cassell, J., Montenegro, M-M., & Sanchez, G. (1989). *The impact of female literacy by adult education on child health and survival* (Mimeograph). Liverpool: Liverpool School of Tropical Medicine.

Street, B.V. (1984). *Literacy in theory and in practice.* Cambridge: Cambridge University Press.

UNESCO. (1992). *Education for all: Purpose and context* (Roundtable Themes #1). Paris: Author.

UNESCO. (1992a). *Education for all: The requirements* (Roundtable Themes #3). Paris: Author.

UNESCO. (1994). *Education for all summit: Final report.* Paris: Author.

Wagner, D.A. (1987). Literacy futures. In D.A. Wagner (Ed.), *The future of literacy in a changing world* (Vol. 1, pp. 9-10). New York: Pergamon Press.

World Bank. (1990). *Primary education.* Washington, DC: Author.

World Bank. (1993). *World development report.* Oxford: Author.

World Bank. (1994a). *Higher education: The lessons of experience.* Washington, DC: Author.

World Bank. (1994b). *Priorities and strategies for education* (Mimeograph). Washington, DC: Author.

22

The Experimental World Literacy Program: A Unique International Effort Revisited*

Arthur Gillette

INTRODUCTION

Other chapters of this book look at a number of national efforts, past and recent, to come to grips with adult illiteracy. Illiteracy has not, however, been a solely national concern; nor has literacy work been an exclusively national enterprise. Since the end of World War Two, for example, many international nongovernmental organizations have been active in this area, as have a number of bilateral government-to-government programs of aid and cooperation.

At the multilateral level, the United Nations Educational, Scientific and Cultural Organization (UNESCO) was entrusted, from its creation 50 years ago, with both a standard-setting responsibility and a technical-cooperation function concerning adult education generally and adult literacy more specifically.

*Please note that this chapter is drawn in part and updated from a previously published chapter in R.F. Arnove & H.J. Graff (1987). (Eds.), *National literacy campaigns*. New York: Plenum.

A high point in UNESCO's literacy efforts came in the period from 1967 to 1974 with the organization of the Experimental World Literacy Program (EWLP). EWLP was an unprecedented, and remains in educational history an unequalled, multilateral literacy venture in terms of international resources mobilized, political and technical interest aroused, and controversy unleashed. These unique dimensions, coupled with the unusually large body of relatively reliable and comparable data generated by EWLP and analyzed in its final report, *The Experimental World Literacy Program: A Critical Assessment*, (UNESCO, 1976; see also UNESCO, 1979) suggest that it may be worthwhile to revisit the Program, with the purpose of attempting to derive some still-valid lessons for national and international planners and practitioners.

This return trip cannot be relaxed tourism, however, because there is still disagreement over the value, results, and even intentions of EWLP. Also, to do justice to its objects, this chapter's itinerary, while proceeding as dispassionately as possible, must not take evasive detours around any of the landmark (or stumbling block) issues that continue to raise controversy even today.

To situate the climate of discussion about EWLP in proper perspective, the chapter will, by turns, outline factually what EWLP actually was, discuss the Program's strategy, attempt to derive some practical lessons from EWLP's major variable, and examine EWLP's results in terms of new literates' profiles; it will end with a word about the current situation and international cooperation's role in the field of literacy.

THE NATURE OF EWLP

The program had many parents: decolonization, with its attendant demand for basic education, growing acceptance by governments of out-of-school education, the persistent perception of education as a universal human right, and U Thant's call at the beginning of the first U.N. Development Decade for a development that was social as well as economic. The *primus inter patres* was a 1961 U.N. General Assembly that asked UNESCO for a report on world illiteracy and recommendations for action. According to Kenneth Levine (1982), UNESCO reacted "with a massively ambitious plan for a worldwide frontal assault on illiteracy" (p. 252). Even revised, the proposal was to teach literacy to 330 million people, at an approximate total cost of two billion dollars spread over a decade (Blaug, cited in Levine, 1982).

Although the 1963 General Assembly offered general support to this plan, it was dropped. One reason was cost. It was at one and the same time too expensive (a two hundred million dollar-a-year sustained outlay for 10 years was perhaps not an entirely realistic expectation) and too cheap (a unit cost per new literate of 6.06 dollars certainly seems unrealistically low). An additional reason for the abandonment of the mass design was probably the then-ascendant influence of educational-qua-investment economists, for who literacy work should be focused selectively on the actual or potential producers of a given society.

Whatever the reasons, the mass approach wad discarded, or at least postponed, and replaced, at the 1964 session of UNESCO's General Conference, by "a five-year experimental world literacy program designed to pave the way for the *eventual* execution of a world campaign in this field" (cited in UNESCO, 1976, p. 9; emphasis added). How would a limited program "pave the way" for a broader campaign? By providing, in the words of the U.N. Secretary General when he presented the new UNESCO proposal to the General Assembly, "valuable information on the relationship of literacy with social and economic development" (Thant, cited in UNESCO, 1976, pp. 9-10), that is, through experimental and research activity as well as actual literacy work.

To prepare implementation of the 1964 decision of UNESCO's General Conference (to launch an EWLP as yet without upper-case letters), Unesco convened a World Congress of Ministers of Education on the Eradication of Illiteracy at Tehran, in 1965. This gathering gave political support and technical content to the Experimental World Literacy Program, which began to get under way the next year.

THE EWLP STRATEGY

Widely touted as something of a breakthrough at very least a way of paving the way for a possible future world campaign when there was not the will to launch such a campaign immediately, the EWLP's strategy was never clearly, completely, and definitively spelled out before or during the Program. It evolved as EWLP when along. In retrospect, however, it seems possible to identify five chief components of the strategy: functionality, intensity, selectivity, innovativeness, and experimentation.

Generally opposed to "literacy for its own sake," *functionality* was defined as follows by the 1965 Tehran Congress:

> Rather than an end in itself, literacy should be regarded as a way of preparing man for a social, civic and economic role . . . reading and writing should lead not only to elementary general knowledge but to training for work, increased productivity, a greater participation in civil life and a better understanding of the surrounding world and should . . . open the way to basic human culture. (Thant, cited in UNESCO, 1976, p. 10)

Who would quarrel with the above definition? What major literacy program in process or recently terminated at the time of Tehran advocated literacy for its own sake? At a period when education was increasingly viewed as an important contributing factor to multifaceted development, *dys*functional literacy appeared to be something of a straw man concept.

A real issue did emerge, however, in 1966 and 1967, when the Tehran guidelines of 1965 were forged into operational definitions in the various countries' project documents. On the one hand, as will be seen later, the Program did innovate, insofar as it integrated unusually large quantities of functional material into the literacy curricula, which in turn had repercussions on the kinds of teaching staff required and the methods they used.

On the other hand, however, and in contrast with the broad, balanced, and multipurpose social, economic, civic, and cultural functionality advocated at Tehran, the central (albeit far from only) criterion adopted by the Program was rather narrowly work-oriented functionality. In all participating countries, literacy was closely linked with industrial, agricultural, and craft training, although secondary activity did take place in other areas (e.g., homemaking and family planning for women).

This conceptual narrowing or reduction of functional literacy to a primarily production-related role appears to have been largely the result of economic-oriented thinking then current at EWLP's major funding agency. According to a recent memoir of one of the Program's artisans, "the UNDP had made its participation in EWLP conditional on the orientation of literacy to vocational training (de Clerck, 1984).

Looking back, it now seems possible to clarify some of the confusion that has surrounded discussion of functional literacy. The real debate is not between literacy for its own sake and functional literacy, but between different kinds of functional literacy. Seen in this light, the 1980 Nicaraguan Literacy Crusade was, for example, just as functional as EWLP, the difference being that the first had largely political functionality while the second was vocationally functional.

A second element in the EWLP strategy was *intensity*. Much used during the Program, the term seems to have had several meanings. In one interpretation, literacy became intensive when something (usually vocational content) was added to the three Rs. In another, intensity implied that the overall time required to achieve literacy would be telescoped, presumably with more hours of learning per week making it possible to reduce the number of weeks needed. Focusing of resources—more inputs per learner to achieve fuller and/or shorter learning—was a possible related interpretation of intensity.

In sum, it appears that intensity took on a life of its own as a term or slogan (rather than a well-defined concept), meaning different things to different people in different contexts. If such ambiguity did not actually harm the EWLP strategy, it cannot be said to have contributed to its clarity—or solidity.

Selectivity was, in contrast, a sturdy cornerstone of the Program's strategy. According to it, teaching was on the whole focused on groups most likely to turn literacy and allied vocational training into increased production. Thus, EWLP displayed "more than occasional preference for the most favored of the impoverished—a kind of 'élite'—seen as needing only a small educational push to move over the threshold of modernity" (cited in UNESCO, 1976, p. 162). Who were these "élites of the impoverished"? Farmers with access to arable and irrigable land in areas where sharecropping or peonage was the rule, and workers with salaries, no matter how small, in cities where unemployment was widespread.

Such selectivity was perhaps the only realistic approach in certain of the countries participating in EWLP. It did, however, raise the problem of equity, particularly in countries that were anxious, and perhaps able, to move more quickly toward mass literacy action (Guinea, Madagascar, Sudan and possibly Tanzania).

An issue at stake here is the degree of rigidity and uniformity that is necessary and possible in an international literacy strategy. Selective, vocationally functional literacy could have been offered as one possible approach, appropriate for some countries, less so in others. Unfortunately, EWLP thinking seemed to harden into something of a dogma, which assumed that selective, vocationally functional literacy was the best (if not the only) approach. Since EWLP, Unesco has fortunately returned to a much more flexible and diversified policy.

As stated at the beginning of this chapter, EWLP was an unprecedented international effort in the literacy field. As such, the Program was, by nature as well as intent, a breeding ground for educational innovation. *Innovativeness* was, in fact, a major, if largely unstated, element of the EWLP strategy. In country after country, teams of international and national staff worked out new curricula, materials, and methods, developed improved training packages, and generally gave fresh impulse to literacy work and adult education. In Mali and Tanzania, the Program is recalled nostalgically by specialists who took part as something of a halcyon period of innovation.

Yet, EWLP was not exempt from an overemphasis on the technical aspects of its work. Innovation is a necessary, but not sufficient, condition for successful literacy. When the Program was being formulated, a developmentalist (or, more crudely, technocratic) approach to economic growth and social change prevailed in international circles. Thus, literacy work then being carried out was assumed to fail primarily because of inadequate know-how. The problem was thought to be mainly technical in nature, and it was only logical that is solution should also be sought primarily through technical innovation (i.e., the work-oriented functional approach).

It was perhaps also logical (but nonetheless curious) that the EWLP strategists virtually ignored the recently completed Cuban literacy Campaign, which was anything but innovative in technical terms (the actual teaching was very close to directive school pedagogy), which indeed violated several basic EWLP precepts (it was massive rather than selective, it was politically rather than vocationally functional, it used a single curriculum and manual rather than a diversified/adapted approach, and it was definitive rather than experimental)—and which was nevertheless a resounding success. The Cuban effort demonstrated forcefully that pedagogically *uninnovative* literacy action could succeed. It perhaps prompted the EWLP's final report to suggest that "a crucial lesson of EWLP seems . . . to be the need to avoid viewing or designing literacy as an overwhelmingly technical solution to problems that are only partly technical" (cited in UNESCO, 1976, p. 122).

A final major element of EWLP's strategy was, as its title indicates, its *experimental character*. What, in global terms, the experiment was supposed to be and do was never made entirely clear, however. The nature and purpose of the experiment seemed to evolve over time and vary as a function of the expectations of different entities involved in the Program.

At first, it was apparently intended to test the hypothesis of a positive correlation between literacy and (particularly economic) development, by determining, with experimental groups of learners and control groups of nonlearners, if and how the acquisition of work-oriented literacy skills went hand in hand with increased productivity, improved consumption patterns, and other manifestations of better socioeconomic well-being. Then, the emphasis shifted from testing—with the possibility for inconclusive or negative results—to demonstrating the hypothesis—with no option for failure. Finally, it seemed that the correlation was assumed to be an already-proven thesis.

Within EWLP, moreover, there were at least two schools of thought on experimentation. For the first, "windtunnel" school, the Program was a laboratory in which technical improvements in various aspects of literacy work would be made through controlled scientific experimentation before massive expansion would take place. For the second, "runway" school, EWLP was a process of incremental pragmatic enrichment, leading naturally to expanded action. It viewed EWLP "as a plane full of passengers rather than a prototype flown by a test pilot" (cited in UNESCO, 1976, p. 132).

On the face of it, *conclusions* for strategists emerging from EWLP seem contradictory.

Where the Program did have clear and solid components of strategy—its mainly vocational functionality and its selectivity—they were not well-suited to the policies of all participating countries, and were looked on as something of an imposition by certain of them, accepted mainly in hope of obtaining international resources for literacy that would not otherwise have been available.

On the other hand, EWLP strategy components that were ill-defined, changing, or otherwise elusive—intensity, innovativeness, and experimentation—contributed to confusion and gave rise on occasion to irritation and even conflict, none of which helped the Program, its implementers, or the illiterates it was meant to serve. So it appears that one is damned if one has a clear, solid strategy, and damned if one doesn't.

In the event, however, the double-bind concerned not the fact of having a strategy, but the nature of the components of EWLP's strategy. When clear and solid, they were too limiting; and those that were neither clear nor solid did not have the virtue of being intentionally flexible and adaptable. Major criteria for a successful international literacy strategy would seem, then, to include a mix of clarity, solidity, flexibility, and adaptability.

MAJOR VARIABLES AND SOME PRACTICAL LESSONS

The previous section concerns the EWLP's architecture, and may be chiefly of interest to international planners, we now look at the Program's nuts and bolts—hopefully of equal concern for national and international specialists. Who staffed the Program? What curricula were used? what methods? What institutional arrangements were adopted? On what premises did classes take place? What languages were used for instruction? What postliteracy follow-up was provided? Answers to these questions will, it is hoped, yield some practical pointers.

Regarding *staff*, and turning first to the top-level policy makers, continuity was a problem in several EWLP countries. The first three years of one project were severely disrupted by no less than seven changes of the Minister of Education. Some polity makers were reticent because then viewed the Program "as designed to disseminate a pre-packaged, self-contained innovation with which national innovators were not expected to tamper" (cited in UNESCO, 1976, p. 132).

At the middle level, EWLP found the usual complement of bureaucrats for whom the Program was a wearisome imposition, and field work as exile. Because of its unique nature, however, it also does seem to have sparked enthusiasm in an exceptional number of cadres. In addition, it showed that the link with functional subject matter and the intention to innovate in terms of materials require the mobilization of a wide variety of professionals whose skills are not normally allied with literacy work: extension officers, factory foremen, journalists, graphic artists, and so forth.

The Program did not (and did not set out to) solve the old argument of professional versus volunteer/amateur literacy instructors. In India, more instructors were, in fact, village schoolteachers who worked at literacy part time. At the other extreme was Mali, which used no teachers but called on skilled workers and students. Most participating countries fell in an intermediate position. They used teachers (with special training, as in Tanzania) while also calling on skilled workers, students, literate farmers, and the like (in Algeria, one-third of project instructors had not completed primary school). Training was provided to these nonprofessionals, who in some cases taught vocational subjects as well as (or instead of) three-R lessons. The impression emerged that technicians who taught literacy got better results than schoolteachers who also gave vocational instruction.

In most EWLP countries, a task profile of the ideal literacy instructor appeared that overlaps with, but extends well beyond, the skills profile and attitude pattern of many primary-school teachers. The ideal literacy instructor should be capable of "teaching the three Rs, classroom vocational teaching, practical training via demonstrations, animation and understanding of—and sensitivity to—adults of the least favored socio-economic strata" (cited in UNESCO, 1976, p. 134).

Many approaches to training were used in the different national projects. There was, at the end, consensus that long preservice training with no systematic follow-up was not as effective as short initial training followed by regular refresher sessions. The latter method had three advantages: it provided repeated reinforcement; it enabled trainees to use their personal classroom experience as raw material in the follow-up sessions; and it provided instructors—often working in isolated villages—a chance to get together, socialize, and build an *espirit de corps*.

"Integration" was the guiding principle according to which vocational subject matter was added to basic three R teaching in EWLP *curricula*. At one extreme was Sudan, where heavy stress was put on vocational subjects, and relatively less importance accorded to literacy. At the other were Mali and Algeria, where the three Rs occupied 80% of class time. In between were eight other countries where the vocational-to-three-R ratio was 1:2.

The vocational subjects were supposed to be designed on the basis of an analysis of problems actually encountered by workers and farmers during their projective activity. Statistically significant research results suggested that when this happened, literacy programs were "more effective" (cited in UNESCO, 1976, p. 159) But who identified the problems to be covered in curricula? Problem-detection surveys were run in all countries, but did not always include the illiterate producers among respondents. In some cases, only supervisory personnel were polled; in two countries, the economic development authorities alone set vocational curriculum objectives; in another, expatriate experts were left to make curricula decisions on their own.

When workers were surveyed, it happened that the problems they identified did not lend themselves to solution through education (e.g., low wages), but required social change. This led EWLP evaluators to postulate that literacy "brings about a change for the better *on condition* that it is associated with a process of genuine innovation (of a political, social, or technical nature) in which the participants themselves are involved" (cited in UNESCO, 1976, p. 160; emphasis added). Similarly, it was concluded that vocational subject matter should not be linked too narrowly, rigidly, or mechanically to performance of learners' jobs.

There is perhaps there a kernel of more general wisdom about education and social change. Human beings resist being reduced to machines. It is their humanity, not perversity, that makes the planner's equation

Input (education) + *Process* (individual and/or group)
$$= Output \text{ (economic development)}$$

often unpredictably dysfunctional. On a recent visit to rural Tanzania, I stopped at a number of village libraries. From carefully kept loan registers, librarians, borrowers, and a look at the shelves, it was clear that books on farming, clean water supply, latrine digging and the like are not best-sellers. Rather, newly literate villagers seem to favor love stories and stories more generally, politics, religion, and a biography of the Brazilian footballer Pelé. EWLP's empirical evidence suggests, then, that a general climate of socioeconomic change that personally concerns the lives of illiterates can help motivate them to learn, but also that, once they have learned, they may prefer to read about football rather than food production. Is that somehow futile, wrong? Is not the delivery of choice real empowerment?

In terms of *teaching methods*, EWLP experience seems to have confirmed the validity of three tenets of andragogy that, if not particularly new (much less revolutionary), are not yet put into practice where school-based pedagogy is still used with adult learners. The first is an inductive approach to knowledge acquisition. Group discussions were the starting point of each class meeting in several EWLP countries, for example.

Naturally, discussion that seems superficially nondirective can be subtly structured by instructors or "natural leaders" present in the group. Nonetheless, several projects explicitly recognized adults' ideas and insights as valid starting points for learning. Albert Meister, critical of many other aspects of EWLP projects he observed, concluded that "overall, the teacher's view of the adult pupil has been enriched by the realization that the illiterate adult knows and understands many things; their approach has therefore become more andragogic" (Meister, 1973, p. 137).

Experiential learning was a second widespread method used in EWLP. Workshops, fields, demonstration plots, and the like were recognized as legitimate locales for learning. In at least one case, Tanzania, profits from the sale of produce from literacy-demonstration plots helped offset the cost of the classes, although this was not their central purpose, which remained pedagogical.

In Iran, a study attempted to identify different rates of adoption of new crops and techniques between older autonomous farmers, whose classes had demonstration plots, on the one hand, and classes without demonstration plots, on the other. Statistically significant differences judged positive were found. Results suggest that adoption of new-taught techniques is also a function of learners' actual postlearning prospects for applying those new techniques. Thus, positive effects were not found among farmers under 25 years of age with no access to land (UNESCO, 1976).

Finally, and although no research was carried out on the subject (which was not an explicit part of the methods tested during EWLP), stimulus variation appeared in a number of projects as a kind of intuitive way of maintaining adult learners' interest. Recourse to a variety of methods and techniques typified classes in Sudan, for instance; there, sequences included oral expositions (by the class instructor, then visiting technicians), group discussion (problem- and solution-oriented), audiovisual aids, individual and joint use of written materials, field visits, and practical demonstrations.

The major lesson to be derived from EWLP as regards the most appropriate *institutional arrangements* for literacy is that there is no magic solution to the problem. At the national level, with the understandable desire to confer a dynamic identity on the EWLP project, several countries set up autonomous structures, outside the institutional framework of other educational and developmental activities. This created friction among programs and staffs, and in virtually all cases the responsible structure was merged into preexisting institutions, generally the Ministry of Education.

In turn, a single-ministry setting made it difficult to have access to the services of other vertical parts of the bureaucracy, crucial though such services were for literacy work attempting to integrate vocational and other development-related elements. The predictable results: in one country, agricultural extension workers attached in principle to the project had no contact with literacy instructors who taught the same pupils but were responsible to another ministry.

Even attempts to achieve compromise or intermediate solutions did not have notable success. Cooperation bodies, ranging from national advisory committees to coordinating councils with (in principle) more executive muscle, were created, modified, disbanded, resuscitated, to little avail. In no case does it seem possible to attribute project success or failure to the structural formula ultimately, if uneasily, settled on, or even correlate the with it. "Finally," according to the EWLP evaluation, "there seems to have been no satisfactory and replicable solution to the autonomy/coordination dilemma" (cited in UNESCO, 1976, p. 145).

Much of the same may be said of the centralization/decentralization question. This is the more regrettable since a measure of local learner self-government was part of the EWLP's approach. In 1973, the UNESCO Secretariat affirmed that:

> functional literacy work cannot be designed from outside, in accordance with the mechanistic approaches of traditional pedagogy. It presupposes active participation on the part of those concerned at all stages of preparation and implementation. (cited in UNESCO, 1976, p. 146)

Attempts were made in Algeria, Guinea, and particularly Tanzania to provide for a degree of devolution of responsibility to this class itself. In Tanzania, elected class committees were empowered inter alia to enforce participant discipline, spend money made from demonstration plots, and schedule classes. This last function was not without importance, wince it could result in classes deciding to extend schedules that, in turn, could require extra government spending for additional teaching hours.

Internationally, the institutional relationships were also complex. UNESCO and UNDP were both involved in all projects, and there was between them, according to the final report signed by both, a "fundamental disagreement at various times . . . about the relative priority to be accorded to literacy programs in the framework of economic development and scarce international resources" (cited in UNESCO, 1976, p. 148). Further complicating relationships was the participation in some projects of other technical or finding agencies, both bi- and multilateral.

One disappointment noted by the EWLP evaluators was the unrealized potential for involvement in the Program of international nongovernmental organizations (NGOs) and their national branches in project countries. After some initial efforts, "the movement of joint and active international NGO participation in EWLP slowed, and then stopped. . . . Joint action in the framework of EWLP . . . died a premature death, depriving the Program of an important consortium of partners" (cited in UNESCO, 1976, p. 149). Why this happened is still not entirely clear. Inter-NGO cooperation has, however, again become a real possibility with the creation by Unesco in 1984 of an annual Collective Consultation of NGOs on Literacy.

As for *premises*, EWLP dealt a body blow to the "edifice complex." Many classes did, of course, take place in rural primary schools, often a village's most modern and (costly) construction, with cement walls and a tin roof. But churches, mosques, factories and other work places, private homes, and even the shade of trees were also used, and shown to be adequate locales in which literacy could be taught successfully.

From the pedagogical point of view, the organization of classes in varied setting offered the advantage of providing a physical link with reality, particularly the reality of learners' actual working situations. Sometimes the link was not fully exploited by instructors who did not themselves view such settings as pedagogically worthy places. Elsewhere, unthinking organizers appear to have followed instructions rather ineptly: one demonstration plot was hardly bigger than the UNESCO expert's office. But on the whole, EWLP did confirm that successful literacy work does not require a "normal" or "modern" classroom.

From the economic point of view, diversification of premises enabled most Program countries to make fuller use of already-existing educational and other plants, thereby reducing costs. Also, economies were achieved when, as in Ethiopia, learners built their own facilities; a similar practice in Tanzania led to a national policy under which villages only receive government assistance to build educational facilities if they themselves provide labor and materials.

With regard to *language*, statistically significant research results led EWLP evaluators to postulate that "the closer the language used to present the content and materials of the course to the workers' everyday language, the more effective the literacy program" (cited in UNESCO, 1976, p. 170). This sounds a reasonable, even banal, proposition today; but at the time of the Program there was still considerable reticence about breaking away from the former colonial language as the medium of instruction outside, as well as inside, the school. In Mali, new ground was broken thanks to EWLP: national languages were transcribed, a lexicon and grammar were prepared in Bombasa, teaching materials developed and used, and a popular rural newspaper issued for new literates. Still today, the responsible government unit is called National Directorate of Functional Literacy and Applied Linguistics.

Elsewhere, however, program was far from remarkable. In some multilingual countries such as India, programs arose in maintaining full fidelity to the meaning of the language in which materials were prepared while making them thoroughly comprehensible to speakers of the language(s) into which they were translated. The international element compounded the complexity on occasion. In one case, original drafting was done in Russian, then translated into English, then from English into the major national language for distribution to learners who did not speak that language (much less English or Russian). In this connection, the possible use of international funds to promote literacy as a means of spreading the national language to assimilate (subdue?) minority groups appears to have raised sensitive cultural, and thus political, questions in certain instances.

If the Experimental Program's creators gave thought to post-EWLP work, it was primarily with a view to the possible World Campaign toward which EWLP was to pave the way. There was a widespread (if not universal) implicit assumption in the Program that once people had become literate they would stay literate. The major focus had, therefore, to be on making him or her literate.

In reality, EWLP countries encountered serious difficulties in providing *postliteracy follow-up* reading materials. Indeed, "the very term 'follow-up' seems to have lulled several projects into assuming that such materials were of secondary or auxiliary importance only" (cited in UNESCO, 1976, p. 139). Nothing, EWLP demonstrated, could have been farther from the truth. Literacy, of the levels to which it was taught in most national projects, was not self-sustaining. Unless nourished by periodicals, books, and other reading matter, and unless developed by further education, newly acquired literacy tends to wilt, wither, and die.

Even in highly literate societies, the care and feeding of the three Rs is more than a marginal activity, as Britain, America, West Germany, and France found out when in the late 1970s or early 1980s they discovered that perhaps as many as 15% of Johnnies, Johanns, and Jeannots could not really read (Espérandieu, Lion, & Bénichou, 1984; Hamadache, 1984). How much more awesome, then, is the task of postliteracy work in situations where the majority is illiterate, where the printed message is an exception rather than the rule, and where writers, publishers, libraries, and other facilities for its production and wide dissemination (often in more than one previously uncodified language)—not to forget opportunities for continuing education—are few and far between.

In such setting, according to the EWLP final report, creation almost *ex nihilo* of indispensible postliteracy facilities "may be tantamount to setting up the material infrastructure of a literate society" (Espérandieu, Lion, & Bénichou, 1984; Hamadache, 1984). This lesson has been well illustrated by a country like Tanzania, whose experimental EWLP project bloomed into a full-scale national literacy campaign which, in turn, has given birth to a whole new written literature in Kiswahili, an extensive network of rural libraries, eight widely real rural newspapers, and a pervasive and varied menu of postliteracy learning opportunities: residential, in villages, and by correspondence.

Yet, the magnitude of the postliteracy work required for initial literacy to have a good likelihood of success appears to be occasionally ignored and often underestimated, even on the part of serious promoters of literacy. Hurried to engage in mass literacy activities as soon as possible after liberating the national territory, the Nicaraguan Sandinista authorities do not, for example, seem to have given sufficient initial thought to postliteracy; and if postliteracy is a working proposition today in that country, it is largely a result of psychological mobilization of the population (which could perhaps have been helped by better initial planning for the transition from literacy to postliteracy) (Torres, 1983).

In conclusion, major "nuts-and-bolts" outcomes that can be culled from EWLP may be grouped into four categories.

First, the Program could not but restate certain dilemmas that are as familiar as they seem to be inextricable. No breakthrough was evident with regard to certain institutional problems (autonomy vs. coordination, centralization vs. decentralization, UN interagency relations), and the professional vs. amateur/volunteer staff argument persists unresolved.

Second, EWLP plotted a number of hopeful avenues which, disappointingly, it then explored hardly at all. Among these: full learner participation in preparing and implementing literacy work, and the unfulfilled potential of mobilizing an NGO consortium.

Third, the Program did break ground—or at least reconfirmed earlier ground breaking on a comparatively broad international scale—on some questions. These included: successful integration of functional subjects in literacy curricula on the basis of actual problems facing learners in contexts of socioeconomic change; the pedagogical and economic advantages of using diverse and unusual locales for learning; andragogical methods (inductive, experiential, and varied); staff issues (the possibility of sparking enthusiasm, broadened skill profiles of functional literacy instructors, mobilization of a wide range of technical staff for instructional and backup tasks, and the effectiveness of short initial training followed by periodic refresher encounters).

Finally, EWLP pointed the way (not always intentionally) to certain new issues, or a t least called attention to the need to view certain issues with a new intensity. The complex problem of language used for literacy work was one; the decisive importance of postliteracy follow-up was another.

EWLP'S NEW LITERATES: CREATORS OR CREATURES?

The most critical part of the assessment of EWLP issued in the Program's final report, a section strangely ignored by most reviewers concerns its human results. How did the new literates change, in terms of socioeconomic behaviors, as a result of EWLP?

Causality proved difficult indeed to establish, as was to be expected. Nevertheless, it does seem that EWLP caused behaviors to change. Some 160 measures and observations were run on various projects, doubtless with differing degrees of reliability. In all, the "influence of functional literacy [on changes observed and measured] was judged to be plausible" (cited in UNESCO, 1976, p. 176) in about 42% of the cases.

Not only "plausible," but "favorable" (cited in UNESCO, 1976, p. 176). In other words, the Program assigned positive or negative value to changes that took place, and attempted to determine what favorably valued (and statistically significant) changes attributable to functional literacy took place, in three categories of new literatures' relationships with their surroundings. These were: insertion into the milieu, mastery of the milieu, and transformation of the milieu.

Indicators used to assess *insertion into the milieu* reflected, among other things, efforts made to obtain vocational/technical advise, interest in further education, participation in formal organizations and management of personal finances. 86% of changes found were judged to be satisfactory, 56% with statistical significance. Analysis of data from several countries enabled the final report's authors to establish a provisional qualitative profile of the new literate judged to be successfully "inserted" in the milieu. Such a person seemed to:

> (a) actively seek information likely to help solve mainly personal problems, generally posed in vocational terms; (b) prefer such activity to participation in formal community organizations; (c) take advantage of his or her new literacy and numeracy skills to maintain personal bank and savings accounts; and (d) aspire to reduce the size of his or her family in exchange for the prospects of a higher material living standard. (cited in UNESCO, 1976, p. 178)

Clearly, the Program judged itself most successful "when it reproduced the narrowly economic interpretation of functionality" (cited in UNESCO, 1976, p. 178) This kind of functionality reflects, in turn, a certain model of socioeconomic development which, while dominant in certain countries, is far from universally accepted.

The second broad class of intended socioeconomic changes examined concerned new literates' *mastery of the milieu*. Here, such effects as adoption of new technical practices were measured, and 93%

of changes recorded were deemed satisfactory, 51% significantly so. Focusing its analysis on agricultural subprojects in India, the EWLP final report suggested that a major effect had been to enable small peasants to joint the Green Revolution. This step had advantages (higher personal income) but servitudes too (greater expenditure for new seeds and other accessories). Also, the approach is not massively replicable, since the Green Revolution tends to be neither green nor revolutionary outside land irrigated with sure water (about 10% of cultivated land in India).

EWLP did, then, increase new literates' mastery of the milieu, but in a narrowly technical and productivistic way akin to the kind of functionality promoted with regard to insertion into the milieu, as outlined above. This leaves a number of important and not entirely rhetorical questions to be dealt with:

> In acquiring this kind of mastery of the milieu, to what extent does the new literate become dependent on which external socio-economic processes and forces? Has literacy enabled the new literate to know and understand these processes and forces? To come to grips with them? To have a voice in controlling them? What implications has the new literate's accession to mastery of the milieu for the fate of his or her less favored neighbors and compatriots? (cited in UNESCO, 1976, p. 181)

The final class of behavior changes sought and measured by EWLP involved *transformation of the milieu*. In this category, attempts were made to detect effects on behaviors concerning, for example, the means and volume of production, cash income, and consumption of goods such as bicycles, sewing machines, and pressure lamps. Of changes recorded, 90% were judged satisfactory, 41% significantly so.

One must ask, however, whether increased consumption can (or should) be made a proxy for the humanistic aspiration to achieve mastery over the conditions in which one lives. Proceeding from this line of questioning, the Program's final report outlines a global profile of the positively judged new literate, who:

> "inserted into the milieu" has been stimulated by the prospect of personal material gain and equipped with knowledge . . . to supply appropriate response to that stimulus. As a "master of the milieu," the new literate does seem effectively to supply the appropriate response. It is only logical then that, completing the circle, the new literate should be rewarded: he or she (and family) appears to gain access to increased personal consumption of material goods. (cited in UNESCO, 1976, p. 182)

This may seem something of a caricature, or at least an oversimplification, considering that during EWLP, over one hundred thousand people were made literate in diverse provinces of 11 very different countries in Africa, the Arab States, Asia, and Latin America. Yet, the Program's basic vocational and productivistic logic made it vulnerable to precisely the kind of stimulus/response and instrumental thinking that pervaded its evaluation design and the values by which results were judged under that design.

Literacy however, like education more generally, cannot be reduced to behavioral conditioning. It endows people with skills that they can (although do not always) use to receive and emit messages of an almost infinite range. a range that in any event largely escapes the control of those who imparted literacy to them. Literacy is potential empowerment.

President J. Nyerere could have been (but probably wasn't) referring to some of EWLP's excesses on this score when he made "a serious distinction between men and women who are skillful users of tools, and a system of education which turns men and women into tools. I want to make quite sure that [ours] is an education for creators, not creatures . . . " (1975, p. 67).

POSTSCRIPT: JOMTIEN AND SINCE

The foregoing is adapted from a text drafted some ten years ago, a decade after the end of EWLP. What has happened since? What does a revisit to the revisit reveal, or—more modestly—suggest?

The good news is that there does appear to have been progress, perhaps in absolute as well as relative terms: there may well, contrary to statistical projections of a few years ago, be less complete illiterates among our fellow world citizens in the year 2000. The Jomtien Education for All Conference, and indeed the 1990 International Literacy Year operation as a whole, may have steeled resolve, and successfully nudged at least a few international as well as national decision-making hands towards their billfolds.

The money is certainly there: The "peace bonus" released by reductions in military spending since the end of the Cold War has been estimated at $700 billion. How much as gone for literacy work, or education more broadly?

The People's Republic of China, for one, has rededicated itself to the pro-literacy struggle. At a ceremony marking the creation of the Young Chinese Volunteers Association at Beijing, in December 1994, I and other international participants were taken aback to hear the leaders of the new body apologize for the modesty of their goal: volunteers would "only" strive to teach basic literacy to one-third of China's 30 million illiterates by the year 2000!

Elsewhere, the situation is far from hopeful. In Ethiopia (an ex-EWLP country), regression has been a main feature of the educational scene in the last few years. School attendance has declined from 1/3 to 1/4 of the relevant population group—with the pupil:teacher ratio often as high as 100:1. Estimates of absolute illiteracy given to me in Addis Ababa in January of 1995 floated around 70% of adults, against 50% a decade ago.

The problem of *literacy maintenance* already mentioned above, has also come to the forefront of concerns in many countries. Jonathan Kozol's *Illiterate America* was followed, at the end of the 1980s by Jean-Pierre Vélis' prize-winning *La France Illéttrée* (20% of the native-born, schooled population over 18), and the same author's *Through a Glass Darkly* (*Lettre d'Illettrie*, published by UNESCO) on the situation in industrialized countries more generally.

Whatever the official rates and trends of absolute illiteracy (that was the good news), many examples lead me to believe that the *functional use* of the three Rs may actually be declining in the world.

Then, there is the problem of evolving definitions of literacy.

I astonished my peers thirty-plus years ago by packing out high school homework on an Olivetti portable typewriter; my 18-year-old son swishes through his on a P.C., and my 24-year-old daughter is a headhunter in a consultant firm that specializes in . . . computer whizzes. Gone forever, my Olivetti has left me an orphan: I am a total computer illiterate, and am in fact writing this "P.S." *by hand*!

To conclude: an ultimate irony of EWLP is that it appears (a) to have had little or no influence, for better or worse, on pre-Jomtien, Jomtien or post-Jomtien thought and action, indeed (b) to have been largely forgotten.

One would have thought the world education community's collective memory less fickle.

REFERENCES

de Clerck, M. (1984). *L'Educateur et le villageois: De l'education de base a l'alphabétisation fonctionnelle* [The educator and the villager: From basic education to functional literacy]. Paris: L'Harmattan.

Espérandieu, V., Lion, A., & Bénichou, J.-P. (1984). *Des Illettrés en France* [Illiterates in France]. Paris: La Documentation Francaise.

Hamadache, A. (1984, February). Illiteracy in the fourth world. *Unesco Courier*.

Levine, K. (1982). Functional literacy: Fond illusions and false economies. *Harvard Educational Review, 2,* 252.

Meister, A. (1973). *Alphabétisation et developpement* [Literacy and development]. Paris: Anthropos.

Nyerere, J. (1975). Education for liberation in Africa. *Prospects 1.* Paris: Unesco.

Torres, R.M. (1983). *De alfabetizando a maestro popular: La post-alfabetización en Nicaragua* [Literacy and the people's teacher: Post-literacy in Nicaragua]. Managua: Instituto de Investigaciones Economicas y Sociales and Coordinadora Regional de Investigaciones Economicas y Sociales.

UNESCO (1976). *The experimental world literacy program: A critical assessment.* Paris: The Unesco Press and UNDP.

UNESCO (1979). *The experimental world literacy program.* Paris: Author.

23

Does Rising Literacy Spark Economic Growth? Commercial Expansion in Mexico

Bruce Fuller
University of California at Berkeley

John H. Y. Edwards
Tulane University

Kathleen Gorman
University of New Hampshire

Farming is for people who can't read or write . . . those who have to work with the kodalo [hand spade] and carry the doko [basket used for portering]. R. B. Khatri, a subsistence farmer in Nepal (Ashby, 1985, p. 72)

I. OVERVIEW

The economic magic of literacy is widely accepted within developing countries. Whether speaking to a rural Nepalese peasant or a Third World political leader, many claim that literacy holds miraculous power in providing upward mobility for the individual and in boosting eco-

373

nomic development for a nation. Human capital theorists have formalized this faith by offering empirical evidence suggesting that the young *individual* often does benefit economically from increased levels of schooling within developing nations (Psacharopoulos and Woodhall, 1985).

However, empirical researchers are just beginning to examine (a) whether actual gains in literacy yield economic benefits similar to investment returns from formal schooling, and (b) whether literacy leads to economic growth at the *national* level, comparable to the individual-level payoff of schooling. Earlier confidence in the alleged potency of literacy has given way to a sharp questioning over whether economic structures must change before literacy or school investments will yield significant economic benefits (for instance, Bowles & Gintis, 1976). Advocates of the alternative proposition (though arguably short on empirical evidence) suggest that gains in literacy and schooling follow rather than precede economic growth (Collins, 1977). In addition, the most advantaged classes may gain the most from rising levels of literacy and schooling, reinforcing social and economic inequality (Soltow & Stevens, 1981).

We ask and empirically assess a related question: Do rising levels of literacy help explain economic growth within a Third World nation over time? We attempt to identify the forces that explain Mexico's period of early commercial expansion within agrarian and manufacturing sectors over the 1900-1940 period. This period was split by a significant social revolution, offering the chance to study sources of growth alternatively within a free market and a largely state-planned economy. Like other post-revolutionary societies, Mexico placed an enormous priority on boosting literacy as a primary method of raising living standards and improving social equality. Acrimonious debate continues over whether Mexico's documented progress in improving literacy in fact did generate these material and social effects (Ruiz, 1963; McGinn & Street, 1984). The present study sheds empirical light on this question—an issue that holds relevance to other developing countries in assessing the likely impact of literacy on national growth.

First, we review the theoretical debate over literacy's role in boosting growth or in reinforcing the social structure. Second, Mexico's pattern of national development is outlined, highlighting the rising investment in literacy instruction and change in the country's economic structure during the 1900-1940 era. Third, our empirical model and method for estimating potential economic effects of literacy are presented. Fourth, findings are summarized, followed by our conclusions on the future—and realistic—role of literacy in spurring economic change.

II. LITERACY AND ECONOMIC GROWTH: HUMAN CAPITAL FORMATION OR STRUCTURAL REINFORCEMENT?

At first, the question of whether literacy growth precedes or follows economic growth may appear to be simply an academic chicken-or-egg dilemma. However, for centuries societies have invested in literacy projects and have allocated scarce resources to formal schooling under the assumption that economic returns would be sizeable. At other times social communities (at the village or national scale) have chosen to invest in physical capital—irrigation, oxen, power plants, or factories—in hopes that these inputs would yield economic growth. A better understanding of the direction of causality could help boost the efficiency with which resources are expended for national development.

This debate may be framed in terms of the relationship between school investment (not literacy per se) and economic growth, given the present state of the research literature. Distinctions are then raised between investment in discrete school institutions versus the operation of literacy within a culture. More indigenous forms of literacy may stem from different factors and create quite different effects than investments in rationalized school organizations.

Few doubt that the propensity to enroll in school (an individual action) or to build additional schools (an institutional action) covaries with economic wealth among nations. But individual-level *human capital* versus institutional-level *structural reinforcement* theories differ sharply on several questions: What causal model best distinguishes causes from effects? Are the dynamic processes that explain this correlation rooted in individual decisions or in widely institutionalized social beliefs and formal organizations? How can one best observe and estimate these competing models? What is the magnitude of effects between school investment and economic growth?

Proponents of human capital theory make the rationalist assumption that the individual (or one's family) maximizes his or her economic returns in choosing between alternative actions, such as deciding between additional schooling or moving into the labor market. A neoclassical economic assumption is then made regarding the occupation and wage structure, namely that higher wages are allocated to more productive workers. Therefore, additional investments in human capital formation by families and nations—allegedly lead to higher productivity, private income gains, and aggregate economic expansion (Schultz, 1961). Researchers then typically analyze the rate of return to investments in literacy or schooling, taking into account direct costs of schooling and opportunity costs associated with forgone income. Rates of return have been found to be substantial in both industrial and developing nations, based on cross sectional surveys. These rates of return for individuals and for societies (both estimated from individual income gains) appear to be at least as high as alternative investment strategies, such as the return to investing in technological inputs to production (Psacharopoulos & Woodhall, 1985).

The *causal assumption* contained within human capital theory is that the individual's investment in literacy and schooling precedes the economic returns he or she eventually gains. Like the infusion of material capital into the production process, the human capital stock varies in technical skills that variably boost individual productivity and income. Yet social theorists, emphasizing institutional-level processes, argue that causality may flow more strongly in the opposite direction. That is, rising national investments in schooling and the propensity of individuals to enroll in schools *follow* economic development and correspond to social class patterns (that are defined by the organization of capital). The demand for schooling or higher levels of literacy can spring from (a) individuals searching for both technical skills and symbolic credentials to maintain or advance their status and income; (b) social groups (especially churches) seeking to advance group membership and solidarity; and (c) states seeking to advance their own legitimacy and to integrate plural communities into a national market and consciousness (Collins, 1977). In short, social theorists argue that school expansion follows the desire of groups to enhance their position or to reinforce the rules that define existing social classes.

Initial empirical evidence backs the structural reinforcement position advanced by social theorists, at least for later stages of industrial development. Walters (1984), for instance, found that the level of demand for young workers in the U.S.A. significantly explained school enrollment levels over the 1922-1979 period (testing a multivariate time-series model). Contemporary enrollment rates also can be largely explained by a family's social class position in Mexico (Goldblatt, 1972); Nicaragua (Wolfe & Behrman, 1984); Brazil and India (Bowman, 1984; employing correlational and multivariate empirical methods). Rising technological complexity helps to explain the growth of primary and secondary enrollments in the U.S.A. during the twentieth century (Rubinson & Ralph, 1984). In addition, demand for schooling often stems from efforts to reinforce (nonmaterial) social structures which are organized around religious or social values. The preindustrial rise of grammar schools in the U.S.A. was associated with a rural Protestant commitment to literacy and formal socialization through schooling (Fishlow, 1966; Meyer et al., 1979). This influence of rural cultural values was much stronger than subsequent labor structure effects on school expansion during the early industrial era (Fuller, 1983). The historical rise of schooling in both colonial Latin America and Africa also may have been more strongly linked to attempts at church expansion and religious solidarity than to material economic factors (Yates, 1980).

This evidence backs the structural reinforcement model, showing that the organization of capital at times determines the reproduction and expansion of social institutions, including the school—the secular organization dedicated to the spread of literacy. Social class position clearly shapes the *distribution* of individual-level demand for schooling. However, even when economic factors drive the spread of literacy and schooling (in Time 1), rising educational levels could boost subsequent economic growth (in Time 2). This proposition has received empirical support for later periods of industrial growth in the United States (Denison, 1979; Walters & Rubinson, 1983). Yet very little is known about the economic effects of rising literacy in earlier periods of commercial expansion typically present in contemporary Third World nations.

The *process assumption* underlying human capital theory is that the *individual* (or one's family) decides how long to remain in school based on a strategy to maximize the present value of lifetime income. Social theorists counter that both demand for schooling and any economic effects of school expansion flow from institutionalized beliefs and formal organizations, not from rational decisions by each individual. Particularly within early stages of economic growth, school investment may be part of an institution-building process designed to integrate local communities into regional and national markets. This requires achievement of a national language,.reduction of ethnic insularity and cultural diversity, and universal systems of exchange that are often encased in formal organizations (Bendix, 1964; Meyer, 1977). Schools help to socialize children toward a national consciousness and equip youth to work within bureaucratic firms. From an institutional viewpoint, investing in literacy and schooling is important not only in providing technical skills to the individual. This investment also helps break down ethnic or regional loyalties and socialize youth to accept "modern" ways of organizing work and life.

We argue that this latter assumption of the structural reinforcement model does not necessarily contradict the direction of causality claimed by human capital economists (that is, school investment causing economic growth). But institutional rather than individual-level processes are emphasized in explaining *how* school investment boosts economic development.

Literacy Versus Schooling Efforts

When studying the role of literacy, rather than specific investments in schooling, three distinctions must be drawn. First, literacy often serves non-economic social functions. Illustrations are abundant: an otherwise unwieldy Chinese state advanced literacy and ideological hegemony (centered in Confucian writings) by choosing government officials from among top performers on the national exam (Borthwick, 1983). Following Mexico's war of independence in the 1820s and again after the social revolution (1911-1917), strong steps were taken to deliver literacy (in Spanish) to indigenous Indians—with the explicit goal of building a national consciousness (Vaughan, 1982). And early growth in literacy among Western European states occurred prior to industrial development, energized by a cultural commitment to reading the Bible and competition for members among religious sects (Archer, 1982). In each instance the function of literacy emphasized social goals, not material development.

This early cultural or religious commitment to literacy has often occurred prior to the rise of a modern state and concurrent investments in formalized schools. For example, the church was the primary purveyor of literacy—pursuing spiritual, not material goals—in both Latin America and parts of Africa prior to the rise of secular schools. Here early literacy may have sparked economic growth within a nation prior to any effects of formal schooling. Mitch (1984) shows that the economic return of literacy to the *individual* was high in early nineteenth-century England. The central government began investing in schooling at this point in time. But the rate of return to formal schooling (and presumably to literacy) began to fall as literacy spread and the costs of instruction (now within a formal structure) began to rise.

Second, the growth of literacy in many nations occurs in a segmented fashion, following social class lines. For example, the rise of literacy prior to the expansion of formal schooling in the U.S.A. was not experienced equally by all segments of the society. Occupational and social position largely determined the reproduction of literacy even early in the nineteenth century (Soltow & Stevens, 1981). As described later, the growth of literacy in Mexico was associated with differing levels of wealth among regions within the nation. This pattern is similar to that reported in other contemporary developing countries.

Third, literacy is a benchmark for the level of learning which actually occurs, not simply a measure of resources invested in schooling. Most research examines how long children spend in school, not the levels of literacy or cognitive skills that are actually attained. The relationship between achieved literacy and economic benefit may be stronger than using length of schooling as the explanatory variable. For instance, young workers' levels of actual school achievement in Kenya and Tanzania appeared to have more strongly influenced their subsequent earnings, compared to their length of school attendance (Boissiere, Knight, & Sabot, 1985).

III. CONTRASTING METHODS AND EVIDENCE: HUMAN CAPITAL VERSUS STRUCTURAL REINFORCEMENT MODELS

To substantiate the human capital model, economists typically estimate the rate of income-return gained by the individual from completing more years of school. These studies often observe a correlation between individual school attainment and income, then infer: (a) that higher wages signal greater productivity, and (b) that this productivity differential is due to formal schooling. A pivotal assumption is that labor markets, free of institutional rules, consistently reward more productive workers. Two methodological weaknesses in this method of individual-level analysis are currently being debated. First, little empirical work exists to substantiate the claim that higher wages reflect higher productivity at the individual level. The empirical studies which have been done reveal a low association between wages and productivity (Frank, 1984; Fuller, 1976). Empirical refutation of these central neoclassical assumptions may be especially true in the Third World where institutional rules often influence both the supply of schooling and wage policies (Dore, 1976). Hinchcliffe's (1976) study of Nigerian textile workers suggests that schooling's effect on wages may only occur for those technical occupations which rely heavily on academic credentials for entry.

High covariation between school attainment and income could exist at the individual level without any increase in national productivity. Advanced industrial economies, for instance, rely heavily on educational credentials as a screening device in hiring and promoting workers. Even in periods of economic decline the correlation between schooling level and income will be observed. But *aggregate* levels of national income or productivity may remain static. In addition, schools may simply sort out youth who have benefited from better family backgrounds or demarcate those who have learned requisite social mores required for higher-status jobs. This does not imply, however, that schools offer higher levels of technical skills which then boost individual productivity (Thurow, 1974).

Second, individual-level rate of return analyses implicitly assume stable labor demand and income allocation patterns over time. Relying on cross-sectional survey data, this method ignores how short-term economic cycles might affect rates of return to schooling, and how labor demand may shift for certain groups. Historical changes in labor demand patterns must be recognized before inferring long-run rates of return from cross-sectional snapshots, especially during early stages of economic growth. Within Third World countries, rates of return may be much higher for youth who are located closer to the modern economic sector. School credentials are scarce commodities during early periods of development;

economic rewards for marginal increases in school attainment are great. But as the number of schooled youth rises relative to labor demand, rates of return decline (Psacharopoulos & Woodhall, 1985).

Very little work has been reported that looks at the relationship between aggregate (not individual) levels of literacy and economic growth. The recent article by Boissiere and his colleagues (cited above) suggests that higher literacy levels held by individuals do lead to higher wages. But it is not known whether higher literacy levels among regions of a nation boost economic growth. The empirical strategy described below examines whether differences in the literacy rate among Mexico's states help to explain their level of economic output. Before turning to this empirical model and method, we outline the Mexican context.

IV. EDUCATION AND ECONOMIC CHANGE IN MEXICO

A. Shifting Economic Structure

The first period examined in Mexico includes the three decades preceding Mexico's social revolution, 1880-1910. This era was dominated by the national regime of Porfirio Diaz, a strong advocate of free market capitalism, growth in the export of raw materials, and investment by foreign entrepreneurs. New Spain was founded to provide precious minerals and agricultural products. Diaz successfully accelerated this dependent, peripheral position in the world economy with a post-colonial, more ecumenical strategy for attracting foreign capital. As Diaz cut back customs duties and other investment barriers, the value of all exports increased more than ten-fold between 1885 and 1894 (in constant pesos); minerals represented three-fourths of the value of all exports. At the turn into the twentieth century Mexico provided 30% of the world's silver and 6% of all gold produced. Of the (U.S. $647 million invested in the mining industry in 1910, the United States owned $499 million of the capital, $97 million came from the English and French, and only $29 million in Mexican capital was invested (Hager, 1916).

Mexico's agricultural exports increased by 47% during the last decade of the nineteenth century. As early as 1810 commercialized crop and livestock production comprised 56% of all output, providing raw materials (cotton, wool, and indigo) for Spanish and British textile manufactures. Agriculture was originally organized around feudal-like *haciendas* which eventually engaged in a mix of wage-labor and debt peonage to secure a steady workforce. The modern agricultural sector was concentrated around mining or administrative centers where population growth stimulated regional demand for wheat and livestock production, in addition to indigenous cultivation of corn (Van Young, 1981).[1] As late as 1910, 840 families controlled almost all the productive land and employed inexpensive farmworkers and tenants rather than investing in more productive technology. Ninety-seven percent of rural family heads owned no land at all (Callcott, 1931). By the late nineteenth century Mexico's agricultural productivity was low relative to international standards. However, preoccupied with attracting capital to support mining and manufacturing activity, the Diaz administration did little to boost agrarian production.

Following the 1911-1917 revolutionary period, Mexico's newly centralized government exercised a variety of economic reforms aimed at spurring growth in agriculture and manufacturing. These efforts included redistributing farm land, organizing marketing cooperatives in rural areas, financing the expansion of factories, and discouraging foreign investment via the nationalization of major industries and tax reform. Annual rates of growth increased in agriculture and manufacturing during the 1925-1940 period compared to the last decade of the Diaz regime. Traditional export industries, especially mining, were hurt badly (in terms of output, not necessarily in earnings returned to Mexico) by the discouragement of foreign investment. Between 1925 and 1940 mining and petroleum output fell by 1.9% per year on average. Imports dipped 3.5% annually during this period. The result was a drop in real per capita GDP from a 2.2% annual growth rate prior to the revolution to no aggregate growth during the 1920-1940 period. Growth within agricultural and manufacturing sectors, however, was significant following the revolution. The value of manufactured products rose 32% in the first decade of the 1900s, an additional 68% prior to the depression in 1929, and another 112% by the end of World War II (Reynolds, 1970). By 1945 the ratio of manufactured to agricultural output (value) equalled 35 to 1.

The growth in manufacturing significantly altered the labor structure, moving from a caste-like social pattern centered around mining and feudal land ownership toward a more diversified, open commercial economy. Our first hypothesis was that this growth in urban-based output and employment stemmed, in part, from rising levels of

---

[1]Historically, Spanish families in Mexico controlled the high-return enterprises that produced goods for European and eventually U.S. markets, including mining and manufacturing firms, cattle ranching, and cultivation of sugar and indigo. Low-return sectors were left to indigenous peoples, who produced corn and vegetables, gathered firewood, and grew labor-intensive crops such as silk, cotton, and cacao (Frank, 1979).

literacy and schooling. After the revolution, planned growth in the agricultural sector also may have boosted the economic return to literacy (for individuals and states). Land reform proceeded very slowly. Yet by 1926 almost 20% of all rural peasants had received parcels. Growth in the rural sector, both in terms of social expectations and material productivity, boosted the share of the labor force engaged in agriculture from 61.9% in 1900 to 70.2% in 1930 (Reynolds, 1970). Our second hypothesis was that expanded investments in literacy instruction helped to increase agricultural output.

B. A Shift in Educational Investments

Levels of literacy and school investment varied enormously in Mexico, both for the nation across pre- and post-revolutionary eras and among states during the early twentieth century. Corresponding to the pre-revolutionary economic structure, schooling was largely centered in urban ports or commercial centers, governed and financed by local groups. As late as 1875, 87% of all primary schools were operated by municipalities. Within Mexico City, 40% of all primary schools were privately operated. Private schools were of higher quality, spending 24 pesos per student annually in the 1870s, versus 5.4 pesos in public schools. (Farm workers earned three pesos (US$ 1.50) a week during the late nineteenth century). Residents of the more rural states, not surprisingly, were less frequently literate, benefited from fewer municipal schools, spent less per student on education, and earned less per capita (Fuller, Gorman, & Edwards, 1986). Even by 1907 less than one-fifth of all school-aged children within rural states ever entered school, such as within Oaxaca and Chiapas (Vaughan, 1982).

Following the revolution, the structure of educational investment was determined by the central government, and expenditures grew rapidly in rural areas. Education was a key ingredient of the array of social reforms initiated during the 1920-1940 period, emphasized more strongly than changes in the economic structure (Ruiz, 1963). Rural schools provided the modest organizational base for cultural missions, composed of government staff who organized the redistribution of land, farming and marketing cooperatives, and health care initiatives. Between 1921 and 1947 the number of rural schools rose from just over 1,000 to 13,700. Despite uncertainties caused by the revolution, federal support of schools grew from $9 million to $29 million per year (in constant pesos; Stanley, 1948). By 1925 municipal governments contributed less than 10% of all school aid. The federal government bolstered existing mandates on factory- and hacienda-owners to provide schools for workers. Vocational schools also were expanded.in both urban and rural areas.

Gains in literacy levels were substantial following implementation of these post-revolution educational programs. Rates of literacy are reported in Table 23.1 for urban and rural areas of the nation and for representative states. Data from 355 municipalities in Mexico were analyzed for 1900 and 1940 (a one-seventh random sample of these contiguous political units).

TABLE 23.1. Rise in Literacy Among Mexico's States for Urban and Rural Municipalities, 1900-1940.

	Literacy rate (5)	
	1900	1940
National literacy		
1. Urban municipalities	26	49
2. Rural municipalities	14	31
State literacy[a]		
3. Jalisco		
Urban	46	66
Rural	20	37
4. Coahuila		
Urban	37	53
Rural	30	56
5. Yucatan		
Urban	40	67
Rural	11	35
6. Oaxaca		
Urban	20	31
Rural	6	21
7. Chiapas[b]		
Rural	8	18

[a]States representing the range of literacy rates are reported.

[b]No villages in Chiapas exceeded the criterion used to define urban municipalities (less than 20% of labor force working in agriculture).

Source: Direccion (1900-1907); Direccion (1943).

Those *municipios* with less than 20% of the workforce employed in agriculture were classified as urban areas, comprising 15% of the sampled local jurisdictions. Between 1900 and 1940, literacy increased among urban areas from 26% to 49%. Within rural *municipios* literacy increased from 14% to 31%. Variation in literacy was wide among Mexico's states: in the more affluent state of Jalisco (within which the city of Guadalajara is located), urban literacy increased from 46% to 66% among urban areas. In contrast, rural literacy in Oaxaca (heavily populated by indigenous Indians) was only 6% in 1900, climbing to 21% by 1940.

Mexico provides a good example of a centralized government that sharply realigned educational investments, in part attempting to boost agricultural and manufacturing production. But whether rising levels of school support aided the documented economic growth during the 1920-1940 era remains an unexplored empirical question. The rapid expansion of schooling did not overcome very low levels of school quality apparent in many areas. In 1920, for example, the state of Sonora's schools were spending 15 times more than expenditures prior to the revolution; yet this equalled only 6 pesos annually per student. Rural teachers earned as little as one-fourth the wages paid in the commercial sector (Vaughan, 1982). Yet, independent of these questions, Mexico did place enormous faith in human capital theory prior to, and especially after, the revolution, arguing that expanded school investments would help drive economic growth. The next section describes our empirical test of the human capital model's efficacy within the Mexican context.

V. STUDY DESIGN

Did variation in literacy rates among Mexico's states significantly influence economic output during the late nineteenth and early twentieth centuries? The present method of analysis builds from earlier work that models the aggregate influence of schooling, not literacy, on economic growth over historical periods (Denison, 1979; Walters & Rubinson, 1983). These analysts used an aggregate production function to examine the influence of rising schooling levels on output after controlling for the effects of physical inputs to production (land, labor, and capital investment). Since annual time-series data are not available for Mexico (nor for other Third World countries) from early periods of development, state-level data were used (n=30 states for 1900; n=32 for 1940). The question here is whether interstate variation in economic output can be explained by variation in literacy for each of the years 1900 and 1940. An analysis at this aggregate level tells how literacy rates within particular states influence economic output relative to other states.[2]

---

[2]A potential problem with this form of analysis is that economic effects of schooling and literacy for individuals who migrate to other states will not be observed, or will bias estimates. Yet during the period under study, migration was not substantial: in 1900, 89% of the population lived in the state where they were born. In addition, all models initially controlled on state migration rates. Inclusion of this variable did not alter the results.

A. Model

The basic model suggests that the value of aggregate output (Q) is a function of land under cultivation (N), size of the labor force (L), amount of capital stock (K), and literacy (T). The model can be summarized as follows:[3]

$$Q = f(N, L, K, T)$$

A Cobb-Douglas production function was employed which has major advantages over other multivariate models (Walters, 1970). First, the model does not necessarily assume a linear relationship between the independent and dependent variables. Since inputs may hold non-linear relations with economic output, the model is commonly employed to flexibly fit this form of function. Second, the parameters of the Cobb-Douglas model can be interpreted as elasticities which aid in the interpretation of the magnitude of influence between antecedent and dependent variables. In addition, the model assumes full interaction between factors in terms of marginal effects; yet specific elasticities indicate the independent contribution of each variable.

B. Data and Measures

For 1900 the model estimated the value of total output and output within two specific economic sectors: (a) the value of agricultural production for basic crops (corn and beans), and (b) the estimated value of tobacco related production. Firms in the latter sector generally were located in

---

[3]The basic Cobb-Douglas model can be represented in the following way:

(1) $Q_{it} = A \, N^{\alpha}_{t} \, L^{\beta}_{t} \, K^{\psi}_{t} \, T^{\phi}_{t} \, e^{\xi}$

The model is then transformed by taking the natural log of each term. The equation reduces to an additive log-linear model that can be analyzed with an ordinary least-squares regression procedure:

(2) $q_{t} = a + \alpha n_{t} + B l_{t} + \psi k_{t} + \phi t_{t} + \xi$

Where $q = \log(Q)$, $n = \log(N)$ and so on. Each beta coefficient in this log-linear model represents the elasticity between the particular input and the dependent output variable. For instance, in Equation (2), if $B = 2.00$, then a 1% increase in land under cultivation is associated with a 2% increase in output.

urban areas, providing a more valid indicator of urban-based manufacturing.[4] For 1940, data availability improved and the model estimated output for several sectors in addition to total output and production of basic crops. State-level data for the value of all manufacturing firms were available, as well as the value of livestock assets (not output) and the value of production from collective farms. To allow comparison of the effects of literacy in urban versus rural areas, literacy rates were calculated separately for each of these two areas within each state based on the random sample of 355 local *municipios* as described earlier. According to archival records, census-takers determined adults' literacy either by asking whether they considered themselves to be literate (Direccion, 1943) or whether they knew the Spanish alphabet (Ruiz, 1963). No evidence indicates that individuals were required to actually demonstrate their reported literacy. This procedure probably led to overestimates of functional literacy levels. In addition, numbers of newspapers published were available for individual states for 1900 but not 1940. This provided another aggregate indicator of literacy and demand for written material. Data on economic inputs (land, labor, and capital), levels of output, and literacy for individual states came from several archival sources published by agencies of the Mexican government. These measures and their sources are detailed in the footnote.[5]

---

[4]In an earlier study a composite measure of urban-based wealth was calculated from the level of each state's value of tobacco-related manufacturing and from the number of property-owners. This index was internally consistent (alpha = 0.92) and was negatively correlated in 1900 ($r = -0.67$, $p<0.001$) with the number of residents living in towns with populations under 25,000 (Fuller et al., 1986).

[5]Economic data come from irregularly published surveys of agricultural, industrial, and commercial activity reported by federal agencies (Penafiel, 1901; Secretaria de la Economia, 1943). Literacy data are from decennial census reports (Direccion, 1900-1907, 1943). Data on 30 states were reported prior to the revolution, including the Federal District or Mexico City. For the post-revolution period, reports were from 32 jurisdictions, including former territories that were awarded the status of statehood. Dunng the revolutionary period, 1911-17, little information was collected by successive governments.

For 1900 the value of aggregate output included total product from agriculture, livestock, textile, mining, and tobacco-related manufacturing sectors. The agricultural output measure included production of corn and beans. This comprised 75% of all crop production in 1900. The model was calculated separately for the agricultural sector.

The value of tobacco-related production (V) by state was estimated from the actual level of taxes (TX) paid by cigarette and cigar manufacturers and an average tax rate (TR) faced by manufacturers in the state of Jalisco during this era (Banda, 1873): $V = (TX) \times (1/TR)$.

Measures of total capital investment were available from firms engaged in mining, textile manufacturing, and tobacco-related sectors. The census also

VI. FINDINGS

A. Literacy and Economic Output

Simple correlations between literacy rates and elements of the economic structure among Mexico's states are reported in Table 23.2. For 1900, literacy within urban areas of the states was positively related to aggregate economic output, value of livestock, and mining production. Interestingly, literacy in rural municipalities was significantly correlated with the value of tobacco-related manufacturing. Possibly some production in this sector occurred within rural areas.

For 1940, all literacy rates were correlated with livestock value and with manufacturing output. States with a larger share of workers involved in agriculture had lower literacy rates than more industrial states. As observed in 1900, those states with lower migration rates also had lower total rates of literacy. This may be explained by the fact that the more rural states had lower rates of interstate migration (Fuller, et al., 1986).

B. Multivariate Findings, 1900

Results from the production functions for 1900 are reported in Table 23.3. The model first was estimated by entering all physical production inputs and the four measures of literacy. Second, given that we were working with a small number of cases (30 and 32 states in 1900 and 1940, respectively), a partial stepwise procedure was employed to better identify

---

reported participation in the formal labor market (or in subsistence farming) by occupational category. The labor force measure was simply the total number of workers for the aggregate output model, and workers in agriculture or industry for rural and urban production models, respectively. No measure of capital investment for agriculture was available. Levels of capital investment in agriculture did vary during this period, particularly in the availability of draft animals for plowing or transport (oxen or mules) and simple irrigation. Otherwise technology was primitive and labor-intensive (Wells, 1887). Land under cultivation was estimated on the basis of crop volume in 1900 and contemporary yields per hectare to adjust for soil and climate quality.

For 1940, more extensive data were available for economic output and physical inputs. Aggregate input included production from agriculture (all crops), mining, and manufacturing (all subsectors). Total capital investment figures were available for all manufacturing and mining firms. For collective farms established through land distribution and rural organizing efforts, the value of machinery was used as a capital measure. Actual data on land under cultivation were available, as were labor participation data by sector. Individual models were constructed to estimate the value of production in manufacturing, all agriculture, collective farms, and for the *value* of livestock (not output).

TABLE 23.2. Correlations Between Literacy and Economic Features Among Mexico's States for Urban and Rural Areas 1900 (n=30) and 1940 (n=32).

	Literacy rate, 1900			Literacy rate, 1940		
	Total	Urban	Rural	Total	Urban	Rural
Economic output per capita						
1. Aggregate output[a]	0.15	0.67***	0.03	0.54**	0.43*	0.19
2. Agriculture (crops)	0.04	-0.15	0.16	-0.02	-0.14	0.31
3. Livestock	0.57***	0.48	-0.04	0.49	0.48	0.70
4. Collective farms[b]				0.20	-0.08	0.01
5. Mining	0.09	0.72***	-0.08	0.30	0.08	-0.13
6. Manufacturing						
All firms				0.59***	0.68***	0.47**
Textile	0.18	0.05	-0.15			
Tobacco-related	0.12	-0.11	0.48***			
Job structure						
7. Share of workers in agriculture	-0.45*	-0.55**	0.21	-0.70***	-0.52**	0.08
8. Share of workers in industry	0.00	0.75***	-0.07	0.50**	0.89***	0.07
Migration						
9. No. of native residents of state (as percentage of all)	-0.55**	-0.35	0.01	-0.73***	-0.25	-0.28

[a]The aggregate output variable for 1900 is an estimate based on available reports from a subset of economic sectors

[b]Collective forms did not exist prior to the revolution; data reported only for 1940.

*$p < 0.05$; **$p < 0.01$; ***$p < 0.001$.

which particular indicator of literacy helped to explain economic output. Literacy rates statewide, within urban *municipios*, and within rural *municipios*, did vary independently of each other. For the first period the number of newspapers published provided a fourth indicator of literacy.

In estimating total economic output, for instance, the full model revealed that none of the four literacy variables significantly entered the equation. However, the stepwise model (using $p < 0.10$ as a minimum criterion for entry) indicated a positive relationship between urban literacy and total output (beta=0.11, p<0.10), controlling for the effects of capital investment and labor force size. For tobacco-related manufacturing, a similar finding was apparent for the total literacy rate (beta=1.53, $p < 0.10$). The results for agricultural output were ambiguous. Both the total literacy rate and urban literacy entered the model. However, note that the high beta-value (0.94) for land under cultivation and the high F-value (282.30) for the entire equation. The cultivated-land variable was so strongly related to output that a very small residual remained. Since the literacy variables were regressed on such a small residual, the literacy findings should be interpreted cautiously.

TABLE 23.3. Influence of Literacy on Economic Output Among Mexico's States, 1900 (Elasticities and Errors Reported, $n = 30$).

Independent literacy variables	(a) Total output (estimate)		(b) Tobacco-related manufacturing		(c) Agriculture	
	Full model	Stepwise model	Full model	Stepwise model	Full model	Stepwise model
Economic inputs						
1. Land cultivated	0.02 (0.02)	0.02 (0.02)			0.94**** (0.03)	0.94**** (0.33)
2. Capital	0.15*** (0.04)	0.15**** (0.04)	0.21** (0.09)	0.19** (0.08)		
3. Labor	0.45** (0.19)	0.39** (0.16)	1.93*** (0.59)	1.85*** (0.55)	0.32 (0.23)	0.33* (0.19)
Literacy						
4. Total literacy	0.02 (0.37)		1.46 (1.06)	1.53* (0.79)	1.03** (0.49)	0.97** (0.45)
5. Urban literacy	0.10 (0.07)	0.11* (0.06)	-0.29 (0.38)		-0.26** (0.12)	-0.26** (0.10)
6. Rural literacy	0.06 (0.13)		0.30 (0.41)		-0.19 (0.21)	
7. Number of newspapers per capita	0.07 (0.14)		0.24 (0.45)		0.13 (0.22)	
Full model						
F-value	8.53****	18.77****	4.29***	8.77****	179.76****	282.30****
R^2	73%	72%	53%	50%	98%	98%

Dependent output measures

*$p < 0.10$; **$p < 0.05$; ***$p < 0.01$; ****$p < 0.001$.

C. Multivariate Findings, 1940

Results from our 1940 estimates of the aggregate production function are illustrated in Table 23.4. No relationship between literacy and total output was apparent after controlling for capital investment (where the effect was strong), land under cultivation, and labor force size. Turning to manufacturing output, the total literacy rate did hold an effect (beta=0.42, $p<0.05$) even in the presence of sizeable impacts of capital and labor force size.

Empirical findings for agricultural subsectors in 1940 are reported-in Table 23.5. The literacy variables failed to significantly enter the estimated function for the value of crop production. However, the value of livestock was significantly related to total literacy (beta=1.65, $p < 0.01$) and was *negatively* associated with rural literacy (beta=-0.28, $p < 0.05$). This may represent a sharp division of the social structure in states which were more productive in highly valued—and frequently exported—livestock and meat products. Finally, literacy was not related to the

TABLE 23.4. Influence of Literacy on Total and Manufacturing Output Among Mexico's States, 1940 (Elasticities and Errors Reported, n = 32).

	Dependent output measures			
	(a)		(b)	
	Total output		Manufacturing	
Independent variables	Full model	Stepwise model	Full model	Stepwise model
Economic inputs				
1. Land cultivated	0.07	0.05		
	(0.11)	(0.09)		
2. Capital	0.77****	0.80****	0.68****	0.69****
	(0.11)	(0.07)	(0.08)	(0.08)
3. Labor	0.13	0.12	0.23**	0.22**
	(02)	(0.11)	(0.10)	
Literacy				
4. Total literacy	0.16		0.33	0.42**
	(0.36)		(0.22)	(0.19)
5. Urban literacy	-0.02		0.05	
	(0.06)		(0.05)	
6. Rural literacy	-0.04		0.03	
	(0.13)		(0.10)	
Full model				
F-Value	42.43****	94.04****	78.71****	135.53****
R2	91%	91%	94%	94%

*$p < 0.10$; **$p < 0.05$; ***$p < 0.01$; ****$p < 0.001$

TABLE 23.5. Influence of Literacy on Output in Agricultural Subsectors Among Mexico's States, 1940 (Elasticities and Errors Reported, $n = 32$).

Independent literacy variables	Dependent output measures					
	Agriculture/Crops		Livestock (Asset value)		Collective farms	
	Full model	Stepwise model	Full model	Stepwise model	Full model	Stepwise model
Economic inputs						
1. Land cultivated	0.82***	0.80****	0.08	0.06	0.54***	0.53****
	(0.09)	(0.09)	(0.15)	(0.15)	(0.16)	(0.14)
2. Capital					0.61****	0.61****
					(0.12)	(0.11)
3. Labor	0.02	0.06	0.67***	0.70***	0.01	0.07
	(0.12)	(0.09)	(0.20)	(0.19)	(0.51)	(0.30)
Literacy						
4. Total literacy	0.13		1.78****	1.65****	-0.23	
	(0.22)		(0.37)	(0.43)	(1.09)	
5. Urban literacy	-0.06		-0.07		-0.02	
	(0.05)		(0.08)		(0.24)	
6. Rural literacy	-0.08		-0.33**	-0.28**	0.00	
	(0.08)		(0.13)	(0.12)	(0.44)	
Full model						
F-value	43.73****	114.24****	11.99****	14.90****	30.75****	68.60****
R^2	89%	89%	70%	69%	88%	88%

*$p < 0.10$; **$p < 0.05$; ***$p < 0.01$; ****$p < 0.001$.

output of collective farms. Physical capital investments (irrigation, draft animals, and machinery) appear to have had strong effects, eclipsing any influence of literacy.[6]

VII. CONCLUSIONS

In sum, these findings paint a mixed portrait of the extent to which rising literacy rates helped to spark economic growth. In 1900, prior to Mexico's revolution, levels of literacy did appear to positively influence total economic output among the states. Here urban literacy was the most efficacious factor, not total literacy nor literacy within rural *municipios*. This suggests that the effect was limited to urban centers of trade. Clearly literacy effects were felt most consistently within the urban manufacturing sector, not within agrarian segments of the economy. The rural literacy rate was not associated with output in any sector during this pre-revolutionary era. Given the noted limitation of estimating the production function for agricultural output, more work is needed to clarify the possible effects of literacy in this sector.

The spread of literacy in post-revolutionary Mexico was impressive. Gains occurred both in urban centers and in the rural hinterlands. But even following the government's aggressive initiative centered within rural schools, the economic impact of rising literacy rates continued to be most strongly felt in urban centers. For 1940, literacy levels helped to explain differences in states' levels of manufacturing output. The magnitude of this effect was comparable to the contribution made by physical capital (machinery, technology, and construction) and labor force size. However, within agrarian sectors an economic effect from literacy appears only in the case of livestock value. No effect is apparent for the growth in crop production; and the level of livestock and meat production was highest around urban areas where demand by the upper classes and export traders was strongest (Van Young, 1981).

---

[6]Here we do not detail the magnitude of literacy's effect, beyond reporting levels of statistical significance. As an example, however, take the elasticity (beta) of 0.42 for the effect of total literacy on manufacturing output in 1940 (Table 23.5). This indicates that a 1% increase in literacy is associated with a 0.42% difference in manufacturing output at the margin, looking among Mexico's states. This would have to be adjusted downward based on the mean level of literacy. Nevertheless, this level of magnitude is certainly important from the viewpoint of development policy. To assess the cost-effectiveness of literacy we would have to estimate the cost of increasing state-level literacy by 1% (a problematic question) and calculate the value of a 0.42% difference in manufacturing output.

In general, this evidence offers support for the human capital model. Rising literacy did influence economic growth among Mexico's diverse states, after controlling for the effects of physical inputs to production. We also looked at aggregate economic effects of literacy across states and employed direct measures of output. This approach avoids the questionable assumptions of traditional human capital studies. In particular, we do not assume that individual-level wages can be used as sound proxies for actual productivity. Nor do we infer the level of national economic benefits from individual-level income, as commonly employed by many human capital economists. Our aggregate production functions do *not* establish conclusively a causal relationship—that growth in literacy led to higher levels of economic output. However, controls for the three physical inputs to production strengthen our ability to infer this direction of causality. In addition, empirical testing of similar models that controlled on prior levels of economic activity found similar simultaneous effects from states' literacy rates and lagged effects from school investment over the same period (Fuller et al., 1986).

Despite this overall support for the human capital model, the structural reinforcement model can also help clarify *when* rising literacy levels might influence economic output. In Mexico, urban centers clearly benefited most from the spread of literacy. Despite a sharp emphasis by the postrevolutionary government on developing the hinterlands, the impact of literacy on rural agrarian growth was slight at best. Therefore the human capital prediction that economic effects would accrue to expanded investment in literacy was valid. But this relationship is evident only in urban centers. Thus the resulting gains in economic productivity were realized by urban residents involved in high value-added, manufacturing enterprise. In effect, literacy helped to reinforce the position of those towns and individuals involved with manufacturing, notwithstanding some degree of mobility for industrial workers.

It should be reiterated that this study looked at the economic effects of the spread of literacy, *not* formal schooling. During this period the average length of school attendance by Mexican children equalled 2 years. The quality and popular acceptance of formal schooling remained limited until after World War II. Literacy rose in Mexico's urban areas long before schooling became a mass institution, stemming in part from the immigration of upper-class administrators from Spain and from an active Church pressing for knowledge of the Bible. On the other hand, the rural school movement in Mexico was successful over time in boosting literacy levels of the rural population. Here the formal school may have held an influence in eventually raising economic output and productivity after 1940. Additional work on the post-war period would be very helpful.

394 Fuller, Edwards, and Gorman

What do these findings suggest about the future role of literacy in spurring economic development? We have seen that literacy can play a role in boosting growth during a nation's early period of commercial expansion. Yet this effect may occur only within urban centers of manufacture and trade. The influence of literacy on farm output and rural development in Mexico may have become significant as the quality of schooling and the time children spent in classrooms was strengthened. But the limited effects during the early commercial era suggest that the claims of true believers in literacy will be realized only under certain conditions. Finally, we must think more carefully about why growth in literacy may yield economic benefits only in cities, but not among the rural poor where literacy and economic output remain disturbingly low.

ACKNOWLEDGEMENTS

We thank Daniel Wagner, who nudged us to refine our ideas and our language. Hearty thanks also to Stephen Heyneman and George Psacharopoulos of the World Bank, for their early financial and intellectual support of this project.

REFERENCES

Archer, M. (Ed.). (1982). *The sociology of educational expansion: Take-off, growth, and inflation in educational systems.* Beverly Hills, CA: Sage.

Ashby, J. (1985). Equity and discrimination among children: Schooling decisions in rural Nepal. *Comparative Education Review, 29,* 68-79.

Banda, L. (1873). *Estadisticas de Jalisco.* Guadalajara: Tipografia de Banda.

Bendix, R. (1964). *Nation-building and citizenship.* New York: Wiley.

Boissiere, M., Knight, J., & Sabot, R. (1985). Earnings, schooling, ability, and cognitive skills. *American Economic Review, 75,* 1016-1030.

Borthwick, S. (1983). *Education and social change in China: The beginning of the modern era.* Stanford, CA: Hoover Institution Press.

Bowles, S., & Gintis, H. (1976). *Schooling in capitalist America: Educational reform and the contradictions of economic life.* New York: Basic Books.

Bowman, M. (1984). An integrated framework for the analysis of the spread of schooling in less developed countries. *Comparative Education Review, 28,* 563-583.

Callcott, W. (1931). *Liberalism in Mexico, 1857-1929.* Stanford, CA: Stanford University Press.

Collins, R. (1977). Some comparative principles of educational stratification. *Harvard Educational Review, 47,* 1-27.

Denison, E. (1979). *Accounting for slower economic growth: The United States in the 1970s*. Washington: Brookings Institution.

Direccion General de Estadistica (1900-1907). *Segundo Censo de Poblacion, 1900*, Volumes 1-21. Mexico, DF: Gobierno de Mexico.

Direccion General de Estadistica (1943). *Sexto Censo de Poblacion, 1940*. Mexico, DF: Gobierno de Mexico.

Dore, R. (1976). Human capital theory: The diversity of societies and the problem of quality of education. *Higher Education, 5*, 79-102.

Fishlow, A. (1966). Levels of nineteenth century investment in education: Human capital formation or structural reinforcement? *Journal of Economic History, 26*, 418-436.

Frank, A. (1979). *Mexican agriculture, 1521-1630*. Cambridge: Cambridge University Press.

Frank, R. (1984). Are workers paid their marginal product? *American Economic Review, 74*, 549-572.

Fuller, B. (1983). Youth job structure and school enrollment, 1890-1920. *Sociology of Education, 56*, 145-156.

Fuller, B., Gorman, K., & Edwards, J. (1986) School quality and economic growth in Mexico. In S. Heyneman & D. White (Eds.), *The quality of schools in developing countries*. Washington, DC: The World Bank.

Fuller, W. (1976). More evidence supporting the demise of pre-employment vocational trade training: A case study of a factory in India. *Comparative Education Review, 20*, 31-41.

Goldblatt, P. (1972). The geography of youth employment and school enrollment rates in Mexico. In T. LaBelle (Ed.), *Education and development: Latin America and the Caribbean*. Los Angeles: University of California, Latin America Studies Center.

Hager, G. (1916). *Plain facts about Mexico*. New York: Harper & Row.

Hinchcliffe, K. (1976). Earnings determinants in the Nigerian textile industry. *Comparative Education Review, 20*, 48-64.

Meyer, J. (1977). The effects of schooling as an institution. *American Journal of Sociology, 83*, 55-77.

Meyer, J., Tyack, D., Nagel, J., & Gordon, A. (1979). Public education as national building: Enrollments and bureaucratization in the American states, 1870-1930. *American Journal of Sociology, 85*, 591-613.

Mitch, D. (1984). Underinvestment in literacy? The potential contribution of government involvement in elementary education to economic growth in 19th-century England. *Journal of Economic History, 44*, 557-566.

McGinn, N., & Street, S. (1984). Has Mexican education generated human or political capital? *Comparative Education, 20*, 323-338.

Psacharopoulos, G., & Woodhall, M. (1985). *Education for development: An analysis of investment choices*. Baltimore: Johns Hopkins University Press.

Reynolds, C. (1970). *Changing trade patterns and trade policy in Mexico: Some lessons for developing countries*. Stanford, CA: Food Research Institute.

Rubinson, R., & Ralph, J. (1984). Technical change and the expansion of schooling in the United States, 1890-1970. *Sociology of Education, 57,* 134-152.

Ruiz, R. (1963). *Mexico: The challenge of poverty and illiteracy.* San Marino, CA: Huntington Library.

Schultz, T. (1961). Investment in human capital. *American Economic Review, 51,* 1-17.

Secretaria de la Economia Nacional, Direccion General de Estadistica (1943). *Anuario Estadistica de los Estados Unidos Mexicanos.* Mexico, DF: Talleres Graficos de la Nacion.

Soltow, L., & Stevens, E. (1981). *The rise of literacy and the common school in the United States.* Chicago: University of Chicago Press.

Stanley, J. (1948). La Casa del Pueblo: Mexico's Experiment in Rural Education. Unpublished doctoral dissertation, Stanford University, School of Education.

Thurow, L. (1974). *Generating inequality: Mechanisms of distribution in the United States economy.* New York: Basic Books.

Van Young, E. (1981). *Hacienda and market in eighteenth century Mexico: The rural economy of the Guadalajara region, 1675-1820.* Berkeley: University of California Press.

Vaughan, M. (1982). *The state, education, and social class in Mexico, 1880-1928.* Dekalb: Northern Illinois University Press.

Walters, A. (1970). *An introduction to econometrics.* New York: Norton.

Walters, P. (1984). Occupational and labor market effects on secondary and postsecondary educational expansion in the United States, 1922-1979. *American Sociological Review, 48,* 480-493.

Walters, P., & Rubinson, R. (1983). Educational expansion and economic output in the United States, 1890-1969. *American Sociological Review, 49,* 659-671.

Wells, D. (1887). *A study of Mexico.* New York: Appleton.

Wolfe, B., & Behrman, J. (1984). Who is schooled in developing countries? The role of income, parental schooling and sex. *Economics of Education, 3,* 231-245.

Yates, B., (1980) White views of black minds: Schooling in King Leopold's Congo. *History of Education Quarterly, 20,* 27-51.

What Next for World Literacy: An Afterword

Wadi D. Haddad
Former Deputy Secretary,
The World Bank

The year 1990 was a watershed for international education and for world literacy. It not only was the UN International Literacy Year, but was marked by the World Conference on Education for All, held in Jomtien, Thailand. One could say that this year was an important turning point for nations—more than 155 of which were represented at the Jomtien meeting—to reflect on and to recommit themselves to a new vision for basic education, of which literacy is clearly one of the most central components.

What was most significant was that basic education was no longer to be compartmentalized by age or delivery system. National representatives, as well as representatives of the major intergovernmental and nongovernmental organizations, committed themselves to an education for all that meets the basic learning needs of all children, youth, and adults. This commitment translated into national educational targets, such as improving access to primary schooling, reducing gender disparities, and improving literacy rates in all developing countries. But more importantly, for the literacy field, this represented a broad political consensus on the importance of learning in the everyday lives of all people and peoples in today's world. It also evidenced a break with past practice, by contributing to a refocus on learning achievement, rather than the simplistic "head counting" of past literacy programs in many countries.

In a number of ways, the original publication of the present volume presaged this turning point, as the chapters deal with many of the difficult issues that connect with real learning achievement in literacy programs for adults and for children. The revised and updated chapters, now 10 years since the original publication, build on this early sense of what is needed to improve literacy worldwide.

As the Executive Secretary of the 1990 World Conference in Jomtien, I have taken a personal interest in how various institutions and agencies are progressing in meeting the goals and commitments that flowed from that meeting. Some major gains have been made in a number of countries (such as South Africa, Bangladesh, China, and elsewhere), and also in terms of methodology (as we have seen greater and better reliance on national and international assessments of learning achievement). Institutionally, it is important to mention the advent of the International Literacy Institute, set up by UNESCO at the University of Pennsylvania in Philadelphia with the mission to advance research and innovation on the best practices in literacy in developing countries.

My own view is that significant progress in literacy will be made only when decision makers at all levels come to the full realization that illiteracy cannot be afforded—either economically, socially, or politically. In a very real sense, to be deprived of the skill of literacy is to be deprived of an essential tool for modern living. Without the skills to participate in a literate, technological world, people will remain on the margins of society, and society itself will lose vast potential contributions. This is more true than ever before as all countries face the challenge of knowledge-based and globalized economies, escalating information that requires life-long learning and adaptation, and an enlightened and empowered citizenry to practice and sustain democracy, civic participation, human rights, peace, and environmental protection.

Author Index

E

Eastman, P. D., 147, *149*
Edwards, J., 382, 387, 393, *395*
Eggan, F., xvi, *xxii*
Ehri, L. C., 44, *51*
Eickelman, D. F., 187, *197*
Elkins, J., 41, *53*
Elkonin, D. B., 42, *51*
Elley, W. E., 222, 222*n*, 226, 227, 233, *238*, 267, *268*
Elley, W., 7, *17*
Engle, P. L., 194, *197*
Englebrecht, G., 220*n*, *239*
Enoch, H., 205, *209*
Esperandieu, V., 365, *370*
Esposito, Y. L., 114, *129*
Ezzaki, A., 4, 11, 14, 16, *19*, 185, *197*

F

Fairclough, N., 57, *71*
Faires, R., 281, *288*
Federico, H., 139, *149*
Feitelson, D., 200, 202, 203, 204, 205, 206, 207, *209*
Feldman, D. H., 30, *51*, 115, *129*
Feng, S., 102, 105, 106, *108, 109*
Ferguson, C. A., xix, *xxii*, 185, *197*, 215, *238*
Ferrerio, E., 40, 41, *51*, 115, 116, *129*, 132, *149*
Fiering, S., xvii, *xxii*
Fijalkow, J., 45, *51*
Fingeret, A., 244, 249, *249*, 297, *312*
Finnegan, R., xix, *xxii*
Fischer, F. W., 43, *52*
Fish, S., 252, *268*
Fishlow, A., 376, *395*
Fishman, J. A., 303, 304, *312*
Fodor, M., 135, *149*
Fox, L. C., 82, *92*
Frank, A., 381*n*, *395*
Frank, R., 379, *395*
Freeland, J., 71, *71*
Freire, P., 64, *71*, 79, *91*, 249, *249*
Fridman, I., 202, *210*
Friedman, M. P., 116, *129*

Frith, U., 115, *129*
Fuller, B., 376, 382, 387, *395*
Fuller, W., 379, 393, *395*
Furet, F., 58, *72*

G

Gadsen, V., 9, *17*
Galifret-Granjon, N., 124, *129*
Garcia de Lorenzo, M. E., 44, *51*
Gardner, R. C., 193, *197*
Gardner, R., 345, *351*
Gates, A. L., 189, *197*, 204, *210*
Gaur, A., 259, *268*
George, K. M., xix, *xxii*
Geraghty, P., 216, 216*n*, 217, 220, *238*
Gharib, G. S., 64, 65, *72*
Gibson, E. J., 207, *210*
Gillette, A., 4, *17*
Gintis, H., 374, *394*
Glass, G. V., 337, *339*
Glassie, H., xviii, *xxii*
Gleitman, L., 152, *171*
Glenn, C. G., 256, *268*
Glenn, E. S., 256, *268*
Glick, R., 222, *238*
Goldblatt, P., 376, *395*
Goldfield, B. A., 135, *149*
Goldstein, Z., 202, 203, 204, *210*
Golonka, S., 87, 89, 90, *91*
Goodman, K. S., 8, 9, *17*, 37, 44, *51, 52*
Goodman, K., 232, *238*
Goodman, Y., 132, *149*, 200, *210*, 232, *238*
Goody, J., 33, *52*, 60, 62, *72*, 267, *268*, 292, *312*
Gordon, A., 376, *395*
Gorman, K., 382, 387, 393, *395*
Gough, K., 46, *52*
Gould, S. J., 15, *17*
Graff, H. J., 221*n*, *238*
Graff, J. H., 247, *249*
Grandguillaume, G., 186, *197*
Graves, D., 232, *238*
Gray, W. S., 5, 6, *17*
Green, J., L., 137, *149*
Green, K. R., 296, 297, 303, 304, *312, 313*

Schultz, T., 375, *396*
Scollon, R., 132, *149*
Scollon, S. B. K., 132, *149*
Scott, J. A., 79, *90*
Scribner, S., 15, *18*, 26, *28*, 70, 72, 87, *92*, 120, *130*, 215, *239*, 245, *250*, 259, 261, 267, *269*, 277, 292, 297, 307, *313*
Searle, C., 45, *53*
Secretaria de la Economia Nacional Direccion General de Estadista 386n, *396*
Segall, M. H., 276, *288*
Senner, W., xx, *xxiv*
Shankweiler, D., 43, *52*
Shao, W., 106, *109*
Shimron, J., 206, *211*
Shultz, T. W., 15, *18*
Shuman, A., 297, *313*
Silva, A. C. da, 114, *130*
Sinclair, A., 41, *53*
Sinclair, H., 41, *53*
Sisco, B., 244, *249*
Skinner, A., 276, *289*
Smilansky, M., 195, *197*
Smith, L., 86, *92*
Smith, M. L., 337, *339*
Snow, C. E., 135, *149*
Snow, C., 86, 87, *91*, 132, 150, 200, *211*
Snyder, S. S., 82, *92*
Soares, M. B., 126, *130*
Soltow, L., 374, 378, *396*
Song, J., 102, 103, 104, 105, 106, 107, *108*, *109*
Sotsky, R., 152, *171*
Souali, M., 193, *197*
Spiro, R. J., 259, *268*
Spivey, E. M., 41, *54*
Spolsky, B., 44, *53*, 220*n*, 304, *313*
Spolsky, B., 187, 195*n*, *198*
Spratt, J. E., 13, *19*, 68, 70, 72, 186, 196*n*, *198*
Staal, F., xx, *xxiv*
Stanley, J. 282, *396*
Stanley, J. C., 328, *339*

Stedman, L. C., 89, *91*
Steegman, A. T., Jr., 275, *290*
Stein, N. L., 204, *211*
Stern, D., 9, *18*
Stevens, E., 374, 378, *396*
Stevenson, H. W., 156, 160, *171*
Stewart, W. A., 44, *53*
Sticht, T. G., xv, *xxiii*, 81, 83, *92*
Stigler, J. W., 156, 160, *171*
Stotsky, S., 89, *92*
Street, B. V., 67, 69, 70, 72, 215, *239*, 244, *250*
Street, S., 348, *351*, 374, *395*
Stubbs, M., 230, *239*, 303, 304, *313*
Sultman, W. F., 41, *53*
Sulzby, E., 131, 132, 135, 139, 145, 146, *150*
Swain, M., 215, *239*
Sweeney, M., 303, *313*
Szwed, J., 303, *313*

T

Takala, S., 258*f*, 263, 265, *269*
Tax, S., 44, *53*
Taylor, D., 90, *100*, 132, 133, *150*, 245, *250*
Taylor, G., 273, *289*
Taylor, H., 33, *51*
Taylor, I., 151, *171*
Taylor, M. M., 151, *171*
Teale, W. H., 131, 132, 133, 135, 137, 139, *150*, 200, *211*
Teberosky, A., 40, *51*, 115, 116, 126, 129, 132, *149*
Tedlock, D., xix, *xxiv*
Teit, J. A., xxi, *xxiv*
Templeton, S., 41, *54*
Templeton, W. S., 39, *54*
Thackray, D., V., 31, *51*
Thomas, C., 138, 139, *149*
Thompson, C., 338*n*, *339*
Thomson, D., 32, 39, 44, *50*
Thorndike, E. L., 87, *92*
Thorndike, R. L., 75, 87, *92*
Thurow, L., 379, *396*
Tierney, R. J., 204, *211*

Subject Index

DATE DUE
